Kris Jamsa's
STARTING
with

Microsoft®
Visual C++®

Check the Web for Updates:

To check for updates or corrections relevant to this book and/or CD-ROM visit our updates page on the Web at **http://www.prima-tech.com/support**.

Send Us Your Comments:

To comment on this book or any other PRIMA TECH title, visit our reader response page on the Web at **http://www.prima-tech.com/comments**.

How to Order:

For information on quantity discounts, contact the publisher: Prima Publishing, P.O. Box 1260BK, Rocklin, CA 95677-1260; (916) 787-7000. On your letterhead, include information concerning the intended use of the books and the number of books you want to purchase.

Kris Jamsa's
STARTING
with

Microsoft®
Visual C++®

CHARLES WRIGHT

Prima Tech is a division of Prima Publishing. Prima Publishing and colophon are registered trademarks of Prima Communications, Inc. PRIMA TECH is a trademark of Prima Communications, Inc., Roseville, California 95661.

Publisher: Stacy L. Hiquet

Associate Marketing Manager: Jennifer Breece

Managing Editor: Sandy Doell

Acquisitions Editor: Stacy L. Hiquet

Production and Editoral: Argosy

Technical Reviewer: Greg Perry

Cover Design: Prima Design Team

ISBN: 0-7615-3444-X

Library of Congress Catalog Card Number: 2001-086665

Printed in the United States of America

00 01 02 03 04 BB 10 9 8 7 6 5 4 3 2 1

Dedication

To James Bort, my friend and mentor as I made the transition from newsroom geek to computer geek. Jim was City Editor at The Fresno (California) *Bee* during the time I was a reporter, and later became Assistant Managing Editor while I was responsible for the newsroom computer system. He was one of the famous *Fresno Four*, who made journalism history by defying a judge's order to divulge confidential information.

Acknowledgments

Writing a book is not a solo experience. While the author's name goes on the cover, the ultimate product actually is the culmination of the efforts of many people involved in the process. Even before the author puts the first word down, there are a number of people in the background ready to help and to transform the author's efforts into a finished book.

The first person who deserves thanks is my wife, Tammy, who puts up with my long hours of holding down a full-time job while I pursue my writing. Without her support, there would not be time to write or to program. Adding to that support is The Bear, my three-year-old Pomeranian who loyally keeps me company during the early morning and late night writing and programming sessions.

Thanks also to the staff at Argosy in Boston for their efforts in editing the text. Although I was a newspaper reporter and editor for many years before becoming involved in computers, my writing skills had atrophied over the years and the Argosy staff put me back on the track.

Kris Jamsa and the folks at Jamsa Media Group helped me through this experience by providing writing tips (let's face it, writing a book is not the same as writing a news story) and providing feedback based on their many years of experience in book publishing.

Finally, thanks to the many, many unnamed programmers on the World Wide Web who contributed code to the many C++ interest groups on the Internet. Over the years, I have learned a lot studying their sample code and incorporating the ideas into my programs.

Contents
at a
Glance

Contents

Part 1

The Basics

Lesson 1

Getting Started with Visual C++

Somewhere out there is a program with your name on it. You may not know what that program is, but the fact that you have decided to learn how to program means you have taken the first step toward creating it. Maybe you have been dabbling in programming with a language such as BASIC or Pascal, and you are tired of the limits and speed of these other languages. Or maybe you are a professional programmer who has decided to look into the possibilities of C++, a language that in a very brief time has become the de facto programming language of the personal computer industry. The fact is that most of the programs you and others will use in the next 10 to 20 years have not been written yet.

This lesson will introduce you to Microsoft Visual C++. By the time you finish this first lesson, you will understand the following key concepts:

- ◆ Programming is writing instructions for a computer in a language you can read and write, such as Visual C++.

- ◆ Compiling is the process of converting the program you wrote into the ones and zeros the computer understands.

- ◆ You write and store your program in a source code file. The Visual C++ compiler reads this file and converts it into instructions the computer understands, then stores these instructions in another file called an *executable*.

- ◆ Visual C++ is part of the Microsoft Visual Studio, which contains many tools to help you write and develop programs.

- ◆ Debugging is the process of finding and correcting errors in a program. To help you debug your programs, the Visual Studio contains a powerful debugger program.

Understanding Computer Programs

A computer program, or *software*, is a series of numbers your computer uses as *instructions* to perform a specific task. In the computer, these numbers are composed of zeros (0) and ones (1) that represent the absence or presence of electrical signals. Different numbers activate different combinations of transistors, or *gates*, in the computer circuitry and cause it to perform certain operations. You create a program first by writing a list of *statements* in a programming language such as BASIC, C++, or Pascal. Then, using another program called a *compiler*, your statements get translated into the numbers that are meaningful to a computer.

Learning programming is a matter of persistence and reinforcement. Few things worth doing are easy to master. If you are trying to learn the Morse Code, for example, it is more important that you study 15 minutes *every* day than that you study four hours a week, perhaps all in one day. As your skills advance, you will find yourself encountering "plateaus," periods when you just do not seem to advance as rapidly as you would like. You will find some programming constructs difficult to master. This is where persistence pays off. If you keep at it, eventually you will break out of a plateau, and your skills will seem to rocket for a while. Keep tinkering and experimenting with a difficult construct, and you will suddenly get an insight and exclaim, "Of course!"

Visual C++ is one of the tools used by a program called *Visual Studio*, which is Microsoft's offering of an *integrated development environment*. Often you will see it called the "IDE." The package contains a source code editor, a compiler, and a debugger, as well as other programming tools, that you can run from the Visual Studio. You can perform all the tasks within the Visual Studio program, or you can write your programs and compile and run them from a command-line prompt. (Compiling is the process of converting your source code into the binary instructions your computer understands). In the course of this book, you will do both.

The first purpose of Visual C++ is to provide you with an environment in which you can write Windows programs. To do that, of course, you need a basic understanding of C++ programming. Windows programming and C++ programming are broad topics, and no book could hope to do either justice by combining both topics. In this book, you will learn the basics of the C++ language within the Visual C++ environment with the goal of placing you in a position to better understand those books you will use to write Windows programs. You can use this book by itself, with a more specialized book on C++ basics such as *Rescued By C++*, or with a book that concentrates more on Windows programming with Visual C++ such as *1001 Microsoft Visual C++ Programming Tips*.

Installing Visual C++

Visual C++ comes in three editions. The Standard Edition often is called the Learning Edition and is relatively inexpensive. You can write some powerful programs with the Standard Edition, and the license for it lets you distribute and sell your programs and include the required Visual C++ modules. The next level is the Professional Edition, which includes several additional tools, including a number of tools used for database programming. The Enterprise Edition is the highest, and the most expensive, version. It includes a developer's edition of Microsoft SQL Server and other tools that you can use to develop professional applications.

Visual C++ 6.0 requires a 32-bit version of Windows such as Windows 95, Windows 98, or Windows NT. In Visual C++, an integer—the representation of a whole number without a fractional part—is given 32 *bits* of storage, or four *bytes*. (A bit is a 1 or 0 that indicates whether a signal is on or off; when you use eight bits to represent a number, the combination is called a byte). In the documentation, you may see references to "Win32" to differentiate this environment from the older versions of Windows and DOS, in which an integer was given only 16 bits of storage. You cannot use Visual C++ 6.0 to write programs for the 16-bit versions of DOS and Windows.

To install the Introductory Edition of Visual C++ 6.0 that comes with this book, insert the CD into your CD-ROM drive. After several seconds, the Installation Wizard should appear on your screen. If it does not, double-click your mouse on the My Computer icon on the desktop and then right-click on the entry for your CD-ROM drive. Select Explore from the menu that pops up. Double-click the mouse on the the *SETUP.EXE* program to start the Installation Wizard.

The Installation Wizard will ask you to enter your name and to accept the Microsoft End User Agreement. You cannot install Visual C++ if you do not accept the agreement.

The installation will take several minutes. When it finishes, the wizard will prompt you to install the Visual C++ 6.0 Introductory Documentation. This is the Microsoft Developers Network (MSDN), the help system for Visual C++. Make sure the box is checked (there should be only one box) and click on the Next button to start the installation.

Running Visual C++

Visual Studio is a Windows program. When you install it, the installation program creates a group of menu items that let you run it from the desktop without starting a command window. Select the Start button on the taskbar, then select Programs. From this list, you should see an entry for "Microsoft Visual C++ 6.0." Select this item and you get another menu list containing tools the installation program added when you installed Visual C++. The actual tools will depend on the edition you installed, but each edition includes an item labeled "Microsoft Visual C++ 6.0." Select this item to start Visual C++. The Visual Studio window will appear, as shown in Figure 1.1.

Without a doubt, the Visual Studio is a busy place. The labels in Figure 1.1 point out the major areas of the studio, and in Lesson 3, "Exploring the Visual Studio," you will learn the primary purpose of each of area. But, first, you want to get to the point where you can write and launch your own programs.

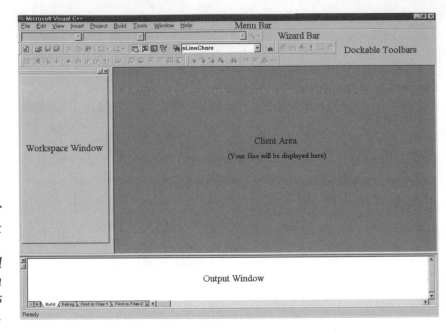

Figure 1.1

An empty Visual Studio as it first appears on your screen. Depending upon setup and custom options, your screen may not look exactly like this figure.

In Lesson 3, you will learn the purpose of the various portions of the Visual Studio window and how to use them. Think of the Visual Studio as the computerized equivalent of a wood-working shop. You place various tools around the workshop, and you might set aside certain areas for a specific task. In a workshop, for example, you might set up a table saw in the corner, and that is where you do most of your work with wood. Another area might contain a lathe and drill press where you do your metal work. Similarly, each section of the Visual Studio has a purpose, and you will perform specific tasks in these areas.

Visual C++ does not limit you to developing your programs in the Visual Studio, however. There will be times when you will want to write a utility program—a "quick hit" program—that you run from the command line. The command line is the prompt you get when you select the Start button, then Run and type in "command." It also can be the command window you get when you select the MS-DOS Prompt from the Start menu. Lesson 4, "Using Visual C++ from the Command Line," will teach you how to create and edit program files, then compile and run them without ever entering the Visual Studio.

Loading a C++ Program in Visual C++

Visual Studio is designed to help you develop many different types of projects, not only C++ projects. You cannot just create a C++ program file and expect to compile and run it. You first must create a *workspace*. The workspace is a holder—imagine it as a workbench—for your programs. Then you must create a *project*. The project defines the tools and file types your program will use and determines how the Visual Studio handles your source files.

You will build these in the next lesson, "Building, Running, and Saving Your First Visual C++ Program," and you also will learn about the files the Visual Studio creates for you and how it uses them. For now, you can use the sample program in the Lesson01 directory of the code files available for dowload at *http://www.prima-tech.com/books/book/5536/903*. In that directory, run the *SAMPLE1.EXE* program. The program will ask you for a disk and subdirectory where you want to install the files, and then the program will create a Project01 sub-directory.

When the program ends, open the project in the Visual Studio by performing these steps:

1. Start Visual C++ as described in this lesson's section entitled *Running Visual C++*.

2. Select the File menu, then Open Workspace. You will get a File Open dialog box.

3. In this dialog box, change to the Project1 subdirectory that you just created and look for a file named *Hello.dsw*. This is the workspace file for the program.

4. Select this file and then click the mouse on the Open button. The workspace and project file will load in the Visual Studio.

This is how you will open workspaces when you want to return to a program to work on it. The Visual Studio will create new workspaces in separate directories. To open a different program, simply maneuver to the direc-tory and open the workspace file. The Visual Studio will open any projects that you have created in the workspace at the same time.

Locate the Build MiniBar as shown in Figure 1.2. If the toolbar is not visible, click the right mouse button in a blank area to the right of any toolbar. Visual Studio will display a list of toolbars. Toolbars that are visible will have a check mark next to their names. Select Build MiniBar from the list to make it visible.

Figure 1.2

The Build MiniBar contains the buttons you need to build and run your program.

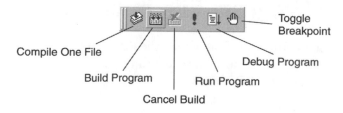

Compile One File

Build Program

Cancel Build

Run Program

Debug Program

Toggle
Breakpoint

Building your program involves running a program—the compiler. This program reads your source files and converts them to the numbers that are instructions for the computer. The compiler then writes this converted code to another file with an *.exe* extension. This file is the *executable*.

If you have not opened the Lesson01 project as previously described, do it now. To build this program, click the mouse on the Build Program button or press the F7 key. Visual Studio will begin building the project, and in a few seconds, a line similar to the following will appear in the Output Window at the bottom of the screen:

```
Hello.exe - 0 error(s), 0 warning(s)
```

When this message appears, the program is ready to run or debug. *Debugging* is when programmers test run their program to look for program errors and fix them. The Visual C++ debugger lets you run your program one line at a time to test your code.

Click the mouse on the Debug Program button to start the debugger. Shortly, your program displays a message box with the words "Hello, Visual C++ World!" as shown in Figure 1.3.

The message box may appear simple, but it contains several smaller *objects*, as noted by the labels in Figure 1.3. Within the message box is a button with the word "OK" on it. Click the mouse on this button to close the message box and exit the program.

Figure 1.3

When you build and run the hello.exe *program, your screen will display a window similar to this. This is a Windows message box.*

In the next lesson, you will go through the steps of actually creating this program

Printing a Program File in Visual C++

Visual C++ lets you to print a file from within the Visual Studio, or to print just a portion of it. You will find the partial print option handy when you need to print only a specific section of your source code. To print a file from Visual C++, perform the following steps:

1. Select the file in the client area. To do this, click the mouse anywhere on the editing window that contains the file. The bar at the top of the window should appear in blue.

2. Select the File menu, then move down to the Print item (if you have not selected a file in Step 1, the Print item will be "grayed out," and you cannot select it).

3. A Print dialog box will appear with the name of your default printer highlighted. Notice that there is a box labeled "Selection" in the Print Range area, but it is disabled.

4. Click on the OK button. The Visual Studio will begin sending the file to the printer, and the Print dialog box will disappear.

To print just a portion of a file, select the file as in the preceding Step 1, then follow these steps:

1. Place the caret (the window cursor) in front of the first character of the portion you want to print.

2. Hold the Shift key down. While holding the Shift key down, use the arrow keys to move to the *last* character in the portion you want to print. This will cause the text to appear in white against a black background. This is the *selection,* and by holding the Shift key down you have *highlighted* it.

3. Select the Print item from the Visual Studio File menu. Do not click on the editing window again or move the caret. If you do, you will cancel the selection.

4. In the Print dialog box, notice that the Selection item is enabled and Visual C++ has selected it for you.

5. To print just the text you highlighted, click the OK button.

If you change your mind and decide to print the entire file, click the left mouse button on the All box before selecting the OK button.

Setting Up Visual C++

If you do not like the way the Visual Studio appears or the location of the various windows and toolbars, you can move them around to suit your taste. All of the toolbars may be moved to other places around the studio by grabbing the left side of them with the left mouse button and dragging them to where you want them. They can be left "floating," unattached to the window frame as tool windows. Figure 1.4 shows two views of the Visual Studio. The top view has all the toolbars attached to the Visual Studio frame, and the bottom view shows them floating. With the exception of the Menu Bar, they all may be hidden when you do not need them.

Figure 1.4

You can detach and move any of the toolbars or tool windows in the Visual Studio and move them where you want them. The top view shows all the toolbars attached. At bottom, the Edit, Debug and Build MiniBar and the Workspace Window are floating.

To hide or show a toolbar, right-click the mouse on a blank area of the frame (the area to the right of the toolbars is a good place), and a selection menu will appear. If a toolbar is visible, it will have a check mark next to it. Move the mouse cursor over a toolbar and click the *left* button to turn it on or off.

The selection menu that appears does not show all the toolbars available to you. The list will change according to the task you are performing. For example, if you are in the process of debugging a program, several of the selections will change so you can select toolbars that are used only for debugging. You should practice using this menu and make yourself familiar with the various toolbars. You will need this knowledge when you start debugging your programs.

The specialized windows such as the Output Window and the Workspace Window also may be moved or hidden. The Workspace Window "grabber" is at the top and the Output Window grabber is to its left. Individual panes in the Workspace Window may be toggled on and off by right-clicking the mouse button on the corresponding tab and selecting it in the menu.

Saving Your Program Code

You may configure the Visual Studio to save your program files automatically when you compile a file or build your program. As you develop more complicated programs, this is important because Visual C++ is not a perfect program and it has been known to *crash* during debugging sessions. A crash is caused by an unexpected error in a program that makes it impossible to continue.

From the Tools menu, select the Options... item to get the Options dialog box. This is a tabbed dialog box, and the various pages are used to set options throughout the Visual Studio. Right now you are interested in the Editor options, so select that tab by clicking it with the left mouse button. In the middle of the page is a group called Save Options, and within that group is an item labeled "Save before running tools." Make sure this box is checked, and the Visual Studio will save your files automatically when you compile or build your program.

 Saving Your Files Within Visual C++

If you need to save a file without running the compiler, make sure that you have selected the window containing the file in the client area, then select the Save item on the File menu. You also can select Save All to save all the files that you have modified since your last save operation.

When you exit the Visual Studio or close a workspace, the Visual Studio will check whether you have modified any files and not yet saved them. If it finds any, it will prompt you for each file to ask whether you want the changes saved.

What You Must Know

In this lesson, you learned how to install and run the Visual C++ compiler and how to set up the Visual Studio to save your program files when you build your program. You also learned how to view and print your program source code from within the Visual Studio. In Lesson 2, "Building, Running, and Saving Your First Visual C++ Program," you will create your own programs using Visual C++.

Before you continue with Lesson 2, however, make sure you have learned the following key concepts:

◆ When you write a program, you are writing instructions for the computer in a language you can understand. Visual C++ is a tool that lets you write programs in C++.

◆ After you have written your program in Visual C++, a program called a compiler translates your program from C++ to the ones and zeros that the computer understands.

◆ You keep your program code in a source file. The Visual C++ compiler reads this source file and converts it to the binary instructions (the ones and zeros) that the computer can understand.

◆ You find and correct errors in your program through a process called debugging. The Visual Studio contains a debugging tool that helps you through this process.

◆ Like most Windows programs, the Visual Studio contains commands that let you print your source files.

Lesson 2

Building, Running, and Saving Your First Visual C++ Program

One of the characteristics of a language—whether it is spoken, written, or a computer language—is that its syntax must allow a finite number of elements (words, punctuation, and so on) to be used to create an infinite number of constructions. Computer programming is the process of turning your thoughts into the language syntax that the language compiler (a special software program) can understand. The compiler then translates the program statements you write into the binary ones (1) and zeroes (0) that the computer understands as instructions and data.

In this lesson, you will begin writing your own programs. As you begin programming, you should remember that there is more than one way to accomplish the same result, just as in a spoken language, there may be more than one way to express the same thought. While you need to learn the words and syntax of C++, you should remember to concentrate on the *intent* of your program and not be too concerned with the *mechanics* of the language. The more you program, the more natural it will become to you.

After you type in your program, the compiler will tell you when you have made a syntax error, such as forgetting a semicolon at the end of a statement. When syntax errors occur, you will simply return to the editor and fix the mistakes, using the error information the compiler provides you as a guide. Unfortunately, the compiler will not necessarily tell you when you have made a program error (which programmers refer to as *logic errors*). Such an error might be directing your program to execute a section of instructions repeatedly (looping) without providing your code with any way out of the *loop*. Only experience will teach you to recognize these problems. In this lesson, you will run, build, and save your first Visual C++ program. By the time you finish this lesson, you will understand the following key concepts:

◆ Use the Visual Studio project wizards to create your workspace and project files. The wizards also create the basic source files for you. These files contain code that is common to most programs.

◆ Syntax errors are grammatical or spelling errors. The Visual C++ compiler will tell you about these errors in the Output Window.

◆ When you make changes to your source files, you must recompile your program for the changes to take effect.

◆ Visual Studio creates several files to help it maintain your project and hold optional settings for the project and workspace.

◆ The Visual Studio displays the words and lines in your source files in different colors. This is called *syntax highlighting* and helps you to identify the parts of your source file.

◆ From within the Visual Studio, you can edit your program files, compile your program, and debug errors.

Creating a Project

As you learned in Lesson 1, "Getting Started with Visual C++," you cannot just create a source file in the Visual Studio. Rather, the workspace and project files help the Visual Studio to identify the type of program files you are creating so it can invoke the proper tools.

In this section, you will go through the steps to create a program like the one you compiled and ran in Lesson 1. You will name this first project *First*. The project will be a Windows application that creates a window, then writes some text to the window, as shown in Figure 2.1. The Visual Studio will create your first source files, and you will edit them to change the message that appears in the window.

Figure 2.1

In the First *project, the Visual Studio will create program source code files for you. You will edit the source code to display the window shown here.*

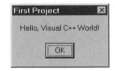

To create your project, perform these steps:

1. Within the Visual C++ Studio, select the File menu New option. Windows will display the New dialog box.

2. Within the New dialog box, select the Project tab. Windows will display a Projects sheet similar to that shown in Figure 2.2. (Note: This image was taken from an Enterprise edition of Visual Studio, so your dialog box may not show all the items.)

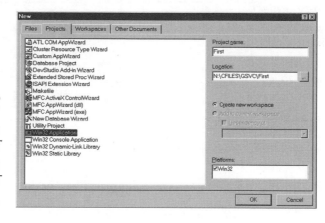

Figure 2.2

The New dialog box Projects page lists the various types of applications you can create with your version of Visual C++.

3. Select the "Win32 Application" item from the dialog box list. The items are in alphabetical order, so this item will appear near the bottom.

4. Click the mouse in the Location field at the upper-right to move to it. Enter the directory where you want to place your application. If the directory doesn't exist, the Visual Studio will create it.

5. Use the Tab key or click the mouse on the Project Name field. Type **First** in this field to name your project. Notice that Visual Studio adds the project name to the path in the Location box.

6. Click the mouse on the OK button to start the wizard.

In the Project Name field, enter **First**. Notice that Visual Studio has added the project name to the path in the Location box. Click the mouse on the OK button to start the wizard, as shown in Figure 2.3. (A *wizard* is a special dialog box that requires you to perform steps one page after another. Installation programs, for example, often use wizards to walk the user through a setup process). This wizard has only one page, but soon you will encounter others that take several pages.

Figure 2.3

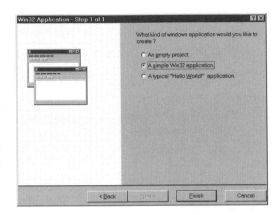

The Win32 Application wizard is a single-page dialog box offering you three choices. When this page first appears, notice that "An empty project" is the default selection. You need to click the mouse on the button next to "A simple Win32 application" to select that choice.

Within Figure 2.3, you will find the wizard offers you three choices:

◆ "An empty project" creates workspace and project files but does not create any start up program files. This is the default.

◆ "A simple Win32 Application" will create your main program source file along with a couple of others the compiler uses to speed compilation.

◆ "A typical 'Hello, World!' application" will create a window and draw the text "Hello, World!" at the top of the window.

For now, select the "simple Win32 application" and click the mouse on the Finish button. The wizard will display a New Project Information box telling you what program files it will create for you and how the program will perform initially. Click the mouse on the OK button to create the project.

Visual Studio used your selections to determine what files to create for your project. First, on the Projects page of the New dialog box, you told it you wanted to create a Win32 application. Next, you selected the application type, a simple Win32 application. The wizard used that information to prepare only the basic files you need to start writing a Win32 application.

The application wizard actually created three source files for you. Visual C++ uses two of them, *stdafx.cpp* and *stdafx.h*. You will place your source code in the third file, *First.cpp*. For right now, *First.cpp* does nothing. It now is up to you to add the statements that will make the program display the window.

To view your source files, use the following sequence:

1. Select the FileView tab on the Workspace Window. This is the tool window at the left center of the Visual Studio with tabs at the bottom.

2. Click the mouse button on the "+" next to "First files." The FileView list will expand and show several categories of files.

3. Click the mouse on the "+" sign next to "Source files." The list will expand again to show the .cpp files in your project, *stdafx.cpp* and *First.cpp*.

4. Double-click the mouse on the First.cpp item, and the file should appear in an editing window.

You can view more than one source file. If you double-click on the *stdafx.cpp* item, the Visual Studio will create another editing window and display the contents of *stdafx.cpp* in the window.

You are not ready to compile your program yet. If you do compile and run the program, it will simply exit without doing anything. That is because the only statement in the *WinMain* function is a *return* statement as shown below. The Visual Studio provided this code to give you a template to begin writing your program. This saves you the repetitive task of having to enter the same code for every program you write:

```
// First.cpp : Defines the entry point for the application.
//


#include "stdafx.h"


int APIENTRY WinMain(HINSTANCE hInstance,
                     HINSTANCE hPrevInstance,
                     LPSTR     lpCmdLine,
                     int       nCmdShow)
{
    // TODO: Place code here.
    return 0;
}
```

To make the program pop up a small box with the words "Hello, Visual C++ World!" add the line *MessageBox (0, "Hello, Visual C++ World!", "First", MB_OK);* to the *First.cpp* source file between the line starting with "TODO:" and the *return* statement. (The "TODO:" line begins with two slash marks (//) and is a *comment* line. The compiler ignores comment lines). Your source file now should look like the following:

```
// First.cpp : Defines the entry point for the application.
//

#include "stdafx.h"

int APIENTRY WinMain(HINSTANCE hInstance,
                     HINSTANCE hPrevInstance,
                     LPSTR     lpCmdLine,
                     int       nCmdShow)
{
    // TODO: Place code here.
    MessageBox (0, "Hello, Visual C++ World!", "First", MB_OK);
    return 0;
}
```

To compile your program, click the mouse on the Build button on the Build MiniBar or press the F7 key. Watch the Output Window for the following line:

```
First.exe - 0 error(s), 0 warning(s)
```

If, for some reason, your Output Window displays error messages, double-check your previous typing closely to ensure that you typed the statement exactly as follows, including the use of upper and lowercase letters, the number of commas, quotes, and the ending semicolon:

```
MessageBox (0, "Hello, Visual c++ World!", "First",  MB_OK);
```

If you find a mistake, simply correct the error and press the F7 key again (or click the Build button) to compile your program.

After you successfully compile your source code, click the mouse on the Debug button or press F5 to run the program within the Visual Studio debugger. Your program should display a small pop up window with the message "Hello, Visual C++ World!" as previously shown in Figure 2.1.

Within the program, *MessageBox* is a function in the Windows Application Programming Interface. The text inside the parentheses are *arguments*. In the *MessageBox* function, the first argument corresponds to the parent window. If the program has no parent window, you enter 0 to indicate the desktop. The second argument specifies the text that the message box displays. The third argument is the title that appears in the blue bar at the top of the message box. Finally, the *MB_OK* argument is a *flag* that indicates the button or buttons that will appear on the message box.

Take time now to experiment with the *First.cpp* source file. For example, you might change the message-box text to "My First Program!" or you might change the message box title. Also, try using other buttons for the last argument such as *MB_YESNO*, *MB_OKCANCEL*, *MB_RETRYCANCEL*, or *MB_YESNOCANCEL*. Each time you change a source file, you must recompile your program before the changes will take effect. If you make a change and forget to recompile the program, Visual C++ will display a message as shown in Figure 2.4. Click the mouse on the Yes button, and Visual C++ will compile your program and then run it.

Figure 2.4

If you see a message box such as this when you run your program, it means you forgot to rebuild your program after you made changes to your program files.

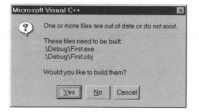

In the *First.cpp* source code file on your screen, notice that Visual Studio displays certain words in different colors. For example, Visual Studio displays the words "include" and "return" using blue. As you will learn, *include* and *return* are C++ *keywords*, which means your programs must use them only in specific ways. The line beginning with "//" is green to indicate C++ *comments*. Within your programs, you will use comments to place notes to yourself or other programmers about your program's processing. The comments are only for the benefit of programmers. The C++ compiler ignores commented text.

The colors that the Visual Studio displays on the screen are not part of your source file. Instead, the Visual Studio sets the colors when it displays your files to help you identify certain parts of your program quickly. Using colors within an editor in this way to assist programming is called *syntax highlighting*. If you open your source file within another editing program, such as *Windows NotePad*, all the text will appear in black.

Creating a DOS (Console) Program

The message box is one way to display text in Windows. Unfortunately, the message box won't work on other operating systems such as Unix or Linux because the *MessageBox* function is specific to Windows. Programmers call this type of code *nonportable,* meaning, you cannot move the code from one operating system to another and successfully compile it.

You can, however, use Visual C++ to write *command-line* programs that are more portable. In Windows, these types of programs often are called *DOS programs,* but the name is misleading. Remember from Lesson 1 that Windows 95 and later are 32-bit operating systems, MS-DOS is a 16-bit operating system, and you can use Visual C++ only for 32-bit Windows programs. When you start the MS-DOS Prompt in Windows (it's called Command Prompt on Windows NT), you actually are launching a window that accepts DOS commands. From this prompt, you can run 16- and 32-bit programs.

To create a command-line program, perform the following steps:

1. Select New from the File menu, then select the Projects tab from the dialog box that appears.

2. Near the bottom of the list on the Projects tab is an item labeled "Win32 Console Application." Click the mouse on this item.

3. Make sure that the Location box in the upper-right has the path to your program files.

4. Enter "Second" in the Project box. If you haven't closed the *First* project, the Visual Studio will close it before creating the next project.

5. Be sure that "Create new workspace" is selected and click the mouse on the OK button. This will display the one-page wizard.

6. Select "A 'Hello, World!' application" and press the Finish button.

7. The wizard again will display a list of the program files it will create for you. Click on OK to create the project.

The Visual Studio will respond by creating your second project. Open the *Second.cpp* source file. To do this, select the FileView tab on the Workspace Window, then click the mouse on the "+" next to "Second files" and then the "+" sign next to "Source files" as you learned in the last section. Double-click the mouse on the file named *Second.cpp,* and the file shown below should appear in an editing window:

```
// Second.cpp : Defines the entry point for the console application.
//

#include "stdafx.h"

int main(int argc, char* argv[])
{
    printf("Hello World!\n");
    return 0;
}
```

Within Visual Studio, click on the Build button to compile your program. Then click on the Debug button to run it. The program appears to do nothing, but it really does display the words "Hello, World!" to the console screen. The Visual Studio creates a console window in which the program runs. The program outputs the text and then exits, and Visual Studio closes the command window.

If you start a command prompt (select the Start menu Programs and choose MS-DOS Prompt), change to the program's directory and run the program the same as you do any DOS program; you will see the output.

But you want to run the program in Visual Studio to take advantage of the debugger. To pause the program to view the output, you can set a *breakpoint* at the end of the program. A breakpoint pauses the program in the debugger. You can use breakpoints only when you are running debug versions of your program in the Visual Studio.

To set a breakpoint at the end of the program, select the *Second.cpp* file and move the caret to the line that says "return 0;". (In Windows, the caret marks the *insert* position in a text window, the position where the next character typed will appear; in Visual Studio source windows, it's a vertical line. The word *cursor* is reserved for the mouse pointer.)

On the Build MiniBar that you used to compile and run the program is a button with an image like an open hand. Select a file in the editor, then move the caret to the line where you want to set a breakpoint. Click the mouse on that button, and the Visual Studio will place a brown dot on the left side of the window, as shown in Figure 2.5.

Figure 2.5

Near the bottom of the window, the Visual Studio has placed a dot on the left side of the window to indicate a breakpoint. The vertical line next to the dot is the caret.

```
Second.cpp
// Second.cpp : Defines the entry point for the consol
//

#include "stdafx.h"

int main(int argc, char* argv[])
{
    printf("Hello World!\n");
    return 0;
}
```

Now, run the program again. Once more, the program appears to run and exit. However, look at the breakpoint dot again. The debugger program has placed a yellow arrow inside it. This arrow indicates the current *execution point* in the program. In this case, the program has stopped at the *return* statement. You also will see that Windows has placed an MS-DOS Prompt item on the Windows taskbar at the bottom of your screen. Click on that item to see output of your program You should see a window similar to Figure 2.6.

Figure 2.6

When you test run a console program, the Visual Studio creates a command window for you. Your console program writes to this window.

Click the mouse on the Debug button again to resume your program. That will make the program exit normally.

Understanding Your Program Files

Except for the way they display your message, *First.EXE* and *Second.EXE* perform the same task, but there are some important differences in the source code files.

In *First.cpp*, you have a *function* named *WinMain*, which is the *entry point* for Windows programs. Each Windows program must have the *WinMain* function as part of the program. When you compile your program, the compiler creates intermediate files that another program, called the *linker*, puts together to create the executable file. Later, when you run your program, a special program called the *loader* loads your program from disk into the computer's RAM and then uses the *WinMain* function as your program's entry point.

In the command-line program, *Second.cpp*, you do not have a *WinMain* function. Instead, the entry point is *main*, which is the standard entry point for C++ programs. All command-line programs must have the *main* function. Like the *WinMain* function, the loader looks for *main* and transfers control to the function when you run your program. You will learn more about the *main* function later.

Near the top of each source file is a line similar to the following:

```
#include    "stdafx.h"
```

The "#include" portion is called a *preprocessor directive*. This directive tells the compiler to locate a file and include it as part of the program. When you use files in this way, they are called *header* files and usually are given the extension *.h*. In this case, the file is *stdafx.h*. Files that you include in a program may include other files, and compiling these files every time you build your program can take a lot of time. You do not change these files very often, so Visual C++ uses *stdafx.h* to create a *precompiled header file*. Once it creates this file, Visual C++ reads the compiled information from it rather than spend a lot of time recompiling everything.

The *stdafx.h* file from *Second.cpp* is shown below. You will learn about the preprocessor directives later, so you can ignore most of the file's contents for now. You should pay attention to the line near the middle that includes *stdio.h*. This file defines the functions and values that are part of the standard C++ interface. You will include this file in most of the programs you write:

```
// stdafx.h : include file for standard system include files,
//  or project specific include files that are used frequently, but
//      are changed infrequently
//

#if !defined(AFX_STDAFX_H__1CB6671F_A029_11D4_85DC_66F691000000__INCLUDED_)
#define AFX_STDAFX_H__1CB6671F_A029_11D4_85DC_66F691000000__INCLUDED_

#if _MSC_VER > 1000
#pragma once
#endif // _MSC_VER > 1000

#define WIN32_LEAN_AND_MEAN  // Exclude rarely-used stuff from Windows headers

#include <stdio.h>

// TODO: reference additional headers your program requires here
```

```
//{{AFX_INSERT_LOCATION}}
// Microsoft Visual C++ will insert additional declarations immediately before
the previous line.

#endif //
!defined(AFX_STDAFX_H__1CB6671F_A029_11D4_85DC_66F691000000__INCLUDED_)
```

In the *First* project, the *stdafx.h* header file is very similar. However, instead of including *stdio.h*, it includes a different file called *windows.h*. This file defines the functions and definitions that are part of the Windows interface. You will always include this file when you write a Windows program. You can include both files if you need to use both the Windows and standard interface, but often you only need one or the other.

Using the Compiler

For most projects, the Visual Studio will set up two versions of your program. To help you find and correct errors in your program, the Visual Studio creates a *Debug* version. The Debug version is the version you compiled in both the *First* and *Second* projects. When you compile the Debug version, Visual C++ adds a lot of extra information to the program file to help the debugger trace your program when you run it.

You do not have to run the debug version in the debugger. You can run it from the command line, or start it from the desktop in the case of a windows program. You cannot necessarily copy the debug version to another computer and run it. The debug version requires special files that also include debugging information be installed on the computer. Unless the same version of Visual C++ has been installed on the other computer, chances are you will not be able to run your program on it.

To copy the program to another computer, you need to compile the *Release* version of your program. This version does not require the special files needed by the debug version.

Figure 2.7

The Active Configuration dialog box allows you to select the version of your program that Visual C++ will compile.

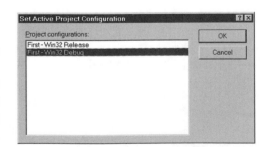

To switch to the release version, you need to change the active configuration in the Visual Studio by performing these steps:

1. Select the Visual Studio's Build menu and click the mouse on the Set Active Configuration item. Visual Studio will display the Active Configuration dialog box as shown in Figure 2.7. This dialog box should list two versions, "Win32 Release" and "Win32 Debug." The Visual Studio highlights the current configuration selection with a blue line.

2. Within the Active Configuration dialog box, click the mouse on the "Win32 Release" version to select it.

3. Click the OK button to save your selection and close the dialog box.

4. To return to the debug version, repeat the process, except select the "Win32 Debug" version instead.

To compile the selected version, press the Build button on the Build MiniBar. Assuming there are no errors in the compilation, your program is ready to run when the compiler reports there are "0 error(s)." Visual Studio places the debug version of your program in a *DEBUG* subdirectory and the release version in a *RELEASE* subdirectory. If you make changes to your program, you have to recompile both versions.

Using the Build Window

When you are building and testing your program from within the Visual Studio, the tools the Studio invokes, such as the Visual C++ compiler, will display information in the Output Window, which normally is at the bottom of the Visual Studio screen.

The Output Window contains several panels, depending upon the version you have installed. The compiler reports its results in the Build panel, as shown in Figure 2.8. When you test run the debug version of your program, the window will change to the Debug panel automatically. The debugger will write information about the program in this panel. You will learn how to use the Find in Files panels later.

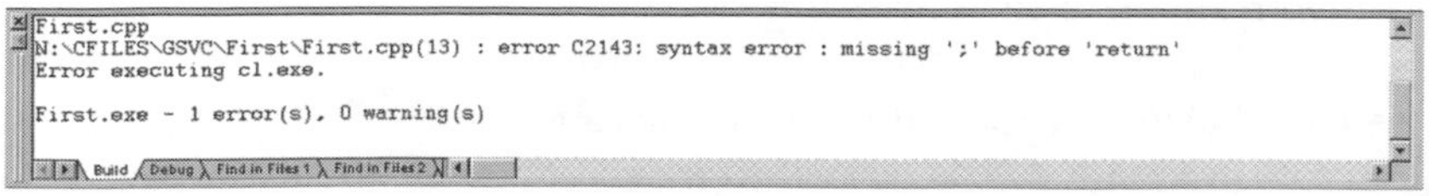

Figure 2.8

The Build panel of the Output Window shows the results when you compile your program in the Visual Studio.

```
First.cpp
N:\CFILES\GSVC\First\First.cpp(13) : error C2143: syntax error : missing ';' before 'return'
Error executing cl.exe.

First.exe - 1 error(s), 0 warning(s)

Build  Debug  Find in Files 1  Find in Files 2
```

You can display or hide this window using the toolbar list. Right-click on a blank area of the Visual Studio and select Output at the top of the list. If the Output Window is hidden, it will be displayed; if it is displayed, it will be hidden.

Examining the Results

The Output Window is a helpful tool, and it also serves as a navigation point for your project. From the Output Window, you can move to the file containing an error or look up help on an error message that you do not understand.

An intentional error has been introduced in the *First* project in Figure 2.8 to show you a sample of the error output. The semicolon in the *MessageBox* statement has been removed. If you double-click the mouse on the Output Window line where the compiler reported the error, the Visual Studio will open the source code file and move to the line containing the error.

Also, if you single-click the mouse on the line to place the caret in the line, and then press the F1 key, the Visual Studio will open the help file and display an explanation of the error.

Running Your Program

When you run your program in the Visual Studio debugger, the Output Window will switch automatically to the Debug panel. The debug version of the special files that you added to your computer when you installed Visual C++ contain special code to write information to this panel.

Normally, Visual Studio will hide the Output Window when you are running your program and display it when your program exits. You can display it during the debugging process, however, using the toolbar list. Alternatively, you can use a button on the Main toolbar to toggle the window on and off. The button has an image of a hammer in front of a small window.

You can start your program using the buttons on the Build MiniBar. You have already used the debug button to launch your program, but next to this button is another with an exclamation point on it. This button is the Run button, and it will start your program outside the debugger. You will need to do this from time to time because the debugger provides a protected environment for your program, and you'll need to see how it runs normally. When you start the debug version of your program using the Run button, the program still will stop at any breakpoints you have set.

Instead of using the toolbar buttons, you can press the F5 key to start your program in the debugger and press Ctrl+F5 to run it.

Examining Visual C++ Project Files

To keep track of your workspace and project settings between sessions, the Visual Studio needs to create some housekeeping files. Microsoft warns about editing these files, and with good reason. Unless you know what you are doing, you can damage the project files seriously.

The workspace information is kept in a file with an extension of *.dsp*. If your project name is *First*, the workspace file will be called *First.dsw*. This file contains a list of the projects that you have added to the workspace.

The project information is kept in a file with the same name as the project but with an extension of *.dsp*. You can have more than one project in a workspace, but each must have a unique name. This file contains source file names as well as compiler and linker information.

Workspace options are kept in a file with an extension of *.opt*. When you change the Visual Studio appearance using the Options item from the Tools menu, these changes are written to this file. Later, when you restart Visual C++ and open your project, Visual Studio reads this file to restore the options you selected.

Closing and Saving Your Program

You can close individual files that you have open in the client area using the Close item on the File menu. When you are debugging a program, you may find that Visual C++ has opened some files to help you locate an error, and you may want to close these files after fixing the error.

To close a file, first select it in the client area. From the File menu, select Close. If you have modified the file since the last time you compiled the program, Visual C++ will ask you if you want to save the file before closing it. Select Yes or No from the message box that appears. If you haven't changed a file, Visual C++ will close the file without prompting you.

You also can left click the mouse on the "X" button that appears in the upper-right corner of the editing window that contains the file.

When you are ready to exit Visual C++, you should close any projects you have open. Closing your projects will assure that the Visual Studio properly saves any changes you have made and any project options you have selected.

To close your projects, select the File menu, then select the Close Workspace item. Visual C++ will ask you if you want to close all the open windows. Select Yes to close the project.

At any time during your session, you can save the workspace and all the files in it by selecting the Save Workspace item on the File menu.

What You Must Know

In this lesson, you learned how to install and run the Visual C++ compiler, and how to create Windows- and console-based programs. You also learned how to run your program from within the Visual Studio debugger.

In Lesson 3, "Exploring the Visual Studio," you will learn how to use the tool windows in the Visual Studio and how to set up the syntax highlighting the way you want. Before you continue with Lesson 3, however, make sure you have learned the following key concepts:

◆ Syntax errors are grammatical and spelling errors in the programming language you are using. The Visual C++ compiler detects these errors and reports them in the Build panel of the Output Window.

◆ The Visual Studio uses syntax highlighting to display the elements of your source files in different colors.

◆ Portability is the ability to move your program source files (not the executable files) from one operating system to another such as Linux and to compile them on another operating system. Your command-line programs may be portable, but programs that display windows usually are not portable.

◆ Visual C++ is a development tool for Windows. It will run only under Microsoft Windows operating systems such as Windows 95, 98, and ME or Windows NT and 2000.

Lesson 3

Exploring the Visual Studio

As you will learn, Visual C++ provides you with more than a programming language. To improve your programming productivity, Visual C++ provides an integrated development environment called the *Visual Studio*. To a newcomer, Visual Studio can seem overwhelming at first. So, although you probably want to keep writing more programs right now, you will become a much more effective Visual C++ programmer if you take some time now to learn how to use the Visual Studio.

In the previous lessons, you have created, compiled, and tested projects using the Visual Studio and Visual C++. In this lesson, you will learn about the major components of the Visual Studio and how to use them. By time you finish this lesson, you will understand the following key concepts:

◆ Visual Studio contains several tool windows to help you to perform specific tasks during the process of writing and debugging your program.

◆ As you work, you can hide the task windows when you do not need them in order to make room for editing source files. Later, you can display specific task windows as your needs require.

◆ The Visual Studio toolbars are visual aids you use with the mouse. Different toolbars are available to you when you edit and debug your program.

◆ The Visual Studio tools will help you find and display specific functions and variables in your source files.

◆ Using the Find command, you can search a single program file for a word, such as a specific variable name. Using the Find In Files command, you may search *all* the files in your project.

Setting Visual Studio Options

For this lesson, start the Visual Studio and then open the *Second* project you created in Lesson 2, "Building, Running, and Saving Your First Visual C++ Program," by performing these steps:

1. Select the File menu on the Visual Studio Menu Bar.

2. Within the File menu, select the Open Workspace item. The Visual Studio will display an Open Workspace dialog box. The Open Workspace dialog box is similar to the File Open dialog box in many other applications.

3. Within the Open Workspace dialog box, locate the directory where you created the *Second* project and double-click the mouse the entry.

4. Within the directory box, you should see a file called Second.dsw, which is the workspace file. Double-click the mouse on this file to open the project.

Visual Studio also maintains a list of the last four projects you had open. Rather than using the preceding sequence, you can open your project from this list using the following steps:

1. Select the File menu on the Visual Studio Main Menu Bar.

2. From the File menu, select the Recent Workspaces item toward the bottom of the menu. Visual Studio will display a list of the last four workspaces with which you worked.

3. Within the list, click the mouse on the entry for Second.

Later in this section, you will learn how to change the number of recent projects that appear on the Recent Workspaces list.

The Visual Studio contains many tools and a number of work places. You can customize the appearance of most of these tools using the Options dialog box, which you access from the Tools menu. The Options dialog box, shown in Figure 3.1, contains a number of tabs from which you may set the behavior of the tools.

In the following steps, if you cannot see the tab for a page, use the *scroll* buttons at the upper-right of the dialog box. Click the mouse on the arrow that points to the right to scroll the tabs right and reveal more tabs. Click the mouse on the arrow that points left to scroll the tabs to the left. When you click on a tab, the dialog box will display a different page of options.

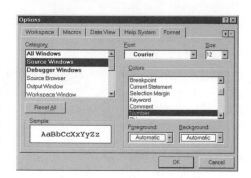

Figure 3.1

The Options dialog box lets you customize the appearance of the Visual Studio, including the fonts and colors used for syntax highlighting.

Within the Options dialog box, select the first page by clicking the mouse on the Editor tab. From within the Editor tab, you may select how the editor interacts with the rest of the Visual Studio. You should at least select the "Save before running tools" item. The Visual Studio is not a perfect program and sometimes may "crash." Visual Studio's most vulnerable time is when you are debugging a program. By setting the "Save before running tools" option, you assure that the Visual Studio will save your files every time you compile your program.

The second page, the one with the Tabs label, contains tab options. As you saw in Lesson 1, "Getting Started with Visual C++," most Visual C++ programmers use four spaces for the tab and indent sizes. Others use two or three spaces. For now, you should enter 4 in both the Tab Size and Indent Size boxes. For efficiency, check the Keep Tabs option. If you leave the Keep Tabs option unchecked, Visual Studio will save your files with spaces in place of the tab characters. A source file with spaces rather than tabs may use up to 10 percent more disk space.

Next, click the mouse on the "Debug" tab to select the Debug page. At the lower-right corner of the page, the "Just-in-time debugging" item causes Visual C++ to embed information in your program file that lets the program start the Visual Studio debugger if the program encounters an error, which is especially useful when you test run your program outside the Visual Studio.

Another option on the Debug page is "Debug commands invoke Edit and Continue." Checking this item lets you modify the code during a debugging session. When you pause your program at a breakpoint or by clicking the Pause button on the Debug toolbar and make a change to the code, Visual Studio will compile the new code before resuming the program. Without this option, you would have to stop the debugger, then recompile the program and restart it from the beginning to make the changes take effect.

Click the mouse on the "Workspace" tab. (The Workspace tab probably is not visible, so click the mouse on the scroll arrow that points to the right until the tab appears, then click on the tab). You may change the number of recent workspaces on this page. At the lower-right of the page is a box labeled "workspaces." If you have not changed it already, this box should contain the number 4. This is the number of recent workspaces the Visual Studio will list on the menu item that you used earlier in this section to open the *Second* workspace. Enter the number you would like in this space. As you develop more projects, four may be too few, and you may want to increase this number.

Finally, click the mouse on the "Format" tab to select the Format page. The options here let you customize a feature known as *syntax highlighting*. You can make the various components—keywords, numbers, comment text, and such—appear in different fonts and/or colors. The defaults are pretty good, but take some time to study this page. As your programming skills develop and you use more and more of the Visual Studio tools, you might want to return to this page to customize the displays.

 Increasing the Font Size within Your Source Code Window

If you find that you have difficulty reading programming statements within the source-code windows, you might want to use the Format page to increase the size of the text display in the windows. To do this, use the following steps:

1. *Make sure the "Format" page is selected by clicking on the tab. If the tab is not visible, click on the right scroll arrow until it appears.*

2. *Select the window type in the Category list. To change just the source file windows, click on the "Source Windows" item.*

3. *Change the size of the text in the Size box. The sizes are in points, which is a printing measure. The default is 10 points, about one-seventh of an inch. Seventy-two points is about an inch, so 12 points would be about one-sixth of an inch and 16 points about one-fourth of an inch.*

4. *Click the mouse on the OK button to save your changes.*

Using the New Menu Command

The starting point for new workspaces, projects, and files is the New item on the File menu. Most Windows-based programs simply display an Open File dialog box when you select the New item. Visual Studio, however, displays a more complex tabbed dialog box that contains entries for files, projects, workspaces, and application documents. Do not let the range of options on this dialog box confuse you. Visual Studio is designed for all levels of programmers, and you will be concerned with only a few of the options.

Exactly what appears on these tabs will depend upon the Visual Studio options you have installed and what other applications you have on your computer.

You can create individual source files using the Files tab on this dialog box. To select it, click the mouse on the tab with the label "Files." Once again, this list contains many file types. For the lessons in this book, you will use only the "C/C++ Header File" and "C/C++ Source File" items.

 Creating a Word Document from within Visual Studio

If you have Microsoft Word installed on your computer, you can create a Word document from the New dialog box. Click the mouse the Other Documents tab. You should see an item labeled "Microsoft Word Document." If you double-click on this item, Word will create a document in the Visual Studio. Notice that the title bar still says "Microsoft Visual C++," but the menu and toolbars you see are from Word. When you close the document, Visual Studio restores its menus and toolbars.

This feature gives you the ability to create and maintain the documentation for your program, or to write a help file, as part of the project.

Next, click the mouse on the Projects tab to list the various types of projects you can create with the Visual Studio. You will examine these options in the next topic.

Next, click on the Workspaces tab. The list should contain only one item, "Blank workspace." The Blank workspace option, which is for advanced and intermediate programmers, lets you create an empty workspace from the Workspaces tab. Later, you can create projects in the workspace.

Finally, click the mouse on the Other Documents tab. The dialog box, in turn, will display a page that provides the Visual Studio interface to other applications on your computer.

Selecting a Project Type

Microsoft designed the Visual Studio for all levels of programmers, from beginner to professional, and all types of applications, from single-purpose programs to commercial applications. The project options available to you when you click the New dialog box Projects tab, as shown in Figure 3.2, reflect that range. As a newcomer to C++ and Visual C++, the options you will need are near the bottom of the list, "Win32 Application" and "Win32 Console Application."

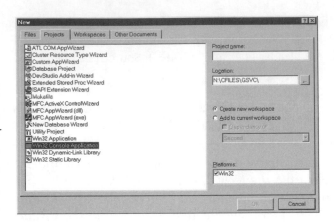

Figure 3.2

The Projects tab of the New dialog box lists a wide range of project types. You may never use all of them, but as your programming skills advance, you will need several of them.

When you select an item from this list, the Visual Studio uses your selection to create the basic source files you will need to write your program.

The Win32 Application option creates a skeleton Windows program using the Windows *application program- ming interface* (API). An API is a library of functions that exist to make it easier for you to program for a specific task. In this case, the API functions help you to access the underlying Windows operating system. The Win32 Application option is the item you selected to create the *First* application in Lesson 1.

The "Win32 Console Application" selection creates the basic files for a command-line program, one that you run from the DOS command prompt in Windows. You used the Wind32 Console Application option to create the *Second* project in Lesson 1.

You should note the "Win32" in the name for each of these selections. Visual C++ 6.0 is a tool to help you write programs for 32-bit versions of Windows, which includes versions from Windows 95 and later. You cannot use it to write programs for older DOS or 16-bit Windows systems.

Using Visual Studio Windows

The Visual Studio contains several windows. The outer window that includes the blue title bar at the top is called the *parent* window and often is called the *frame window*. As you will learn through the course of this book, each toolbar and tool window in the Visual Studio is a *child* window. It is like building a house out of bricks. Each brick may have a special shape and color for its position in the overall construction project, but when they all are assembled, the appearance is that of a brick house.

This modular construction makes it easier to manipulate and use the various elements that make up a program window. The studio with the *Second* project is shown in Figure 3.3.

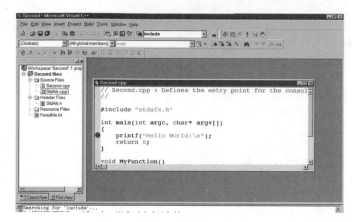

Figure 3.3

The Visual Studio as it appears with the Second project open.

There is no "typical" Visual Studio appearance because the menus and toolbars and the content of the various windows will change according to the task you are performing and the type of project you are creating. The studio may be used for projects other than Visual C++. In addition, you may move all the elements around to suit your tastes.

At the top of the Visual Studio just below the blue title bar is the Menu Bar. Until you learn the various toolbars, the Menu Bar will be your primary point of interaction with the Visual Studio. The Visual Studio Menu Bar is moveable, and you may detach it from the frame and move it to another location. You also may make it *float*, or appear unattached to the window frame.

To move the Menu Bar—or any other toolbar—to a new location, perform these steps:

1. Click and hold the mouse on the double bars at the far-left of the Menu Bar. Visual Studio will draw an outline around the Menu Bar or toolbar.

2. Move the mouse to drag this outline to a new position. Notice that the outline changes shape depending upon the location in the Visual Studio.

3. When the outline appears where you want to place the toolbar, release the mouse button, and the bar will reattach itself to the frame in the new position.

4. If you release a toolbar away from the frame, such as in the large client area, it will float there and Visual Studio will give it a blue title bar. For example, a floating Menu Bar will appear with the words "Menu Bar" in the title bar. To move a floating toolbar, use this title bar instead of the double bars.

Immediately below the Menu Bar is the WizardBar, which is shown in Figure 3.4. The contents of the Wizard-Bar will change according to the current *context* of your project and what task you are performing. While you are working in the Visual Studio, a portion of the Visual Studio program is watching what you do. This part of Visual Studio will change the contents of the WizardBar when you open and select different source files or move the caret around in a source file. The help file describes this feature as *context tracking*. The WizardBar also will help you to navigate the files in your project.

Figure 3.4

The Visual Studio WizardBar will help you to move from file to file and from function to function in your project.

To see an example of context tracking, add the code that corresponds to *MyFunction* to the *Second.cpp* source file so that the file appears as follows:

```
// Second.cpp : Defines the entry point for the console application.
//

#include "stdafx.h"

int main(int argc, char* argv[])
{
    printf("Hello World!\n");
    return 0;
}


void MyFunction()
{
    printf ("My Function\n");
}
```

Referring to Figure 3.4, display the drop-down function list by clicking the mouse on the down arrow to the right of the Members List. The list will contain the names of the two functions that now are in your *Second.cpp* source file. Select one of the functions and click the left mouse button on it. If *Second.cpp* is not visible in the client area, the wizard will open the file and display it. Then the wizard will locate and highlight the function in the file. Select another function from the list, and the wizard will move the caret to that function and highlight it.

Success HINT: Moving Quickly to a Specific Function's Code Using the Members List

If your source file contains many functions, you can move directly to one or another by selecting the function name from the Members List. This is called navigating your code, *and the Visual Studio contains many tools that help you navigate.*

Now, using the arrow keys, move the caret between the *MyFunction* and *main* functions. When the caret is in *MyFunction*, that function's name appears in the Members List. When you move the caret to *main*, the display changes to show *main* instead of *MyFunction*.

The other lists deal with C++ *classes* and Windows *messages*. These lists do not mean much in *Second.cpp*. You will learn how to use these later.

Next is the Toolbar area. *All* the toolbars used in the Visual Studio including the WizardBar are *dockable*, meaning you may use the mouse to detach them from their current locations and move them to another position on the Visual Studio frame, or leave them unattached as floating tool windows. Initially, they will appear in this area. You can display a partial list of available toolbars by right-clicking the mouse on a blank portion of this frame. The list is partial because its contents will change depending upon what you are doing. For example, if you are in the process of debugging a program, this list will contain a number of debugging tools that may be turned on and off, as seen in the right side of Figure 3.5. In addition, you may design your own toolbars, and they will appear in this list.

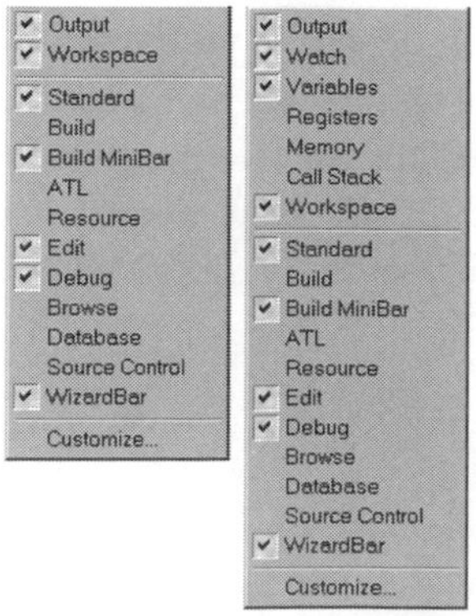

Figure 3.5

The toolbar list at left is the one you will see when editing your program files. If you pause your program while running it, the toolbar list at the right will be displayed. A check mark next to a toolbar name means it is being displayed.

At the far-left and in the middle of the screen is the Workspace Window. This area will contain one or more panels according to the type of the project and the Visual Studio edition you have installed. For all projects, the FileView pane will display a list of files in your project. For a Windows application, a ResourceView pane will give you access to the resource file and all the dialog boxes, cursors, images, and other objects that a Windows program needs. If you write your program in C++, a ClassView pane will list all the classes in your project along with the member functions and variables. The Workspace Window may be moved to another area around the frame. For example, putting this window on the right side of the screen might be more to your liking, or you can leave it floating as any other toolbar.

To the right of the Workspace Window is the Client area. This is where your project files will appear when you create or open them for editing. The individual file windows are limited to this area, and if you try to move outside it, the edges of the windows will be "clipped" and appear to disappear under the edges of the frame.

At the bottom of the Visual Studio is the Output Window. This position is shared with the Watch Window, which is displayed while you are debugging a program, as shown in Figure 3.6. When you start debugging your program, the studio normally will hide the Output Window and display the Variables Window on the left and the Watch Window on the right, as shown in the bottom image of Figure 3.6.

Figure 3.6

The Output Window (top) appears when you are editing your source files. During debugging, the Visual Studio replaces it with the Variables and Watch windows (bottom).

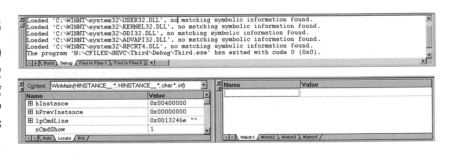

The Output Window contains several tabs, again depending upon your installation. It always will contain at least four tabs, however. The Build tab shows the results when you compile a program. The compiler will write any error or warning messages here. You can go to the file and the exact line where an error appears by double-clicking the mouse on the error message. The Debug pane displays diagnostic information when you are debugging a program. Two Find In Files panes display the results of the Find In Files command, which you will learn about later in this lesson.

Exploring Visual Studio Menus and Toolbars

The Menu Bar contains the menus that you will use to create and build your program. The menus drop down from the Menu Bar when you select one by clicking the mouse on its name.

The toolbars below the Menu Bar duplicate many the menu items. Toolbars provide you with a visual aid and shortcuts when you use the mouse. Instead of text, toolbars contain buttons with pictures, or *icons*, that indicate the purpose of the buttons.

The File menu contains the commands you will use to create and open and save projects as well as files. It also contains the Print commands. Next to it is the Edit menu, which contains the commands you will use to cut and paste text in your program files. It also contains Undo and Redo commands that allow you to correct an editing mistake. Every time you make a change to a program file, the Visual Studio adds the change to the Undo list. The studio stores up to 20 edit operations.

The View menu lets you turn Visual Studio windows on and off. The Insert and Project menus allow you to add new objects to your project. The Build menu contains the commands that you used on the Build MiniBar and lets you start and stop debugging and pause a debugging session.

The Tools menu lists the tools used by Visual C++ or other tools you might need in the course of building a project. From this menu, you also access the dialog boxes to customize the Visual Studio and set options.

The Window menu generally is used to control and display the windows in which you are editing source code. At the bottom of this menu is a list of the first 10 source files you have open in editing windows. You can switch to a window by selecting the window name from the list. If you have more than 10 windows open, selecting Windows at the bottom of this menu will display a list of all the windows.

 Splitting a Window to View Multiple Locations within Your Source File

You may want to spend some time experimenting with the first two items on the Window menu. These can make editing a single file much easier. If you select an edit window in the client area and then select New Window from the Window menu, Visual Studio will create another window containing the same source file. Any changes you make in one window also will appear in the other window.

The Split item allows you to divide a single editing window into as many as four smaller windows—or panes—and to scroll the code in each of the smaller windows separately. When you select it, a crosshair pattern appears in the source code window. Move the center of the crosshairs to select the sizes of the panes, then click the mouse to split the window. Any changes you make to one of the panes will be made in the other panes as well.

To remove a split from the editing window, move the mouse cursor over the bar. When the cursor changes from an arrow to something that resembles a vise, click and hold the left mouse button. Move the mouse cursor to the edge of the editing window, and the splitter bar will follow. At the edge, release the mouse button, and the split will disappear.

Before you continue with the next topic, remove any splits and close any editing windows.

During the course of building your program, Visual C++ may add other menus you need to the Menu Bar. For example, when you are building a dialog box, Visual C++ will add a Layout menu to the bar.

Using the Workspace Window

Within the Visual Studio, the Workspace Window is a center of information about your project and a focal point for getting to various parts of your program. Figure 3.3 earlier in this lesson shows the Workspace Window open with the FileView pane visible for the *Second* project. Figure 3.7 shows the ClassView pane. At the bottom, you will see up to three tabs. The first is the FileView pane, which contains a list of all the files in your project. The second is the ResourceView tab, which gives you access to the resource file. The last is the ClassView pane. For a more advanced Visual C++ project, it contains a list of all the *classes* and *structures* in your project along with their members. For any Visual C++ project, it contains a list of functions and variables.

Figure 3.7

The ClassView pane of the Workspace Window.

Select the ClassView pane by clicking on it with the mouse. The entire name may not be visible because the tabs are too narrow, but if you let the mouse cursor hover over it for about a half second, Visual Studio will display the full name.

If the ClassView pane shows only "Second classes" with a plus sign next to it, click on the "+" to show the items under it. For the *Second* project, the pane will list only "Globals." Next, click the mouse on the "+" next to Globals to expand the items under it and you should see a list similar to Figure 3.7.

The window may be too narrow to display the entire name of an item, but if you move the mouse cursor over it the Visual Studio will display the full name.

Select the *WinMain* item and double-click the left mouse button on it. The studio will open the file containing the function and display it in an editing window, then place the caret on the line containing the function. Next, select and double-click the mouse on the *WndProc* item. The Visual Studio scrolls the file to that function and places the caret at the beginning of the line.

Using the Find Command

You probably have used the Find command in other Windows programs. You use it to find words or groups of characters within a file. Of course, Visual C++ has such a command, but for a program as sophisticated as the Visual Studio that might seem too simple, Microsoft has added a lot of features to the Find command.

Open the *Second.cpp* file in the Visual Studio and select it. From the Edit menu, select Find, or hold the Ctrl key down and press the F key. You can use the Find dialog box the same as you would in any other program such as Microsoft Word. On the right side of the dialog box is a button labeled "Mark All" that you have probably not seen in any other Windows program, however. This button places a *bookmark* on every line that contains the search word or phrase.

Refer to Figure 3.8 and make sure the Edit toolbar is visible. Open and select *Second.cpp* in an editing window, then click the Find button on the toolbar. Enter **printf** in the dialog box, then click the Mark All key. The Visual Studio places color squares in the margin to the left of each line containing the word "printf." These are *book-marks*, and they are the electronic equivalent of placing a slip of paper between the pages of a book.

Figure 3.8

The Edit toolbar enhances the Find command.

The buttons on the Edit toolbar allow you to move to the next or previous bookmark, turn a single bookmark on or off, and remove all the bookmarks. The buttons to increase and decrease indent are "grayed out" because you cannot use them with Visual C++ source files, but they will become active if you edit a World Wide Web page in the Visual Studio.

The Toggle White Space button places markers in the editing window to show you individual spaces, tabs, and end-of-line characters.

The bookmarks and the white space markers are not saved as part of your source file.

The ClassWizard button summons a very special tool that you will get to know better in a later lesson.

Using the Find In Files Command

In addition to the Find command, Visual C++ also has a command that will search *all* the files in your project. Select the Edit menu and choose the Find In Files option to select this command. Visual Studio, in turn, will display the Find In Files dialog box, as shown in Figure 3.9.

Figure 3.9

The Find In Files dialog box allows you to select groups of files to search.

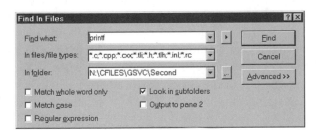

By default, the Find In Files command will search all the source files in your project, but you may use the dialog box to select other files. Clicking on the Advanced button to the right will let you specify other directories for the search.

The Find In Files command works in conjunction with the panes on the Output Window. The command will write the results to the Find In Files pane. You can select this pane by clicking on the tab labeled "Find In Files 1." There are two panes for the search results, and you can select the second pane by checking the Output To Pane 2 box in the dialog box. This means you can have the results of two searches available at the same time.

To try it, select the Find In Files command, enter **include** in the Find What box, then click the Find button. The *Second* project contains three files, and "include" appears several times in the files. When you clicked the Find button, Visual Studio selected the "Find In Files 1" pane in the Output Window and listed seven places in your files where the word "include" appears. Double-click the mouse on an item in the list, and the Visual Studio will open the file containing the search word and display the line in an editing window.

What You Must Know

In this lesson, you learned about the various tool windows in the Visual Studio and how to use them. You also learned how to use the Find and the Find In Files commands. This knowledge will make your programming easier. In Lesson 4, "Using Visual C++ from the Command Line," you will learn how to use Visual C++ from the command line. Before you go to the next lesson, make sure you understand the following key points:

◆ The Visual C++ menus let you select the commands you want to execute.

◆ Toolbars contain buttons with an image called an icon. Toolbars are shortcuts to menu commands. You select toolbar buttons using the mouse.

◆ To remove screen clutter, you can hide and later display the Visual Studio toolbars by clicking on a blank area of the window frame and selecting the toolbar from the list that appears.

◆ Visual C++ displays the results of running the compiler in a pane in the Output Window. When you run your program in the debugger, Visual C++ hides the Output Window and displays the Watch Window.

◆ The WizardBar helps you locate named sections of code called functions. Select the function name in the list to display it in the editing window.

◆ The Find command lets you set bookmarks in your program file. You then can use the Edit toolbar buttons to move to these bookmarks.

◆ The Find In Files command searches all the files in your project and displays the results in one of two panes in the Output Window.

Lesson 4

Using Visual C++ from the Command Line

In the previous lessons, you created, compiled, and ran your programs from within the Visual Studio environment. Visual Studio, however, runs only under Microsoft Windows operating systems. An operating system is the software that controls the use of computer resources such as memory and disk space. Depending on the systems that your user's use, there may be times when you must write a program that you can move to and from other operating systems, such as Linux.

To make the development of such programs easier, you might want to avoid the Visual Studio and develop your program from the *command line*. At other times, you may not want to go through the steps to create a workspace and project for short utility programs that you use for a single task.

Windows users sometimes refer to the command line as the "DOS prompt." To get a command-line prompt from Windows, select the Start menu Programs option and then choose the MS-DOS Prompt item. (On Windows NT, it is called "Command Prompt." On Windows 2000, to get the command line window you select the Start button, then Run and type **command** in the Run box). Windows, in turn, will open a window that programmers often refer to as the "command-console window," because the window gives you a prompt at which you can enter commands. The advantage of using the command line is that virtually every operating system has one.

In this lesson, you will learn how to use Visual C++ from the command line and how to create the source files that the Visual Studio wizards made for you in the previous lessons. By the time you finish this lesson, you will understand the following key concepts:

◆ You must store program source files as ordinary text files. Popular *word processor* programs such as Corel WordPerfect and Microsoft Word add (often hidden) formatting characters to the source file that will cause errors when you compile your program.

◆ The entry point for a C++ program is a function named *main*. To run your program from the command line and move it to other operating systems, you must include this function in your program.

◆ Your program writes to the command console using standard C++ functions such as *printf*. These functions are available to you on other operating systems.

◆ When you make a change to your program code, you must recompile the program for the change to take effect

◆ If you make a language or *syntax* error in your source code file, you must correct the errors before you can compile your program.

Selecting a Program Editor

C++ is a compiled language, and the compiler requires you to store your source code in a text file called a *source file*. The compiler reads the program code from this file to generate the intermediate object files, which it *links* with other object and library files to create your program file.

You can use sophisticated word-processing programs such as Corel WordPerfect or Microsoft Word to create your source files, but you must remember to save them as *ASCII text files*. The compiler will not be able to read the code if you save the source files as *document* files in the word processor's format. The reason is that the word-processing programs store various formatting, font, and color information in the document files, and this information is meaningless to the compiler.

On DOS-based systems, you can use the *EDIT.EXE* program, and on Windows platforms, you can use the *NotePad.Exe* program. Both of these platforms store files as plain text files and can be used to create and modify source files. *NotePad.Exe* has a fixed tab setting of eight spaces, while most programmers use only four spaces for a C++ program. *EDIT.EXE* defaults to eight spaces for tabs, but you can change that by selecting Display from the Options menu and setting the Tab Stops value to four.

You want to select an editor that can use a *fixed pitch font*. A *font* is the collection of all the characters of a given typeface, style, and weight; and in a fixed pitch font, all the characters have the same width. Using a fixed pitch font makes indents and tabs line up properly. An example of a fixed pitch font on Windows is Courier New.

A good program editor that supports various fonts and syntax highlighting similar to the Visual Studio editor is the *SciTE* editor, written by Neil Hodgson and others. This versatile editor uses the *Scintilla* library (also written by Hodgson), and versions of it can be compiled or obtained for several operating systems, including Linux and various versions of Unix and Windows. Figure 4.1 shows a screen from the SciTE editor.

The SciTE editor is free under the GNU General Public License, and you can download it from *sourceforge.net*. You also will need the *scintilla* library. It, too, is available under the GNU license.

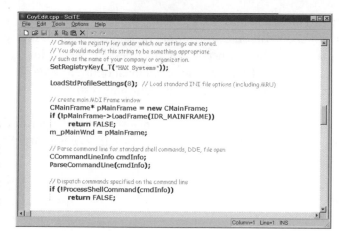

Figure 4.1

The SciTE editor supports a user-definable display including complete syntax highlighting in various fonts and colors.

The Windows version on the companion CD is set up to use syntax highlighting similar to Visual C++ and includes commands to compile your program from within the editing program. You can install the editor by running the *SETUP.EXE* program in the *SCITE* directory.

When you are instructed to compile your program, you can select Compile from the SciTE editor's Tools menu. If you are using another editor such as *EDIT.EXE* or *NotePad.Exe*, you will have to save your program code and exit the editor to compile it. The next topic will describe how to do it both ways.

(You also will find the source code for the editor and its libraries at *http://www.prima-tech.com/ books/book/5536/903/*. At this point, you probably will not understand the source code, but the GNU license requires giving the source code to users.)

Understanding the *main()* Function

Functions are the basic building blocks of Visual C++. You can *declare variables* and *define objects* outside of a function, but all of your programming code must be inside named blocks of code that form functions.

You can have as many functions as you need in a Visual C++ program, but every program must have a function called *main*. That said, you already have seen that a Windows program does not need *main* and instead uses a function called *WinMain*. This is a peculiarity of Windows and not the C++ programming language, and in fact makes the Windows code *non-portable*, meaning you cannot compile and run the program on another operating system. You should remember that all standard C++ programs must have a *main* function.

You can write your entire program in the *main* function, and for short programs that is not a problem. However, as your program gets more complex, you will want to break it into smaller blocks of code—functions. Each function should have a unique name, and usually you will want to use a name that describes its purpose.

You must *declare* each function before your can use it. Declaring a function is the process of telling the compiler about the form the function will take. The *main* function is unique in that you do not have to *declare* it before using it. You will learn more about functions in a later lesson. Meanwhile, you need to know about them for the samples in this lesson. In its undeclared form, *main* must return a value. When your program *calls*, or executes, a function, the function will perform its task and return its result.

The block of code you write in a function must be enclosed between open and close braces. This is called a *block* in the C++ jargon. A block can be empty, in which case it does nothing. Start your program editor and enter the following lines:

```
main()
{
    return (1);
}
```

Remember that C++ is a *case-sensitive* language. The C++ compiler treats *main* and *Main* as separate functions. When you name a function, you always must refer to it with the same name, including the uppercase or lowercase letters. The *main* function always is in lowercase.

If you have decided to use the *SciTE* editor, select the Tools menu and then the Compile item, or simply hold the Ctrl key down and press F7. The program will ask you for a name for the file. Call it *empty.cpp* and press the Save button. A window will appear at the bottom showing the results of the Compile command. When the compiler has finished, you will get a message like the following:

```
>Exit code: 0
```

Select Go from the Tools menu or press the F5 key. The editor will display the following message that indicates it ran the EMPTY.EXE program, which in turn, exited and returned to the operating system the value 1:

```
>Empty.exe
>Exit code: 1
```

Within a command-line environment, it is common for a program to return 0 if it succeeded in its task, and a non-zero value if it failed.

If you are using another editor, you will have to save the file as *empty.cpp*, then exit the editor. From the command line, enter the following and press the Enter key:

```
C:>cl empty.cpp   <Enter>
```

The compiler, in turn, will respond by showing the progress of the compile:

```
empty.cpp
Microsoft (R) Incremental Linker Version 6.00.8168
Copyright (C) Microsoft Corp 1992-1998. All rights reserved.

/out:empty.exe
empty.obj
C:>
```

When your system redisplays the command prompt (the *C:>*), type **EMPTY** and press the Enter key. The program will simply run and exit without doing anything:

```
C:> EMPTY  <Enter>
C:>
```

In the next section, you will learn how to make the program write to your screen.

 Understanding void *main()*

> *The* main *function may have different forms. When you write* main *as shown in this lesson, the function must return a value or the compiler will issue an error. Often you will see it written as* void main() *or* void main(void). *In these forms, the function cannot return a value, and attempting to do so will make the compiler issue an error. The* void *return type indicates that the function does not return any value.*

Performing Basic Output Using the *printf()* Function

A program that does nothing is not without value. On Unix operating systems, there are a couple of programs, *true* and *false*, that do nothing intentionally. Usually, however, you will want your program to perform a task before it ends.

The C++ language contains very few built-in functions that you can use. Instead, when you compile your program, the compiler *links* some additional functions that perform basic input and output operations. *Input* occurs when you read some external information into your program, such as characters from the keyboard or information from a file. In contrast, *output* occurs when your program writes information to some device, such as the screen or the disk.

One of these functions is *printf*, which you can use to write text to the computer screen. You encountered both *main* and *printf* in the *Second* project during Lesson 2, "Building, Running, and Saving Your First Visual C++ Program."

The *printf* function is defined in a special *header file* named *stdio.h*, which you must include in your program. Using your program editor, create a file called *Hello.cpp* that contains the following lines of code:

```
#include    <stdio.h>

void main()
{
    printf ("Hello, Visual C++ world!\n");
}
```

Next, save the file and compile the program. When you run it, the program will print the following line to the screen:

```
C:> Hello   <Enter>
Hello, Visual C++ world!
```

In Lesson 2, you learned that there often is more than one way to accomplish the same result. The C programming language—the predecessor to C++—used *printf* to write text to the screen. It was included in C++ so programmers could compile older programs with C++ without having to rewrite them.

To write to the screen or a file, some programmers prefer to use C++ *streams*. You probably have seen stream methods in other books, such as *Jamsa's Rescued By C++*. There are some advantages to using C++ streams, as you will learn in a later lesson. For example, *printf* always writes to the console device. To write to a file, you must use a different—but similar— function, *fprintf*. With streams, the actual output device may be identified with a *variable*, which your program code may change to output to a different device, such as a printer using the same program statement.

The stream that writes to the screen is identified by a variable called *cout*. You can direct your output to this variable, and it will appear on the screen. To write "Hello, Visual C++ World!" from the previous program, you would use the following line instead of the line containing the *printf* statement:

```
cout << "Hello, Visual C++ World!\n";
```

Success HINT: Do Not Mix Standard Output and Stream Output Operations

You may learn to prefer one method over the other, but you should not mix printf *and* cout *in the same program. The operating system handles the output differently, and the results are unpredictable. To show this, create a simple program called* output.cpp, *as shown below. Be sure to include the* iostream.h *file, which defines the streams:*

```
#include     <stdio.h>
#include     <iostream.h>

void main()
{
    printf ("Hello, printf\n");
    cout << "Hello, streams\n";
}
```

With streams, the double less than symbol (<) is called the insertion operator, *and the statement inserts the string into the stream. When you compile and run the program, you get the following output:*

```
Hello, streams
Hello, printf
```

Even though the printf *statement appears before the* cout *statement in your program code, the program wrote the* cout *line first! This is caused by the way the operating system flushes the buffers that hold the output text. To avoid this sort of problem, always use the same method in a program to write your output.*

Using Strings and String Constants: "Hello, Visual C++ World!"

There are a couple of things you should notice about the program code and the text written to the screen. First, the text appears within a set of double quotes. Programmers call a sequence of text within quote marks a *string* constant, a *string literal*, or often simply a *string*. Every computer language needs to deal with strings as a means of accepting information and displaying it on the screen. The double quote marks indicate the beginning and the end of the string but are not part of it, so they are not printed to the screen.

If you leave out the first quote mark and try to compile the program, the compiler will think the text is part of the program instead of a string and treat the individual word in the string as *variables*, and it will issue several errors:

```
Empty.cpp(5) : error C2065: 'Hello' : undeclared identifier
Empty.cpp(5) : error C2017: illegal escape sequence
Empty.cpp(5) : error C2065: 'World' : undeclared identifier
Empty.cpp(5) : error C2001: newline in constant
Empty.cpp(5) : error C2146: syntax error : missing ')' before identifier 'n'
Empty.cpp(7) : warning C4508: 'main' : function should return a value; 'void'
return type assumed
```

Because of the missing quote mark, the compilation process gets out of sync, and the compiler fails to locate other parts of the code such as the ending parenthesis. In fact, just from one missing character, there are more errors than there are lines in the program. If you leave off the ending quotes, the results are not as traumatic, but you still get errors:

```
Empty.cpp(5) : error C2001: newline in constant
Empty.cpp(6) : error C2143: syntax error : missing ')' before 'return'
Empty.cpp(7) : warning C4508: 'main' : function should return a value; 'void'
return type assumed
```

When this happens, locate the first error in the list, fix the error, and recompile the program.

Secondly, you may be wondering about the sequence "\n" in the string. Visual C++ has several special character sequences that begin with the backslash character. This combination is an *escape* sequence (but do not confuse it with the *escape* character, which is an actual character that may be sent to the screen or printer). The "\n" sequence tells the compiler to insert a newline character in the string. For Windows, this actually is two characters: a *carriage return*, which returns the console cursor to the beginning of the line, and a *line feed*, which moves the cursor to the next line. (In the early days of computing, the console usually was a printer with a keyboard, which is how we get the names for these characters).

There are other escape characters that you will learn to use. For example, "\t" inserts a tab character, "\a" causes the PC speaker to beep, and "\f" causes the printer to feed out a sheet of paper. These escape sequences are translated into the proper characters by the compiler.

Neither the *printf* function nor the C++ stream *cout* inserts a new line sequence automatically. This makes it possible to build a single line on the screen using more than one output statement. Using your program editor, create a new program called *string.cpp,* as shown below:

```
#include      <stdio.h>

void main()
{
    printf ("Hello, ");
    printf ("Visual C++ ");
    printf ("world!\n");
}
```

In this example, notice that the first two *printf* lines have spaces at the end of the string. Neither *printf* nor *cout* provides these spaces automatically, so you must include them to keep the words from running together. Compile and run the program to display the following output:

```
C> string  <Enter>
Hello, Visual C++ world!
```

The newline sequence occurs only in the last statement. In practice, if you are writing to the screen, Windows will provide a newline when the program ends, but other operating systems such as Unix do not. Make it a practice to include the newline sequence whenever you want to end a line.

Compiling Your Visual C++ Program from the Command Line

When you compile your program, you actually are starting a sequence of events that invokes several Visual C++ programs.

You start the compile process using the *cl.exe* program. At the command prompt, enter **cl** followed by the name of your source file. For the *String.cpp* from the last section, the entire command line is shown here:

```
C:> cl string.cpp   <Enter>
```

First the compiler starts a *preprocessor*, which reads your source files and all the files you added using the *#include* directive. It puts these files together into one file, which it then compiled. It also reads and responds to other preprocessor directives.

The compiler creates an *object* file with an *.obj* extension. This file contains the numbers your computer uses as instructions, but it contains no *run* information. The file does not contain the code the Windows loader needs to place it into memory. After you compile the *String.cpp* program from the previous section, the compiler will create a *String.obj* file.

If the compiler encounters an error in the compilation, it will not create the object file. Instead, it will report the errors to your screen and stop. You must return to your program code and fix any errors before you attempt to recompile your program.

The compiler may issue *warnings* during the process. Warnings are not language errors. The compiler will continue to build the object file, but warnings may indicate problems in your program that might cause it to fail when you run it.

The object file contains *linkage* information. To create the run information, the compiler next invokes a *linker*. The linker uses the linkage information to add functions from the standard C++ *libraries*. One of these functions is the *printf* function that you used in *String.cpp*.

When the linker finishes, you have an *executable* with an extension of *.exe*. This file contains run information the Windows loader can use to place it in memory and then transfer control to the *main* function.

Running Your Visual C++ Program

If the linker does not encounter any errors, it will create an executable file that you may run directly from the command line. For your programs, the executable file will have an extension of *.exe*.

For basic programs, this executable file will have the same name as your source code file, except for the extension. You may rename the executable file to something else, but you must keep the *.exe* extension. When you run your program, Windows uses the extension to determine how to place the program code into your computer's memory.

To run your program, type the name of the executable file at the command prompt and press the Enter key. You don't have to include the extension (*.exe*) when you type the program name. The Windows loader has some built-in rules to look for files with executable extensions.

To run the *string.exe* program, enter just **string** at the command prompt as shown here:

```
C:> string   <ENTER>
```

Window will respond by loading the *string.exe* program file into memory and transferring control to it. The computer will *execute* the instructions in the program code. When all the instructions have executed, the program will *exit*, and Windows again will display the command prompt.

Making Changes to Your Visual C++ Program

When you compile a program, the executable file is separate and independent from the source code file. If you make a change to the source code file, the changes will not take effect in the executable file until you recompile the program.

Using your program editor, open the *string.cpp* file that you created earlier and change one of the *printf* statements, such as changing "Hello" to "Howdy," as shown below:

```
#include      <stdio.h>

void main()
{
    printf ("Howdy, ");
    printf ("Visual C++ ");
    printf ("world!\n");
}
```

Run the *string.exe* program without recompiling the program. The output is the same as it was, without the changes you made to the source file:

```
C> string  <ENTER>
Hello, Visual C++ world!
```

If you recompile the program, the compiler will read the changes you made to the program and create a new executable file:

```
C:> cl string.cpp  <ENTER>
string.cpp
Microsoft (R) Incremental Linker Version 6.00.8168
Copyright (C) Microsoft Corp 1992-1998. All rights reserved.

/out:string.exe
string.obj
```

```
C:> string  <ENTER>
Howdy, Visual C++ world!

C:>
```

You must recompile your program *every* time you make changes to the source code file, no matter how small or minor the change.

Understanding Syntax Errors

Syntax errors are language errors such as a misspelled *keyword*, a misplaced *operator*, or a punctuation error. Keywords are words Visual C++ has set aside to indicate specific attributes or actions. An example of a keyword is *return*, which you used to pass a number back to the operating system in earlier programs. Operators are the symbols Visual C++ uses to indicate actions such as arithmetic operations. These include symbols such as the "+" and " {ms} " characters.

You will learn more about keywords and operators in later lessons, but you should understand how they figure into the C++ language and syntax.

Visual C++ cannot compile your program or create an executable file if your program contains *any* syntax errors. The compiler output will identify lines where it found syntax errors, and you can use this information to fix the errors.

In Visual C++, you must type all keywords in lowercase letters. C++ is a case-sensitive language, and a common error among new programmers is to type with the Caps Lock function turned on. In a language such as BASIC, which is not case sensitive, this is not a problem. C++, however, will not recognize keywords that you type in capital letters. To the compiler, a keyword containing a capital letter is a misspelling, and the compiler prints an error message.

Punctuation marks such as the parentheses, the comma, the period, and the semicolon actually are operators because they signify specific actions. For example, the parentheses are used to group other operators and identifiers (an identifier is any word that is not a keyword, such as a variable or function name), and the semicolon marks the end of a statement.

A statement is a collection of one or more operators, keywords, and identifiers that indicates a complete instruction. These statement parts must be written in a specific order, which is determined by the *notation* of the language. C++ uses *algebraic* notation. Fortunately, this is the same notation that you learned in your arithmetic classes.

In algebraic notation, you write the first identifier, the operator, and the second identifier (for some operations called *unary* operations, a second identifier is not required). Writing *b* {*ms*} *c*, for example, means to take the value of *b* and subtract from it the value of *c*. If you write *a* = *b* {*ms*} *c*, you mean the program should perform the subtraction, then assign the result to *a*.

If you write the identifiers and operators out of order, the compiler will issue a syntax error. It is like misplacing the punctuation marks when you write a letter to a friend.

What You Must Know

In this lesson, you learned how to create Visual C++ programs from the command line and how to compile them. You also learned about strings, basic C++ output, and syntax errors. In Lesson 5, "Understanding a Few C++ Basics," you will learn about C++ basics and how to add comments to your Visual C++ source programs. Before you continue with Lesson 5, however,, make sure you understand the following key points:

  To write a program, you create source code files. You must save your source files as ordinary text files.

  The entry point for a command-line program is a function called *main*.

  Visual C++ is a case-sensitive language. The function *main* is not the same as *Main*.

  Your program can write to the command console using a function called *printf* or by using Visual C++ streams. Mixing the two methods in the same program may cause unexpected results.

  Changes in your source files do not take effect until you recompile your program.

  If you make a syntax error in your program, the compiler will issue an error and will not create an executable file. You must fix the errors first.

  When you write statements in Visual C++ language, you must use the algebraic notation. The notation is part of the syntax of the C++ language.

Lesson 5

Understanding a Few C++ Basics

U ntil now, your programs have been short and little more than experiments in code. Understanding the program's purpose involved only looking at a few statements. Soon, however, you will add variables and functions to your program. To make your programs more readable, you will need to use *white space* (such as blank lines), and you will want to add *comments* to remind yourself and to inform other programmers why you wrote code in a certain way, why you declared a variable of specific type, and to describe the purpose and result of a function.

In this lesson, you will learn how to use white space to make your programs readable and how to comment your code. By the time you finish this lesson, you will understand the following key concepts:

◆ C++ files contain tokens and white space. A token is anything that is not white space. The Visual C++ compiler uses white space only to separate *tokens*.

◆ Within Visual C++ programs, statements may span several lines. You can use this fact to make your programs more readable.

◆ The Visual C++ compiler ignores text that you enter in comments. Within Visual C++, there are two ways you can create a comment.

◆ Within your source files, comments serve as memory jogs. When you return to a program much later, they help to remind you about the parts of your program.

◆ Header files (files with .h extensions) make it possible for you to share information between different source code files.

Commenting Your Code

As you develop your program, the number of lines of code will mount, and any sizeable program will span several source files. Providing newlines and indents makes a program more readable and easier to maintain, but these techniques do not guarantee that you will remember *why* you did something in a particular way.

It would be handy to have some method of inserting explanatory text into your code to refresh your memory when you return to the code weeks or months later to modify or maintain the code. After all, developing an application may be a long-term project, and you cannot be expected to remember *everything*.

Most languages provide some method of inserting comments in the code (there actually are a few languages that do not). These blocks of non-code text allow you to explain certain constructs and give other programmers some idea of the purpose of a function or block of code.

C++ has two methods of commenting code. The original C programming language, which serves as the base for C++, used the sequence "/*" to indicate the start of a comment block and "*/" to mark the end of the block. To keep the older C program compatible, C++ lets you use this system of inserting comments.

The compiler will ignore everything from the "/*" until the ending comment marker, "*/," including newline characters. For every *begin comment* ("/*") sequence, you must have an *end comment* sequence ("*/"), even if it is at the end of a file. If the markers are mismatched, the compiler will issue an error. Many Visual C++ programmers use these comment markers to put information at the beginning of a file and to describe the purpose of functions as shown here:

```
/*
   Nada().
   This function does nothing. It takes no parameters
   and returns no values.
 */


void Nada ()
{
}
```

You also may use the comment markers at the end of a line. Programmers often add comments in this way to explain the purpose of a variable or an unusual construct:

```
int nPos;        /* Position in converted line */
```

The compiler does not recognize comment markers between open and close double quote marks. In the following statement, for example, the compiler will not recognize the comment markers and will include them as part of the *string constant*. Your program then will print them when you run the program:

```
printf ("Hello, Visual /* this is not a comment */ C++!\n");
```

C++ also has its own comment marker, a set of double slash marks, "//." When the compiler encounters this set of characters, it ignores everything to the end of the *current* line. The comment *does not* span lines, as does the C comment.

Actually, the C++ comment is much more efficient. When the compiler encounters the "/*" marker, it must search through the text until it finds a matching "*/." But when the compiler encounters the double slash marker, it simply moves on to the next line.

Everything has a cost, however. The cost of this efficiency is that you must include the double slash on every line where you want to continue the comment.

You could rewrite the above sample as shown here using the double slash at the beginning of each line:

```
//
// Nada().
// This function does nothing. It takes no parameters
// and returns no values.
//

void Nada ()
{
    int nPos;          // Position in converted line
}
```

Notice that you do not have to use an end comment marker. The commented text terminates at the end of the current line.

New programmers have a tendency to add too many or too few comments. Many comments are self-evident and only tend to confuse the text. In the following line, the comment tells you nothing that the code does not:

```
    nPos = 5;          // Set nPos to 5
```

As you begin programming, remember that it is better to add too many comments than to add too few. If you have any doubts as to whether you should add a comment, add one. The practice will be good, and you will add only a few bytes to the source code file. It is easier to remove a comment later than it is to add one.

Understanding Tokens and White Space

In C++, there are *tokens* and *white space*. White space is any character or sequence of characters that produces only caret movement such as a space, a tab, a newline, or a form feed. Anything else that is not within *comment* markers is a token. These include the identifiers, the keywords, the constants, the string literals, operators, and other separators.

Other than the fact that the compiler needs white space to separate certain tokens such as identifiers and keywords, the Visual C++ compiler ignores white space. There is no requirement that you indent the lines of code or even write the code statements on separate lines. Writing x *<space>* = *<space>* 2; is the same as writing x=2;. You also may use as much white space as you want. This is fortunate because it lets you write programs that are more *readable*. Writing statements on separate lines and following some informal indenting rules makes reviewing and debugging your program much easier. Compare the following code with what the compiler recognizes:

```
for (x = 1; x < 10; ++x)
{
    y = x + 1;
    z = y + 4;
}
```

For the compiler, this is the same as writing *for(x=1;x<10;++x){y=x+1;x=y+4;}*. By writing the code on several lines and indenting the lines within the loop, the code is much easier to read.

Tab characters in a C++ program generally are four spaces each, but some programmers use two or three, and others use more than four, especially if they are used to programming in another language such as FORTRAN or COBOL. This book will use four-character indenting, but you can get an idea of what is comfortable to you by studying other code.

Using the Semicolon to Mark the End of a Statement

You write C++ code as a sequence of *statements*. A statement ends when the compiler encounters a semicolon. This is the same as placing a period at the end of a sentence. If there is more code on the same line, the Visual C++ compiler will treat it as part of a new statement, just as you may have more than one sentence in a paragraph.

Normally, however, you will write only one statement on a line. In most cases, writing multiple statements on one line makes the code more difficult for you to read.

You can, however, write a single statement on several lines. The compiler will put the lines together until it encounters the semicolon. To keep them *unique*, variable and function names in larger programs can become long, and writing a function call on a single line would make a very long line. For example, the following call to the Windows function to create a window is 170 characters long:

```
hWnd = CreateWindow("MyWindow", "Hello, Visual C++ World!",
WS_OVERLAPPEDWINDOW, CW_USEDEFAULT, CW_USEDEFAULT, CW_USEDEFAULT,
CW_USEDEFAULT, NULL, NULL, hInstance, NULL);
```

The function call is difficult to read, and it is very hard to locate individual arguments in it. To read the entire function call, you would have to scroll the screen horizontally, and some arguments always would be out of view. If you use the fact that the compiler treats each line as part of the same statement until it encounters the semicolon, you can rewrite the line as follows:

```
hWnd = CreateWindow("MyWindow",         // The window class
                    "Hello, World!",    // Window name
                    WS_OVERLAPPEDWINDOW, // Window style
                    CW_USEDEFAULT,      // Horizontal pos
                    CW_USEDEFAULT,      // Vertical pos
                    CW_USEDEFAULT,      // Window width
                    CW_USEDEFAULT,      // Window height
                    NULL,               // Parent window
                    NULL,               // Menu handle
                    hInstance,          // Instance handle
                    NULL);              // Creation data
```

White space is cheap, and using some here not only makes the function more readable, but also leaves room on the right to add a comment that describes each argument. You can see all the arguments on the screen at the same time. The cost is that it takes 11 lines to write it this way.

To the compiler, either call is OK. The compiler will generate a call to the function with the arguments in the proper order using either method.

Using Header Files

A *header file* is a source file that is read into another source file by the Visual C++ preprocessor. Although Visual C++ does not place any restrictions on what you may put in a header file, usually you will use header files for definitions and declarations that are used by more than one source file.

Header files usually have an extension of *.h*. You cannot compile a file with an *.h* extension directly. The only way to compile a file with an extension of *.h* is to read it into a source code file using the *#include* preprocessor directive.

Visual C++ contains many header files. You have already used *stdio.h*, which declares the functions used for basic input and output, and *iostream.h*, which declares the C++ streams. These are but two of the more than 900 header files in the Visual C++ *include* directory. The Visual C++ installation program placed these files in a subdirectory where you installed Visual C++. If you installed Visual C++ in the *C:\Program Files* directory, which is the default, you will find them in the *C:\Program Files\Microsoft Visual Studio\VC98\Include* directory. The preprocessor looks for header files in this directory, which is part of the *include path*. The include path is the list of directories where the Visual C++ preprocessor will look for header files.

You also may create your own header files, and the Visual Studio wizards usually create one or more header files when you create a project. For example, suppose your program contains several functions that you will call from more than one source file. Within C++, you must declare a function before your program can use it. Normally, you would have to write a declaration in each program file where you call one of these functions.

Instead, you may place the function declarations in a header file, then use the *#include* directive to add that header file to your source code files.

The preprocessor looks for header files according to some preset rules that depend upon how you write the *#include* directive. You may have noticed in the earlier programs that some header file names were in double quote marks, while others were between the less-than and greater-than symbols (< and >), as shown in the following two lines:

```
#include    "stdafx.h"
#include    <stdio.h>
```

In the first line, where the header file name is between quote marks, the preprocessor will look for the header file in the same directory as your source file. It the preprocessor does not find the file in this directory, it then will look in the directories in the include path.

In the second form, where the header file name is between less-than and greater-than symbols, the preprocessor will *not* look in the same directory as your source files. Instead, the preprocessor will look for the header file only in the directories in the include path.

Using these rules, you normally will include your own header files using the double quote marks, and you will include the *standard* header files using the less-than and greater-than symbols.

You may open the standard header files in your program editor, but you should be careful not to make any changes to them. If you make a change that causes a syntax error, then you will not be able to compile any programs that use the header file containing the error.

To look at a header file in the Visual Studio, first start the Visual Studio program. Select the Start menu Programs option, choose Microsoft Visual Studio 6.0, and finally select Microsoft Visual C++ 6.0. Next, perform the following steps:

1. Within Visual Studio, open the *Second* project that you created Lesson 2, "Building, Running, and Saving Your First Visual C++ Program." Select the File menu Recent Workspaces option. Then, click your mouse on the *Second* menu item.

2. Click your mouse on the FileView tab on the Workspace Window. If the "Second files" item has a plus mark next to it, click on the plus mark to display the list of file type.

3. Within the list of file types, look for the "Header Files" item. If the item has a plus mark next to it, click on the plus mark to display a list of header files.

4. Within the header-files list, you should find an entry for "Stdafx.h" (it should be the only header file listed). Double-click your mouse on this line to open the *stdafx.h* header file in an editing window.

5. Scroll through the editing window until you find a line that reads "#include <stdio.h>." *Right-click* your mouse on this line to display a menu of file options.

6. About one-third of the way down the menu of file options is an item labeled "Open Document <stdio.h>." Select this item, and the Visual Studio will create another editing window and display the *stdio.h* file, as shown in Figure 5.1.

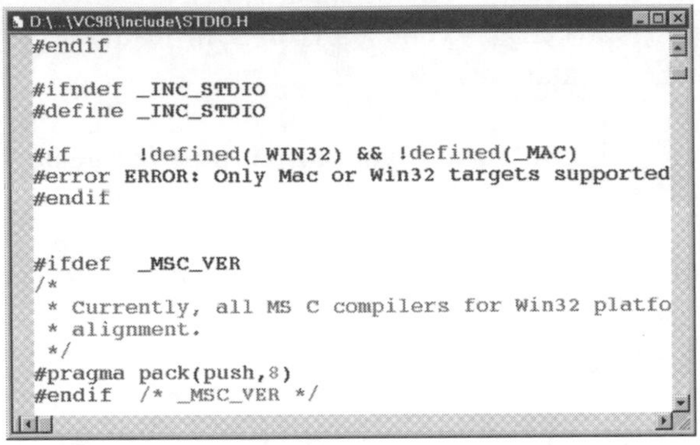

Figure 5.1

The Visual Studio displays the stdio.h *in an editing window. Be careful not to make any changes to this file.*

At this point, you may not understand most of the symbols and definitions in *stdio.h*. Later, you may want to open a header file in this way to look up a particular definition or to look at the members of a particular item.

To close the file without making any changes to it, click your mouse on the "X" symbol at the upper-right of the window. If the Visual Studio asks you whether you want to save any changes, click on the No button.

What You Must Know

In this lesson, you learned about tokens and white space in Visual C++ and how to use white space to make your programs more readable. You also learned how to enter comment text in your program to write notes to yourself and to explain why you wrote certain code in a particular manner. You learned how to use the C-style comment markers using the "/*" and "*/" markers, and the C++ comment markers using the "//" marker. You also learned how to share definitions and declarations between source files by using header files. In Lesson 6, "Using Variables to Store Information within Visual C++ Programs," you will learn how to store information in your program using *variables*. Before you continue with Lesson 6, however, make sure you have learned the following key points:

◆ White space characters are those that cause caret (or cursor) movement on the screen only. They do not display as visible characters.

◆ White space characters are spaces, tabs, and line-ending characters. Tokens are any character, group of characters, or symbols that are not white space. The Visual C++ compiler uses white space to separate tokens.

◆ The semicolon marks the end of a statement in Visual C++.

◆ To improve readability, you may write statements on more than one line. A statement ends when you enter the semicolon character.

◆ To include header files from your source code directory in a source code file, use the #include directive with the name of the header file between double quote marks.

◆ To include standard header files, write the #include directive with the name of the header file between less-than and greater-than symbols.

◆ You may display standard header files in your program editor, but you should be careful not to make any changes to them.

Lesson 6

Using Variables to Store Information within Visual C++ Programs

As your programs begin to perform useful work, they will need to store information in a form your code can use within statements and pass to other functions. When your program performs an *operation,* such as a statement that divides 12 by 3, the result is temporary. The computer will discard the result when it performs the next statement. To save the result for use within your program, you must use *variables.* A variable is a memory location where your program can place and retrieve values. That value may be anything from a simple character to a very large number. This lesson will teach you how to declare and use variables in a program. By the time you finish this lesson, you will understand the following key concepts:

♦ An *identifier* is a name. Visual C++ uses identifiers to keep track of variables and functions.

♦ The name of a variable refers to a memory location where your program stores a value.

♦ You must *declare* the variables your program will use by telling the computer the variable's name and what type of value it will hold.

♦ The *type* of a variable tells the compiler what kind of value it will hold and what operations you may perform on the variable.

♦ When you declare a variable, you should use a name that describes the purpose of the variable. This helps you and other programmers to read and understand your code.

♦ C++ defines a list of special, *reserved words* whose names your programs cannot use for variables or for functions.

♦ Programs use the Visual C++ output functions to display a variable's value on the screen.

Understanding Identifiers

One of the reasons programmers use languages is that a programming language lets them refer to memory locations indirectly through names, or *identifiers*. To the computer, there are no names. There are only memory locations called *addresses* where your program can store and retrieve information or mark the beginning code of a function.

A memory address is very much like the address of your house. When a friend or relative writes you a letter, it is not enough simply to write your name on the envelope. For the post office to deliver the letter, your friend or relative also must write your address. The address tells the post office to send the letter to a particular state, then to a particular city. When the letter arrives in that city, the mailman takes it to a particular street, then to a house on that street.

If you had to keep track of these addresses yourself, you quickly would become lost in a sea of numbers. In a programming language, the compiler lets you assign a name—an identifier—to a memory address. The compiler assigns an address to each identifier and uses that address each time you write the identifier's name.

For example, you may declare a *variable* using the name *var* to hold the value of a number. The compiler sets aside enough memory to hold the value. Later, when you use the variable's name, your program will look in that location to get the value.

In C++, you can write a statement such as *12/3;* to instruct the computer to divide 12 by 3. When the computer performs the division, it places the result in a special temporary location in the computer's central processing chip. The next line in your program will use the same location and destroy the value of the first operation. Later, when you want to use the result, you will have to write *12/3* again. If, instead, you write *var=12/3;* the computer will do the division and place the result in the memory location set aside for *var*. Programmers call this operation an *assignment*, and within C++, the equals sign (=) is the *assignment operator*.

An identifier name can be any number of characters, but the compiler may impose a limit on the length of a name. In Visual C++, that limit is 247 characters. Those 247 characters must include the variable name and its *type*. For a function, you must be able to write the function's type, name, and the names and types of all the *parameters* within 247 characters. That number is large enough that you may never face the limit, but you should be aware of it.

In addition, the first character of an identifier must be an uppercase or lowercase letter or an underscore (_). You cannot begin an identifier name using a number or any of the special characters used by Visual C++. These special characters include the punctuation marks such as the comma or semicolon and the symbols used to perform an arithmetic operation such as the plus sign or division symbol. As you will learn through your programming, C++ uses nearly all the special characters, except for the underscore, available on most keyboards.

A Variable's Type Defines the Values a Variable Can Store and Operations Your Program Can Perform on the Variable

Different types of variables need different amounts of memory to hold the values of the variables. The computer stores everything as a series of ones and zeros called *bits*. When you put eight bits together, you have a *byte*. A byte is the minimum amount of storage the compiler can reserve for a variable.

For programs using Visual C++, for example, you can represent the character A in bits as 01000001, and you can place all these bits in a single byte. In Visual C++, however, an *integer* (a whole number without a decimal part) may be as large as 2,147,483,647. To store this number, you need at least four bytes of memory. Other numbers, such as those with a decimal point in them, need even more memory.

To set aside the correct amount of memory, Visual C++ requires you to declare what type of value you are storing. If you try to store a value that is too large for the amount of memory for that type, the compiler will issue a warning. In some cases, it will issue an error and will not let you perform the operation.

Understanding Fundamental C++ Types

There are two kinds of variable types in Visual C++, *fundamental* and *derived*. The fundamental types provide memory storage for numbers of different sizes. The derived types are those you build from the fundamental types, such as *structures* and *classes*. You will learn about the derived types in later lessons.

The actual sizes of the fundamental types depend upon the compiler and the operating system. Your compiler is Visual C++, and your operating system is 32-bit Windows. Table 6.1 lists the fundamental types for Visual C++ and the range of numbers these types may store.

Table 6.1 The Visual C++ Fundamental Variable Types

Type	Value stored
bool	0 or 1. Programs use this type to indicate *true* (1) or *false* (0).
char	Values in the range −128 to 127. Programs use this type to store letters of the alphabet.
int	Values in the range −2,147,483,648 to 2,147,483,647.
unsigned	Values in the range 0 to 4,294,967,295.

continues

Table 6.1 The Visual C++ Fundamental Variable Types, Continued

Type	Value stored
long	Values in the range $-2,147,483,648$ to $2,147,483,647$.
float	Values in the range 3.4×10^{-38} to 3.4×10^{38}.
double	Values in the range 1.7×10^{-308} to 1.7×10^{308}.

The data type not only tells the compiler how many bytes are needed for the variable, but also what type of *operations*, such as addition, multiplication, or subtraction, you may perform on the variable.

Other languages such as BASIC that do not use data types set aside enough memory for the *largest* value possible for every variable. Commonly on personal computers, the storage needed is 16 bytes, even though you need only one byte for a character value. Storing variables this way is not very efficient and tends to slow down a program.

 Working with Exponents

Within a Visual C++ program, use the float *type to store a number with a decimal point but* without *an exponent. Use the* double *type to write a number with an exponent. The compiler does not understand exponents in the method you learned in math classes. Instead, you write the exponent using the letter* e *or* E. *For example, you would write Avogadro's number as 6.022E23. The 6.022 is the* mantissa, *and the 23 is the* exponent *of 10. The compiler reads this as* 6.022×10^{23}.

Use the other types to store numbers without decimal points.

Declaring Variables within a Visual C++ Program

Your program must *declare* a variable before using the variable. This introduces the variable to the C++ compiler, which then determines how much storage to set aside for the variable's values. To declare a variable in your program, you must specify the variable's type and the name (the identifier) that your program will use to refer to the variable, as shown below:

```
variable_type   variable_name;
```

Notice that the terms "variable type" and "variable name" are joined by an underscore. In most cases, a variable's type is one word and will not contain any spaces (although, as you will learn, you may apply *modifiers* to the variable type that may contain spaces). Variable names *may not* contain spaces, however. If you want to use more than one word for a variable's name, you must join the words with another character such as the underscore.

Also, notice that the line ends with a semicolon to mark the end of the statement for the compiler. In C++, this is a *declaration statement*. Often you will see more than one variable name in a declaration statement, as in the following line:

```
variable_type   variable_one, variable_two;
```

This statement declares two variables of the *same* type. To declare more than one variable in a declaration statement, you must separate the names with a comma. The variables must be of the same type. You cannot have more than one type in a declaration statement.

If you do not declare a variable before using it, the compiler will tell you that it is an "undeclared identifier." If this happens, the compiler will not create the executable file you need to run your program. You must edit your source code to declare the variable in a line *before* you use it, then recompile your program.

You should use a meaningful word or words for the variable's name. Choose a name that describes the variable's use to someone reading your program. The following program declares three variables using meaningful names:

```
#include     <iostream.h>

void main (void)
{
    int test_score;
    long distance_to_mars;
    double Avogadro;
}
```

This program does nothing but declare the variables. The compiler only sets aside storage for the values, but you have not yet assigned values to the variables. If you compile and run this program, it will not display any output.

You may declare more than one variable *of the same type* in a declaration statement by separating the names of the variables with commas. For example, if you want to declare three variables to hold the values for a student's age, test score, and grade, you could write it as shown below:

```
int student_age, test_score, grade;
```

In the Visual C++ punctuation rules, using the comma is grammatically the same as using "and." When you use the comma to declare multiple variables, you cannot declare variables of different types on the same line. The compiler would generate and display an error for the following line:

```
int student_age, double test_score;
```

Visual C++ reserves some words for its own use, and you cannot use these words as names for your variables. These are the C++ *keywords*, listed in Table 6.2.

Table 6.2 C++ Keywords

C++ Keywords

and	and_eq	asm	auto	bitand
bitor	bool catch	break	case	char
class	compl	const	const_cast	continue
default	do	delete	double	dynamic_cast
else	enum	extern	explicit	export
false	float	for	frient	goto
if	inline	int	long	mutable
namespace	new	not	not_eq	operator
or	or_eq	private	protected	public
register	reinterpret_cast	return	short	signed
sizeof	static	struct	static_cast	switch
template	this	throw	true	try
typedef	typeid	typename	union	unsigned
using	virtual	void	volatile	wchar_t
while	xor	xor_eq		

 Understanding Variables

> *A variable is the name of a storage location in your computer's random access memory (RAM). Your program stores information in variables. When you create your programs, you must declare the variables by telling the compiler the variable's type and name. For example, the following statement declares a variable of type* int *with the name* age:

```
int age;
```

Variable names are case-sensitive. Once you have declared the variable age *as just shown, you cannot later refer to it as* Age *with a capital "A." To the compiler, that is the name of a different variable, and the compiler will tell you* Age *is an "undeclared identifier."*

Assigning Values to Variables

Earlier in this lesson, you learned that variables hold values as your program runs. You also learned that Visual C++ uses the equals sign as the *assignment operator*. After you declare a variable, you use the assignment operator to give a value to the variable.

If your program attempts to use a variable before your program assigns a value to the variable, the compiler will generate and display a warning. A warning is not an error, and the compiler still will generate the executable file. A warning indicates code that may cause problems when you run your program, so you should attempt to correct lines that generate warning messages.

The following statements assign values to variables:

```
score = 92;
distance_to_moon = 238858;
Avogadro = 6.022E23;
```

Each assignment statement ends with a semicolon. In other code, you sometimes may see multiple assignments on one line. Visual C++ lets you write multiple assignments on a line if you separate them with commas, as shown below:

```
score = 92, distance_to_moon = 238858, Avogadro = 6.022E23;
```

(When you write multiple assignments on one line, the compiler lets you use different types. This is because you already have *declared* the variables on separate lines and the compiler is aware of the variable types.)

However, until you have more experience, you should write only one assignment on a line. The line must end with a semicolon to mark the end of the statement.

Note that in both samples, the *distance_to_moon* value was written *without* commas within the number; that is, the value is *238858* and not *238,858*. If you write it with a comma, the compiler will think you are trying to write a multiple statement on one line. The compiler will assume you want to assign 238 to the variable *distance_to_moon*. Then, the compiler will evaluate the *expression* 858 and simply discard the result without so much as a warning. In the first part of this lesson, you learned that just writing a number or expression is a valid statement in C++.

The following program first declares the variables you just encountered and then assigns the values to the variables:

```
#include <iostream.h>
void main(void)
{
    int score;
    long distance_to_mars;
    double Avogadro;

    score = 92;
    distance_to_moon = 238858;
    Avogadro = 6.022E23;
}
```

Once again, this program will not produce any output. So far, you only have declared the variables and assigned values to the variables. In the next section, you will learn how to write them to your screen.

Programmers call the operation that assigns a starting value to a variable "initializing a variable." Sometimes it is convenient to initialize the variable at the same time you declare the variable. Visual C++ lets you combine the declaration statement and the assignment statement—to declare and initialize a variable—on the same line, as shown in the following:

```
int score = 92;
long distance_to_mars = 238858;
double Avogadro = 6.022E23;
```

In this book, many of the sample programs will assign values to variables at the same time the programs declare the variables.

 Assigning One Variable's Value to Another

Variables store information while your program executes. To store a value in a variable, you use the C++ assignment operator, the equals sign. After your program uses the value of a variable, you may assign another value to the same

variable later using the assignment operator. The following code fragment assigns 6 to the variable lesson, *then calls a function called* MyFunc *using the variable. Then it changes the variable's value to 7:*

```
Lesson = 6;
MyFunc (lesson);
lesson = 7;
```

To make it easier for you, C++ lets you assign a value to a variable at the same time you declare the variable, as shown below:

```
int lesson = 6;
MyFunc (lesson);
lesson = 7;
```

*Note that the second assignment—*lesson = 7;—*does not declare the variable again. You can declare a variable only once.*

Displaying a Variable's Value

After you assign a value to a variable, your program may use the value by referring to the variable's name. The following program, *ShowVars.cpp,* declares several variables and then uses the C++ stream *cout* to write them to the screen:

```
#include  <iostream.h>

void main (void)
{
    int test_score = 92;
    double Avogadro  = 6.022E23;
    long distance_to_moon = 238858;

    cout << "The test score is " << test_score << endl;
    cout << "Avogadro's Number is " << Avogadro << endl;
    cout << "The distance to the moon is " <<
            distance_to_moon << " miles" << endl;
}
```

Notice that the last *cout* statement is too long to write on one line. The program continues the statement to the next line. The program *wraps* the text to the next line. There is no semicolon at the end of the first line of the statement, so the compiler continues reading on the next line.

When your program wraps a line, you should take care that the end of the line does not fall in the middle of a string (text between double quotes). If the end of the line does fall in the middle of a string, end the line with a double quote mark and do not put any punctuation marks after the quote mark. Begin the rest of the string on the next line with another double quote mark, as shown in the following code:

```
cout << "The distance to "
        " the moon is " <<
        distance_to_moon << " miles" << endl;
```

Notice also that there is no *inserter* at the end of the first line or the beginning of the second line. With no punctuation marks or operators between two strings, the compiler will put them together in a single string. Programmers say the compiler "concatenates" the strings.

When you run the *ShowVars* program, your screen will display the following output:

```
C:> ShowVars   <ENTER>
The test score is 92
Avogadro's Number is 6.022e+023
The distance to the moon is 238858 miles
```

As you can see, to use the value of a variable, you refer to the variable's name in your program. Your program knows where the value is stored, and it retrieves the value when you refer to the variable's name.

Take some time now to experiment with different values for the variables in your program. For example, try changing the value of *Avogadro* from 6.022E23 to 6022E20 (remove the decimal point and change the exponent to 20). Compile and run your program to see the results.

When the computer stores a *float* or *double* type, it sets aside part of the memory location for the mantissa and another part for the exponent. This lets the computer store larger numbers in *scientific notation* than it normally would be able to store. If you assign a *float* or *double* variable a number with many digits, your computer may not be able to store all the digits. Your program will try to store the value *nearest* the actual value, and you should understand there might be some slight errors as a result. These *precision* errors are difficult to locate. Fortunately, however, precision errors do not cause problems often if the program is aware of how the computer stores values.

In the following program, *Precise.cpp,* the program assigns a value slightly less than one-half, but with more digits than the computer can store. The computer tries to compensate by storing the closest value that it can hold, which is 0.5:

```cpp
#include  <iostream.h>

void main (void)
{
    float f_almost_half = 0.49999990;
    double d_almost_half = 0.49999990;

    cout << "Floating point 0.49999990 is " <<
            f_almost_half << endl;
    cout << "Double 0.49999990 is " << d_almost_half << endl;
}
```

When you compile and run *precise.cpp,* your screen displays the following output:

```
C:> precise  <ENTER>
Floating point 0.49999990 is 0.5
Double 0.49999990 is 0.5
```

The values the program assigns to the variables and the values the computer actually stores are not exactly the same. Normally, given the scale of most *float* and *double* numbers, this does not cause problems. Still, you have to keep it in mind when dealing with *float* and *double* variable types.

What You Must Know

In this lesson, you learned how programs store information in variables. The variable name is the identifier your program assigns to a memory location. Before your program can use a variable, you must declare the type and name of the variable. Your program also needs to assign initial values to variables. If you attempt to use a variable name, the compiler will generate a warning.

You also learned how to use the assignment operator. In Lesson 7, "Getting Started with Visual C++ Operators," you will learn how to use other Visual C++ operators, such as addition and subtraction, on variables. Before you continue with Lesson 7, make sure you understand the following key points:

◆ Variables are names a program uses to store and retrieve information from locations in your computer's memory.

◆ The Visual C++ compiler uses identifiers to keep track of variable and function names in a program. Error messages usually will use the word "identifier" rather than "variable."

◆ To use a variable in your program, you first must declare the variable's type and name.

◆ Variable names must begin with an uppercase or lowercase letter or the underscore character. Variable names are case-sensitive in Visual C++.

◆ A variable's type determines the amount of storage the compiler will set aside for the variable's value. This, in turn, determines what type of values a variable may hold. Common variable types are *char, int, long, double,* and *float.*

◆ Once your program declares a variable and assigns a value to the variable, your program later may assign it a different value without again declaring the variable.

◆ Floating point types (*float* and *double*) may experience precision errors if you attempt to assign a number with too many digits.

Lesson 7

Getting Started with Visual C++ Operators

In Lesson 6, "Using Variables to Store Information within Visual C++ Programs," you learned how to declare and use variables to store information in your program. At some point, your program will need to perform arithmetic operations such as addition and subtraction on the values your variables contain. The C++ language contains a rich set of operators that help you to manipulate numbers and perform arithmetic. This lesson will teach you how to use these operators. By the time you finish this lesson, you will understand the following key concepts:

◆ Your programs use the Visual C++ arithmetic operators to perform mathematical operations.

◆ C++ represents most operators as symbols. The variables and numbers you use with operators are *operands*.

◆ Unary operators require only one operand. Binary operators require two operands. C++ contains one ternary operator that requires three operands.

◆ An expression is a combination of identifiers, values, and operators. Your program evaluates an expression to get the result. Your program can then assign that result to a variable.

◆ Relational operators compare two values and return a true or false condition.

◆ Bitwise operators combine the bits in two values in a logical manner.

Reviewing Operators

At some point, nearly every program performs some arithmetic operation on the values it stores in variables. It will use one of the basic arithmetic operators to add, subtract, multiply, or divide two values. An example of an arithmetic operation might be to add 3 and 4 by combining them with the addition operator. To do this, you would write 3 + 4.

When you combine one or more values, identifiers, and operators, you are writing an *expression*. In the expression 3 + 4, the plus sign is the operator, and the 3 and 4 are *operands*. The operands may be numbers or variables.

An expression by itself does nothing but yield a *result*. The result of 3 + 4, for example, is 7. You may use the assignment operator, the equals sign, to store the result in a variable, as in *var = 3 + 4;* or you can use the result as an argument to a function or as part of a larger expression.

It is a rare program that will not use any of the C++ operators. Even the simple task of assigning a value to a variable, such as *int var = 0;*, is an example of using the *assignment operator* (the equals sign).

C++ has a rich set of operators, more than most computer languages. Some of these, such as the arithmetic operators, perform basic operations and are the same in most computer languages. Others are unique to C++. Most languages provide only one assignment operator. In C++, there are 11 assignment operators. Ten of these let you combine an assignment with another operation.

Operators fall in three broad categories. The *unary* operators use only one operand. Some programmers call these operators *monadic* operators. An example is the increment operator, ++, which you will learn to use in the next lesson. The increment operator instructs the program to add one to the value of the operand.

Most operators require two operands. These are *binary* operators, and some programmers refer to them as *diadic* operators. An example is the addition operator, which causes the program to add two values, such as in 3 + 4.

Most languages do not have operators that require more than two operands, but C++ contains one *ternary* operator, which requires three operands. This operator is the *conditional expression* operator, and you will learn about it in Lesson 11, "Making Decisions within a Visual C++ Program."

This book will refer to operators as unary, binary, or ternary. You may see "monadic" and "diadic" in other books, so you should be aware that these words refer to unary and binary operators.

Understanding Unary Operators

Some C++ operators perform their action on a single operand. These are the *unary operators*. C++ contains several unary operators, many of which emulate instructions in a low-level language called *Assembly*. It is partly because of these operators that the C and C++ languages incorrectly became known as low-level languages.

Unary operators include those to increment and decrement a value, to get the address of a memory location, to store a value directly into a memory location, and to manipulate the bits in a variable. Table 7.1 summarizes the unary operators.

Table 7.1 Visual C++ Unary Operators

Operator	Operation	Result
~	Ones (1) complement	Reverses the sense of the bits in a variable. The ones are changed to zeros, and the zeros are changed to ones.
!	Negation	Returns *true* if a value of the operand is zero or *false* if the value is non-zero.
*	Indirection	Returns the contents of a memory location.
&	Address	Returns the address where the value of a variable is stored.
−,+	Minus and Plus	Unary minus and plus.
++	Increment	Adds one to the value of a variable.
−−	Decrement	Subtracts one from the value of a variable.
new	Allocate	Reserves a memory location where a value may be stored.
delete	Deallocate	Releases a reserved memory location.
sizeof	Size of	Returns the number of bytes required to store the value of a variable.

You may not be familiar with all the operators in Table 7.1. By the time you finish this book, you will have used and should understand each of them.

However, you may be wondering about the plus and minus symbols in the table. Customarily, you have used these symbols to add or subtract one value from another. Actually, these symbols each represent *two* operators. The minus sign, for example, can be unary or binary depending upon how you use it. The compiler will determine how to apply it from the *context* of your program. In its unary form, the minus sign means to take the negative of a value or variable. For example, −5 tells the compiler to use the negative value of 5, and −*var* tells the compiler to retrieve the value of *var*, then use its negative value.

The unary plus sign operates similarly to the unary minus sign. However, the unary plus seldom has any effect, and you rarely see it used. You also will see the minus and plus signs in Table 7.2, the binary operator list. You should remember that, although these two unary and binary operators use the same symbols, they are different operators.

The following program, *Minus.cpp*, uses the plus and minus signs both as unary and binary operators. First, the program uses the minus sign to subtract the value of one variable from another variable. Then it uses the minus sign as a unary operator to change a positive value to a negative value:

```
#include   <iostream.h>

void main (void)
{
    int first = 5;
    int second = 8;
    int result;
//
// Use minus sign as a binary operator
//
    result = second - first;
    cout << "result equals " << result << endl;
//
// Use minus sign as a unary operator
//
    result = -result;
    cout << "result now equals " << result << endl;
//
// Use plus sign as a unary operator
//
    result = +result;
    cout << "result now equals " << result << endl;
}
```

The program first subtracts the value of *first* from the value of *second* and assigns the difference to *result*. Then the program displays the value of *result* on your screen. Using the unary minus operator, the program next changes the value of *result* to negative and displays the new value on your screen.

The last two lines show that you also may use the plus sign as a unary operator. Its use is "window dressing," however, and it has no effect on the sign of the value.

When you compile and run *Minus.cpp,* your screen will display the following output:

```
result equals 3
result now equals -3
result now equals -3
```

Later in this lesson, you will learn about the *sizeof* operator. In Lesson 8, "Using Increment and Decrement Operators," you will learn about the increment and decrement operators.

Understanding Binary Operators

Although you might not have known the name, you have used *binary* operators for most of your life. This group includes the basic arithmetic operators—plus, minus, addition, and subtraction. A binary operator is an operator that requires two operands.

Table 7.2 summarizes the binary operators in C++.

Table 7.2 The Visual C++ Binary Operators

Operator	Operation	Result
+, −, *, /, %	Arithmetic	The result of the arithmetic operation.
<<, >>	Shift	Shifts the bits (the ones and zeros) in the left operand the number of times specified by the right operand.
<. >, <=, >=, ==, !=	Relational	*true* or *false.*
&, |, ^	Bitwise	Combines the bits in the left operand with the bits in the right operand.
&&, ||	Logical	*true* or *false.*
=	Assignment	Sets the value of the left operand to the value of the right operand.
,	Comma	Evaluates the left expression, then the right expression. No operation is performed on the operands.

Once again, you might not be familiar with all of these symbols, but you will learn and use the operators throughout the course of this book.

To use a binary operator, you must have a starting value, the value or name of the variable that you write on the left side of the operator. Then you must have a value or variable that the operator will apply to the first value.

You write this second value to the right side of the operator. In the expression 3 + 4, the 3 is the starting value, and the 4 is the value the operator will apply to the first value. In this case, it will add 4 to 3.

The order in which C++ performs the arithmetic operations is important. When you write an expression this way, programmers say that the operator *associates* the values from left to right. That is, the program always evaluates the value on the left first, then the value on the right. The program then applies the value on the left to the value on the right using the binary operator.

For a simple expression such as 3 * 4, this may sound trivial, but the value on each side of the operator might be another expression containing other operators. For example, instead of 3 * 4, you might write the following expression:

```
int result = (24 / 8) * (64 / 16);
```

Your program first will evaluate 24 / 8, then 64 / 16 before applying the multiplication (*) operator. The parentheses place the values and operators into a single expression; you will learn about them in Lesson 9, "Writing Expressions in Visual C++."

In Lesson 6, "Using Variables to Store Information within Visual C++ Programs," you learned how to use the assignment operator (=) and that Visual C++ lets you write multiple assignments on a single line using the *comma* operator.

In the next section, you will learn how to use the arithmetic operators. Later in this lesson, you will learn how to use other binary operators.

Using Arithmetic Operators

You will start out this part of the lesson by building expressions using the basic arithmetic operators. Table 7.3 lists the basic operators.

Table 7.3 The C++ Basic Math Operators

Operator	Purpose	Example
+	Addition	total = cost + tax;
−	Subtraction	change = payment − total;
*	Multiplication	tax = cost * tax_rate;
/	Division	average = total / count;
%	Modulo	remainder = numerator / denominator;

You learned about most of these symbols in basic math classes, but there are some special rules for C++. You learned to write multiplication using an x as the operator, as in *12 = 3 x 4*. However, the x is an alphabetical character that might represent a variable, so C++, like most computer languages, represents multiplication with an asterisk (*). In Visual C++, you need to write *3 * 4* to multiply 3 by 4. The result, of course, is 12.

The modulo operator, %, returns the *remainder* of a division operation. The most common form of division in Visual C++ is *integer* division. An integer is a whole number, and the result of an integer division has no fraction part. Your program simply discards the remainder after integer division. Often, you will need the remainder for some reason, and you can obtain it with modulo division. In your math classes, you learned to write 93 divided by 8 as in the following:

```
   11 (Integer quotient)
 8)93
    8
   13
    8
    5 (remainder)
```

In C++, writing the expression *93 / 8* gives a result of 11, and your program discards the remainder of 5. To obtain the remainder as a result, you would write *93 % 8* (when you read this expression, you say "93 modulo 8"). Modulo division gives only integer results, so you may use the operator only on integer variables. Integer variables are those with types that do not use a decimal point, such as *int, char,* or *long*.

To get the result of division as a value with a decimal point, you would have to write one of the operands as a floating-point value (a value with a decimal point in it). For example, *93.0 / 8* gives a floating result of 11.625. You also could write *93 / 8.0* to obtain the same result of 11.625. The important point to remember is that to get a floating-point result, *at least one* of the operands must be a *float* type.

The following program, *ShowMath.cpp,* uses *cout* to display the result of several simple arithmetic operations:

```cpp
#include   <iostream.h>

void main (void)
{
    cout << "5 + 7 = " << 5 + 7 << endl;
    cout << "12 - 7 = " << 12 - 7 << endl;
    cout << "1.2345 * 2 = " << 1.2345 * 2 << endl;
    cout << "15 / 3 = " << 15 / 3 << endl;
```

```
    cout << "93 / 8 = " << 93 / 8 << endl;
    cout << "93.0 / 8 = " << 93.0 / 8 << endl;
    cout << "93 / 8.0 = " << 93 / 8.0 << endl;
    cout << "93 % 8 = " << 93 % 8 << endl;
}
```

Examine *ShowMath.cpp* closely. Each expression first appears in quotation marks, which causes the program to output the expression as text (such as $5 + 7 =$) on your screen. Next, the expression appears without quotation marks, which causes the program to evaluate the expression and use the value of the result. Finally, each line ends with an *endl*, which causes the program to end the line and start the next output at the beginning of the next line.

When you compile and run *ShowMath.cpp,* your screen will display the following output:

```
5 + 7 = 12
12 - 7 = 5
1.2345 * 2 = 2.469
15 / 3 = 5
93 / 8 = 11
93.0 / 8 = 11.625
93 / 8.0 = 11.625
93 % 8 = 5
```

Examine the results of the expression 93 / 8. As you just learned, the result is an integer, and the program discarded the remainder. But when you write one of the operands as a floating-point value (using a decimal point and a zero) in the next two lines, the result of the expression is a floating-point value.

This program uses *constant* values in the expressions. In Lesson 6, you learned how to assign values to variables. You can use a variable in an expression after you assign the variable a value. The following program, *MathVars.cpp,* uses variables to perform mathematical operations in expressions:

```
#include   <iostream.h>

void main (void)
{
    float cost = 15.50;         // The cost of an item
    float sales_tax = 0.06;     // Sales tax is 6 percent
    float amount_paid = 20.00;  // Amount the buyer paid
    float tax, change, total;   // Sales tax, buyer change
                                // and total bill
```

```
    tax = cost * sales_tax;
    total = cost + tax;
    change = amount_paid - total;


    cout << "Item cost: $" << cost << "\tTax: $" << tax <<
            "\tTotal: $" << total << endl;
    cout << "Customer change: $" << change << endl;
}
```

MathVars.cpp uses floating-point variables to represent a cash register transaction. The program assigns values to several of the variables when the program declares them. The program then uses mathematical operations on the variables to calculate the amount of sales tax, the amount of change, and the total cost of the transaction. When you compile and run the program, you will see the following output:

```
Item cost: $15.5   Tax: $0.93   Total: $16.43
Customer change: $3.57
```

Edit the program to change some of the values held by the variables. Try assigning the variable *cost* the value *25.00* and the variable *amount_paid* the value *100.00*.

In Lesson 6, you learned about *precision* errors when using floating pointer numbers. *MathVars.cpp* provides an example of how precision errors *might* cause problems.

The following experiment will show you some of the dangers of using floating-point variables for money transactions. The change is 3.57, so you might reasonably expect *change * 100* to equal *357*. You then could use the *357* to determine the number of dollar bills, quarters, dimes, nickels, and pennies to give back to the customer. However, look at what happens. Add the following lines to the end of the program (but before the closing "}"):

```
int cents_back;
cents_back = change * 100;
cout << "Cash back in cents: " << cents_back << endl;
```

When you compile and run the program, you get *356* instead of *357* as the number of cash back in cents. The customer has lost one cent in the transaction. This result may not seem significant for one transaction, but in a bank, where many thousands of transactions occur every day, the difference could add up quickly.

Because of the way computers store floating-point values, programmers usually compute money transactions in whole numbers using the number of cents rather than the number of dollars. To get the number of dollars, you use integer division. To get the number of cents, you use modulo division. The amount 5.76, for example, would be stored in an integer as 576. Integer division, *576 / 100*, returns the number of dollars, *5*, and modulo division, *576 % 100*, returns the number of cents, *76*.

The following program, *IntVars.cpp*, uses integer arithmetic to compute the same values as *MathVars.cpp*, then uses the variable *change* to compute the number of dollar bills and coins to return to the customer:

```cpp
#include   <iostream.h>

void main (void)
{
    int cost = 1550;          // The cost of an item
    int sales_tax = 6;     // Sales tax is 6 percent
    int amount_paid = 2000; // Amount the buyer paid
    int tax, change, total;   // Sales tax, buyer change
                                  // and total bill


    tax = cost * sales_tax / 100;
    total = cost + tax;
    change = amount_paid - total;

    cout << "Item cost: $" << cost / 100 << "." <<
            cost % 100 << endl;
    cout << "Tax: $" << tax / 100 << "." <<
            tax % 100 << endl;
    cout << "Total: $" << total / 100 << "." <<
            total % 100 << endl;
    cout << "Customer change: $" << change / 100 << "." <<
            change % 100 << endl;
//
// Compute the change in dollars and coins
//
    int cash;
    int dollars, quarters, dimes, nickels, cents;
```

```
    cash = change;
    dollars = cash  *100                // How many dollars
    cash = cash - do*llars * 100;       // Subtract dollars
    quarters = cash */ 25;              // How many quarters
    cash = cash - qu*arters * 25;       // Subtract quarters
    dimes = cash / 1*0;                 // How many dimes
    cash = cash - di*mes * 10;          // Subtract dimes
    nickels = cash /* 5;                // How many nickels
    cents = cash - n*ickels * 5;        // Subtract nickels to
                     *                  // get pennies
//
// Show the change to return to the customer
//
    cout << "\t" << dollars << " dollar bills" << endl;
    cout << "\t" << quarters << " quarters" << endl;
    cout << "\t" << dimes << " dimes" << endl;
    cout << "\t" << nickels << " nickels" << endl;
    cout << "\t" << cents << " pennies" << endl;
}
```

Using only integers, you are able to calculate the same results as you did with floating-point values. Then you used the change to help the sales clerk determine what coins to return to the customer. When you compile and run *IntVars.cpp,* you will see the following output:

```
Item cost: $15.50
Tax: $0.93
Total: $16.43
Customer change: $3.57
     3 dollar bills
     2 quarters
     0 dimes
     1 nickels
     2 pennies
```

Experience will teach you when to use floating-point values and when to use integer values. In a scientific experiment where the scientist assumes some degree of error, floating-point values are okay. But people are very picky about money, and customers expect your calculations in a transaction to be exact.

Understanding Assignment Operators

In Lesson 6, you learned how to store information in a variable. To do this, you used the *assignment* operator, the equals sign, to tell the compiler and your program that you wanted to place a value in a particular variable.

Most languages use the equals sign as the only assignment operator. In C++, it is only one of the assignment operators. There are no fewer than 10 other assignment operators. Table 7.4 lists the operators. In each case, the operation assigns the result to the left operand.

Table 7.4 The C++ Assignment Operators

Operator	Example	Description
=	x = y	Assigns the value of the right operand to the left operand.
+=	x += y;	Adds the right operand to the left operand.
−=	x −= y;	Subtracts the right operand from the left operand.
*=	x *= y;	Multiplies the left operand by the right operand.
/=	x /= y;	Divides the left operand by the right operand.
%=	x %= y;	Divides the left operand by the right operand and assigns the remainder to the left operand. Both operands must be integral types.
<<=	x <<= y;	Shifts the bits in the left operand to the left the number of places indicated by the right operand.
>>=	x >>= y;	Shifts the bits in the left operand to the right the number of places indicated by the right operand.
&=	x &= y;	Combines the bits in both operators using a bitwise AND operation.
|=	x |= y;	Combines the bits in both operators using a bitwise OR operation.
^=	x ^= y;	Combines the bits in both operators using a bitwise XOR operation.

C++ has lots of shortcuts when it comes to operators. Usually, these shortcuts make writing common operations much easier and reduce the amount of typing you have to do when you write a program. The more you have to type, the more chance there is of an error, such as misspelling the name of a variable. As a result, these shortcuts reduce the chance of you making a typing error.

A common operation in programming is to add a value to that of a variable, or to add the value of one variable to the value of another variable. Say you have a variable *var* that contains a value of 14 and you want to add 28 to it to get a value of 42. In most languages you would have to write *var* = *var* + 28 to set the new value for *var*. C++, however, lets you combine one of the binary operators with the assignment operator. In C++, the following statements both add 28 to the value of *var:*

```
var = var + 28;
var += 28;
```

The statement *var += 28;* means "take the value of *var* and add 28 to it, then assign the result of the addition to *var.*" That really is what the first statement, *var = var + 28;,* means. The difference is that you do not have to type the variable's name twice.

You may write any of the binary operators except the comma operator, the logical operators (*&&* and *||*), and the assignment operator itself in this shorthand method. Always write the name of the variable first, then the operator, next the assignment operator (the equals sign), and finally the value you want to apply to the variable. Do not put a space between the operator symbols. The following statements show some examples:

```
var -= 28;      // Subtract 28 from var
var /= 28;      // Divide var by 28
var *= 00;      // Multiply var by 28
var <<= 4;      // Shift the bits in var to the left 4 times
```

The following program, *Assign.cpp,* shows how these operators work and how you can use them.

```
#include  <iostream.h>

void main (void)
{
    int var = 2;

    cout << "Starting value for var = " << var << endl;
//
//  Add 1 to var
    var += 1;
    cout << "After var += 1, var = " << var << endl;
//
//  Multiply var by 2
    var *= 2;
```

```
      cout << "After var *= 2, var = " << var << endl;
//
//   Divide var by 2
      var /= 2;
      cout << "After var /= 2, var = " << var << endl;
//
//   Shift the bits in var three spaces to the left
      var <<= 3;
      cout << "After var <<= 3, var = " << var << endl;
//
//   Shift the bits in var three spaces to the right
      var >>= 3;
      cout << "After var >>= 3, var = " << var << endl;
}
```

The program sets the value of *var* to 2, then adds *1* to it using the += assignment operator. The result, 3, is assigned to the value of *var*. Next, the program uses the *= and /= operators and displays the result. You can see, for example, that writing *var *=3;* is the same as writing *var = var * 3;*. The program displays the following output:

```
Starting value for var = 2
After var += 1, var = 3
After var *= 2, var = 6
After var /= 2, var = 3
After var <<= 3, var = 24
After var >>= 3, var = 3
```

You might note with interest that shifting the bits in *var* to the left three places is the same as multiplying *var* by 8. Also, shifting the bits to the right is the same as dividing by 8. Your computer stores numbers in a sequence of bits, and each bit can have a value of 0 or 1. The *number base* for this type of storage is 2 because each bit can have one of two values.

Shifting the bits to the left is the same as multiplying the value by the number base. In the *decimal* number base that you normally use, the base is 10. If you multiply 8 by 10, you get 80. In other words, the operation shifts 8 one place to the left.

The same is true in your computer. Shifting the bits to the left three times is the same as multiplying the value by 2^3, which is 8. Similarly, shifting the bits to the right three times divides the value by 2^3.

Using Relational Operators to Compare Two Values

At the heart of your computer is a machine, the central processing chip. If you examine it closely, you will not see any moving parts, but it still is a machine. What distinguishes it from other machines is that it is capable of making decisions. You, the programmer, must give it the information it needs to make decisions, however.

C++ produces this information using the *relational* and *logical* operators. The relational operators compare two values to determine whether the values are equal or one is greater than the other. Table 7.5 summarizes the relational operators. You will learn about the logical operators in the next section.

Table 7.5 The C++ Relational Operators

Operator	Operation	Result
<	Less Than	*true* if first operand is less than the second. Otherwise *false*.
>	Greater Than	*true* if the first operand is greater than the second. Otherwise *false*.
<=	Less Than or Equal	*true* if the first operand is less than or equal to the second. Otherwise *false*.
>=	Greater Than or Equal	*true* if the first operand is greater than or equal to the second. Otherwise *false*.
==	Equal To	*true* if the first operand is equal to the second. Otherwise *false*.
!=	Not Equal To	*true* if the first operand is not equal to the second. Otherwise *false*.

From Table 7.5, you can see that relational operators return a *boolean* value. A *boolean* value can hold only *1* to indicate *true* or *0* to indicate *false*. In Lesson 11, you will learn how to use these results to write a decision-making statement in your program. For now, you need to understand that a relational operator returns only a *true* or *false* value.

The following program, *Compare.cpp*, shows the return values when the relational operators are applied to the values 2, the first operand, and 7, the second operand:

```
#include   <iostream.h>

void main (void)
{
    int var1 = 2;
    int var2 = 7;
```

```
    cout << var1 << " is less than " << var2 <<
            " (2 < 7) = " << (var1 < var2) << endl;
    cout << var1 << " is greater than " << var2 <<
            " (2 > 7) = " << (var1 > var2) << endl;
    cout << var1 << " is less than or equal to " <<
            var2 << " (2 <= 7) = " << (var1 <= var2) <<
            endl;
    cout << var1 << " is greater than or equal to " <<
            var2 << " (2 >= 7) = " << (var1 >= var2) <<
            endl;
    cout << var1 << " is equal to " << var2 <<
            " (2 == 7) = " << (var1 == var2) << endl;
    cout << var1 << " is not equal to " << var2 <<
            " (2 != 7) = " << (var1 != var2) << endl;
}
```

In the program, the relational operations are within parentheses. This is because of the order in which C++ evaluates operators. If you do not enclose these expressions in parentheses, the compiler will try to associate the variable with the inserter "<<" as an operator first and will issue and display an error. Most of the time you use relational operators, you will need to enclose the operator and its operands within parentheses.

When you compile and run *Compare.cpp*, your screen will display the following output:

```
2 is less than 7 (2 < 7) = 1
2 is greater than 7 (2 > 7) = 0
2 is less than or equal to 7 (2 <= 7) = 1
2 is greater than or equal to 7 (2 >= 7) = 0
2 is equal to 7 (2 == 7) = 0
2 is not equal to 7 (2 != 7) = 1
```

In each case, the return value is either 0 (if the relationship is false) or 1 (if the relationship is true).

The "==" (is equal to) and "!=" (is not equal to) operators also are called the *equality* operators because they return *true* or *false* depending upon whether the two operands are equal to each other.

Notice that the "is equal to" (==) operator is *two* equals signs written together. A common error even among programmers with some experience is to write the operator with a single equals sign. The compiler *will not* issue or display an error if you do this. Instead of a boolean value of *true* or *false*, the expression will return the value of the assignment, and decision-making statements with this error may not perform as expected.

The following short program, *BadTest.cpp*, shows the result of making this type of error:

```
#include   <iostream.h>

void main (void)
{
    int var1 = 0;
    int var2 = 2;
//
// The test written properly
//
    cout << var1 << " is equal to " << var2 <<
            " (2 == 7) = " << (var1 == var2) << endl;
//
// The test written with "=" instead of "=="
//
    cout << var1 << " is equal to " << var2 <<
            " (2 == 7) = " << (var1 = var2) << endl;
}
```

When you compile and run this program, you will see the following output:

```
0 is equal to 2 (0 == 2) = 0
2 is equal to 2 (0 == 2) = 2
```

As you can see from the first output line, the intent of the expression is to return *false*, or 0, as the result of the test. Written with the equals sign error, the expression sets *var1* to the same value as *var2*, and returns the new value of *var1*.

This can be a particularly difficult error to find, especially if you are used to working in another language such as BASIC, which uses just a single equals sign to test for equality.

Using Logical Operators to Test for True and False Conditions

The logical operators test the results of two values or expressions. The operators simply test whether the values or expressions are zero or non-zero, then they return a boolean value to represent the result.

There are only two logical operators. The logical AND operator returns *true* only if both expressions are non-zero. You write the logical AND operator with two ampersands (&&) between the values or expressions. The logical OR operator returns *true* if *either* of the two values or expressions is non-zero. You write the logical OR operator with two vertical bars (||) between the two operands.

You will see examples of these operators shortly, but it is important that you understand the difference between *true* as used with the relational operators and non-zero. The word *true* refers to a boolean truth value and is always 1. Non-zero, on the other hand, is any value, positive or negative, that is not zero. The logical operators test the operands for non-zero values and return boolean *true* or *false* depending upon the result of the expression. Table 7.6 is a truth table showing the result of the logical operators.

Table 7.6 Truth Table for Logical Operators

Expr1	Expr2	Expr1 && Expr2	Expr1 || Expr2
Non-Zero	Non-Zero	true	true
Non-Zero	Zero	false	true
Zero	Non-Zero	false	true
Zero	Zero	false	false

Using a logical operator, a program evaluates the expression on the left of the operator first, then the expression on the right. The interesting characteristic of a logical operator is that some part or all of the expressions actually may not be evaluated. The operation will end and the result known as soon as the program can determine the *truth value* of the operation.

The following program, *Logical.cpp*, shows how to use the logical operators:

```
#include   <iostream.h>

void main (void)
{
    int var1 = 0;
```

```
    int var2 = 2;
    cout << var1 << " AND " << var2 <<
            " (0 && 2) = " << (var1 && var2) << endl;
    cout << var1 << " OR " << var2 <<
            " (0 || 2) = " << (var1 || var2) << endl;
//
// Set new values for var1 and var2
//
    var1 = 4096;
    var2 = -8192;
    cout << var1 << " AND " << var2 <<
            " (4096 && -8192) = " << (var1 && var2) << endl;
    cout << var1 << " OR " << var2 <<
            " (4096 || -8192) = " << (var1 || var2) << endl;
}
```

When you compile and run *Logical.cpp,* you will see the following output:

```
0 AND 2 (0 && 2) = 0
0 OR 2 (0 || 2) = 1
4096 AND -8192 (4096 && -8192) = 1
4096 OR -8192 (4096 || -8192) = 1
```

In each case, the program simply evaluates whether the values are zero or non-zero. In the first line, the program evaluates only *var1*. Because it is zero, the expression cannot possibly return anything but *false*. In the last line, the program also evaluates only *var1*, which is non-zero. From the truth table, you can see that if either expression is non-zero, the test *must* return *true*, so the program does not need to evaluate the second value.

Using the *sizeof* Operator to Determine an Object's Size in Bytes

In Visual C++, an integer variable requires four bytes to store its value. Other variable types may require more or less memory to store values. There are times when you will find it useful to know the amount of memory a particular variable type requires. When you begin using *arrays* and *class* and *structure objects*, often you will need to know their sizes to perform operations on these objects.

The *sizeof* operator returns the number of bytes required to store a particular data type. The *sizeof* operator requires only one operand, which may be a data type, a value, or the name of a variable. The following program, *Size.cpp*, shows some samples of the *sizeof* operator:

```cpp
#include  <iostream.h>

void main (void)
{
//
// First, use some constant values
//
    cout << "sizeof(6) = " << sizeof (6) << endl;
    cout << "sizeof ('A') = " << sizeof ('A') << endl;
    cout << "sizeof (\"This is a string)\" = " <<
    sizeof ("This is a string") << endl;
//
// Show the sizes of some data types
//
    cout << "sizeof(int) = " << sizeof (int) << endl;
    cout << "sizeof(char) = " << sizeof (char) << endl;
    cout << "sizeof(long) = " << sizeof (long) << endl;
    cout << "sizeof(float) = " << sizeof (float) << endl;
    cout << "sizeof(double) = " << sizeof (double) << endl;
}
```

When you compile and run this program, you will see the following output:

```
sizeof(6) = 4
sizeof ('A') = 1
sizeof ("This is a string)" = 17
sizeof(int) = 4
sizeof(char) = 1
sizeof(long) = 4
sizeof(float) = 4
sizeof(double) = 8
```

The output reveals an interesting fact about strings. Notice that the number of bytes needed to store a string is one more than the length of the string *without* the quote marks. As you know, the quote marks are not part of the string. However, C++ adds an extra byte to the end of the string to mark the end of the string. It places a 0 in this byte.

Understanding Bitwise Operators

The Visual C++ *bitwise* operators combine the bits of one operand with those of a second operand. The operators work on corresponding bits in the two variables using the operator. For example, the lowest order bit, bit 0, of the first operand is combined with the lowest order bit of the second operand. Then bit 1 of the first operand is combined with bit 1 of the second operand. The operation is complete when all of the bits have been combined.

Table 7.7 summarizes the three bitwise operators, and Table 7.8 is a *truth table* for the bitwise operations.

Table 7.7 The C++ Bitwise Operators

Operator	Operation	Result
&	AND	1 if both bits are 1, otherwise 0
|	OR	1 if either bit is 1, otherwise 0
^	XOR	1 if both bits are *different*, otherwise 0

Programmers sometimes call the XOR operators the "exclusive OR" operator. As you can see from the truth table, the result is 1 if one and only one exclusively is 1. If both bits are 1 or both bits are 0, the result is 0.

Table 7.8 Truth Table for C++ Bitwise Operators

Bit1	Bit2	Bit1 & Bit2	Bit1 | Bit2	Bit1 ^ Bit2
1	1	1	1	0
1	0	0	1	1
0	1	0	1	1
0	0	0	0	0

The XOR operator has some special properties. Programmers sometimes call it the "toggle operator." If you XOR a bit with 1, the result is always the *opposite* of the original bit. For example, 1 ^ 1 is 0, and 0 ^ 1 is 1.

The following program, *Bitwise.cpp,* gives examples of the bitwise operators. The values and the result are shown in *binary* form, using the ones and zeros as they are stored in the memory location.

For now, do not try to understand the *ShowBits()* function. Its purpose here is to output the values as ones and zeros. In the course of this book, you will learn how to construct functions such as *ShowBits()*:

```cpp
#include  <iostream.h>

template <class T> void ShowBits (T x);

void main (void)
{
    int var1 = 7324;
    int var2 = 1693;

    cout << "      var 1 = ";
    ShowBits (var1);
    cout << endl;
    cout << "      var 2 = ";
    ShowBits (var2);
    cout << endl;
    cout << "var1 & var2 = ";
    ShowBits (var1 & var2);
    cout << endl << endl;

    cout << "      var 1 = ";
    ShowBits (var1);
    cout << endl;
    cout << "      var 2 = ";
    ShowBits (var2);
    cout << endl;
    cout << "var1 | var2 = ";
    ShowBits (var1 | var2);
    cout << endl << endl;

    cout << "      var 1 = ";
```

```
    ShowBits (var1);
    cout << endl;
    cout << "        var 2 = ";
    ShowBits (var2);
    cout << endl;
    cout << "var1 ^ var2 = ";
    ShowBits (var1 ^ var2);
    cout << endl;
}

template <class T> void ShowBits (T x)
{
    int i;
    unsigned long Bit = 1 << (sizeof (x) * 8 - 1);
    for (i = sizeof (x) * 8; i > 0; --i)
    {
        cout << ((Bit & x) >> (i - 1));
        Bit = Bit >> 1;
    }
}
```

When you compile and run *Bitwise.cpp,* your screen will display the following output:

```
      var 1 = 00000000000000000001110010011100
      var 2 = 00000000000000000000011010011101
var1 & var2 = 00000000000000000000010010011100

      var 1 = 00000000000000000001110010011100
      var 2 = 00000000000000000000011010011101
var1 | var2 = 00000000000000000001111010011101

      var 1 = 00000000000000000001110010011100
      var 2 = 00000000000000000000011010011101
var1 ^ var2 = 00000000000000000001101000000001
```

Compare the bits in the original variable with the bits in the result, then compare them with what you think they should be using Table 7.8. Try changing the values of *var1* and *var2,* then try changing the type of both *var1* and *var2* to *char*.

What You Must Know

In this lesson, you learned about Visual C++ operators and how to use many of them. Some operators require one operand and others require two operands. You learned how to use the relational and logical operators to obtain a boolean result, which will be important when you start writing programs that make decisions. In Lesson 8, "Using Increment and Decrement Operators," you will learn how to use the increment and decrement operators. Before you continue with Lesson 8, however, make sure you understand the following key points:

◆ Programs use C++ operators to perform mathematical and logical operations. The result of the operation depends upon the operator.

◆ Visual C++ represents most operators with symbols you type on your keyboard. You cannot use these symbols as part of a variable name.

◆ The operands used by an operator may be a value, the name of a variable, or an expression. C++ evaluates expressions from left to right.

◆ Relational and logical operators are used to obtain a boolean value, which is either 1 or 0. The boolean value may be used in a decision-making expression.

◆ Bitwise operators act on one bit at a time in the operands. The resulting bit is assigned to the corresponding bit in the result.

Lesson 8

Using Increment and Decrement Operators

In Lesson 7, "Getting Started with Visual C++ Operators," you learned about operators in Visual C++ and how to use the operators. In this lesson, you will learn how to increment and decrement the value of a variable by adding or subtracting 1 from its value. First, you will do this using the arithmetic and assignment operators, then by using C++ operators to perform the task. By the time you finish this lesson, you will understand the following key concepts:

♦ *Incrementing* a variable is the process of adding a fixed value to the variable's value. You can use increments to step the value up by a certain value.

♦ *Decrementing* a variable is the process of subtracting from the variable's value. You can use increments to step the value down by a certain value.

♦ C++ provides operators that let you increment or decrement the value of a variable by 1 without using the arithmetic and assignment operators.

♦ Prefix operations modify the value of a variable before your program uses the value. Postfix operations modify the value of a variable after your program uses the value.

Incrementing and Decrementing Variables

Throughout your programming, you often will need to modify the value of a variable to keep track of a certain operation. You may have to increase or decrease the value of the variable, using the new value in a decision-making statement to repeat portions of your code until the variable's value reaches a certain amount.

For example, you may need to print a number of files. Your program could use a variable named *count* to keep track of how many files you have printed already. Starting with a value of 0 for *count*, each time you print a file, you add 1 to the value of *count*. You can use the Visual C++ assignment operator as shown:

```
count = count + 1;
```

This statement obtains the current value of *count* and then adds 1 to it. Next, the statement stores that new value back into the variable *count*. When the value of *count* is the same as the number of files you need to print, your program will know to stop printing files.

When you increase the value of a variable this way, you are *incrementing* the value of the variable. The most common increment is 1, but you may use other variables as the increment value. The following program, *Inc-Count.cpp*, starts with a value of 1000 for *count*, then uses the addition operator to increase the value by 1:

```cpp
#include  <iostream.h>

void main (void)
{
    int count = 1000;

    cout << "The starting value for count is " <<
            count << endl;
    count = count + 1;
    cout << "The ending value for count is " <<
            count << endl;
}
```

When you compile and run the *IncCount.cpp* program, your screen will display the following output:

```
The starting value for count is 1000
The ending value for count is 1001
```

Incrementing the value of a variable by 1 is a common operation in programming. Because it is so common, C++ provides an *increment operator* to perform this operation. You write the operator using two plus signs together as "++." The increment operator is sort of a shorthand method of adding 1 to the value of a variable. For example, the following two lines both increment the value of *count* by 1:

```
count = count + 1;
++count;
```

The second line requires much less typing, however. As you learned earlier, the more you have to type, the greater the chance of making an error such as misspelling the name of a variable.

The following program, *IncOper.cpp,* uses the increment operator to increase the value of *count* by 1:

```
#include  <iostream.h>

void main (void)
{
    int count = 1000;

    cout << "The starting value for count is " <<
            count << endl;
    ++count;
    cout << "The ending value for count is " <<
            count << endl;
}
```

As in *IncCount.cpp,* the program starts by assigning a value of 1000 to the variable *count,* then prints the starting value. Next, the program increments the value of *count* using the increment operator instead of repeating the variable's name and adding 1 to it. Finally, it displays the new value of *count* on your screen.

The output of *IncOper.cpp* is the same as *IncCount.cpp.* The difference is the method you used to increment the *count* variable.

In addition to incrementing a variable, you often may need to subtract a certain amount from the value of a variable. When you decrease a variable's value, you are *decrementing* the variable.

The following program, *DecCount.cpp*, shows how to decrement the value of a variable. The process is much the same as incrementing the value, except you use the subtraction operator instead of the addition operator:

```cpp
#include  <iostream.h>

void main (void)
{
    int count = 1000;

    cout << "The starting value for count is " <<
            count << endl;
    count = count - 1;
    cout << "The ending value for count is " <<
            count << endl;
}
```

When you compile and execute *DecCount.cpp*, your screen will display the following output:

```
The starting value for count is 1000
The ending value for count is 999
```

Once again, the program starts with an initial value of 1000 for *count*. However, in *DecCount.cpp*, the program *subtracts* 1 from the value. The output shows the ending value for *count* is 999 instead of 1001.

In programming, decrementing a variable's value is almost as common as incrementing a value. In addition to the increment operator, C++ provides a *decrement operator*. You write the decrement operator using two minus signs together as "−−." The following two lines decrement the value of *count* by 1:

```cpp
count = count - 1;
--count;
```

The following program, *DecOper.cpp*, changes the code in *DecCount.cpp* to use the decrement operator instead of the assignment operator:

```cpp
#include  <iostream.h>

void main (void)
{
    int count = 1000;
```

```
    cout << "The starting value for count is " <<
            count << endl;
    --count;
    cout << "The ending value for count is " <<
            count << endl;
}
```

When you compile and run *DecOper.cpp*, you should see the same output you saw with *DecCount.cpp*.

In all the samples in this topic, the increment and decrement operators have been written in front of the variable names. When you write them this way, they are *prefix* operators. You also may write them as *postfix* operators by placing the operator after the variable name, as in *count++*. As you will learn in the next two sections, there is a significant difference between prefix and postfix operators.

Using Prefix Expressions

A common operation in any programming language is to add or subtract 1 from the value of a variable. When you do this, you are *incrementing* (adding 1 to) or *decrementing* (subtracting 1 from) the value of the variable. Incrementing and decrementing are particularly useful in *loops*, a group of statements a program repeats. The incremented or decremented variable is used as the *test variable* to determine when the program should *exit* the loop.

Adding or subtracting 1 from a variable's value is so common that C++ provides operators for those purposes, a sort of programming shorthand. To add 1 to a variable's value, you write the increment operator with the name of the variable. For example, if you have a variable named *var* and it contains a value of *4*, writing *++var* will change the value to *5*. To subtract 1 from the value of a variable, write the decrement operator with the name of the variable. If *var* now contains a value of *5*, writing *--var* will change the value to *4*.

When you increment or decrement a variable in a separate statement, it does not matter whether you use the operators as prefix or postfix operators. The following two statements, for example, achieve the same result. Either statement will increment *count* before the next statement executes:

```
++count;
count++;
```

You do not have to write the increment or decrement operation as a separate statement, however. You may combine it with another operator. Assume you have two variables, *var1* and *var2*, that contain the values *2* and *3*, respectively, and a third variable, *count*, that contains the value 3. The following code fragment will increment the value of count, add it to the value of *var2*, and assign the result, *7*, to *var1*:

```
int var1 = 2;
int var2 = 3;
int count = 3;


var1 = var2 + ++count;
```

It is important that you understand that the program will increment the value of *count* before it uses the value. In the preceding code, the value of *count* when the program adds it to the value of *var2* will be *4*. This is the result of using the increment operator as a *prefix* operator. As you will learn in the next section, the operation of the *postfix* operator differs considerably.

Whether you write the increment and decrement operators before or after the variable name determines how your program will use them in an expression. The following program, *PreOpers.cpp*, shows the result of using the increment and decrement operators as prefix operators:

```
#include    <iostream.h>


void main (void)
{
//
//   Prefix increment
//
     int count = 4;
     cout << "Initial value of count: " << count << endl;
     cout << "Prefix increment: " << ++count << endl;
//
//   Prefix decrement
//   Reset the value of count to 4
     count = 4;
     cout << "Initial value of count: " << count << endl;
     cout << "Prefix decrement: " << --count << endl;
}
```

Before each operation, the program first sets the value of *count* to 4. In the first few lines of the program, when the operator appears before the operand, as in ++*count*, the value is incremented before the program displays the value. The same sequence occurs when you use the prefix decrement operator instead of the increment oper-ator. The program decrements the value of *count* before displaying the value. When you compile and run *PreOpers.cpp*, you will see the following output:

```
Initial value of count: 4
Prefix increment: 5

Initial value of count: 4
Prefix decrement: 3
```

Success HINT: The Comma Operator: Combining Increment or Decrement Operations

The increment and decrement operators will add or subtract 1 from only one vari-able. There are times that you may want to increment two variables. Visual C++ lets you do this by writing the operations in the same statement if you separate them with the comma *operator. For example, suppose you have two variables,* count1 *and* count2, *and you want to increment both of them. You could write the operations as separate statements as shown:*

```
++count1;
++count2;
```

Alternatively, you could write them in the same statement using the comma, as shown in the following line:

```
++count1, ++count2;
```

When you use the comma operator, the operations on the two variables do not have to be the same. For example, you could increment count1 *while decrement-ing* count2, *as in the following statement:*

```
++count1, --count2;
```

Effectively, the comma operator combines two independent statements on one line. You may have more than two operations, but there must be a comma opera-tor between each. The comma operator guarantees the program will evaluate the expressions from left to right. In this case, the C++ language guarantees that the program will perform the ++count1 operation before it performs the ——count2 operation.

(You should not confuse the comma operator in this sample with the commas that you used to declare more than one variable on a line. For variable declarations and for the expressions in a function call, the comma is merely a separator, and C++ does not guarantee the program will evaluate the expressions from left to right.)

Using Postfix Expressions

You have seen that, when written before the variable name, the increment or decrement operators cause the program to perform the operation before the value of the variable is used. You also may write the operators as *postfix* operators, that is, you append an operator to a variable's name.

When you write the increment or decrement operator as a postfix operator, the program will use the value of the variable *before* it performs the operation. In the following statement, the program will add the value of *count* to the value of *var2* and assign the result, 6, to the variable *var1:*

```
int var1 = 2;
int var2 = 3;
int count = 3;


var1 = var2 + count++;
```

In the last section, you learned that a similar group of statements that use the prefix increment operator assigned a value of 7 to *var1*. In the preceding, code, however, the value of *count* is 3 when the program performs the addition. After the addition is complete, the program then increments the value of *count* to 4.

This may seem like a fine distinction, but you must understand the difference before you get to Lesson 12, "Repeating Statements within a Visual C++ Program." In Lesson 12, you will begin writing *loops*, repeating blocks of code. If you write a postfix operator when you really mean to write a prefix operator, your loop will execute one time more than you intend it to execute.

The following program, *PostOper.cpp,* shows the results of using postfix increment and decrement operators:

```
#include    <iostream.h>

void main (void)
{
//
//   Postfix increment
//
    int count = 4;
    cout << "Initial value of count: " << count << endl;
    cout << "Postfix increment: " << count++ << endl;
    cout << "Value after postfix increment = " <<
            count << endl;
//
//   Postfix decrement
//   Reset the value of count to 4
    count = 4;
    cout << "Initial value of count: " << count << endl;
    cout << "Prefix decrement: " << count-- << endl;
    cout << "Value after postfix decrement = " <<
            count << endl;
}
```

When you compile and execute *PostOper.cpp*, your screen will display the following output:

```
Initial value of count: 4
Postfix increment: 4
Value after postfix increment = 5
Initial value of count: 4
Prefix decrement: 4
Value after postfix decrement = 3
```

At the time the program evaluates the expressions containing the postfix operations, the value of *count* is 4, and that is the value the program displays on your screen. Then the program performs the postfix operation, and the line following shows the new value for *count*.

Compare the output of *PostOper.cpp* with the output of *PreOpers.cpp* in the previous section.

Success HINT: Using Values Other Than 1 to Increment or Decrement a Variable

The Visual C++ increment and decrement operators let you adjust the value of a variable in steps of 1 only. There are times, however, that you will need to add or subtract a larger value from the variable's value.

C++ does not provide a specific operator to increment or decrement by values greater than 1. However, you can combine the arithmetic and assignment operators into a single symbol to achieve increments and decrements greater than 1. To do this, write the variable's name, the plus or minus operator, the assignment operator, and finally the amount by which you want to change the variable's value. The following statement, for example, increments the value of count *by 2:*

```
count += 2;
```

Similarly, you may use the minus sign with the assignment operator to decrement a variable's value by more than 1. The following statement decrements count *by 4:*

```
count -= 4;
```

What You Must Know

In this lesson, you learned about the Visual C++ increment and decrement operators and how to use them. You also learned about prefix and postfix operations and how to write the different operations in a statement. You also learned how the choice of prefix or postfix affects the value of a variable in your program. In Lesson 9, "Writing Expressions in Visual C++," you will begin writing expressions and assigning the result to variables. Before you continue with Lesson 9, however, make sure you have learned the following key points:

◆ The increment operator increases the value of a variable by 1. Write the increment operator using two consecutive plus signs with the name of a variable.

◆ The decrement operator decreases the value of a variable by 1. Write the decrement operator using two hyphens with the name of a variable.

◆ A prefix increment operation increases the value of a variable before your program uses the value. A prefix decrement operation decreases the value of a variable before your program uses the value.

◆ Write a prefix increment or decrement operation using the operator before the variable's name.

◆ When you use a postfix increment or decrement operation, the program uses the value of the variable before the increment or decrement operation takes place.

◆ Write a postfix increment or decrement operation by appending the operator to the variable's name. That is, you write the operator immediately following the variable name.

Lesson 9

Writing Expressions in Visual C++

In Lesson 8, "Using Increment and Decrement Operators," you learned about the increment and decrement operators in Visual C++ and how to use the operators to add or subtract 1 from the value of a variable. In this lesson, you will learn how to write other expressions in Visual C++. You also will learn about operator precedence, or the order in which Visual C++ evaluates the part of an expression. By the time you finish this lesson, you will understand the following key concepts:

◆ An *expression* is a sequence of operators and identifiers that computes a value or generates an effect in C++.

◆ Expressions may contain other subexpressions that are evaluated first.

◆ To make sure a program evaluates expressions in a consistent and orderly manner, C++ assigns a precedence to each operator.

◆ Parentheses group operators and indentifiers. You may use parentheses to change the order of evaluation.

How C++ Evaluates Expressions

In your lessons so far, you have learned how to assign a value to a variable and how to increment or decrement the value. You also have seen the results of using some of the Visual C++ operators in your program.

When you write a variable's name or simply a value in C++, or when you combine variable names or values with operators, you are writing an *expression*. An expression can be very simple, nothing more than a value or a variable's name. C++ does not require that you do anything with a value. For example, it may surprise you to learn that the following line is a perfectly acceptable statement in C++:

```
42;
```

C++ does not require that a statement do anything useful. In this case, your program simply *evaluates* the expression. Because you did not assign the result to a variable or use it in a function call, your program discards the value.

Of course, you want to save the results of an expression, so you use the assignment operator to store it in a variable, such as when you write *int count = 42;* in a declaration statement.

The important point here is that the variables and operators on the right side of the assignment operator make up an expression. Your program evaluates all of the variables and operations in the expression before assigning the result to a variable.

When you read and write an expression, you normally proceed from left to right. For example, you would read the statement *result = 5 + 8 * 2;* as "*result* equals five + eight times 2." As you will see in the next section, C++ evaluates certain parts of the expression first because some operators are more important than others.

The following program, *C2F.cpp*, uses an expression to convert degrees Celsius to degrees Fahrenheit. This program also introduces you to *parameters* to the *main* function:

```
#include    <iostream.h>
#include    <stdlib.h>

void main (int argc, char *argv[])
{
    int celsius;
    int fahrenheit;
    if (argc < 2)
    {
```

```
        cout << "usage: c2f degrees" << endl;
        return;
    }
    celsius = atoi (argv[1]);
    fahrenheit = 9 * celsius / 5 + 32;
    cout << celsius << " degrees C = " <<
            fahrenheit << " degrees F" << endl;
}
```

C2F.cpp uses a *command-line argument*. After you compile the program, run it by typing a number after the program name, as shown below:

```
C2F 24 <Enter>
```

The program will respond by displaying the following output on your screen:

```
24 degrees C = 75 degrees F
```

Your programs so far have used *void* as the parameter list to *main* to indicate that you will not use any parameters in your code. Regardless of whether you use them, Windows still delivers parameters to the *main* function of your program. The first parameter is the number of arguments that were typed on the command line. Programmers often give this parameter the name *argc*. The second parameter is a *pointer* to an *array* of strings that contain the command-line arguments. Programmers often call this array *argv[]*. (*Arguments* and *parameters* essentially mean the same thing. When you call a function, the values, variables, and expressions you use in the function call are *arguments*. Within the function itself, however, these arguments are *parameters* because your program already has evaluated them.)

The first argument in the array *always* is the name of your program. In Windows, this is the full *path* of your program, including the drive letter, all the subdirectories, and the *.EXE* extension. You will learn more about arrays in Lesson 13, "Using Array Variables to Store Multiple Values." For now, understand that C++ arrays begin with a subscript of 0, so this first member is *argv[0]*.

Next in the *argv[]* array are the command-line arguments that you typed. *C2F.cpp* needs only one argument, so C++ will place it in *argv[1]*. Although you type a number for this argument, C++ passes all parameters to *main* as strings. The program uses a *library* function to convert it back to a number.

C2F.cpp also uses a *decision-making* statement, *if (args < 2),* to make sure you actually entered an argument on the command line. You will learn about decision making in Lesson 11, "Making Decisions within a Visual C++ Program," but right now you need to use it. If you run your program without entering an argument, it could crash because it will attempt to convert a string that does not exist to a number. This test causes the program to remind you to enter a temperature value when you run the program; it then uses the *return* statement to exit.

Success HINT: Controlling the Order in Which C++ Evaluates Expressions

You might have learned in elementary algebra that you can change the order in which you evaluate an expression by writing part of it inside a set of parentheses. The same is true for Visual C++. Consider the following expression:

```
result = 5 + 8 * 2;
```

*You just learned that your program will perform the 8 * 2 multiplication first add then 5 to the value and assign the value 21 to the variable* result. *However, there are times when you really want to do the addition first, then the multiplication. You could rewrite the expression as follows:*

```
result = (5 + 8) * 2;
```

A C++ program always evaluates the portion of an expression inside the parentheses first. In this case, your program will assign the value 26 to result.

In the C2F.cpp program, you converted degrees Celsius to degrees Fahrenheit. The following program, F2C.cpp, uses parentheses to make sure the program performs the subtraction first:

```
#include     <iostream.h>
#include     <stdlib.h>

void main (int argc, char *argv[])
{
    int celsius;
    int fahrenheit;
    if (argc < 2)
    {
        cout << "usage: f2c degrees" << endl;
        return;
```

```
        }
        fahrenheit = atoi (argv[1]);
        celsius = 5 * (fahrenheit - 32) / 9;
        cout << fahrenheit << " degrees F = " <<
                celsius << " degrees C" << endl;
}
```

This program evaluates fahrenheit − 32 *first because it is surrounded by paren-theses. Without the parentheses, the equation would give a very different, and incorrect, result.*

You may nest parentheses as well. Nesting parentheses involves writing one expression in parentheses inside another set of parentheses, as in the following statement:

```
x = 2 * (8 * (4 + 3) + 42);
```

Your program will evaluate the expression inside the innermost parentheses, 4 + 3, first. Then your program will evaluate the expression within the outer set or parentheses using the result of the first expression, making it 8 * 7 + 42. Finally, your program evaluates the rest of the expression and assigns x *the result, 196.*

Understanding Operator Precedence

When you write an expression in C++ that involves arithmetic operations, you must be aware that C++ considers some operators more important and will perform the operations in a special order. C++ assigns a *precedence* to each operator depending upon its importance. For example, C++ considers the multiplication operator more important than the addition operator, so your program will perform multiplication before it performs any addition in an expression. Consider the following expression:

```
result = 5 + 8 * 2;
```

Your program first will evaluate *8 * 2* before it performs the addition operation. After performing the 8 * 2 multiplication, it adds the result, 16, to 5, and assigns the value of the expression, 21, to *result*.

Basically, this is the same order you learned in math classes to evaluate equations. You learned to perform all multiplication and division before you performed addition and subtraction. If you or your program does not follow these rules, the result will be very different, as shown in the following example:

```
result = 5 + 8 * 2;          result = 5 + 8 * 2;
       = 13 * 2;                    = 5 + 16;
       = 26;                        = 21;
```

The sample on the left performs the operations from left to right, encountering the addition operator first. In this case, it yields an incorrect result, 26. The sample on the right performs the multiplication first and calculates the correct result, 21.

Table 9.1 lists the C++ operators in order of operator precedence. Some of them, such as the addition and subtraction operators and the multiplication and division operators, have the same precedence. In Table 9.1, operators within each section have the same precedence. You may not have seen many of the operators in the table. By the time you finish the lessons in this book, you will have used and will understand all of them.

Table 9.1 Visual C++ Operator Precedence

Operator	Name	Example
::	Scope resolution	ClassName::ClassMemberName
::	Global resolution	::MessageBox()
.	Member of	object.member_name
−>	Member of	object_pointer−>member_name
()	Function call	FunctionName (arguments)
()	Sub expression	(Expression)
++	Postfix increment	variable++
++	Prefix increment	++variable
−−	Postfix decrement	variable−−
−−	Prefix decrement	−−variable
&	Address	&variable
*	Dereference	*pointer
new	Allocate memory	new type
delete	Deallocate memory	delete pointer
delete []	Deallocate array	delete [] pointer
~	Ones complement	~variable
+	Unary plus	+42 or +variable

Table 9.1 Visual C++ Operator Precedence, Continued

Operator	Name	Example
—	Unary minus	−42 or −variable
()	Cast	(type) expression
.*	Member selector	object.*pointer
—>*	Member selector	object—>*pointer
*	Multiply	expression * expression
/	Divide	expression / expression
%	Modulo	expression % expression
+	Addition	expression + expression
—	Subtraction	expression − expression

This is not a complete list. There are many operators after the addition and subtraction operators, but you should, at least, be familiar with this portion of the list. These other operators, such as the *logical* and *bitwise* operators have lower precedence than those in the list. You will learn about these other operators in later lessons.

 Visual C++ Reuses Many Operator Symbols

Some of the operators have multiple entries in Table 9.1. When you write expressions using these operators, the compiler will determine which you want from the context. The context is the meaning of the operator after taking into account the adjacent operators, variables, and values.

In Lesson 7, "Getting Started with Visual C++ Operators," you learned that the plus and minus signs may be unary or binary depending upon the context. In the expression x = −4; the minus sign is unary because it takes only one operand, the 4, but in the expression x = x − 4; it is binary because it takes two operands, the x and the 4.

Other operators that are context-sensitive *are the* :: *symbol and the parentheses. If you use the* :: *symbol between an object name and the name of a member of that object, then Visual C++ interprets the operator as a* scope resolution *operator. If you use it before an identifier, then it is a* global resolution *operator. You will learn more about these operators in later lessons.*

Although the parentheses appear three times in the operator precedence list, the only use of the parentheses as a true operator is the cast *operator. You may use parentheses to group a subexpression or to contain the arguments to a function call. In these cases, the parentheses are* punctuation marks, *which you will learn about in Lesson 10, "Visual C++, Like All Languages, Follows Rules of Grammar and Syntax."*

C++ already uses most of the symbols on the keyboard that are not letters or numbers. Without reusing the symbols for multiple operations, C++ would have to resort to a confusing array of operators using words instead of symbols.

Using the Comma Operator

In Lesson 8, "Using Increment and Decrement Operators," you learned how to use the comma operator to write two increment or decrement operators in a single statement. The comma symbol is confusing to new C++ programmers because sometimes it is an operator and sometimes it is not. The precedence table in the last section does not list the comma operators. However, the comma operator has the very lowest precedence of all the C++ operators.

Programmers often refer to the comma as the "sequential-evaluation" operator. It allows you to group two or more statements where the Visual C++ compiler normally would expect only one. In the following program, *Comma.cpp,* the comma is an operator:

```
#include    <iostream.h>

void main (void)
{
    int x;
    int y;
    x = 3, y = x * 4;
    cout << "x = " << x << endl;
    cout << "y = " << y << endl;
}
```

When you compile and run *Comma.cpp,* you will see the following output:

```
x = 3
y = 12
```

The C++ rules require your program to evaluate $x = 3$ before it evaluates $y = x * 4$. If you write more than one expression using the comma operator, your program evaluates the leftmost expression first, then the second to the left, and so on until it reaches the last expression.

In other uses, the comma may be a mere separator. Remember that C++ ignores white space except to separate tokens. In a *function call*, for example, you need something other than spaces to separate the arguments. Otherwise, the compiler would read all the arguments as a single argument.

In this case, the comma is *not* an operator. Instead, it merely serves to separate the arguments, and the C++ rules about evaluating the expressions from left to right do not apply. In fact, Visual C++ usually evaluates the argument expressions in a function call from right to left, and other compilers might use a different order. Look what happens in the preceding program when you place the expressions $x = 3$, $y = x * 4$ in a function call. The following program, *Comma2.cpp*, does this:

```cpp
#include     <iostream.h>

void MyFunction (int, int);

void main (void)
{

    int x;
    int y;
    MyFunction (x = 3, y = x * 4);
}

void MyFunction (int x, int y)
{
    cout << "x = " << x << endl;
    cout << "y = " << y << endl;
}
```

When you compile *Comma2.cpp*, the Visual C++ compiler will display a warning similar to the following:

```
local variable 'x' used without having been initialized
```

In this program, the order of evaluation in the function call is from right to left, so in the expression $y = x * 4$ the variable x does not yet have a value. When you compile and run the code, you will see output similar to the following:

```
x = 3
y = 16829624
```

That may not be the value you had in mind for y. When your program *declared* the variable x, it set aside memory to hold the value of x. That memory might already have some information stored there from an earlier operation. If you do not *initialize* the variable, your program will use that old value. To help you avoid this situation, the Visual C++ compiler will warn you when you use a variable without initializing the variable's value.

The distinction between the uses of the comma may seem as thin as a hair, but you should realize how C++ treats this symbol in the different uses and recognize the warning the compiler will print to your screen.

Writing Arithmetic Expressions

Arithmetic expressions are expressions that yield a number value. That number may be used for various purposes. For example, it might just be a plain number that represents a temperature, a distance, or the elevation of a city. Or it might be a *pointer* that contains the address of a variable or object. (Using pointers is a common programming practice in Visual C++.)

To write an arithmetic expression, you must use at least one value or variable. If you use more than one value or variable, you must use an operator to tell C++ what action you want to perform on the values or variables. In other words, you must *explicitly* write the operator.

In high school algebra, you probably learned that you can represent the multiplication of two variables by writing them adjacent to each other. For example, if you have variables a and b, you write the product of the two as ab. The multiplication operator is *implicit*. That doesn't work in programming. The compiler would interpret ab as another variable other than a or b. In C++, and most programming languages, you must write $a * b$ to indicate that you want the program to multiply a by b.

You may use arithmetic expressions in an assignment statement. In fact, this is a common use in assignment statements. In an assignment statement, an expression may use a variable that the program already has evaluated, as in the following:

```
int pre_count = 8;
int count = 3 * pre_count + 2;
```

In this case, your program will evaluate the expression 3 * *pre_count* + 2 before assigning the result to the variable *count*.

As you saw in the last section, you also may write an arithmetic expression as an argument to a function call. Your program will not pass the expression to the function your program is calling. Instead, your program will evaluate the expression as an *argument* to the function. Once your program has evaluated the expression, it will pass a single value, the *parameter,* to the function.

Some C++ articles and help files may refer to the identifier on the left side of the assignment operator as the *lvalue.* The "l" comes from *left,* and literally means the identifier on the left side of the assignment operator, the equals sign, or one of the other assignment operators. This identifier must be *modifiable,* meaning it must be a variable in which you can store a value. For example, 5 = 2 + 3; would cause the compiler to generate and display an error. The 5 is a constant, and is not a memory location where you may store the results of 2 + 3. Instead, you would have to write something like the following:

```
int var;
var =  2 + 3;
```

The identifier *var* describes a memory location where your program can store the result of the expression.

Yes, the expression on the right side of the assignment operator is called the *rvalue,* but you will see that term used very infrequently.

Writing Boolean Expressions

Like arithmetic expressions, a *boolean* expression also returns a number. The boolean expression, however, will return only a *0* or a *1.* In C++, the identifier *true* is defined as *1,* and the identifier *false* is defined as *0.* Thus, a boolean expression returns either *true* or *false.*

The name *boolean* comes from George Boole, an English mathematician who invented a system of algebra dealing with logic. This system later became known as *boolean* algebra, which often is used to represent the state of switches or transistors in a circuit. Deep within the circuitry of your computer, all of your programming efforts are converted to boolean algebra in some form.

Many of the C++ operators return a boolean result. For example, if you write 2 < 5, the result cannot be represented as a numerical result. You are asking, "Is 2 less than 5?" Your program responds by returning *true,* or *1,* as the result of the expression. Of course, that result is obvious, but suppose you wanted to compare two variables that represent the results of two different operations. You would write *var1* < *var2,* or "Is *var1* less than *var2?*" The result—*true* or *false*—will give your program the answer.

Boolean expressions give your program the ability to make decisions. You will cover this topic very soon. Earlier in this lesson, you saw an example of how to use a boolean expression to protect your program in case you forgot to enter a temperature when you ran the program:

```
if (argc < 2)
{
    cout << "usage: f2c degrees" << endl;
    return;
}
```

Here, you are asking, "Is *argc* less than *2?*" If the result is *true*, the *if* keyword instructs your program to execute the *block* of statements immediately following (the block is enclosed in open and closed *braces* { and }). If the result is *false*, your program will ignore the block of statements.

What You Must Know

In this lesson, you learned how to write expressions in Visual C++ and how the compiler and your program evaluate expressions. You also learned that some operators are more important than others, and C++ assigns each operator a precedence. Using this precedence, your program evaluates expressions in a consistent and orderly manner. In Lesson 10, you will learn about C++ grammar and syntax. Before you continue with Lesson 10, "Visual C++, Like All Languages, Follows Rules of Grammar and Syntax," however, make sure you have learned the following key points:

◆ An expression is a group of values, variables, and operators that results in a value such as a number or generates some effect such as a function call in C++.

◆ Expressions give your program the power to perform arithmetic on variables and values and to store the results in a variable.

◆ C++ considers some operators more important than others and assigns each operator a precedence. The precedence assures that your program will evaluate expressions in a consistent and orderly manner.

◆ Expressions may contain subexpressions. You may change the order in which your program evaluates expressions by writing subexpressions inside parentheses.

◆ The comma operator separates multiple expressions written in a single statement. Grammatically, this is like joining two English statements with "and."

◆ Generally, your program evaluates expressions from left to right. In a function call, however, your program does not know and cannot determine the order of evaluation.

◆ Boolean expressions return only *0* or *1* (*true* or *false*) and give your programs the ability to make decisions.

Lesson 10

Visual C++, like All Languages, Follows Rules of Grammar and Syntax

In Lesson 9, "Writing Expressions in Visual C++," you learned how C++ evaluates expressions and how to write expressions. You also learned how to change the order in which your program evaluates expressions by writing subexpressions inside sets of parentheses. In this lesson, you will learn about Visual C++ syntax and punctuation. You also will learn how to recognize different parts of your program using the syntax highlighting in the Visual Studio. By the time you finish this lesson, you will understand the following key concepts:

◆ C++ defines certain rules you must follow when writing a program. These rules are the grammar of the programming language.

◆ Some operators contain more than one symbol, and C++ provides strict rules on how you write them.

◆ A statement is a group of one or more C++ expressions. A simple statement ends with a semicolon.

◆ Compound statements are groups of simple statements contained within a block. You mark the beginning of a compound statement using an opening brace (" { ") at the beginning and a closing brace (" } ") at the end.

◆ Visual C++ contains a number of specialized statements that transfer control of the program to other statements or cause the program to repeat statements in a *loop*.

Visual C++ Definitions and Conventions

In any language, everyone must agree to some basic concepts or no communication can take place. If not everyone agrees on the definition of a "table," for example, it is pretty hard to tell everyone to sit around the table. One person might stand in front the sink, another might sit in front of a window, yet another might do a headstand, and so forth. In a programming language, without agreeing on some basics, no programming can take place.

C++ has some formal conventions that make up its *syntax*. The syntax is the set of grammatical rules that tell you how to use a language. You already have seen some of these syntax rules in C++:

- ◆ White space separates identifiers such as constants and the names of variables.

- ◆ C++ statements end with a semicolon. This is equivalent to writing a period at the end of a sentence.

- ◆ The C++ language assigns all operators a precedence to ensure orderly and consistent evaluation of expressions.

- ◆ Identifiers written together must be joined by an operator. For example, to write "a times b," you must write *a * b* and not simply *ab* or *a b*.

- ◆ To store a value or the result of an expression, you must assign the value to a variable.

You also have seen examples of definitions in C++. For example, boolean *true* is always *1,* and boolean *false* is always *0.*

In a spoken or written language, the syntax rules are open to interpretation by the listener or reader. You can make a mistake, but the other person may be able to determine what you really mean. In programming, C++ *syntax* is more rigorous. The compiler will not attempt to determine what you really meant to write. If you make a mistake in writing a statement according to the syntax rules, the compiler will generate and display a syntax error and will not compile your program.

 Visual C++ Has Unofficial Naming Conventions

Visual C++ programmers also use naming conventions that are not required by the language—that is, they are not part of the C++ syntax. However, it makes it easier to identify the type of a variable from the name. One of the most common

naming conventions is the Hungarian notation *system. Much of the sample code in the Visual C++ help files contains variable names using Hungarian notation.*

To use variable names with Hungarian notation, write the variable's name with a lowercase prefix that indicates its data type, then write the first character of the rest of the name in uppercase. For example, instead of using just count *for the name of an integer variable, you would write it as iCount. In a program using Hungarian notation, you know that every variable with a name beginning with a lowercase "i" is an integer.*

Table 10.1 summarizes the prefixes used in Hungarian notation.

Table 10.1 Hungarian Notation Prefixes

Prefix	Data Type
c	char
by	BYTE (type unsigned char)
n	short int
i	int
x, y	short when used as coordinates
cx, cy	short when used to signify the length (count) of a coordinate
b	BOOL (type int)
w	unsigned int or WORD (type unsigned short)
l	long or LONG
f	float or double
dw	unsigned long or DWORD
p	pointer to an object or variable
fn	pointer to a function
s	character array (string)
sz	a null-terminated string

Sometimes programmers combine these prefixes. For example, a variable name for a null-terminated string might be szString, but a pointer to this variable might be called pszString. Not all variables need to have a prefix. For example, i com-

monly signifies a variable used in a loop or as the index for an array, so you do not need to write it with a prefix.

From this point, all program samples in this book will use Hungarian notation. As the programs become more complex, this notation will help you to follow and understand them.

The Hungarian notation system predates C++ and so does not contain prefixes for C++ objects. Over the years, programmers have added a number of prefixes that relate to C++.

In the intermediate part of this book, you will study classes and structures. You will need to add variables as members of these objects. Programmers often prefix class member variables with m_ to identify the members throughout the code.

In addition, C++ and the Microsoft Foundation Class library contain classes to make strings easier to use. Variables of these classes usually have a prefix of str to distinguish them from ordinary string variables.

Understanding Operator Syntax

As you have seen, C++ syntax is the set of rules that you use when you write your program code. The syntax determines how you use and write tokens and white space. In Lesson 5, "Understanding a Few C++ Basics," you learned that *white space* is any character that only moves the caret and does not display on your screen. These include the space, tab, and Enter keys. *Tokens* are anything that is not white space.

In previous lessons, you learned that the Visual C++ compiler ignores white space except when it is used to separate identifiers, such as variable names. There are times, however, when white space might confuse the compiler and cause it to display a syntax error.

C++ includes several operators that use more than one symbol. These operators cannot be represented by a simple "+" sign, for example. When using these symbols with more than one symbol, you may not insert white space characters between the symbols. The following line, for example, shifts the bits in the variable *var* one place to the left:

```
var = var << 1;
```

If you write this statement as *var = var < < 1;* (inserting a space between the two "<" symbols), the compiler will generate and display a syntax error. It will refuse to compile your program until you fix the error.

When you write the increment (++) or decrement (−−) operators, you may place white space before and after the operators, but you may not place white space between the symbols. For the increment and decrement operators, you should be aware of a quirk in the C++ syntax. The following two lines will compile properly:

```
++count        // No space after the operator
++ count       // A space between the operator and identifier
```

However, if you write the statements as in the following two lines, the compiler will not generate or display a syntax error, but it will not generate the code to increment the variable either:

```
+ +count;      // A space between the operator symbols
+ + count;     // Spaces between the operator symbols and
               // the variable name
```

The compiler will treat the two plus symbols as two unary addition operators rather than as a single increment operator. The statements do not contain syntax errors, but the statements do not perform the increment operation either. The same is true with the decrement operator (−−). If you write the decrement operator with spaces between the minus signs, the compiler will treat the symbols as two unary minus signs, and your code will not decrement the variable's value.

You should be aware of this quirk when you are writing your program code. If you have a variable that does not appear to increment or decrement when you run your program, check to make sure you did not include a space accidentally.

The quirk appears only when you use the increment and decrement operators as prefix operators. When you use them as postfix operators, the compiler will generate and display syntax errors when you compile your code. The following lines will generate syntax errors:

```
count + +;
count+ +;
count - -;
count- -;
```

These statements cause syntax errors because you must have an operand written to the *right* of the unary plus and unary minus operators.

Reviewing Punctuation

Visual C++ has very few punctuation marks. Generally, the symbols used for punctuation help the compiler to determine the intent of your programming statements.

All C++ statements must end with a semicolon, for example. Because the compiler ignores most white space, you may write a single statement over many lines to improve readability. This means you must give the compiler some signal that you intend to terminate the statement. The semicolon serves this purpose.

As with the semicolon, other punctuation marks serve as separators in C++. They tell the compiler where one part of your program or statement ends and the next part begins. Table 10.2 summarizes the Visual C++ punctuation marks.

Table 10.2 C++ Punctuation Marks and Their Uses

Punctuation Mark	Name	Purpose
[]	Brackets	To indicate array subscripts
()	Parentheses	To group expressions, isolate conditions, and indicate function calls
{}	Braces	To indicate the beginning and end of a compound statement
,	Comma	To separate the arguments in an argument list
;	Semicolon	To terminate statements
:	Colon	To indicate labeled statements
...	Ellipsis	To indicate a variable argument list or arguments with varying types

Several of these punctuation marks must be used in pairs. Whenever you use an open bracket, open parenthesis, or open brace, you must include the matching close mark.

You will encounter the ellipsis in Lesson 37, "Writing Functions with a Variable Argument List." When writing an ellipsis, you must write it without any spaces between the individual periods.

Declaration Syntax

You have learned that you cannot use a variable until you declare it. The declaration tells the compiler the data type of the variable and, thus, how much memory to set aside to store its value. In addition, you must declare the names and parameters of functions before you use them.

Frequently, you will see all the variables used in a function declared at the beginning of the function. This is a hangover from the C language, which required you to declare all variables before writing any code. Your programs so far have declared variables at the beginning of your programs. However, C++ lets you declare variables at almost any point in your code. Programmers call this *proximity declaration,* and it improves the readability by letting you declare a variable near the point in your code where you first use it.

The following program, *Declare.cpp,* shows how you can use declaration statements at any point in your code:

```cpp
#include     <iostream.h>
#include     <stdlib.h>

void main (int argc, char *argv[])
{
    if (argc < 2)
    {
        cout << "usage: Declare degrees" << endl;
        return;
    }
//
//  Declare and initialize a variable for degrees fahrenheit
//
    int fahrenheit = atoi (argv[1]);
//
//  Declare and initialize a variable for degrees celsius
//
    int celsius = 5 * (fahrenheit - 32) / 9;
//
//  Display the result
//
    cout << fahrenheit << " degrees F = " <<
            celsius << " degrees C" << endl;
}
```

In *F2C.cpp* in Lesson 7, "Getting Started with Visual C++ Operators," your program declared the *fahrenheit* and *celsius* variables at the beginning the *main* function. *Declare.cpp* does not declare the variables until you are ready to use the variables. Each declaration also includes an expression and an assignment operator to set the variables in the same line.

C++ also lets you declare and initialize multiple variables on the same line, as in the following:

```
int var1 = 2, var2 = 6;
```

In the preceding statement, the variables must be of the same data type. You cannot mix type *int*, for example, with type *float*. The following line will make the compiler generate and display syntax errors on your screen:

```
int var1 = 2, double var2 = 6;
```

In a multiple declaration statement, you should not make the value of one of the variables dependent upon the value of another. You need to be aware that the comma in a declaration statement is a punctuation mark and not an operator. Thus, C++ does not guarantee that the assignments will be made from left to right. The following line, for example, compiles properly using Visual C++, and the program assigns the proper values to the variables:

```
int x = 4, y = x + 2;
```

The preceding line may not compile properly using a compiler other than Visual C++ or on another operating system. Because of this, you should avoid this sort of construction.

Evaluating Expressions

In Lesson 9 and also in this lesson, you learned how C++ evaluates expressions and assigns the results to variables. To evaluate an operation, C++ applies the value on the right of the operator to the value on the left of the operator and proceeds from left to right until it fully evaluates the expression. You may change the order by writing subexpressions inside sets of parentheses.

The *type* of the expression will be the highest precision of any value used in the operation. In other words, if you mix a *float* data type with an *int* type in the same expression, the result of the expression will be a *float* type value. C++ automatically *promotes* values to the next higher precision in an expression. The expression 6.3 / 2 returns a *float* value although one of the two values, the *2*, is an integer:

Ideally, the variable in which the value is stored should be the same type as the expression. If you have a *double* variable, the expression should evaluate to a *double* type. If the values on the left and right sides are not the same data type, C++ will convert the right value to be the same as the left value. The *cast* to another data type, however, is done on the results of the expression. The following program, *Float.cpp*, shows the result of assigning a float value to an integer variable:

```
#include    <iostream.h>

void main (int argc, char *argv[])
{
    int iVar;
    float fVar;
//
//  Test the effect of assigning a float expression to an
//  integer variable.
//
    iVar = 3.0 / 2;
    cout << "iVar = " << iVar << endl;
//
//  Assign the same float expression to a float variable
//
    fVar = 3.0 / 2;
    cout << "fVar = " << fVar << endl;
}
```

When you compile *Float.cpp*, the compiler may issue a warning about a possible loss of precision on Line 11. This is because you are assigning a floating value to an integer. However, the compiler will permit the operation after casting the result of the operation to an integer. When you run *the program*, you will see the following output:

```
iVar = 1
fVar = 1.5
```

The following program, *Int.cpp*, shows that the change in data type—the promotion—occurs *after* the program evaluates the expression:

```
#include    <iostream.h>

void main (int argc, char *argv[])
{
    float fVar;
//
//  Test the effect of assigning an integer expression to an
//  float variable.
//
```

```
    fVar = 3 / 2;
    cout << "fVar = " << fVar << endl;
}
```

Instead of assigning *1.5* to the variable *float_x*, the result is *1*, as shown in the following output:

```
fVar = 1
```

Your program first performed the division as integer division and discarded the fractional portion. Then it assigned the result to the *float* variable.

You must be aware of these automatic promotions when you write your code. The compiler will not always warn you when you are assigning an integer result to a float variable, or vice versa.

Writing Statements

In Visual C++, statements control the flow of your program's execution. So far, you have learned about statements that evaluate expressions or assign values to a variable. C++, however, has several statement types that let you perform loops or transfer control to other statements.

Table 10.3 lists the various statement types available in Visual C++. You may not be familiar with most of these yet, but during the course of this book, you will learn about all of the statement types and use them in programs.

Table 10.3 C++ Statement Types

Statement Type	Purpose
break	To break program execution out of a loop or *switch* statement
continue	To restart a loop before all the loop statements have executed
do-while	To enclose a compound statement inside a loop
for	To repeat a statement in a loop a specified number of times
goto	To cause the program to jump to a labeled statement
if	To provide condition execution of another statement
label	To mark an execution point for a *goto* statement or *switch* statement
null	An empty statement; Contains only a semicolon
return	To transfer control from a function to another function that called it
switch	To provide several optional execution points
while	To repeat a statement in a loop until a condition becomes *false*

In addition to these special statement types, statements may be *expression* or *compound*. Expression statements sometimes are called *simple* statements and contain a single terminating semicolon. Compound statements contain zero or more expression statements and are written using open and closed braces (" {" and "}"). Compound statements have additional properties that control the *scope* or visibility of variables.

The *C2F.cpp* and *F2C.cpp* programs in Lesson 9 each contain a compound statement to guard against a missing parameter:

```
if (argc < 2)
{
    cout << "usage: c2f degrees" << endl;
    return;
}
```

The *if* statement tests the boolean expression within the parentheses. If the expression is *true*, the program will execute *all* the statements between the following braces. The braces enclose the compound statement.

You will learn more about compound statements in the next two lessons. In addition, you will learn about scope in Lesson 17, "Understanding Function and Variable Scope."

What You Must Know

In this lesson, you learned about programming syntax and punctuation in C++. You also learned how to declare and initialize multiple variables in a single expression statement. In addition, you learned how your C++ program evaluates expression and about the various statement types in Visual C++. In Lesson 11, "Making Decisions within a Visual C++ Program," you will learn how to construct compound statements as part of teaching your program to make decisions. Before you continue with Lesson 11, however, make sure you have learned the following key points:

◆ C++ grammar defines the syntax and rules that you use to write programs.

◆ Certain operators contain multiple symbols. You must write these symbols with no white space between them.

◆ Visual C++ punctuation marks are separators and not operators. You must write many of these punctuation marks in pairs with statements between the punctuation marks.

◆ An expression statement is a group of C++ expressions and ends when you write the semi-colon.

◆ A compound statement is a group of one or more expression statements. You mark the beginning of the compound statement with an opening brace and the end of it with a closing brace.

◆ Specialized C++ statements let you transfer program control to another statement or make a statement repeat under certain conditions.

Lesson 11

Making Decisions within a Visual C++ Program

A program, as you have learned, is a list of instructions your computer executes one after the other. Most of your programs so far have used simple statements that started with the first statement in the program and continued to the last statement. In the temperature conversion programs of Lesson 9, "Writing Expressions in Visual C++," you saw how a program can execute an alternate list of statements if a condition is not met. The programs made this "decision" to avoid "crashing" if you did not type a temperature on the command line. In this lesson, you will learn how to use the Visual C++ operators and statements to let your program make other decisions. By the time you finish this lesson, you will understand the following key concepts:

- ◆ Decision making is an important concept in programming and allows your program to select alternate statements to execute based on the result of an expression.

- ◆ The *if* statement is the primary decision-making tool in Visual C++.

- ◆ Using the *if* statement, your program will execute a statement or a block of code if the expression is not 0. If the expression is 0, your program will not execute the statement or block of code.

- ◆ The *else* statement provides an alternate statement or block of code your program will execute if the *if* statement is false or 0.

- ◆ Combining the *if* and *else* statements into an *else-if* statement gives your program the power to select from more than two blocks of code.

- ◆ The *switch* statement lets your program select alternate blocks of code depending upon the value of a variable or expression.

- ◆ You may use multiple tests to help your program make a proper decision.

Understanding Decision-Making Constructs

As you know, a computer is a machine. At the heart of your computer is a *processor* chip that executes the instructions in your program after they have been compiled into the numbers the processor understands as instructions and data. The processor chip recognizes instructions that allow your programs to execute alternate code based on certain *conditions*. In other words, your programs can make *decisions*.

Programs that make decisions perform *conditional processing*. To make a decision, your program performs tests on values in your program. In the temperature programs from Lesson 9, this test involved determining whether there was a *command line argument* present when you ran your program. In other cases, your program might test the value of a variable to determine whether the variable's value is equal to, less than, or greater than a certain value.

For example, your store may require some sort of identification if a customer writes a check for more than $20. At the end of the transaction, your program may test the total value of the sale and prompt you to ask for a driver's license if the sale is greater than $20.

In another instance, you may write a program to assign letter grades to test scores. To do this, your program may compute the score in percentage, then test that score to determine the *range* in which it falls.

Visual C++ provides a number of operators that let your program perform these tests. These *relational operators* help your program to determine whether a value is less than, equal to, or greater than another value. Table 11.1 summarizes the relational operators.

Table 11.1 The Visual C++ Relational Operators

Operator	Test	Example
==	If two values are equal	(cost == 50)
!=	If two values are not equal	(cost != 50)
<	If the first value is less than the second	(cost < 50)
>	If the first value is greater than the second	(cost > 50)
<=	If the first value is less than or equal to the second	(cost <= 50)
>=	If the first value is greater than or equal to the second	(cost >= 50)

Notice that four of the six operators use more than one symbol. You must write these symbols with no spaces between them. For example, the "is equal to" symbol is two equals signs written together, as in *(first == second)*. If you write the statement as *(first = = second)*, the compiler will interpret this as two assignment operators and issue a syntax error.

In this case, the "(first == second)" is the *conditional expression*. The *first* and *second* variables are the operands to the == operator. In most cases, you must include the open and close parentheses when you use the expression in a decision-making statement.

Using the *if* Statement

Visual C++ lets your program perform tests using the *if* statement. Your program then might perform a statement if the test is *true*, or *1*. However, if the test is *false*, or *0*, your program will not execute the statement following the test. The *if* statement is the primary decision-making statement in Visual C++, but later you will learn how to use other decision-making statements.

The basic form of the *if* statement determines whether a value is equal to 0. In this test, you need only write the value or the name of the variable without any operators, as in the following code:

```
if (variable)
    statement;
```

The *if* test will return *true* to your program if the variable's value is not equal to *0* and *false* if the value is *0*. If the value is not *0*, your program will execute *statement*. If the value is *0*, your program will ignore *statement*.

At this point, it is important you notice that the line containing *if* does not end with a semicolon. After learning that you must end each statement with a semicolon, a common error at this point is to add the semicolon after the line containing the *if*. However, *statement* is a part of the overall *if* statement. Actually, you could rewrite the code as follows:

```
if (variable) statement;
```

However, writing *statement* on a separate line and *indenting* it to the right of the line containing the *if* makes your code easier to read and follow when you debug your programs.

The following program, *First_if.cpp*, tests whether the value of *iScore* is *greater than or equal* to 90. If the value is 90 or higher, your program will execute the *cout* line following the test:

```
#include    <iostream.h>

void main (void)
{
    int iScore = 95;
```

```
   if (iScore >= 90)
        cout << "Congratulations. You got an A!" << endl;
}
```

After you compile and test run *First_if.cpp*, try changing the value of *iScore* to something less than 90, such as 85. Recompile and run your program to see the result. The program should run and end without printing anything. Next, assign a value of 90 to *iScore* and recompile and run the program.

In the next section, you will learn how your program can execute an *alternate* statement if the test in the *if* statement is *false*.

When using the *if* statement, sometimes your program will need to execute more than one statement if the test result is *true*. You can do this by grouping the statements inside a set of open and close braces, as shown here:

```
if (iScore >= 90)
{
    cout << "Congratulations. You got an A!" << endl;
    cout << "Your score is " << iScore << endl;
}
```

The braces and the statements between them make up a *compound* statement. Programmers sometimes call this a *statement block*. When the test *(iScore >= 90)*, is *true*, your program transfers control to the first statement in the compound statement. Your program then executes the statements within the block. When the test is false, your program ignores the entire block, as shown in the following program, *Compound.cpp*:

```
#include    <iostream.h>

void main (void)
{
    int iScore = 95;

    if (iScore >= 90)
    {
        cout << "Congratulations. You got an A!" << endl;
        cout << "Your score is " << iScore << endl;
    }
}
```

Try changing the value of *iScore* from 95 to 85 to see the result.

Success HINT: Understanding Simple and Compound Statements

The if statement gives your program the power of decision making. As you write your programs, many times you will need only the simple statement after the if *statement. A simple statement is one that contains only a single terminating semicolon, as the in the following:*

```
if (iScore >= 90)
    cout << "Congratulations. You got an A!" << endl;
```

However, there will be other times when your program will need to execute more than one statement when the test statement is true. *Visual C++ lets you build a* compound *statement from more than one simple statement. A compound statement is a group of statements written within a set of open and close braces. To do this, write the braces and statements as shown here:*

```
if (iAge >= 21)
{
    cout << "Don't forget to register to vote" << endl;
    cout << "Remember Florida 1878 and 2000." << endl;
    cout << "Your vote counts!" << endl;
}
```

Using the *else* Statement

In the last section, you learned how to make your program execute a statement or block of statements when the test result was *true.* Often you will need to provide an alternate statement for your program to execute if the test is *false.*

Visual C++ lets you provide alternate code by using the *else* keyword. When your program executes an *if* statement, the program will execute the statement or block of statements immediately after the *if* statement if the test is *true.* However, if the test is *false,* your program will look for the *else* to find an alternate statement. The following program, *IfElse.cpp,* shows how to write an alternate statement:

```
#include    <iostream.h>

void main (void)
{
    int iScore = 95;

    if (iScore >= 90)
        cout << "Congratulations. You got an A!" << endl;
    else
        cout << "You need to try harder next time" << endl;
}
```

When you compile and run *IfElse.cpp*, the program will display the following output:

```
Congratulations. You got an A!
```

Try changing the value of *iScore* to 85 (or any value less than 90). When you recompile and run the *IfElse.cpp*, you will see the following output:

```
You need to try harder next time
```

You must remember that the *else* keyword is a part of the *if* statement and not a separate statement. You cannot use *else* in your program without the *if* statement. In addition, when you use the *else* keyword, you must provide a statement for the program to execute when the test is *true* and a statement for the program to execute when the test is *false*.

You have learned that you may build compound statements by grouping simple statements inside a set of open and closed braces. If your program needs to execute more than one statement when your test is *false*, you may use a compound statement after the *else* keyword.

The following program, *Cmp_Else.cpp*, uses compound statements after both the *if* statement and the *else* keyword to write alternate text to your screen:

```
#include    <iostream.h>

void main (void)
{
    int iScore = 85;

    if (iScore >= 90)
```

```
{
    cout << "Congratulations. You got an A!" << endl;
    cout << "Your score was " << iScore << endl;
}
else
{
    cout << "You need to try harder next time" << endl;
    cout << "You missed " << 100 - iScore <<
            " points " << endl;
}
}
```

 Mixing Compound Statements With *if-else*

You have learned that you may build compound statements by grouping simple statements inside a set of open and closed braces. If your program needs to execute more than one statement when your test is true, *you may use a compound statement after the* if *statement. Similarly, if your program needs to execute more than one statement following the* else *keyword, you may use a compound statement as well.*

When you use the if-else construct, you do not have to use compound statements after both the if *and the* else. *You may use a simple statement after one or the other, and a compound statement after the other, as shown in the following sample code:*

```
if (iScore >= 90)
    cout << "Congratulations! You got an A!" << endl;
else
{
    cout << "You need to try harder next time" << endl;
    cout << "You missed " << 100 - iScore <<
                " points " << endl;
}
```

Building Multiple *if-else* Constructs

You have learned how to use *if* and *else* in your program to test for one condition, then provide alternate statements for the *true* and *false* results. There will be times, however, when you will need to test several conditions and provide alternate statements for each.

Visual C++ lets you "stack" *if* statements by combining them with the *else* statement. The following program, *Grades.cpp*, accepts a score and assigns it a grade. (The *cin* is opposite stream from *cout*. While *cout* prints output to your screen, *cin* accepts input from your keyboard. Notice that the operator is written in the opposite direction, that is >> instead of <<.)

```
#include     <iostream.h>

void main (void)
{
    int iScore;

    cout << "Type in your test score and press enter: ";
    cin >> iScore;
    if (iScore >= 90)
        cout << "Congratulations. You got an A!" << endl;
    else if (iScore >= 80)
        cout << "You got a B" << endl;
    else if (iScore >= 70)
        cout << "You got a C" << endl;
    else if (iScore >= 60)
        cout << "You got a D" << endl;
    else
        cout << "You failed the test" << endl;
}
```

Your program first tests whether the grade is equal to or greater than 90. If that test is *true,* your program executes the next statement and ignores the rest of the *else if* conditions. If the test is *false,* your program tests the next condition, *iScore >= 80*. It continues down until it finds a condition that is *true*. If all the conditions are *false*, your program will execute the statement following the last *else* and display "You failed the test."

Success HINT: Using the Visual C++ NOT Operator

The if statement causes your program to execute the next statement if the result of the test is true. *If the test is* false, *your program will ignore the next statement or block of statements. There will be times, however, that you will want to execute the next statement if the condition is* false. *To do this, you might have to write an awkward construction such as the following, which uses an* empty statement *after the if statement:*

```
int iUserOwnsADog = 0;
if (iUserOwnsADog)
    ;
else
    cout << "You should get a Pomeranian!" << endl;
```

The empty statement does nothing. Essentially, it is just a placeholder. Fortunately, Visual C++ offers an operator to make this condition easier to write. The NOT operator, the exclamation point (often called a bang*), reverses the sense of the expression. If the expression is* true, *the NOT operator will make it* true. *If the result is* false, *the NOT operator will make it* true.

Using the NOT operator, you can rewrite the preceding code as follows:

```
int iUserOwnsADog = 0;
if (!iUserOwnsADog)
    cout << "You should get a Pomeranian!" << endl;
```

You should understand that the NOT operator has a very high precedence, meaning Visual C++ and your program will evaluate the NOT operator before evaluating an expression with most other operators. If you need to test a condition using a relational operator, you need to write the expression inside parentheses and the NOT operator in front of the open parenthesis, as shown in the following code:

```
if (!(iScore >= 90))
    cout << "You did not get an A" << cout << endl;
```

Using the *switch* Statement as an Alternative to Multiple *if-else* Statements

Your program can test multiple conditions by stacking *if-else* statements. In the last section, you used a series of *if-else* statements to test whether a test score fell within a particular range of values. When you found the proper range, your program displayed some text for that range.

Sometimes your program must test for a number of specific values (not ranges of values). In this case, you may use the Visual C++ *switch* statement. To use the *switch* statement, you must specify a condition that evaluates to a whole number. Your program will use the results to select a statement or a block of statements to execute.

The following program, *Switch.cpp*, uses the *switch* statement to display a message depending upon the student's grade:

```
#include    <iostream.h>

void main (void)
{
    char cGrade = 'B';

    switch (cGrade)
    {
        case 'A':
            cout << "Congratulations on your A!" << endl;
            break;
        case 'B':
            cout << "B is OK, but you can get an A" << endl;
            break;
        case 'C':
            cout << "C is an average grade" << endl;
            break;
        case 'D':
            cout << "D is barely passing" << endl;
            break;
        case 'F':
            cout << "You failed! Study harder!" << endl;
```

```
        break;
    default:
        cout << "Your grade is unknown" << endl;
        break;
    }
}
```

When you use the *switch* statement, there are some important points that you must understand:

◆ The *case* keyword marks the alternate blocks of code your program may execute. Your program will execute a block if the test expression equals the value after the *case* keyword. The *case* value must be a constant. You cannot use a value or an expression containing values after *case*.

◆ The statement following the *switch* statement *must* be a compound statement. Even if you provide only one block of code, you must include it as part of a compound statement. This means you must use the open brace to mark the beginning of the compound statement and the closed brace to mark the end of the compound statement.

◆ The *break* statement ends the compound statement after the *switch* statement. When your program encounters the *break* statement, your program will transfer control to the first statement after the closing brace. If you do not include the *break* in a block of code, the program will "fall through" to the next *case* block.

◆ Your program will execute the statements in the *default* block if the test value does not match any of the values in the *case* statements. This lets you perform statements for an unexpected value.

◆ The test expression *must* be a value, variable, or expression that results in an integer value such as *bool, int, long,* or *short int.* You cannot use a *float* or *double* value for the test value.

Be careful how you write the test expression. If you use one of the relational operators, the result will be *boolean* and can only be *0* or *1*. For example, if you write the test expression as *(cScore == 'A'),* your *case* statement may be only *0* or *1*. You can see this in *Switch.cpp* if you change the expression. The compiler will issue a series of warnings similar to the following for all the *case* statements other than *default:*

```
Switch.cpp(27) : warning C4808: case '65' is not a valid value for switch
condition of type 'bool'
```

The *case* 'A' actually is a value of 65, which is not boolean 0 or 1. Thus, the compiler issues the warning that it is not a valid condition. The compiler will continue to compile your program and will create the executable file if it does not find any errors. However, you should examine the warnings and correct the problem.

Evaluating More Than One Expression in an *if* Statement

The ability to make decisions gives your programs the power of selecting alternate statements and blocks of code based upon the value of a certain expression. Sometimes, however, your decisions may not be so easy. You may have to test more than one condition to determine which block of code your program should execute.

Visual C++ provides two *logical* operators that allow you to combine the result of two or more test conditions. Table 11.2 summarizes the logical operators.

Table 11.2 Visual C++ Logical Operators

Operator	Meaning	Example
&&	AND	*condition1 && condition2*
||	OR	*condition1 || condition2*

You learned about these operators in Lesson 7, "Getting Started with Visual C++ Operators." In Lesson 7, however, you used these operators to compare whether two values are zero or non-zero. You also may use the logical operators to join two or more conditions.

The following short program, *MultiTst.cpp*, shows how you can combine two tests in a single *if* statement:

```
#include    <iostream.h>

void main (void)
{
    int iScore = 85;

    if ((iScore < 90) && (iScore >= 80))
    {
        cout << "Work harder. You got an B." << endl;
```

```
        cout << "Your score was " << iScore << endl;
    }
}
```

The *MultiTst.cpp* program first tests whether the score is less than 90. If the score is greater than 90, the student got an A. The real score is 85, so the test result is *true*. Next, the program checks whether the score is greater than or equal to 80. That test is *true*, so the program then combines the result of the two tests using the truth table shown in Table 7.6. The entire expression is *true*, so the program executes the block of code following the *if* statement.

Notice that the two tests inside the *if* statement are written inside parentheses. Another, outer set of parentheses contains both tests. Actually, the logical operators have a relatively low *precedence*, so you do not need the inner parentheses. However, most programmers use them to isolate the tests and make the program more readable. The extra parentheses do no impose any additional computing time for your programs, and you should get used to using them.

Nesting Decision-Making Statements (Placing One Statement within Another)

You have learned that a *compound* statement is a block of statements enclosed by a set of braces. In Visual C++, you may use any type of statement within a compound statement, including another decision-making statement. There are times when you need to refine your condition by testing for another condition within an *if* statement.

When you place a statement such as an *if* statement inside a statement of another type, you are *nesting* the conditional statements. The following program, *NestedIf.cpp*, show how you can test one condition within another:

```
#include    <iostream.h>

void main (void)
{
    int iScore = 85;

    if (iScore < 90)
    {
        if (iScore >= 80)
```

```
    {
        cout << "Work harder. You got an B." << endl;
        cout << "Your score was " << iScore << endl;
    }
  }
}
```

The *NestedIf.cpp* program first tests whether *iScore* is less than 90. If that test is *true,* the program executes the compound statement block following the test. Within the statement block, you may write any other statement. In *NestedIf.cpp,* the first statement is another *if* statement that further refines the first test.

The program will execute the first statement block only if *iScore* is less than 90. If the nested test, *if (iScore >= 80),* is *true,* you know the grade is a B, so your program executed the nested compound statement.

What You Must Know

In this lesson, you learned about testing values and expressions and how to write *if* statements. You learned how to use multiple *if-else* statements to test for a *range* of values and how to select one of several statements for your program to execute. Then you learned about the *switch* statement and how to select alternate blocks when a variable or expression has a certain value. Finally, you learned how to test for multiple conditions and to nest one test within another. Decision making is an important concept in programming, and it lets your program determine what statements it will execute. In Lesson 12, "Repeating Statements within a Visual C++ Program," you will learn how to build *loops,* statements that your program may execute more than once. Before you continue with Lesson 12, however, make sure you have learned the following key points:

◆ A decision-making statement lets your program decide whether to execute a statement or block of statements.

◆ The *if* statement returns a *true* or *false* value depending upon the result of the test, which you write inside parentheses.

◆ Your program may execute more than one statement as the result of a test. To do this, you write the statements inside a block of code marked with open and closing braces. This block is a *compound* statement.

◆ The *switch* transfers program control to a specific block of code depending upon the value of a variable or expression.

◆ In a *switch* statement, the *break* statement ends the block of code and transfers control to the first statement after the compound statement

◆ Your program may determine a condition based on multiple tests, and an *if* statement may be *nested* in the compound block following another *if* test.

Lesson 12

Repeating Statements within a Visual C++ Program

Decision making, which you learned about in Lesson 11, "Making Decisions within a Visual C++ Program," gives your programs a powerful tool. The ability to make decisions means your program can execute alternate statements depending upon the *current* value of variables in your program. You also learned about the C++ *switch* statement, which lets your program select one of many blocks of code based on the current value of a variable.

Another powerful programming concept is *loops,* which let your program repeat a statement or a block of statements until certain conditions are met. Loops let you perform in just a few statements what otherwise would be a long and tedious series of statements. Decision-making statements and loop statements are C++ *control* statements. These statements interrupt the normal flow of sequential instructions. In this lesson, you will learn how to write and use Visual C++ loop statements. By the time you finish this lesson, you will understand the following key concepts:

◆ Looping involves transferring control of the program back to a statement that the program already has executed.

◆ A program continues executing the statements within a loop until certain conditions are met.

◆ The C++ statement that determines when to exit the loop is the *loop control statement*.

◆ The Visual C++ *for* loop lets your program repeat statements a specific number of times.

◆ The Visual C++ *while* loop lets your program repeat statements as long as a condition is *true.*

◆ The Visual C++ *do while* loop performs statements at least once, then repeats the statements based on a specific condition.

Using Visual C++ Loop Constructs to Repeat Statements

You have learned how your program can execute alternate statements based on the current state of a program value or variable and select alternate blocks of code based on a condition. The statement that transfers control to the alternate statements is the *control statement*. Visual C++ contains other control statements, including those that cause your program to loop, or repeat statements over and over.

Looping is a process of transferring control to a statement that the program already has executed. This is useful when you want to repeat a group of statement until a certain condition occurs. For example, your program might open a data file, read a line, and then process the input. When your program has finished processing the line, it might return control to the statement that reads a line. This would continue until your program has read the entire file. At that point, it would transfer control to a statement outside the loop.

Visual C++ offers three different loop control statements, as shown in Table 12.1.

Table 12.1 The Visual C++ Loop Statements

Loop Statement	Purpose
for	Executes a statement or block of statements a specific number of times. It is similar to the FOR . . . NEXT loop in BASIC.
while	Executes a statement or block of statements indefinitely as long as a condition is *true*.
do while	Executes a statement or block of statements *at least once,* then indefinitely as long as a condition is *true*.

In this lesson, you will learn to write programs using each of these loop statements. Looping is an important concept in programming, and it is important that you fully understand how to use these statements.

Looping with *goto* and Label Statements

The crudest, but most instructive, method of building a loop is to use the Visual C++ *goto* statement along with a *label*. A label is a unique name (similar to a variable's name) that ends with a colon. The following program, *Goto.cpp,* shows how such a loop works:

```
#include    <iostream.h>
```

```
void main (void)
{
    int iCount = 0;

JumpToHere:
    cout << "iCount = " << iCount << endl;
    ++iCount;
    if (iCount < 5)
        goto JumpToHere;
}
```

When you compile and run *Goto.cpp,* you will see the following output:

```
iCount = 0
iCount = 1
iCount = 2
iCount = 3
iCount = 4
```

The line *JumpToHere:* is a *label*. It does nothing except mark a point in your program. When the compiler encounters a label, it marks and remembers the *address* of the statement in case your program uses it later.

The *goto JumpToHere;* transfers control unconditionally to the label statement *JumpToHere*. The statement *if (iCount < 5)* determines whether your program will execute the *goto* statement. If *iCount* is less than 5, it will execute the *goto* statement and jump back to *JumpToHere*. When *iCount* has a value of 5 or greater, the program will ignore the *goto* statement.

There are some variations on how you build the loop. For example, you could put the test and *goto* at the top of the loop and the label statement at the bottom. You will not normally build loops this way, but when you compile a program with a loop in the code, the compiler uses one of these variations to build the loop.

The important point to remember here is that your program transfers control back to the top of the loop when it executes the *goto* statement. Visual C++ offers more elegant methods to write loops, as you will see shortly.

 Using an Empty Statement as a Label

You have seen how to transfer control to a label statement using the goto *statement. You should understand that the label itself, including the colon, is not a*

complete statement. It merely identifies, or labels, a statement for the compiler. To make it a complete statement, you must include a semicolon.

A semicolon without any identifiers or operators is an empty statement. It is like you open your mouth but do not actually say anything, but it can be useful in Visual C++ programming.

The following program, Oops.cpp, is a loop variation that uses a label and goto statement to repeat another statement. However, when you compile and run it, the compiler will gripe that you are missing a semicolon in the statement:

```
#include     <iostream.h>

void main (void)
{
    int iCount = 0;

TopOfLoop:
    if (iCount == 5)
        goto JumpToHere;
    cout << "iCount = " << iCount << endl;
    ++iCount;
    goto TopOfLoop;
JumpToHere:
}
```

To make the program compile properly, you need to write the last label using an empty statement, as follows:

```
JumpToHere:
    ;
```

Using the *for* Loop to Perform Statements a Specific Number of Times

Very often, you will find it convenient and necessary to repeat one or more statements a specific number of times. For example, you might need to print five copies of a file using one program. Another program might need to repeat a block of statements 25 times to list the grades of all the students in a class. You could build a loop using a label and a *goto* statement as in the last section. However, the Visual C++ *for* statement (sometimes called a *for loop*) makes it very easy for your program to repeat one or more statements a specific number of times.

To use a *for* loop, you must specify a variable called the *control variable*. The loop will repeat until the variable reaches a certain value. Usually, you will use the control variable to keep track of the number of times the loop executes. The following *for* loop, for example, will execute ten times:

```
for (iCount = 1; iCount <= 10; ++iCount)
    statement;
```

The *for* loop consists of four parts. The first three parts are the *loop control* statements, which you place inside the set of parentheses after the *for* keyword. The first statement, *iCount = 1*, sets the initial condition for the loop. The *for* loop performs this statement only once, just before the loop begins.

Next comes the *condition expression*, which is *iCount <= 10* in the preceding example. Each time the loop executes, your program will perform this test. As long as this condition is *true*, the loop will continue to execute. When the test becomes *false*, the loop will exit and transfer control to the first statement after the loop. You should understand that your program performs this test *before* it executes the loop. If the test is *false*, the first time your program enters the loop, none of the loop will be performed.

The last item inside the parentheses is the *increment*. Despite its name, you may perform virtually any arithmetic operation in the increment step, even decrement a variable's value if necessary. Your program performs this step *after* each time it performs the loop.

The fourth part of the *for* loop is the statement that will execute each time through the loop. This may be a simple statement, or it may be a compound statement that you write between a set of open and closed braces. The following program, *FirstFor.cpp,* uses a *for* loop to print the value of *iCount* on your screen:

```
#include    <iostream.h>

void main (void)
{
```

```
    int iCount;

    for (iCount = 0; iCount <= 5; ++iCount)
        cout << "iCount = " << iCount << endl;
}
```

This *for* loop produces the same result as the loop you built in the last section using the *goto* and label statement. However, note that it is easier to read and stretches over only two lines.

You may build a *for* loop using a compound statement. When you use a compound statement, the first statement after the opening brace marks the beginning of the code your loop will repeat. When the program reaches the closing brace, control returns to the *for* statement, where the program will perform the increment step and then test the control expression. The following program, *Step.cpp*, uses a compound statement:

```
#include    <iostream.h>

void main (void)
{
    int iCount;
    int iTotal = 0;

    for (iCount = 0; iCount <= 50; iCount += 5)
    {
        cout << "Adding " << iCount << " to " << iTotal;
        iTotal += iCount;
        cout << " yields " << iTotal << endl;
    }
}
```

When you compile and run *Step.cpp*, you should see the following output:

```
Adding 0 to 0 yields 0
Adding 5 to 0 yields 5
Adding 10 to 5 yields 15
Adding 15 to 15 yields 30
Adding 20 to 30 yields 50
Adding 25 to 50 yields 75
Adding 30 to 75 yields 105
```

```
Adding 35 to 105 yields 140
Adding 40 to 140 yields 180
Adding 45 to 180 yields 225
Adding 50 to 225 yields 275
```

As you examine *Step.cpp,* you should notice two things. First, the loop initializes *iCount* to 0. This is arbitrary, but you should be aware that Visual C++ performs much of its counting—array subscripts, character positions in a string, and so on—beginning at 0 rather than 1. Unlike BASIC, which lets you start at 0 or 1 using the OPTION BASE statement, C++ *always* begins its counting at 0.

Second, rather than use the increment operator (++) to step the control variable by *1,* the program uses an assignment operator to step the variable's value by five each time the program completes the loop (one time through the loop is called an *iteration*).

 ## Stopping a Loop Before It Finishes

Sometimes your program may encounter a condition in a loop that makes it impossible to continue performing the statements in the loop. In Lesson 11, you learned how to use the break *statement to transfer program control to the first statement after a* switch *statement.*

The break *statement also works inside a loop, and abruptly ends the loop. When your program performs a* break *statement from within a* for *loop, control passes immediately to the first statement after the loop. Your program does not test the condition and it does not perform the increment step.*

For example, suppose your program is reading a series of lines from a file. You expect to read 10 lines in the file, and you set up your for *loop to repeat the steps 10 times. However, if the file contains only seven lines, your attempts to read the file will return an end-of-file (eof) condition, and the data your program read will be invalid. In this case, you could use the* break *statement to end the loop early.*

The following program, BrkLoop.cpp, *normally would perform the loop statements 10 times. However, it uses a* break *to terminate the loop when the value of* iCount *reaches 7.*

```
#include     <iostream.h>

void main (void)
{
    int iCount;

    for (iCount = 0; iCount < 10; ++iCount)
    {
        cout << "iCount = " << iCount << endl;
        if (iCount == 7)
            break;
    }
}
```

When you compile and run BrkLoop.cpp, you can see that the loop only executes seven times.

The *while* Loop Performs Statements while a Condition Is True

In the last section, you learned how to make your program repeat one or more statements a specific number of times. Sometimes, however, you will not know ahead of time how many times your program needs to repeat a loop. If you are reading lines from the keyboard, for example, you may not know how many lines the user will type before issuing a command to stop.

The Visual C++ *while* statement will continue to repeat a loop as long as its test condition is true. Unlike the *for* loop, the *while* loop uses only a condition expression; it does not contain an initializer or an increment step, as shown in the following sample:

```
while (condition)
    statement;
```

The *while* loop will continue to repeat the statement as long as the condition is *true*. The statement must perform some action that eventually will make the expression evaluate to *false* or the loop will continue forever. It is important that you understand that your program will evaluate the condition each time it repeats the loop, even the first time. If the condition is *false* when the loop first starts, your program *will not* perform the loop at all.

The following program, *While.cpp*, prompts you to enter a letter. It will continue looping until you enter the letter Q (in uppercase):

```
#include    <iostream.h>

void main (void)
{
    char ch = ' ';

    while (ch != 'Q')
    {
        cout << "Type a letter and press Enter: ";
        cin >> ch;
        cout << endl << "You pressed " << ch << endl;
    }
    cout << "Goodbye" << endl;
}
```

You declare your test variable, *ch*. Remember that Visual C++ does not intialize automatic variables in a function. The first thing *While.cpp* does is to initialize *ch* to a space (or anything other than Q), then enters the *while* loop. As long as you type any letter other than an uppercase Q, the test expression will be *true*, and the program will continue to execute the loop. When you type an uppercase Q, the test will be *false*, and the loop will terminate.

The *do-while* Loop Performs Statements at Least One Time

You learned that the *while* loop will continue to repeat one or more statements while the test condition is *true*. When the condition becomes *false*, the loop will end. If the condition is *false* when the program first evaluates the condition, the program will not perform the loop even once.

There are times when you want to make sure the loop executes at least once regardless of the test expression, then terminate when the test condition is *false*. As you have seen, the *while* loop tests the condition *before* your program starts the loop. Another form of the loop, the *do while* loop, tests the condition at the end of the loop.

This assures your program will execute the loop at least once, as shown in the following program, *DoWhile.cpp:*

```
#include     <iostream.h>

void main (void)
{
    char ch;

    do
    {
        cout << "Type a letter and press Enter: ";
        cin >> ch;
        cout << endl << "You pressed " << ch << endl;
    } while (ch != 'Q');
    cout << "Goodbye" << endl;
}
```

In the last section, you had to initialize *ch* to make sure it did not "accidentally" contain a capital Q. Using the *do while* construct, however, *ch* is assigned a valid value *before* the test is performed, so you don't need to initialize *ch*.

There are two important points to remember about the *do while* loop. First, you must use a compound statement after the *do*. Even if your program executes only one statement, you must enclose it in open and closed braces.

Second, notice that the *while* keyword and the test expression appear at the bottom of the loop instead of the top. In addition, there is a semicolon after the test expression at the bottom of the loop. In this case, the expression ends the loop statement, so C++ requires the terminating semicolon.

 ## Skipping Statements with the *continue* Statement

In this lesson, you learned how to end a loop early using the break *statement. Sometimes, you may want to end just a single iteration of the loop before all the statements have executed, but have the loop continue repeating. To do this, you can use the* continue *statement.*

When your program encounters a continue *statement, it ignores any statements below the* continue *statement in the loop and returns to the control statement. The following program,* Continue.cpp, *will abort the loop whenever the value of* iCount *is equal to 3:*

```
#include    <iostream.h>

void main (void)
{
    int iCount;

    for (iCount = 1; iCount <= 5; ++iCount)
    {
        if (iCount == 3)
            continue;
        cout << "iCount = " << iCount << endl;
    }
}
```

When you compile and run Continue.cpp, *you will see the following output:*

```
iCount = 1
iCount = 2
iCount = 4
iCount = 5
```

When iCount *is equal to 3, the program executes the* continue *statement and never executes the line where it would print "iCount = 3."*

Using the Visual C++ Loop Control Statements

In this lesson, you have learned how to build the three Visual C++ loops, the *for* loop, the *while* loop, and the *do while* loop. Each construction has particular advantages, and which one you use will depend upon the needs of your program.

◆ The *for* loop lets your program execute a loop a specific number of times. You may specify an initial value for the loop control variable and use the increment step to modify the variable's value each time the loop repeats.

◆ The *while* loop lets your program repeat a loop until a given condition is true. There is no guarantee that the loop will execute even one time if the initial condition is *false*.

◆ The *do while* loop does not test the condition until the loop executes at least once. After that, it operates much the same as the *while* loop.

In the last section, you saw that the *do while* loop requires a terminating semicolon after the test expression. Do not confuse this with the test expression after a *while* loop. If you write a semicolon after the test expression of a *while* loop, your program will interpret the semicolon as a valid simple expression (an *empty expression*), and your program will fall into what programmers call a *forever* loop. The following code shows what a forever loop might look like:

```
while (expression);
    statement;
```

This is the same as writing the code, as shown here:

```
while (expression)
    ;
statement;
```

The semicolon—the empty statement—becomes the object expression for the *while* loop. An empty statement never changes the expression, so once your program begins the loop, it can never find its way out.

Understanding Nested Loops (A Loop within a Loop)

In Lesson 11, you learned about *nesting*. You learned how you could nest one decision-making statement within another. Nestings involve putting a statement of one type inside a statement of the same type.

Nesting also applies to loop constructions. You may nest a loop of any type inside a loop of any type. For example, you may nest a *while* loop inside another *while* loop or a *for* loop inside a *while* loop. When your program encounters a nested loop, it will execute it until the inner condition becomes false, then resume the outer loop. The following program, *NestLoop.cpp*, contains a *while* loop nested inside another *while* loop:

```
#include      <iostream.h>

void main (void)
{
    char ch = ' ';
    int iCount;

    while (ch != 'Q')
    {
        cout << "Type a letter and press Enter: ";
        cin >> ch;
        cout << endl << "Outer Loop: You pressed " <<
                ch << endl;
        iCount = 3;
        while (iCount--)
            cout << "\tNested Loop: You pressed " <<
                    ch << endl;
    }
    cout << "Goodbye" << endl;
}
```

When you compile and run *NestLoop.cpp,* you will see that the inner loop executes three times each time your program performs the outer loop. You should practice writing nested loops. When you begin working with two- and three-dimensional *arrays* in the next lesson, and when you begin writing programs that *sort* lists, nested loops will be useful tools.

What You Must Know

In this lesson, you learned about the three types of loops in Visual C++ and how to write and use loops. You also learned about the *break* statement to terminate a loop early and about the *continue* statement to make the loop abort a single iteration. Finally, you learned how to nest one loop inside another. In Lesson 13, "Using

Array Variables to Store Multiple Values," you will learn how to declare and use *arrays,* which allow your program to store more than one value in a single variable. Before you continue with Lesson 13, however, make sure you have learned the following key points:

◆ To make your program perform a loop, you transfer control to a statement that your program already has executed. Your program uses a control expression to decide when to end the loop.

◆ A loop will continue repeating until the control expression becomes *false.* Your program may terminate a loop early by executing the *break* statement.

◆ The *for* loop lets your program perform the statements in a loop a specific number of times.

◆ The *while* loop lets your program repeat a loop indefinitely until a condition becomes *true.* If the test condition is *false* initially, the *while* loop will not perform the loop statements.

◆ The *do while* loop executes the statements in the loop at least once. Afterward, it operates similar to the *while* loop.

Lesson 13

Using Array Variables to Store Multiple Values

Programs store information in variables, as you have learned in earlier lessons. Until now, your programs have used one variable to store one value. Many times, you will find that you have to store many related values, such as the grades of all 30 students in a class, the hourly temperatures for today, or the names of 100 books. To store related values, your program may use a data structure known as an *array*. An array stores multiple values using a single variable name. In this lesson, you will learn how to use arrays in Visual C++. By the time you finish this lesson, you will understand the following key concepts:

◆ An array is a data structure your program uses to store multiple values in a single variable.

◆ Arrays may contain values of only one data type such as all integers or all double.

◆ When you declare an array variable, you must specify the data type, that is, the type of information your program will store in the array and how many items (called *array elements*) the array will hold.

◆ When accessing an array element, you must identify it by the name of the array and its number, or *index*. Visual C++ *always* uses 0 to identify the first array element, so the second element is 1, the third element is 2, and so on.

◆ To store or retrieve information from an array element, you must specify the array name. You also must specify the index number in square brackets after the array name.

Arrays Let Your Program Store Multiple Values in a Single Variable

Programs store information in variables. Your programs in previous lessons have used one variable to store one piece of information, such as an *int* variable to store one integer or a *double* variable to store one double precision number.

Usually one variable is all you will need to store a value. However, many times your programs will deal with many related values, such as the test scores of all the students in a class. If you have 30 students in the class, you would have to declare 30 variables to store these scores in individual variables, such as *Student01, Student02, Student03,* and so on. Then you would have to write code to access each specific variable by name. This could be a very tedious process.

To make this process easier, Visual C++ lets you declare related variables in an *array.* An array is a data structure that allows a single variable to hold more than one value. (A *data structure* is a method of organizing information to make it easier to perform operations on the information, or data.)

When you declare an array variable, the Visual C++ compiler sets aside a block of memory large enough to hold the values of every member, or element, of the array. For example, you learned earlier that Windows needs four bytes to store a value of type *int.* If you declare an array large enough to hold 10 values of type *int,* the Visual C++ compiler will set aside 40 bytes of memory.

Declaring Arrays in Your Visual C++ Program

To set aside memory to hold multiple values of the same data type, you can declare a variable of the data type. Then you specify the number of elements in the array by writing the size inside square brackets ("[" and "]").

To declare a single variable to hold all the test scores for the 30 students in a class, you would use a declaration statement similar to the following:

```
int iScores[30];
```

As with a variable that holds only one variable, you must declare the data type for the variable. In this example, it is type *int,* meaning you intend to use the array to store multiple integer values. Next, you must specify the variable's name, or identifier.

Next, you need to tell the compiler how many elements you want to store by writing the size of the array inside a set of square brackets. The compiler will multiply the size of the data type by this number and use the result to set aside a block of memory.

The size of the array must be a *constant*. That means you cannot use the name of a variable or an expression containing a variable as the size of the array. The following declaration, for example, would cause the compiler to generate and display syntax errors:

```
int iSize = 10;
int iScores[iSize];
```

Although you know that *iSize* contains a value of 10, in practice *iSize* does not actually contain any value until you run your program and assign it the value 10. When you compile your program, the compiler does not know this and so does not know how much memory to set aside for the array. Thus, the compiler will issue syntax errors similar to the following:

```
Program.cpp(9) : error C2057: expected constant expression
Program.cpp(9) : error C2466: cannot allocate an array of constant size 0
Program.cpp(9) : error C2133: 'iScores' : unknown size
```

In Part 3, "Advanced Visual C++," when you learn about the *free store* or *heap,* you will learn how to allocate arrays *dynamically* using a variable to specify the size.

You may declare arrays of any data type, but *all* the elements of the array must be the same data type. For example, you may not mix values of types *double* and *int* in the same array. All the members must be either type *double* or type *int*. Different data types need different amounts of storage, as you learned earlier. However, C++ requires that all members in an array be the same size. If you attempt to create an array with different data types, the sizes may not be the same, in which case the compiler issues an error message.

As with a single-value variable, you may initialize the elements of an array variable when you declare the variable. To do this, write the assignment operator, the equals sign, followed by the values of the array members inside a set of braces. The following program, *FirstArr.cpp,* declares and initializes an array:

```
#include    <iostream.h>

void main (void)
{
    int iIndex;
    int iTemperatures[5] = {64, 72, 38, 92, 81};

    for (iIndex = 0; iIndex < 5; ++iIndex)
    {
        cout << "iTemperature[" << iIndex << "] = " <<
```

```
                iTemperatures[iIndex] << endl;
    }
}
```

Your program initializes the array elements using the values in the set from left to right. It assigns the first value to the first array member, the second value to the second array member, and continues until there are no more variables in the set. You may initialize only some of the members. For example, in the preceding example, you could specify only four temperatures. In that case, your program would assign the values to the first four elements, leaving the fifth element uninitialized.

However, if you specify *more* values than the size of the array, the compiler will issue a syntax error telling you that you have "too many initializers." In this case, the compiler will not compile your program or create the executable file.

 **Letting the Compiler Determine the Size of an Array**

When you declare and initialize an array, you may let the compiler calculate the size of the array rather than specify it in the declaration. You may let the compiler count the number of values you provide in the set of values. To do this, you write the variable declaration without a size inside the brackets, then assign the values using the assignment operator, as shown here:

```
int iTemperatures [] = {64, 72, 38, 92, 81};
```

When you declare an array variable this way, the compiler will count the number of values between the braces, then set aside enough memory to hold all of the values.

Your program still will need to know how many elements are in the array. In Lesson 7, "Getting Started with Visual C++ Operators," you learned how to use the sizeof operator to determine the size of a value or data type. To determine the size of the array, divide the size of the array by the size of a type int, as in the following:

```
int iSize = sizeof (iTemperatures) / sizeof (int);
```

The following program, Size.cpp, declares an array without specifying the size, then calculates the size with the sizeof *operator:*

```
#include     <iostream.h>

void main (void)
{
    int iIndex;
    int iTemperatures[] = {64, 72, 38, 92, 81};
    int iSize = sizeof (iTemperatures) / sizeof (int);

    for (iIndex = 0; iIndex < iSize; ++iIndex)
    {
        cout << "iTemperature[" << iIndex << "] = " <<
                iTemperatures[iIndex] << endl;
    }
}
```

Understanding Array Types

The C++ programming language gives arrays special properties. The array variable itself does not contain the value of any of the elements themselves. Instead, it contains the *address* of the block of memory your program has set aside to hold the values. In programming jargon, the value assigned to the variable itself is a *pointer*. This pointer directs the program to the memory where it will find the actual values.

As you will learn later, you may perform certain arithmetic operations on a pointer, such as an array variable that you may not perform on pointers to ordinary variables. This gives the programmer considerable flexibility in determining how the program will store and retrieve values in an array.

At the same time, C++ places a lot of responsibility on the programmer. C++ will let a programmer perform operations on an array variable that other programming languages might consider illegal operations. For example, if you declare an array of 30 elements, C++ will let you access the 31st element. Of course, any value your program reads from this element will be invalid. If your program attempts to store information in this element, you may destroy some important information in another variable.

You need to understand that it is your responsibility to make sure your program does not attempt to access or store information that is not within the array.

Accessing Array Elements

Arrays let your program store more than one value in a variable by setting aside a block of memory for the values. To do that, and to retrieve that value when you need to use it, you need a method to access a specific part of the memory block.

C++ provides several methods to access certain elements in an array. The primary method is to use an *index* value as part of the variable name. You write the index value inside a set of square brackets immediately following the variable's name. Programmers sometimes call this method "subscripting." You will learn other methods to access array elements in later lessons, but you need to understand indexing first.

The following statement accesses the value of the third element of an array and assigns it to another variable:

```
int iStudentScore = iScores[2];
```

You should note that although the statement reads the third element of *iScores,* the index value is *2.* This is because Visual C++ *always* begins its indexing at 0, so the first element of the *iScores* array is *iScores[0],* the second element is *iScores[1],* and so on. Whether you think of it as the "zeroth" element or the first element, you must be aware that indexing starts at 0, as shown in Figure 13.1.

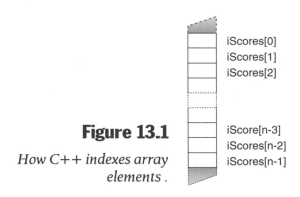

Figure 13.1

How C++ indexes array elements .

iScores[0]
iScores[1]
iScores[2]

iScore[n-3]
iScores[n-2]
iScores[n-1]

The following program, *ScoreArr.cpp,* is a little more advanced than you are used to, but it builds upon previous lessons, and by now you should be able to understand the program statements. First, *ScoreArr.cpp* accepts the letter grades of five students, tests to make sure the grade is an alpha character, stores the scores in an array, and then prints them out to your screen:

```
#include    <iostream.h>


void main (void)
```

```
{
    char ch;
    char cGrades[5];
    int iIndex = 0;

    while (iIndex < 5)
    {
        cout << "Enter student #" << iIndex + 1 <<
                "'s score and press Enter: ";
        cin >> ch;
        if ((ch & 223) == 'Q')
        {
            cout << "Goodbye" << endl;
            return;
        }
        if (((ch & 223) < 'A') || ((ch & 223) > 'F')
            || ((ch & 223) == 'E'))
        {
            cout << ch << " is not a valid grade" << endl;
            continue;
        }
        cGrades[iIndex] = ch & 223;
        ++iIndex;
    }
    for (iIndex = 0; iIndex < 5; ++iIndex)
    {
        cout << "Student #" << iIndex + 1 << "'s grade is "
            << cGrades[iIndex] << endl;
    }
}
```

You may be curious about the statements that *AND* the character with 223. Because of the arrangement of characters in the ASCII character table, if you *AND* an alphabetic character (one in the range A to Z or a to z), it always will be uppercase, regardless of its original case. Similarly, if you *OR* an alphabetic character with 32, it always will be lowercase.

ScoreArr.cpp accepts the grades from the keyboard and tests to make sure they are valid grades, A through D and F. If not, the program prints an error message and goes back to get the score again. The program does not increment the loop control variable until the last line of the loop, assuring that the array index and the student number agree.

Strings Are Arrays of Characters

In previous lessons, you worked with *string constants*. A *string* is a data structure containing a sequence of characters, usually readable text. You did not learn about *string variables* because C++, unlike most programming languages, really does not contain any support for string variables. Instead, it uses an array of type *char* to store strings. Programs store array elements one after another in memory, so an array of *char* contains a sequence of characters, which, in essence, is a string.

Because of the unusual way that C++ treats strings, they may be difficult for a newcomer to the language at first. You likely will use strings a lot in your programming, and a good understanding of arrays will help you to master them.

The following declaration sets aside enough storage for a string containing 24 characters:

```
char szString[25];
```

You should notice that although the string variable is large enough to hold 24 characters, the declaration sets aside 25 array elements. Remember from earlier in this lesson that C++ does not check that you are reading from or storing data outside the size of the array; that is, there is no bounds checking on the array. However, your program and the C++ library functions such as *printf* need to know when the string ends.

To overcome this problem, C++ stores a terminating character as the last character of the string. This character is the *NULL* character, or 0 (technically, it is the ASCII *NUL* character, written with only one "L"). You should write this character using "\0." The backslash tells the compiler to treat this character as a 0 rather than the ASCII zero character, which actually has a value of 48. To declare a character array large enough to hold 24 characters, you must add one element to hold the terminating character.

The following program, *Alphabet.cpp*, sets aside enough memory to hold each uppercase letter of the alphabet, plus one more for the *NULL* terminator:

```
#include    <iostream.h>

void main (void)
{
```

```
char cAlphabet[27];     // 26 characters plus terminator
char cLetter;           // Temporary storage

int iIndex;             // Index variable

for (cLetter = 'A', iIndex = 0; iIndex < 26; ++cLetter, ++iIndex)
{
    cAlphabet[iIndex] = cLetter;
}

cAlphabet[iIndex] = '\0';

cout << "The letters are " << cAlphabet << endl;
}
```

The program assigns a *NULL* character as the last element after first building the string of characters. When you compile and run the program, the last line will print the characters to your screen one at a time until the *cout* operator encounters the *NULL* character.

Using Text in a Character Array

As with arrays of other data types, you may initialize a character array when you declare it. The following declaration sets aside enough memory to hold the string "My String" plus the *NULL* character:

```
char szString[]={'M','y',' ','S','t','r','i','n','g','\0'};
```

In the preceding declaration, when you enclose the terminating *NULL* character inside single quotes, you must include the backslash in front of it.

Alternatively, you may initialize the character array by writing the text inside double quotes, as shown in the following example:

```
char szString[] = "My String";
```

Notice that in this declaration, you do not have to end the string with a *NULL* character. When you enclose the text in a set of double quotes, the compiler automatically adjusts the size and adds the terminator.

Using Arrays of Strings

You have seen that strings are arrays of type *char*. Visual C++ library functions need a *NULL* character (\0) at the end of the string to let them know when the string ends. In addition to the text you want to store in the string, you need to allow an extra element to hold the terminating character.

Sometimes it is convenient to place strings themselves in an array. Often programmers group messages in a string array, then select the string to output using an index number. For example, the array may contain a number of error messages to tell the user why the program failed to open a particular file, and the index may be the return value from a function.

The following program, *StrArray.cpp,* declares and initializes an array of strings:

```cpp
#include    <iostream.h>

void main (void)
{
    char *szStrings[6] =
    {
        "This is not a valid number",
        "C++ is a great programming language",
        "Dalmatians are good",
        "The planes in Spain fall mainly in the rain",
        "Pomeranians are great",
        "It's fun to watch your own programs run"
    };
    char ch = ' ';
    while (ch != 'Q')
    {
        cout << "Type a number from 1 to 5 (or Q to quit) and press enter : ";
        cin >> ch;
        if ((ch & 223) == 'Q')
            break;
        ch -= '0';
        if ((ch > 5) || (ch < 0))
            ch = 0;
        cout << endl << szStrings [ch] << endl;
```

```
        cout << "The string is stored at "<< szStrings + ch
            << endl << endl;
    }


    cout << "Goodbye!" << endl;
}
```

Notice first that the program declares the string array using an asterisk (*) in front of the array name. Remember from earlier in this lesson that your program may store the array itself elsewhere in memory, and the variable itself contains the address of (or *pointer* to) this memory location. When you declare an array of type *char,* your program stores the characters in the array in a particular memory location, then assigns the address of that location to the array variable.

You will learn more about pointers in Lesson 16, "Changing Parameter Values within a Function." For now, understand that the asterisk tells the compiler that the variable contains the memory location of a value rather than the value itself.

Notice also that each string in the array has a different length. As you learned earlier, all members of an array must have the same length. When you declare an array of strings, the compiler creates an array of addresses. These addresses tell your program where it has stored each string. Thus, the size of each element in a string array is exactly four bytes—enough to contain an address—regardless of the length of the string.

Declaring and Using Multidimensional Arrays

Arrays, you have learned, let your program store multiple values in a single variable. You normally access the *array elements* using the index of the element inside square brackets. Up to now, the arrays you have used have been one-dimensional. The values have had just one relationship.

There are times when you want to store an array of values that have more than one relationship. For example, you might want to store the scores of all the students in two or three classes, yet still be able to access the scores of a particular class. In this case, you may use an array with more than one dimension.

To declare an array with two dimensions, write the second dimension inside a second set of square brackets right after the first dimension. The following declaration statement declares an array with four values in the first dimension and six values in the second dimension:

```
int MultiArray[4][6];
```

For example, suppose you teach three algebra classes, and each class has 10 students. The following program, *MultiArr.cpp*, sets up a two-dimensional array using the number of classes, 3, as the first dimension and the student number as the second dimension. (To save you a lot of typing to enter 30 scores, the first loop assigns a random grade between 51 and 100 to each student using the *rand()* library function.)

```cpp
#include     <iostream.h>
#include     <stdlib.h>

void main (void)
{
    int iScores[3][10];     // 3 classes of 10 students each
    int iClass, iStudent;
    int iTotal;
//
//  Use rand() to initialize the scores
//
    for (iClass = 0; iClass < 3; ++iClass)
    {
        for (iStudent = 0; iStudent < 10; ++iStudent)
        {
            iScores[iClass][iStudent] = rand() % 50 + 51;
        }
    }
//
//  Show the scores for each class and calculate the
//  average score
//
    for (iClass = 0; iClass < 3; ++iClass)
    {
        cout << "In Class " << iClass + 1 << ":" << endl;
        iTotal = 0;
        for (iStudent = 0; iStudent < 10; ++iStudent)
        {
```

```
        cout << "\tStudent " << iStudent + 1 <<
                "'s score is " <<
                iScores[iClass][iStudent] << endl;
        iTotal += iScores[iClass][iStudent];
    }
    cout << "\tThe average score for class " <<
            iClass + 1 << " is " << iTotal / 10 << endl;
    }
}
```

Program *MultiArr.cpp* uses nested loops to access every element of the array. The outer loop sets the value of the first dimension, the class; and the inner loop sets the second dimension, the student. Each combination of class number and student number uniquely identifies one member of the two-dimensional array. Notice that the program completely performs all 10 iterations of the inner loop each time the program repeats the outer loop.

Arrays with more than two dimensions are rare, but Visual C++ places no limits on the number of dimensions you may declare. For each dimension, simply add the number of elements inside the array operator (the square brackets) after the previous dimension. For example, the following statement declares a three-dimensional array of 10, 8, and 12 elements, each of type *double*:

```
double fThreeD_Array[10][8][12];
```

What You Must Know

In this lesson, you learned how to store more than one value in a variable using an array. You learned how to write arrays of numbers and strings and how to declare arrays with more than one dimension. You learned how to store values in the arrays and how to access the values when you need to use them. In Lesson 14, "Getting Started with Visual C++ Functions," you will learn how to write and call functions from within your program. You also will learn how to pass values and arrays to functions and how to return a value from a function and use the returned value in your program. Before you continue with Lesson 14, however, make sure you have learned the following key points:

◆ An array is a data structure you may use to store more than one value in a single variable.

◆ You may declare an array of any data type, but all the members of one array must be the same data type.

◆ When you declare an array variable, you must specify the data type and the number of values the array will contain.

◆ To access an element in an array, you must identify it by the name of the array variable and the position, or index, in the array. Visual C++ always uses *0* as the index for the first element.

◆ Strings are arrays of data type *char*. To let library function determine the end of the string, Visual C++ adds one extra element to the array size to hold the *\0* terminating character.

Lesson 14

Getting Started with Visual C++ Functions

As you have learned, programs store information in variables. You may use these variables in decision-making statements and to make your program repeat statements until a certain condition becomes *false*. In Lesson 13, "Using Array Variables to Store Multiple Values," you learned how to store more than one value in a variable using arrays. Until now, however, most of what you have done in your programs has been in the context of the *main* program function. As your programs become longer and more complex, you will find it easier to write and maintain your programs if you break them down into smaller code modules that programmers call *functions*. A function is a named block of code that your program may use as often as it needs. In this lesson, you will learn how to write and use functions in Visual C++. By the time you finish this lesson, you will understand the following key concepts:

◆ A function is a named block of related statements intended to perform a specific task.

◆ To use a function in your program, you *call* the function by writing the function name and argument list. You *must* include the argument list even if the list is empty.

◆ Before you use a function in your program, you need to *prototype* the function. This notifies the compiler of its name, parameters, and return type so the compiler can detect any calling errors in your program

◆ Visual C++ contains many libraries with functions already written that you may use in your programs.

◆ To use library functions, you need to include the header file that contains the prototypes for the library functions.

Breaking Your Program into Smaller, More Manageable Pieces

In previous lessons, most of your sample programs have used only a single function, the *main* function C++ requires that your program contain a *main* function. Your programs contained only statements and variables in *main*.

As your programs grow and become more complex and involved, writing all of your code in a single function becomes impractical and hard to maintain. Rather than have hundreds of lines of code in *main,* you will need to break the statements down into smaller, more manageable pieces.

The following program, *FirstFun.cpp,* places the conversion from degrees Fahrenheit to degrees Celsius in a function, which also displays the temperature values:

```cpp
#include    <iostream.h>

void ShowTemp (int iFahr)
{
    int iCelsius = 5 * (iFahr - 32) / 9;
    cout << iFahr << " degrees F = " <<
            iCelsius << " degrees C" << endl;
}


void main (void)
{
    int iTemp;

    cout << "Enter temperature in Fahrenheit: ";
    cin >> iTemp;
    ShowTemp (iTemp);
}
```

A function is a named block of code that contains related statements. You write the statements inside a compound statement block immediately following the function name. Even if your function contains only one statement, C++ requires that you write it inside a compound statement block.

When you write a function, you first need to declare the function's *return type.* The return type is the same as the data type you use when you declare a variable. The return type tells the compiler that you intend to return a value of that type when the function completes. If you do not intend to return a value, as in the *ShowTemp* function in the preceding program, then you must give the function a return type of *void*. You may remember from Lesson 4, "Using Visual C++ from the Command Line," the *void* type indicates that the function does not return any value.

After the return type, you write the function's name. The name should describe the purpose of the function, just as the name of a variable should describe the value the variable holds. In fact, the same rules that you used to write variable names apply to function names as well. You may begin a function name with an underscore character (_), but you may not use a number or other symbol as the first character of the name.

Immediately after the function name, write the function's *parameter list* inside a set of parentheses. The C++ compiler requires that you include a parameter list even if you do not use any parameters. For example, the following function does not accept any parameters:

```
void EmptyList ()
{
}
```

Some programmers like to write the word *void* for an empty parameter list, as you have done when using the *main* function in previous examples. The parameter list helps the compiler to distinguish between a function and a variable declaration.

After the parameter list, you write the *body* of the function. The body is the collection of statements in a compound statement block that the function will execute.

 ## The Difference between Argument and Parameter Is Argumentative

In this lesson and later lessons, as well as in other books, you will see the words parameter *and* argument *to describe a variable inside a function's parameter list.*

The two words essentially describe the same thing, and the difference is only technical. When you call a function by writing its name and passing values, the values you pass are "arguments." However, when you use these arguments in the function itself, they become "parameters."

An argument may be a value, a variable, an expression, or even another function call. The argument, however, must evaluate to a value that may be used by the function. In the following sample, x / 2 is an argument, and your program will divide the value of x by 2 before calling the function:

```
x = 6;
SomeFunction (x / 2);
```

A parameter must be a variable. When you call the function, C++ assigns the value in the function call to the variable name in the parameter list. You may not use an expression or another function call when writing parameters.

When you list a parameter in a function's parameter list, it is the same as declaring a new variable in the function and assigning it the value passed as the argument in the function call.

Prototyping Functions

In Visual C++, it does not matter in what order you write your functions. In the program in the last sections, for example, you could have written the *main* function first in your program, then the *ShowTemp* function.

However, C++ does require that you *define* or *declare* a function before you use it in your program. *Defining* a function simply means writing the function itself. The following is the *definition* of the *ShowTemp* function:

```
void ShowTemp (int iFahr)
{
    int iCelsius = 5 * (iFahr - 32) / 9;
    cout << iFahr << " degrees F = " <<
            iCelsius << " degrees C" << endl;
}
```

When the function definition appears *before* you call, or use, the function in your program, the compiler already knows the form or pattern of the function. The compiler compares this pattern with the statement that calls the function to detect any errors in your program.

It is not always possible to define a function before you use it in your program, however. For example, you might write the function definition in another program file. In this case, the compiler would not have a pattern to compare with the function call.

When you cannot define a function before you use it, you may *declare* the function. Declaring a function is much the same as declaring a variable. To avoid confusion, however, programmers usually call a function declaration a *function prototype*. The following is a prototype of the *ShowTemp* function:

```
void ShowTemp (int iFahr);
```

To prototype a function, you first write its *return type*. This is the same as the data type for a variable. If the function does not return a value, you specify a *void* return type. You should know that while a function may have a *void* return type, you cannot declare a variable of type *void*. Next, you write the function's name, such as *ShowTemp*. Then you write the *parameter list*, which you must enclose in a set of parentheses. The parameter list must specify the data types (such as *int, double,* or *char*) of the parameter. Finally, you end the prototype with a semicolon after the closing parenthesis. The semicolon tells the compiler the prototype is complete.

You should make it a practice to prototype all of your functions. For most programs, you may place them near the top of the source file and just after the list of include files. For larger programs, you may want to place the prototypes in a separate *header* file. You learned how to use header files in Lesson 5, "Understanding a Few C++ Basics." The following program, *Protos.cpp*, places the prototype for *ShowTemp* in a separate header file, *Protos.h*:

```
#include     <iostream.h>
#include     "protos.h"

void ShowTemp (int iFahr)
{
    int iCelsius = 5 * (iFahr - 32) / 9;
    cout << iFahr << " degrees F = " <<
            iCelsius << " degrees C" << endl;
}


void main (void)
{
    int iTemp;

    cout << "Enter temperature in Fahrenheit: ";
    cin >> iTemp;
    ShowTemp (iTemp);
}
```

Figure 14.1 shows how the *Protos.h* header file looks in your program editor.

Figure 14.1

The Protos.h header file contains prototypes for your program. As you add functions, you may add the function prototypes to this file.

```
Protos.h * SciTE                                    _ □ ×
File  Edit  Tools  Options  Help
//
//  protos.h -- function prototypes for protos.cpp
//

void ShowTemp (int iFahr);
```

As you add functions to your program, remember to add the function prototypes to *Protos.h*, and the compiler will add the prototypes automatically.

A Function Prototype Is a Pattern for the Compiler

C++ requires you to define or declare a function before you use it in your program. When you write a function prototype, you must include the data type of any parameters, but you do not need to include the name of the parameter. All the compiler needs is the data type to determine how much memory it must set aside to hold the value. The following also prototypes the ShowTemp function:

```
void ShowTemp (int);
```

When the compiler examines the prototype, it will determine that every time you call the function, it needs to set aside enough memory to hold a value for type int. If you try to use another data type that is too large for the memory, the compiler will issue and display an error on your screen.

Using Function Return Types

You have learned that when you write a function, you must declare the function's *return* data type. Up to now, your functions have had a *void* return type, meaning they do not return a value when the function ends and control returns to the statement that called the function.

One of the advantages of using functions is that functions are like small programs within your program. You can use a function to perform a specific task, then return the result of that task to the statement that called the function. That statement may assign the return value to a variable, which you may use later in your program. Each time your program needs to perform the task, it only needs to call the function.

The following program, *Return.cpp*, uses a function to convert a number score on a test to a letter grade:

```cpp
#include    <iostream.h>

char CalculateGrade (int iTestScore);

void main (void)
{
    int iScore;

    cout << "Enter your score and press Enter: ";
    cin >> iScore;
    char cGrade = CalculateGrade (iScore);
    cout << "Your grade is " << cGrade << endl;
}


char CalculateGrade (int iTestScore)
{
    char ch;

    if (iTestScore >= 90)
        ch = 'A';
    else if (iTestScore >= 80)
        ch = 'B';
    else if (iTestScore >= 70)
        ch = 'C';
    else if (iTestScore >= 60)
        ch = 'D';
    else
        ch = 'F';
    return (ch);
}
```

The *CalculateGrade* function returns the letter grade to the statement that called the function. That statement then stores the return value in the *cGrade* variable and prints *cGrade* to your screen.

You may assign any data type as the return type for your functions. However, if you assign the return type to a variable, the variable should be the same return type. For example, if your function returns a type *double,* you should assign the return value to a variable of type *double.*

Using the Visual C++ Run-Time Library

You may add statements to your program in named blocks of code called functions. After you write the function and declare it using a function prototype, you may call the function from any place in your program.

In addition to functions that you may add to your program, Visual C++ contains a number of functions that you may add to your program simply by adding a system header file and calling one of the functions. You already have met some of these functions, such as *printf,* which lets you write formatted output to your screen, and *atoi,* which converts a number in string form to a number in *int* format.

These functions are part of the standard C++ run-time library, and they are available with Visual C++ and all C++ compilers. You may use these functions in your program and still be able to compile your program on other operating systems such as Linux. You should understand that these functions are not part of the C++ language, but are standard extensions that have been established as the language evolved.

In Visual C++, there are 18 header files in the standard C++ run-time library encompassing many more functions, far to many to cover here. When you purchased Visual C++, however, you should have gotten a copy of the Microsoft Developers Network (MSDN), which is the help file for Visual C++. You can get an overview and search through the functions using the MSDN search system.

To access the standard C++ library overview, start the MSDN program by selecting the Help menu, then Index. When the help system window appears, as shown in Figure 14.2, enter **Standard C++ Library** in the keyword field and press Enter.

To look up a particular function, type the name of the function in the keyword field of the MSDN window and press Enter. For example, to see details on the *printf* function, type **printf** in the keyword field and press Enter. The MSDN window will display information about the *printf* function, telling you the format (the "prototype") of the function and the required header file you will need to use the function. For many of the standard library functions, the MSDN library also will show you examples of how to use the function.

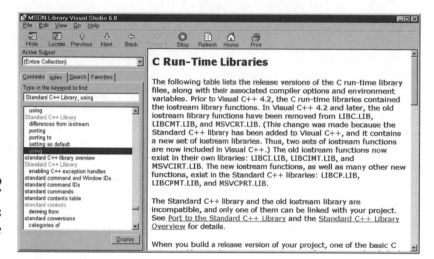

Figure 14.2

The Microsoft Developers Network library is part of the Visual C++ help system.

Declaring Inline Functions

You have learned how to declare and write functions and how to use them in your program. With any function, there is a certain amount of "overhead" involved, however. Even with the fastest computers, it still takes some time to call a function and retrieve the function's return value. First, your program must set aside memory for the arguments, then transfer control to the first statement in the function. When the function ends, your program must retrieve the return value and store it in a variable.

This does not take a lot of time for each function call. In fact, for a single call, the time is negligible. However, there may be times when a program must call a function many thousands of times, such as in a loop. In some cases, the overhead might take more time than it takes to execute the statements in the function.

One way around this overhead is to write every statement in your program rather than call a function to perform the task. However, that means typing every statement each time you want to call your function.

To get around this, Visual C++ offers a mechanism called an *inline function*. When you write an inline function, the compiler replaces calls to the function with the statements in the function. This gives you the ease of using a function, yet provides the speed of writing your code *inline*.

The following program, *Inline.cpp,* uses an inline function to calculate the cube of a number and return it to the statement that called it:

```
#include     <iostream.h>


inline int Cube (int iNumber);
```

```
void main (void)
{
    int iValue, iCube;

    cout << "Type a number and press Enter: ";
    cin >> iValue;
    iCube = Cube (iValue);
    cout << "The cube of " << iValue << " is " << iCube
        << endl;
}


inline int Cube (int iNumber)
{
    int iCubed = iNumber * iNumber * iNumber;
    return (iCubed);
}
```

When you compile *Inline.cpp,* the compiler will expand the call to *Cube* with the actual code in the function. In effect, the statement in *main* that assigns a value to *iCube* becomes the following:

```
iCube = iValue * iValue * iValue
```

The compiler replaces the call to *Cube* each time you call it. For this reason, inline functions should be kept as short as possible. If you write a long inline function and then call it often from your program, your compiled program will become very big very quickly. (You should know that the compiler will perform some tests to determine whether it is practical to place a function inline. If the compiler decides it is not practical, then it will make the function an ordinary function even though you declared it inline.)

What You Must Know

In this lesson, you learned the basics of writing and calling functions in Visual C++. You also learned how to prototype your functions and how to use a function's return value in your programs. In addition, you learned that C++ includes many functions in library files that your program can use by including the proper header files. In Lesson 15, "Passing Variables and Values to Functions," you will learn more about passing arguments to functions and using those arguments in your functions. Before you continue with Lesson 15, however, make sure you have learned the following key points:

◆ A function is a named block of code containing related statements. The function performs a specific task, then returns to the statement that called the function.

◆ To call a function from your program, you write the function name and argument list. If you do not pass arguments to the function, you still must include the parentheses for the argument list.

◆ You must define or declare a function in your program before you call the function. When you declare a function, you are prototyping the function. You should prototype all functions in your program to give the compiler patterns for the functions.

◆ In addition to functions you may write, the Visual C++ library contains many functions that you may use in your program.

◆ To use the Visual C++ library functions, you need to include the proper header files in your source file. The Visual C++ compiler will include the library functions in your program automatically.

Lesson 15

Passing Variables and Values to Functions

As you have learned, programs store information in variables. When you call a function, sometimes you may need to give the function a value so it can perform its task properly. For example, a function that converts a number score to a letter grade will need to know the value of the score you want to convert, and a temperature conversion function will need to know the temperature you want to convert. In Visual C++, you can write the values and variables as *arguments* to the function you are calling. In this lesson, you will learn how to call functions from within your program and pass the function the values it needs to perform its task. By the time you finish this lesson, you will understand the following key concepts:

◆ To pass a value to a function, you write the value, variable name, or expression in the *argument list* when you call the function.

◆ The data type of the values you pass as arguments must match the data type in the function prototype. In some cases, Visual C++ will *promote* one data type to another automatically.

◆ The *stack* is a memory block your program sets aside to store program information when it is running. When you call a function, your program places the *address* of the statement containing the function call on the stack. When the function ends, your program retrieves this address and returns to the statement containing the function call.

◆ When you call a function and pass it values, your program creates space on the stack to hold the values.

◆ Passing the name of a variable to a function causes your program to create a *copy* of the value on the stack. You may modify this copy, but it will not change the value of the original variable.

◆ When you declare additional variables in a function, your program reserves memory on the stack to hold their values.

Understanding Function Arguments and Parameters

In Lesson 14, "Getting Started with Visual C++ Functions," you learned how to write functions in your program, prototype the functions, and call the functions from within your program.

You will use most functions to perform a specific task, thus breaking your program down into smaller blocks of code that are easier for you to maintain. Usually, these functions will need some information to help them perform their tasks. You can give them this information by passing the values they need.

When you pass a value to a program, you write the *argument* in the *argument list* of the function call. You write the argument list inside a set of parentheses immediately after the function name. The following statement passes one value to a function:

```
ShowTemp (iTemp);
```

If you need to pass more than one argument, you separate them with a comma. The following statements call a library function, *strchr,* that looks for the location of a particular character within a string:

```
char *szString = "This is a string";
char *szLocation = strchr (szString, 'a');
```

This function needs to know what string to use for the search and what character to find. You pass this information in the argument list.

How Your Visual C++ Program Stores Values

In programming, and especially in C++ programming, you often will see the word *stack* when referring to variables and function calls. In Visual C++, the stack is an important element of programming. The stack is a block of memory your program sets aside to store program information when the program is running.

The processor chip in your computer contains a special memory location (a *register*) in which the chip stores a pointer to the stack. When you declare and initialize a variable in a function, your program places the value of the variable in the stack memory pointed to by this register. Your program saves the value in the register as the *address* of the value, then adjusts the value of the register to point to the next unused memory location in the stack. The process repeats each time you declare a new variable. When you add a value to the stack, you are *pushing* it onto the stack.

When your function ends and returns to the statement that called the function, your program adjusts the register value so the memory locations may be used by other variables in other functions. Thus, the variables you declare in a function are *local* variables, and their values are lost when the function ends. When you remove a value from the stack, you are *popping* the value from the stack.

It is important for you to realize that variables declared in a function may be used only in that function and are lost when the function ends. Each time you call a function, you must initialize the variables once again. There is one exception, the *static* variable declaration. To declare a static variable, use the keyword *static* as the first word of the variable's declaration.

When you declare a static variable, your program sets aside memory in the program rather than on the stack. A static variable retains its value even when you call the function many times. You can change the value as often as you want, and the variable will retain the new value. The following program, *Static.cpp,* shows how to declare, initialize, and use a static value:

```
#include    <iostream.h>

void ShowCounter (void);

void main (int argc, char *argv[])
{
    int iCount;
    for (iCount = 0; iCount < 5; ++iCount)
        ShowCounter ();
}


void ShowCounter (void)
{
    static int Counter = 1;
    cout << "The function has been called " << Counter
        << " time";
    if (Counter > 1)
        cout << "s";
    cout << endl;
    ++Counter;
}
```

In the *ShowCounter* function, the declaration statement initializes the static variable *Counter* only once. After that, it retains any other value you give it. The last line of the function increments *Counter* each time your program calls the function, thus keeping track of the number of calls.

A static variable declared in a function still is local to the function, and you may use it only in statements within the function.

What Happens When Your Program Calls a Function

The stack is more than just a place to hold variables, however. Whenever you call a function, your program saves the address of the statement containing the function call on the stack. This is how the program "remembers" the statement that was executing when it transferred control to a function.

Before your program saves the statement address, however, it first evaluates all the expressions in the argument list and "pushes" them onto the stack, starting with the last argument. When all the arguments have been placed on the stack, your program then saves the return address along with some related information. Finally, your program passes control to the first statement in the called function.

For example, when your program calls a function as shown in the following code, it first puts the value of y on the stack, then the value of x, as shown in Figure 15.1. Next, it places the address of the statement on the stack and transfers control to the function.

```
FunctionName (x, y);
```

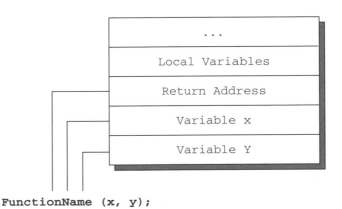

Figure 15.1

The stack grows upward. Visual C++ first pushes the value of y, then teh value of x and finally the return address. Visual C++ creates any local variables on the stack after pushing the return address.

```
FunctionName (x, y);
```

Calling Functions

A function is a named block of code that you use to break your program down into more manageable pieces. Except for the special quality that makes a function perform a block of code, a function is similar to a variable, and you may use it in much the same way.

To use, or *call*, a function, you write the function's name. Immediately after the function name, you write the *argument list* inside a set of parentheses. Even if you do not use any arguments, you must include the parentheses so the compiler can tell the difference between a function call and a variable.

Functions perform specific tasks, and you have learned that some functions may *return* values after they finish processing. You may assign the return value to a variable in your program, but Visual C++ does not require you to use the return value. If you do not save the return value in a variable, you may not use the value later in your program. It is lost, and the only way to retrieve it is to call the function again using the same arguments.

The following program, *Pi.cpp*, uses a function to return the value of the mathematical constant *pi*. The *main* function uses the value in an expression to calculate the circumference of a circle:

```
#include     <iostream.h>

double GetPi (void);

void main (int argc, char *argv[])
{
    int iDiameter;
    double fCircumference;
    cout << "Enter the diameter of the circle and press enter: ";
    cin >> iDiameter;
    fCircumference = iDiameter * GetPi();
    cout << "The circumference of the circle is " <<
            fCircumference << endl;
}


double GetPi ()
{
    return (3.14159);
}
```

The program uses the return value in an expression, but it does not store the value in a variable. The only way this program could use the value return by *GetPi* again is to call the function again.

In *GetPi.cpp,* the *main* function is the *calling function*, and *GetPi* is the *called function.*

Passing Arguments

Sometimes your functions will need values to perform their tasks properly. To give functions the values they need, you pass them as arguments to the function.

In the last section, your function did nothing but return the value of *pi.* That is a very simple function, and you could easily have done the calculation in your *main* function. You could make the function perform the entire calculation, as in the following program, *Area.cpp:*

```
#include    <iostream.h>

double GetArea (int iRadius);

void main (int argc, char *argv[])
{
    double fDiameter, fRadius;
    double fArea;
    cout << "Enter the diameter of the circle and press enter: ";
    cin >> fDiameter;
    fRadius = fDiameter / 2;
    fArea = GetArea (fRadius);
    cout << "The area of the circle is " << fArea << endl;
}

double GetArea (int iRadius)
{

    return (3.14159 * iRadius * iRadius);
}
```

In *Area.cpp,* the program saves the return value in a variable, *fArea,* which it later uses to print the result to your screen. Depending upon the warning level you have set for the compiler, you may get a warning from the compiler about the promotion of *iRadius* to a *double* value. This is normal when you include a *int* value in a *double* expression.

In addition to using a variable as an argument, you may use a value or any expression that evaluates to a value. You may use as an argument any expression that results in value that you may otherwise assign to a variable. The following, *Arg2Func.cpp*, uses an expression that computes the temperature in Celsius, then passes that as an argument:

```cpp
#include     <iostream.h>
#include     <stdlib.h>

void PrintTemp (int iTemp);

void main (int argc, char *argv[])
{
    int celsius;
    if (argc < 2)
    {
        cout << "usage: Arg2Func <degrees Celsius";
        cout << endl;
        return;
    }
    celsius = atoi (argv[1]);
    PrintTemp (9 * celsius / 5 + 32);
}


void PrintTemp (int iFahr)
{
    cout << "The temperature is " << iFahr
        << " degrees Fahrenheit" << endl;
}
```

Your program fully evaluates the expression before giving control to the first statement in the *PrintTemp* function.

When your program begins performing the statements in a function, the argument becomes a *parameter*. The differences between an argument and a parameter are the rules you apply to them. You have seen that an argument may be any expression. A parameter, however, cannot be an expression. Instead, it must be a value. When you write the function, you declare the variables that will hold these values in the *parameter list*.

Declaring a variable this way is the same as declaring it in the function, then assigning it the value you passed as an argument. In the case of a parameter, however, the value may be different for each function call.

You must understand that when you pass a variable as an argument to a function, you are passing only the value, not the variable itself. In effect, you are making a *copy* of the variable's value, and your program then assigns that value to the matching parameter in the function. If you change the value of the function, you do not change the value of the original variable. In computer jargon, this is a *call by value* calling convention. As you will see in Lesson 16, "Changing Parameter Values within a Function," you can use a *reference variable* as the parameter in a function call. Using a reference variable, any changes you make to the parameter in the function will change the original variable.

Using Default Argument Values

You have learned that a function prototype provides the compiler with a "pattern" for the function. The compiler uses this pattern to make sure your function calls provide the number and data types of parameters your function needs. You also learned that your function call must provide the same number of arguments as there are parameters in the function prototype.

However, Visual C++ lets you omit some parameters in your function call if you give them *default values* in the function prototype. To prototype a function with a default parameter value, write the parameter followed by an equals sign and the default value you want to give the parameter, as in the following sample:

```
void ThisFunction (int x = 0);
```

When you call *ThisFunction* with no arguments, your program automatically will substitute *0* as the argument for *x*.

The following program, *DefParam.cpp*, shows how to call a function with a default value:

```
#include    <iostream.h>

void ShowParameter (int iParm = 5);

void main (int argc, char *argv[])
```

```
{
    ShowParameter (2);
    ShowParameter ();
    ShowParameter (7);
}


void ShowParameter (int iParam)
{
    cout << "The value of the parameter is " <<
            iParam << endl;
}
```

The first and third calls to *ShowParameter* passed the values 2 and 7. The second call, however, did not pass any value, so the compiler substituted the default value of 5.

You should notice that the default parameter appears only in the prototype. When you write the function itself, you do not write a default value.

Some special rules apply for prototyping functions with default values and for calling these functions. Default parameters work their way inward from the right. After you set a default value for a parameter, all the parameters to the right of it must have default values. You cannot write something like the following and expect the compiler to understand it:

```
void ThisFunction (int x = 0, int y, int z = 0);
```

Instead, you would have to place the *y* parameter first in the list and follow *y* with the other parameters, as shown here:

```
void ThisFunction (int y, int x = 0, int z = 0);
```

When you call a function with default parameters, you need not include the parameter in the function call. If you do include a value, all parameters to the left of it must have values, but parameters to the right can still use the default values.

Success HINT: Default Parameter Values Can Supply Basic Information

When you prototype your function, Visual C++ lets you assign default values to some or all of the parameters. You can use this to supply the most common values that a function may need to use. For example, if you need to compute an employee's salary for the week, you could pass as the number of hours the most common number, 40, and as the pay rate the most common salary, say, 5.50, as in the following prototype:

```
float Payroll (int iEmployeeNumber, double fHours = 40,
               double fPayRate = 5.50);
```

You then could call the function using only the iEmployeeNumber *parameter. When you need to use different values for the number of hours or the pay rate, you would supply those values in your function call.*

What You Must Know

In this lesson, you learned how your program stores variables on the stack and how your program calls functions. You also learned how to pass information to a function using arguments. In addition, you learned how to write function prototypes and how to declare default values in the prototype. In Lesson 16, "Changing Parameter Values within a Function," you will learn how to pass pointers to a function to modify variables in the calling function. You also will learn how to use reference variables to modify values in the calling function. Before you continue with Lesson 16, however, make sure you have learned the following key points:

◆ The argument list in a function call contains the values, variables, or expressions that will pass a value to a function. If you do not pass any arguments to a function, you must include an empty argument list.

◆ A function prototype provides the compiler with a pattern against which the compiler may compare your function calls with the data types the function needs.

◆ The data types in the argument list must match the data types in the function, and in the same order.

◆ You may provide default values for parameters to a function when you write the prototype for the function.

◆ Visual C++ makes extensive use of the computers "stack." Your program stores variable and parameter values on the stack as well as the address of the statement that calls a function.

◆ When you call a function and give it variables as arguments, your program makes *copies* of the variables on the stack. Modifying the copy in a function does not change the value in the calling function.

Lesson 16

Changing Parameter Values within a Function

In the last few lessons, you have learned how to declare and use variables in your programs. You also learned how to write functions in your program to break it down into more manageable pieces. Functions perform specific tasks, and sometimes they need information from your program to perform those tasks, so you learned how to pass values and variables to functions through arguments. The functions may modify the variables you pass it, but the changes do not affect the original variables in the calling function. Sometimes your program will have to modify the original variables, and Visual C++ provides methods to do this. In this lesson, you will learn how to pass the addresses of variables—*pointers*—and reference variables to change the values of the original variables. By the time you finish this lesson, you will understand the following key concepts:

◆ The information contained in a variable is stored at a particular location in memory. You can use that address to store information or access information in a variable.

◆ A *pointer* is the address of a variable's storage location. A *pointer variable* is a variable that holds the address of another variable's storage location.

◆ To get the address of a variable, you use the *address operator*, which is the ampersand symbol (&).

◆ You may pass pointers as arguments to a function, thus allowing the function to access the original variable's storage.

◆ The information in an array variable is the address where your program stores the array elements. You may use *pointer arithmetic* to access array elements.

◆ The *reference operator* (also an ampersand) lets you create a pointer variable that acts like a normal variable. Once initialized, you may modify another variable indirectly through the *reference variable.*

Understanding Pointers

You have learned that your program stores the value for a variable in a specific memory location. That location is the memory *address* of the variable's value. When you declare a variable, the compiler sets aside enough memory to hold the variable's value. Then when you store information into or read information from the variable, your program accesses the memory location to set or get the value.

Sometimes it is more convenient—or more practical—for your program to use the address rather than the variable's name to access the value. For example, you learned that when your program calls a function using a variable as an argument, the program makes a copy of the value of the variable. When you change the value, you are changing the value of the copy rather than the value of the original variable.

If you pass the address as an argument, you may access the original memory location and modify the value of the original variable. To get the address of a variable's value, write the variable's name preceded with an ampersand (&), as shown here:

```
int iCount = 0;
SomeFunction (&iCount);
```

The preceding declaration declares a variable, *iCount,* and assigns it a value of 0. Then it calls a function using the address of *iCount* rather than the value. In this case, you are giving the function a reference to the variable rather than the variable's value itself.

The function then may modify the value of the original variable using the *indirection operator,* the asterisk (*). Programmers call this "dereferencing" a pointer. To dereference a pointer variable, you write the variable's name preceded by an asterisk.

You may get the address of a variable using the address operator, and you may assign that value to a *pointer variable.* To declare a pointer variable, use the asterisk (the indirection operator) in front of the variable's name when you declare it. The following declaration declares a *double* variable, then declares a pointer to a double variable:

```
double fPi = 3.14159;
double *pfPi = &fPi;
```

You should be aware that Visual C++ strongly enforces the data type used for pointer variables. For example, you cannot declare a pointer to a type *long* and assign it the address of an *int* variable. To do this requires a *cast,* which you will learn about later in this lesson.

The following program, *Address.cpp*, shows how to pass a pointer to a function using the address operator and modify the original variable using the dereference operator:

```cpp
#include    <iostream.h>

void ModifyCount (int *iCounter);
void DontModifyCount (int iCounter);

void main (void)
{
    int iCount = 3;
    cout << "The value of iCount is "<< iCount <<
            " before calling DontModifyCount" << endl;
    DontModifyCount (iCount);
    cout << "The value of iCount is " << iCount <<
            " after calling DontModifyCount" << endl;
    cout << "The value of iCount is "<< iCount <<
            " before calling ModifyCount" << endl;
    ModifyCount (&iCount);
    cout << "The value of iCount is "<< iCount <<
            " after calling ModifyCount" << endl;
}

void DontModifyCount (int iCounter)
{
    iCounter = 42;
}

void ModifyCount (int *iCounter)
{
    *iCounter = 42;
}
```

The preceding program shows that passing the value if *iCount* to *DontModifyCount* does not change the original value, even though the function modifies the parameter. However, when you pass the address to *ModifyCount*, the function uses the indirection operator to modify the original value.

Notice that the declaration (prototype) and definition for *ModifyCount* use the indirection operator to indicate you are passing a pointer as an argument to the function.

 Memory Addresses Are Like Street Addresses

Pointers and addresses are important concepts in Visual C++, and it is important that you understand them. Without pointers, your programming efforts will be limited severely. The following program, Pointers.cpp, *shows how to use the address and indirection operators:*

```
#include    <iostream.h>

void main (void)
{
    int    x;      // Declare an int variable
    int    *px;    // Declare a pointer variable
// using the indirection operator
    px = &x;  // Set the value of px to the address of x
    *px = 4;  // Set the value of x indirectly
    cout << "The address of x is " << &x << endl;
    cout << "The value of x is " << x << endl;
    cout << "The value of px is " << px << endl;
    cout << "The value of the variable pointed to ";
    cout << "by px is " << *px << endl;
}
```

For convenience, think of an address as the location of a house. You put the address of the house in the variable px. *But someone (*x *in this case) lives in that house, and that person has a name (*x*). You refer to the house using* px *and the name (value) of the person living there as* *px. *It's like getting mail addressed to "Occupant." It's really you, but the sender doesn't know your name (*x*).*

Using Pointers to Arrays

In Lesson 13, "Using Array Variables to Store Multiple Values," you learned that an array stores multiple values in a single variable. You also learned that the compiler sets aside a block of memory to hold all the values in the array, and that the array variable contains the address of that memory block.

Thus, an array variable already *is* a pointer variable, although you do not use the address operator when you declare it. You need to understand this when you pass an array to a function as an argument. In addition, Visual C++ does not store any size information in the array information, so when you pass an array to a function, the called function will have no way of knowing how many elements there are in the array. You will need to provide this information in some way, usually as an additional parameter. The following program, *Arr2Func.cpp,* shows how to pass an array to another function and how to access the elements:

```cpp
#include    <iostream.h>

void ShowArray (int *iArray, int iElements);

void main ()
{
// Declare an array of five temperatures
    int iTemperatures[5] = {64, 72, 38, 92, 81};
    ShowArray(iTemperatures,
            sizeof(iTemperatures) / sizeof (int));
}

void ShowArray (int *iArray, int iElements)
{
    int iCount;
// Display the temperatures in the array
    for (iCount = 0; iCount < iElements; ++iCount)
    {
        cout << "Temperature[" << iCount << "] is " <<
                iArray[iCount] << endl;
    }
}
```

You should notice that both the prototype and function definition for the *ShowArray* function use a pointer variable as the array parameter.

Doing Arithmetic on Arrays and Pointers

Thus far, you have accessed array elements by using *subscripts,* that is, you wrote the index of the element you wanted to access within the array operator, the square brackets. You accessed the first element using a subscript of 0, the second element with a subscript of 1, and so on.

You learned earlier in the section that your program does not store any size information about arrays you declare, so you must be careful not to access an element that is not within the boundary of the array.

The compiler, however, does know the size of the *data type* you are storing in the array. For example, if you declare an array of *int* with 10 elements, the compiler knows that the size of each element is four bytes. That is the size of an individual integer in Visual C++.

The compiler lets you use this information to access elements in another manner, using *array arithmetic.* The following program, *ArrArith.cpp,* uses array arithmetic instead of subscripts to access the elements in the array:

```
#include    <iostream.h>

void ShowArray (int *iArray, int iElements);

void main ()
{
// Declare an array of five temperatures
    int iTemperatures[5] = {64, 72, 38, 92, 81};
    ShowArray(iTemperatures,
            sizeof(iTemperatures) / sizeof (int));
}

void ShowArray (int *iArray, int iElements)
{
    int iCount;
// Display the temperatures in the array
    for (iCount = 0; iCount < iElements; ++iCount)
```

```
    {
        cout << "Temperature[" << iCount << "] is " <<
                *iArray << endl;
        ++iArray;
    }
}
```

Notice that in the *ShowArray* function, the program *dereferences* the *iArray* variable using the pointer opera-tor, the asterisk, to output the value. The next line increments the pointer variable to access the next element. When you increment or decrement a pointer variable, your program adds or subtracts the *size* of the data ele-ment. A value of type *int* is four bytes, so when you increment an *int* pointer, the program actually adds 4 to the pointer value.

The compiler treats arithmetic on pointer variables differently from ordinary variables. When you add a value to a pointer variable, your program multiplies that value by the size of the data type. For example, the follow-ing line points to the fourth element of the array, which actually is 12 bytes from the beginning of the array:

```
int iVal = *(iArray + 3);
```

The expression *iArray + 0* points to the first element in the array, *iArray + 1* points to the second element in the array, and so on to the last element of the array. To access an element this way, you must dereference the expression by writing it inside parentheses.

Declaring and Using Pointers to Functions

You have learned how you can access a variable's value indirectly using a pointer variable. The pointer variable contains the address of the information stored in another variable.

Functions also have addresses, and you can access functions using pointers just as you access variable values using pointers. This can be useful when you need to calculate ahead of time which of several functions your pro-gram needs to call. The following program, *pFunc.cpp*, uses your character input to decide which of two functions to call later in the program:

```
#include     <iostream.h>
#include     <ctype.h>

int C2F (int iTemp);
int F2C (int iTemp);
```

```
void main ()
{
    int iTemperature;
    int (^ShowTemp)(int);
    char ch = ' ';
    while (ch != 'Q')
    {
        cout << "Select an option from the list" << endl;
        cout << "\t1. Celsius to Fahrenheit" << endl;
        cout << "\t2. Fahrenheit to Celsius" << endl;
        cout << "\tQ. Quit" << endl;
        cout << "Your choice: ";
        cin >> ch;
        ch = toupper (ch);
        switch (ch)
        {
            case '1':      // Celsius to Fahrenheit
                ShowTemp = C2F;
                break;
            case '2':      // Fahrenheit to Celsius
                ShowTemp = F2C;
                break;
            default:       // Neither. Continue loop
                cout << endl;
                continue;
        }
// Get the temperature to convert
        cout << "Enter temperature: ";
        cin >> iTemperature;
// Call the selected function
        iTemperature = ShowTemp(iTemperature);
        cout << "The converted temperature is " <<
                iTemperature << endl << endl;
    }
}
```

```
int F2C (int iTemp)
{
    return (5 * (iTemp - 32) / 9);
}

int C2F (int iTemp)
{
    return (9 * iTemp / 5 + 32);
}
```

The first thing you should notice is that the prototypes for *F2C* and *C2F* have similar parameter lists and have the same return type. All functions that you might assign to a function pointer must be identical except for the function name.

Next, the declaration of the function pointer variable, *ShowTemp,* in the *main* function also matches the *pattern* of the function prototypes. Notice that you must write the function name and the indirection operator inside one set of parentheses as *int (*ShowTemp)(int)*. This notifies the compiler that the variable is a function pointer. If you omit the parentheses, the compiler will assume you are prototyping a function that returns a pointer to an integer value. In this case, the compiler will not generate an error because of the declaration, but it might when you attempt to use the variable. The second set of parentheses specifies the parameter list for the function pointer.

In the *while* loop, you determine from the user input which function you need to call, and assign the address of that function to the function pointer variable. Notice that in the assignment, you *do not* include the argument list. If you include the argument list, the compiler will assume you want to assign the result of a function call to the variable and will issue an error. Omitting the argument list in the assignment tells the compiler to assign the address of the function to the variable.

Temporarily Changing the Data Type of a Value

You have learned that the compiler will temporarily "promote" a value to a higher data type when you use the value in an expression that contains a value with greater precision. For example, if you divide a value or variable of type *int* by a value or variable of type *double,* the compiler will promote the *int* to a *double* to perform the operation. The data type of the result will be the highest precision data type the compiler found in the expression.

Sometimes you will need to perform your own temporary type conversions to avoid having the compiler issue a warning or error when you assign a variable of one type a value of another type. You can temporarily change the data type of a value by using the *cast* operator, which is represented by a set of parentheses. The following two declarations, for example, both assign the value 3 to the variable *x*:

```
int x = (int) 3.14159;
int x = int (3.14159);
```

Notice that you may write the data type or the expression inside the cast operator. In this case, both declarations have the same result, but you should make it a practice to use the C++ method shown in the second line. When you study C++ *classes* and *inheritance*, you will see the reason for using this form of the cast.

You may temporarily cast variables to another data type in the same way, as in the following sample:

```
double fPi = 3.14159;
int x = (int) (fPi);
```

Using References

As you have learned, passing a variable as an argument to a function will not let you modify the original variable in the calling function. To do this, you must pass a pointer to the variable so the called function can modify the variable's value indirectly.

The process of passing a pointer to a function is so common that C++ provides a special operator to make the task easier. The *reference operator* lets you declare a pointer variable and use pointers without using the indirection operator. To declare a *reference variable,* write the data type, then the name of the variable preceded by the reference operator, the ampersand (&). You *must* initialize a reference variable when you declare it by using the equals sign and the name of the variable to which it refers.

The following short program, *Ref.cpp,* shows how to use a reference variable to set the value of another variable:

```
#include    <iostream.h>

void main (void)
{
    int iTemperature = 32;
    int &refTemp = iTemperature;
```

```
     cout << "iTemperature = " << iTemperature << endl;
     refTemp = 96;
     cout << "iTemperature = " << iTemperature << endl;
}
```

As you can see, when the program assigns 96 to the reference variable, it actually assigns the value to the original variable. You cannot change the value in a reference variable once you initialize the variable. Once you declare and initialize a reference variable, all operations using the variable actually cause the program to perform the operations on the variable to which it refers.

You have learned that a function returns only a single value. Sometimes, however, your program may have to modify more than one variable in the calling program. You learned how to use pointer variables to change values in the calling function. Like pointer variables, reference variables are useful when your program needs to modify more than one variable in the calling function.

When you use reference variables in a function's parameter list, your program initializes them when you perform the function call. Although it appears your program is storing values in the reference variables in the parameter list, the program actually is storing the values in the variables in the calling function that you passed as arguments.

Suppose, for example, your program needs to calculate the points on a circle. It will need to return two values, the position on the x coordinate and the position on the y coordinate. Assuming the center of the circle is at point (0, 0), the following program, *Point.cpp*, passes the radius and angle to the *Point* function along with two reference variables for the x and y coordinates of the point on the circle:

```
#include    <iostream.h>
#include    <math.h>

void Point (int iRadius, int iAngle, int &x, int &y);

void main (void)
{
    int cx, cy;
    Point (300, 60, cx, cy);
    cout << "The point on the circle is at (" <<
            cx << ", " << cy << ")" << endl;
}


void Point (int iRadius, int iAngle, int &x, int &y)
```

```
{
// Convert the angle from degrees to radians
    double fAngle = iAngle / 57.29578;
    x = (int)((double)iRadius * cos (fAngle));
    y = (int)((double)iRadius * sin (fAngle));
}
```

To use the *sin* and *cos* functions, you need to include the *math.h* header file, which prototypes the math-related functions. When you include *math.h,* the Visual C++ compile automatically includes the *sin* and *cos* functions in your program.

Using *const* Arguments

You have learned that when you call a function and pass a variable as an argument, your program actually makes a copy of the value of the variable and passes the copy to your function as an a parameter. Changing the value of the parameter does not change the original variable. The intent of this design is to *encapsulate* your code and keep functions from changing values in another function.

Then you learned how to use pointers and reference variables to override this encapsulation and let your functions modify the original variables. Later, when you learn about C++ *classes* and *structures* and other *objects,* you will find it handy to pass pointers and references to these objects rather than pass copies of the objects as arguments.

However, you may still want to protect these objects so that you do not accidentally change them in a function. You can use the *const* keyword to tell the compiler that you do not want these variables to change and to issue an error if you accidentally try to change them. To use the *const* keyword, simply write *const* in front of the parameter in the function prototype and definition as shown in the following program, *Const.cpp:*

```
#include    <iostream.h>
#include    <math.h>

void Point (const int &iRadius, int iAngle, int &x, int &y);

void main (void)
{
    int cx, cy;
    Point (300, 60, cx, cy);
```

```
    cout << "The point on the circle is at (" <<
            cx << ", " << cy << ")" << endl;
}


void Point (const int iRadius, int iAngle, int &x, int &y)
{
//   Ooops. Attempt to change the radius
    iRadius = 300;
// Convert the angle from degrees to radians
    double fAngle = iAngle / 57.29578;
    x = (int)((double)iRadius * cos (fAngle));
    y = (int)((double)iRadius * sin (fAngle));
}
```

You may need to use the *iRadius* value in further calculations, so you do not want to change it. In the preceding sample, even though you are setting *iRadius* to the same value as in the calling function, the compiler issues an error telling you of the attempt to modify *iRadius*:

```
Const.cpp(17) : error C2166: 1-value specifies const object
```

You can safely pass a variable without having to worry about accidentally changing the variable's value.

 ## Variables Declared *const* Do Not Have to Be Parameters

You have learned that the const *keyword protects parameters from accidental change in a function that your program calls. You may protect any variable from accidental change by using the* const *keyword.*

For example, the following function declares a variable, fRadian, *and protects it using the* const *keyword:*

```
void Point (int iRadius, int iAngle, int &x, int &y)
{
    const double fRadian = 57.29578;
// Convert the angle from degrees to radians
    double fAngle = iAngle / fRadian;
```

```
    x = (int)((double)iRadius * cos (fAngle));
    y = (int)((double)iRadius * sin (fAngle));
}
```

You cannot accidentally change the value of fRadian, *and you probably would not want to change it.* A radian, *you will remember from your math classes, is the angle formed when you draw an arc on the circle as long as the radius.*

Normally, you would declare constants in global *memory. You will learn more about global memory in Lesson 17, "Understanding Function and Variable Scope."*

What You Must Know

In this lesson, you learned how to pass the addresses of variables as pointers and reference variables. When you pass the addresses in this way, you give the called function the ability to modify the original variable in the calling function. You also learned how to protect a variable from accidental change using the *const* keyword. In addition, you learned how to change the data type of a variable or value by using the cast operator. In Lesson 17, you will learn how to declare and use variables in different *scope* and how the scope affects the *visibility* of a variable. Before you continue with Lesson 17, however, make sure you have learned the following key points:

◆ You can access the value of a variable indirectly by using the address operator. This operator lets your program modify the value of a variable indirectly in other functions.

◆ To access the value of a variable, you may use a pointer to the variable. A pointer is the memory address of the variable's value.

◆ To get the address of a variable, you use the address operator. You may store the address in another variable, a *pointer variable*.

◆ A reference variable allows you to pass a pointer to a variable in a function call, yet use the variable in the called function without using the indirection operator.

◆ To declare a pointer variable, you use the indirection operator, an asterisk, in the declaration statement or function prototype. To declare a reference variable, you use the ampersand symbol in the declaration statement or function prototype.

Lesson 17

Understanding Function and Variable Scope

You have learned how to break your program down into blocks of code called functions and how to pass variables and values to your functions. In Lesson 16, "Changing Parameter Values within a Function," you learned how to pass pointers to variables and references to variables to functions. Pointers and references allow a function to change the value of variables in the calling process. To perform their tasks, functions need to store information in variables. The variables you declare in a function are *local* variables, and your program may use them only in the function in which you declare them. In fact, when you declare a local variable in a function, other functions do not even know the variable exists. In this lesson, you will learn about *scope*, which determines when and where your program may use a variable. By the time you finish this lesson, you will understand the following key concepts:

◆ You declare local variables in a function by writing the data type and the name of the variable. Your program may use local variables only within the functions in which you declare the variables.

◆ Local variable names must be unique within a function. Other functions may declare variables with the same name without interfering with each other.

◆ The *scope* of a variable determines the extent to which your functions may use variables. Variables declared within a function have *local* scope.

◆ Your program may declare variables outside of a function. These variables may be used by more than one function and have *global* scope.

◆ Within a function, you may define variables within compound statements that may be used only by statements within the compound statement. These variables have *block* scope.

◆ *Namespaces* group your code and variables into named sections. You may have functions and global variable with the same name as long as they are in different namespaces.

Understanding Scope

Depending upon how and where you declare variables, only a limited number of statements in your program may use the variables you declare. This range of statements is called the *scope* of a variable. In Lesson 15, "Passing Variables and Values to Functions," you learned that your program sets aside space on the *stack* for the variables a function will use when your program calls the function.

Thus, until your program actually calls a function, the variables you declare within the function do not yet exist. When the function ends, your program adjusts the *stack pointer* to the same condition it had when the function was called. Adjusting the stack destroys any variables you declare within the function, and the values of the variables are lost forever. These variables are *local* variables, and only statements within the function may use the variables.

The range of statements that may access a variable is the variable's *scope*. Within the scope of a variable, the name—or variable identifer—must be unique. You can have a variable called *iVar* in one function and a variable of the same name in another function, and they will not conflict with each other. When a variable is not visible from a statement being executed, then it is *out of scope*.

Another way to look at scope is to consider a room as your program file. Inside that room, you have a number of boxes that represent functions. Inside the boxes are kittens that represent variables. If only one kitten pokes its head out of the box at a time, it cannot see the kittens in the other box. You can have a black kitten in one box and a black kitten in another box, and neither will know about the other. Similarly, your program's execution point is in only one function at a time and cannot see the variables in other functions.

Scope is a very important concept in Visual C++, which defines four groups of scope. The following list summarizes the various scopes, and in the following sections you will write samples of each:

- ◆ **Block scope.** A variable has block scope if you declare it within a function or within a compound statement. The scope of the variable is the point where you declare the variable in the program to the close brace ("}") following it.

- ◆ **File scope.** Variables with *file* scope often are called "global" variables. When you declare a global variable, any function in your program after the point where you declare it may access the variable and use its value. You declare global variables *outside* any blocks of statements.

- ◆ **Function scope.** This is a special scope reserved for labels. Within a function and any subblocks in the function, a label name must be unique. The scope is the entire function.

- ◆ **Function prototype scope.** This is a special scope that applies only to function prototypes.

Function Prototype Scope

The simplest example of scope is the *function prototype* scope. The extent of function prototype scope is the function parameter list when you declare, or prototype, a function. This may seem trivial when writing a program, but it is important for the compiler because it lets you use variables with the same name in different function prototypes without having them conflict with one another. At the same time, function prototype scope still requires the variable names in a prototype to be unique.

The following function prototype will cause the compiler to generate and display an error on your screen because the variable names in the prototype are not unique:

```
void FunctionName (int var, int var);
```

You learned that identifier names must be unique within their scope. Because the two variables in the preceding prototype are in the same scope, they must have unique names. However, the variable names in separate function prototypes have different scope, so you may use the same name for variables, as in the following two prototypes:

```
void FunctionOne (int var);
void FunctionTwo (int var);
```

File (Global) Scope

Variables that you declare with *file* scope often are called "global" variables. This is the largest scope a variable may have. You declare global variables *outside* any function definition, that is, not within a block of code enclosed by the braces. Global scope extends from the point you declare the variable to the end of the source code file. Generally, you will declare global variables at the top of your source file so the variables will be available to all functions in the program.

You learned that variables you declare in a function should be *initialized* before you use them. Howver, the C++ language requires the compiler to initialize all global variables to 0. If you need to initialize the variable to another value, you may give the variable a value when you declare it, the same as you did with variables in functions. Often, many programmers initialize global variables, even though the compiler does not require it, to show their intent.

Programmers often declare global variable names with a "g_" prefix to identify them in the program code. The following program, *Global.cpp*, declares two global variables, one at the top of the file and a second after the *main* function:

```
#include    <iostream.h>

void FunctionOne (void);

int g_var1 = 0;    // Declare a global variable at the top

void main (void)
{
    cout << "In main:" << endl;
    cout << "\tThe value of g_var1 is " << g_var1 << endl;
    FunctionOne ();
}

// Declare a global variable after the main function
int g_var2 = 5;

void FunctionOne ()
{
    cout << "In FunctionOne:" << endl;
    cout << "\tThe value of g_var1 is " << g_var1 << endl;
    cout << "\tThe value of g_var2 is " << g_var2 << endl;
}
```

In this program, both *main* and *FunctionOne* are aware of *g_var1*, and both may use the variable in statements. However, only *FunctionOne* is aware of *g_var2*. If you attempt to use *g_var2* in the *main* function, the compiler will issue an error about an "undeclared identifier."

 Using Global Variables with the Same Name in Multiple Files

Although global variables have the title of file scope, the name is a slight mis-nomer. While a global variable may be used only in the file in which you declare the variable, you cannot have global variables with the same name in more than one file.

To do so will not cause a compile error. However, when the compiler invokes the linker to put the object files together into a single executable file, the linker will complain that the variable is defined in more than one file. To avoid this error, you need to declare the variables with the same name as static, as in the following:

```
static int g_Var;
```

You learned earlier that when you declare a static variable in a function, the compiler creates the variable in program memory rather than on the stack, and the variable retains its value between function calls. However, by default, the compiler creates global variables in program memory, so the static keyword takes on a slightly different meaning for global variables.

For global variables, static essentially means to limit the scope of the variable to the file in which you declare the variable. By using the static keyword, you can use a global variable with the same name in more than one program file.

Using Block Scope

The most common scope for variables is *block* scope. In earlier lessons, you declared all of your variables in block scope. Variables that you declare within a set of braces (these symbols mark the beginning and end of *blocks* of code) may be used only by statements that also are within the set of braces.

Variables with block scope are *local* variables because they are limited to the block of code in which you declare the variables. You learned that decision-making statements and loop statements may use *compound* statements. These compound statements also are blocks of code and may contain their own local variables, as shown in the following program, *Block.cpp:*

```
#include     <iostream.h>

void main (void)
{
    int iVar = 10;
    cout << "The value of iVar is " << iVar << endl;
    if (true)
    {
```

```
    int iBlockVar = 20;
    cout << "The value of iBlockVar in the block is "
        << iBlockVar << endl;
    cout << "The value of iVar in the block is "
        << iVar << endl;
    }
}
```

The preceding program shows that statements within the compound block may use variables that are declared outside the block or variables that you declared local to the function. However, if you attempt to use *iBlockVar* outside the compound block, the compiler will display an error on your screen that *iBlockBar* is not defined. Try adding the following statement as the last line of the program, between the closing brace of the compound statement and the closing brace for the function:

```
cout << "The value of iBlockVar outside the block is "
        << iBlockVar << endl;
```

The compiler will issue an "undefined identifier" error, showing that the scope of *iBlockVar* is the compound statement or the statements between the opening and closing braces of the compound statement. Statements outside the block may not access variables declared within the block.

 Hiding Variable Names

You have learned that within a function, the name of the variable must be unique. That rule is true so long as the function does not have any compound statements. The more general rule is that no two variables in the same *scope may have the same name. Within a compound statement, you may declare a variable with the same name as a variable in the function, as shown in the following program, BlockVar.cpp:*

```
#include    <iostream.h>

void main (void)
{
    int iVar = 10;
    cout << "The value of iVar is " << iVar << endl;
    if (true)
```

```
    {
        int iVar = 20;
        cout << "The value of iVar in the block is "
             << iVar << endl;
    }
    cout << "The value of iVar outside the block is "
         << iVar << endl;
}
```

The program declares two variables named iVar. *Both variables have* block *scope,* but the blocks are different. The first declaration initializes iVar to 10, as shown in the following output:

```
The value of iVar is 10
The value of iVar in the block is 20
The value of iVar outside the block is 10
```

However, declaring a new iVar *inside the block and initializing it to 20 has no effect on the original* iVar. In fact, the statements within the block cannot access the iVar outside the block.

When you declare variables this way, the variable inside the block hides the variable outside the block. The statements in the block are not aware that another variable of the same name exists outside the block.

Determining Function Scope

You rarely will need to be concerned with *function* scope, but you should be aware of it. Function scope is a special scope that is used only for *labels*. You learned about labels in Lesson 12, "Repeating Statements within a Visual C++ Program."

As you will learn in the last section, variables that you declare in a function may not be available to all statements in a function, and you may limit the availability of variables by declaring them in *blocks*. Also, you may declare variables with the same name in different blocks.

Within a function, however, Visual C++ will not let you define two labels with the same name. This is because Visual C++ lets you jump into or out of a block using the *goto* and *label* statements, as shown in the following program, *FunScope.cpp:*

```
#include     <iostream.h>

void main (void)
{
    int iVar = 10;
    goto JumpIn;
    cout << "The value of iVar is " << iVar << endl;
    while (iVar > 0)
    {
JumpIn:
        cout << "The value of iVar in the block is "
            << iVar << endl;
        --iVar;
        if (iVar < 7)
            goto JumpOut;
    }
JumpOut:
    cout << "The value of iVar outside the block is "
        << iVar << endl;
}
```

Certainly you would not want to write a program this way, but it does show you why Visual C++ defines a special scope for labels. The program jumps directly into the *while* loop and then jumps out before the loop control statement ends the loop. If Visual C++ lets you hide a label, you could create an unending loop accidentally.

Understanding Visibility and Duration

Two properties of a variable that you will see from time to time are a variable's *visibility* and *duration*. The visibility of a variable is the range of statements that may access and use a variable's value. It is roughly equivalent to a variable's scope.

For example, you learned that you may declare new variables in compound statements, or blocks of code. The *scope* of such a variable is the block of code beginning at the point where you declare the variable, and the variable is visible only to statements in the block following the variable's declaration. The following example of a block of code contains a statement, then declares a new variable, then continues with other statements:

```
{
    Statement1;
    int iNewVar = 10;
    Statement2;
    Statement3;
}
```

You cannot declare another variable named *iNewVar* inside the block because the block from the point of declaration is the variable's scope. The variable is *visible* only to *Statement2* and *Statement3*. *Statement1* is never aware that *iNewVar* ever exists.

The *duration* of a variable is the time between the point where your program creates the variable and where your program destroys the variable. For variables that you declare in a function, the duration is the time that your program is executing statements in the function. In the above example, your program destroys *iNewVar* at the end of the block.

These are trivial examples, and the visibility and duration are nearly the same. That is not always the case, however. In Lesson 15, "Passing Variables and Values to Functions," you learned that you can declare a variable *static* in a function to make the variable retain its value between calls to the function, as in the following sample function:

```
void ShowCounter (void)
{
    static int Counter = 1;
    cout << "The function has been called " << Counter
        << " time";
    if (Counter > 1)
        cout << "s";
    cout << endl;
    ++Counter;
}
```

In this function, the scope of *Counter* is from the function's opening brace to the function's closed brace. However, your program actually creates *static* variables when you run the program and does not destroy these variables until your program exits. The *duration* of *Counter* is the time your program is running. In addition, *Counter* is visible only to the statements in the function *after* the line where you declare the variable.

The same is true for global variables. Your program creates global variables when you run your program, so the duration of these variables is the lifetime of the program. The scope of a global variable is the point where you declare the variable to the end of the current file. You can extend the scope of a global variable to another file by declaring it *extern* in the other file.

 Using the Global Resolution Operator

In this lesson, you learned that you may declare variables using the same name as long as the variables have different scope. In this case, the variable in the smaller scope hides the variable in the larger scope. In other words, Visual C++ gives the variable with the smallest scope precedence. As you saw, in block scope the statements in the block have no way to access the original variable.

When you hide a global variable, however, Visual C++ provides an operator, the global resolution operator, that lets you access the global variable. You write the global resolution operator with two colons without any space between them. The following short program shows how to use the global resolution operator:

```
#include    <iostream.h>

int Number = 1001;

void ShowNumbers (int Number);

void main (void)
{
    int iValue = 2002;
    ShowNumbers (iValue);
}

void ShowNumbers (int Number)
{
    cout << "The local variable contains "
        << Number << endl;
    cout << "The global variable contains "
        << ::Number << endl;
}
```

The global variable Number *has the same name as the parameter to the* ShowNumbers *function. However, the parameter to* ShowNumbers *has a smaller scope than the globlal variable, so it hides the global variable* Number. *The second statement in* ShowNumbers *uses the global resolution operator to display the value of the global variable* Number.

Grouping Variables and Functions in Namespaces

You have learned how to hide variable names by declaring more than variable with the same name but in different scope. Visual C++ provides another mechanism—the *namespace*—that lets you hide not only variable names but function names as well.

A namespace is sort of like a telephone area code. Within each area code, you can have a full set of telephone numbers, even if the numbers duplicate those in another area code. Within your own area code (the default), you can dial another number without using the area code. But to connect with another number in a different area code, you must dial the area code as well as the number.

In Visual C++, the default area code is the default namespace, which is called the *global namespace*. To get to a function or variable in global namespace, you can use the *global resolution operator* (::), although normally the global namespace is your default and you do not need to use it explicitly.

At the same time, you may create other namespaces (area codes) and access the variables and functions using the namespace name and the *scope resolution operator*, which also is a double colon, as shown in the following program, *NameSpac.cpp*:

```
#include     <iostream.h>

namespace Spice
{
    int Number = 3003;
    void ShowNumbers (int Number);
}


int Number = 1001;


void ShowNumbers (int Number);
```

```
void main (void)
{
    int iValue = 2002;
    ShowNumbers (iValue);
    Spice::ShowNumbers (iValue);
}


void ShowNumbers (int Number)
{
    cout << "\tThe local variable contains " << Number
        << endl;
    cout << "\tThe global variable contains " << ::Number
        << endl;
}


void Spice::ShowNumbers (int Number)
{
    cout << "\tThe local variable contains " << Number
        << endl;
    cout << "\tThe global variable contains "
        << ::Number << endl;
    cout << "\tThe Spice variable contains "
        << Spice::Number << endl;
}
```

You should notice that there now are two identical *ShowNumbers* functions, one in global namespace and the other in *Spice* namespace. There also are four variables named *Number*. Each *ShowNumbers* function has its own local variable *Number*, but there is a *Number* in global namespace and another *Number* in *Spice* namespace. Although this could confuse you very quickly, to the compiler all the variables and functions are distinctly different and do not interfere with each other.

The *main* function first calls the global function *ShowNumbers*. You could call it using the global resolution operator as *::ShowNumbers(iValue)*, but because the global namespace is the default, the operator is *implied* and you do not need to write it. The global function writes the local and global variables to your screen.

Next, the program calls the *ShowNumbers* function in the *Spice* namespace, but to get to it, your program must use the namespace name (the area code) and the scope resolution operators, so the function call becomes

Spice::ShowNumbers(iValue). This function shows how to acess the local, global and *Spice* variables, all of which you named *Number*.

While namespace is a very useful concept, you may never need to use namespaces in your early programming. However, soon you will be studying *classes*, and Visual C++ uses the same concept to identify variables and functions within a class so they do not interfere with similarly named functions in other classes and those in global namespace. You should experiment with namespaces until you are comfortable with the concept.

 Avoid a Lot of Typing with the *using* Keyword

Programmers do not like to type. The more typing you have to do, the greater your risk for making a mistake. In many places, Visual C++ provides short cuts that reduce the amount of typing you have to do. One of these short cuts is the using *keyword that you use with namespaces.*

Suppose you have a variable called iValue *in a separate namespace called* StuffAndStuff *that your program accesses repeatedly. Each time you need to store or use the value of* iValue, *you have to type* StuffAndStuff::iValue. *In Visual C++, you can tell the compiler in advance that when you type just* iValue, *you actually want to use the* iValue *in the* StuffAndStuff *namespace. To do this, you write a statement such as the following:*

```
using StuffAndStuff::iValue;
```

After this statement, anytime you write iValue, *the compiler will use the variable in the* StuffAndStuff *namespace. You also may use the* using *keyword with a function name to tell the compiler the function you want to use is in another namespace, as in the following statements:*

```
using Spice::ShowNumbers;
ShowNumbers (iValue);
```

Each time your program calls ShowNumbers, *the compiler will substitute the function* Spice::ShowNumbers.

What You Must Know

In this lesson, you learned about the scope of variables and how to declare variables with different scope. You also learned how the compiler always uses the variable with the smallest scope when you declare two variables with the same name but in different scope and thus *hides* the varaible with the greater scope. In addition, you learned about the *visibility* and *duration* of variables and how your declaration affects these properties. You learned about the *global resolution* and *scope* resolution operators and how to create different namespaces and to declare and access variables and functions in different namespaces. In Lesson 18, you will learn how to declare and define program *constants* and how to use constants in your program. Before you continue with Lesson 18, however, make sure you have learned the following key points:

◆ Variable names must be unique within the scope of the variable. That is, you may not declare two variables that have the same name and scope.

◆ The scope of a variable determines the extent to which statements in your program may use the variable.

◆ Where you declare a variable determines its *visibility* and *duration*.

◆ You may declare variables in *file scope*. These variables are *global* variables.

◆ When a variable declaration *hides* a global variable, you may access the global variable using the *global resolution operator*, which is two colons written together (::).

◆ Namespaces let you sort your global variables and functions into named sections that do not interfere with each other. To access a variable or function in anther namespace, you use the *scope resolution operator*.

◆ The default namespace for your program is the *global* namespace, which is an unnamed namespace that you don't have to declare explicitly.

Lesson 18

Declaring Constants

Y ou have learned how use functions in your program to perform specific tasks and how to pass variables and values to your functions. You also have learned about prototyping functions. In Lesson 17, "Understanding Function and Variable Scope," you learned about the scope, visibility, and duration of variables and how to declare variables and functions using these properties. In addition, you learned how to use namespaces to group your code and functions into named sections that do not interfere with each other. Then you learned how to use the *global resolution* and *scope resolution* operators to access the variables and functions in the different namespaces. In this lesson, you will learn about *constants,* values in your program that never change. By the time you finish this lesson, you will understand the following key concepts:

◆ Constants are values that do not change throughout your program, and the compiler will not let you write a statement that would change a constant.

◆ A *literal constant* is a value that expresses itself. For example, the number *42* used in a program is a literal constant.

◆ Constants that you create using the preprocessor *#define* directive are literal constants. When the compiler encounters a constant created using the *#define* directive, it substitutes the actual value in the *#define* directive.

◆ A *constant variable* is a variable you declare to hold a value that does not change throughout the course of your program.

Understanding Constants

You have learned how to declare variables, which are named identifiers the compiler and your program use to access memory locations and to store values. Your program may initialize a variable to a particular value and change that value at any point in your program.

Often, however, you may need to use numbers that do not change when you run your program. These are values that should remain *constant* from the time you start your program until the time you exit the program. For example, the value of the mathematical constant *pi* never changes, so it would not be wise to let your program accidentally increment its value or to add another value to it.

Visual C++ provides two methods of using constants. The first is a *literal constant* using the preprocessor's *#define* command. As you will see, the preprocessor substitutes all occurrences of the constant you define with the value you give it in the definition.

The second method is to declare an ordinary variable and assign it the value you want. Then you use the *const* keyword to tell the compiler that the variable should not change during the course of your program. If you attempt to change it in a statement, the compiler will generate an error and display it on your screen.

Both methods have advantages and disadvantages, as you will see in this lesson.

Defining Constants

The Visual C++ compiler does not compile your program directly. Before it begins compiling, the compiler starts a special program called the *preprocessor.* The program first reads your source file and interprets any preprocessor *directives* you have in the file.

Preprocessor directives always begin with the pound symbol (#). You have seen how the *#include* directive causes the preprocessor to read a header file and include the definitions and statements from the header file into your source file.

Once the preprocessor has interpreted all the directives, it writes a temporary file containing the interpreted directives mixed with your source code. Next, the compiler compiles this temporary file. The compiler then removes the file when it no longer needs the file.

Another preprocessor directive is the *#define* directive. This directive always includes an identifier. To differentiate *#define* identifiers from ordinary variables, programmers usually write these identifiers in all uppercase. The following directive defines and identifies, *STUFF,* but does not give it a value:

```
#define   STUFF
```

Because *STUFF* does not have a value, every time the preprocessor encounters *STUFF* in your program, it simply strips it out. A more common use of the *#define* directive is to provide a value the compiler will use to replace the identifier. The following directive causes the preprocessor to replace any occurrence of *PI* with the value *3.14159*:

```
#define   PI      3.14159
```

This type of constant is called a *literal* constant because your program uses the actual value itself rather than the identifier *PI*. The compiler never sees the *PI* identifier. By the time the compiler begins compiling your program, the preprocessor already has replaced it with the value *3.14159*. It is as though you had typed the value rather than the identifier throughout your source file.

For simplicity, the following program, *Pi.cpp*, contains no header files and so cannot write anything to your screen:

```
#define   PI      3.14159

void main (void)
{
    double fArea;
    int iRadius = 8;
    fArea = iRadius * iRadius * PI;
}
```

When you compile *Pi.cpp* with the following command line, you will be able to see the intermediate file *Pi.i*:

```
cl -P Pi.cpp
```

When you use the "-P" compiler option, you are requesting the compiler to save the results of the preprocessor output into an intermediate file. By default, the file name is the same as the program name, but with an extension of ".i". Following are the contents of the intermediate file *Pi.i*:

```
#line 1 "pi.cpp"



void main (void)
{
```

```
    double fArea;
    int iRadius = 8;
    fArea = iRadius * iRadius * 3.14159;
}
```

As you can see, the preprocessor has replaced *PI* in the third line of *main* with the value *3.14159.*

The advantage of a literal constant is that it reduces the chance of a typing error in your program. It is much easier to type *PI* than it is to type *3.14159,* especially if you use the constant many times.

The disadvantage is that you must be careful to give the identifiers descriptive names that others who read your program will recognize.

 Macros Let You *#define* Arithmetic Operations

> *You learned that you can assign a name to a value by declaring a* constant *using the* #define *preprocessor directive. The* #define *directive also lets you define arithmetic operations in an expression and pass arguments to the expression. When you use the* #define *directive this way, you are defining a* macro. *An example of a macro is one that returns the square of a number, as in the following:*
>
> ```
> #define    SQR(x)     ((x)*(x))
> ```
>
> *Notice that there is no space between the macro name,* SQR, *and the open parenthesis for the argument list. Each time the preprocessor encounters the macro name, it will substitute the expression. Also, the preprocessor will substitute the value you give it for the variable* x. *The following short program,* Square.cpp, *shows how to declare and use a macro:*
>
> ```
> #include    <iostream.h>
>
> #define    SQR(x)     ((x)*(x))
>
> void main(void)
> {
>     int iNumber = 6;
>     int iResult;
> ```

```
        iResult = SQR(iNumber);
        cout << "The square of " << iNumber << " is "
            << iResult << endl;
}
```

Macros, particularly complicated macros, can make a program difficult to read.
They also can confuse the debugger in Visual C++ because the line in your source
code is not the same as the actual code (remember, the preprocessor has substi-
tuted your expression). In addition, you should avoid any operations that change
the value of a variable that you pass to the expression, such as the increment (++)
and decrement (−−) operators.

Using the *const* Modifier

The second method of using constants is to declare a *constant variable*. The name may sound contradictory, but a constant variable declaration is simply an ordinary variable that you modify by using the *const* keyword, as in the following:

```
const double pi = 3.14159;
```

The *const* keyword tells the compiler that you want to use the identifier, *pi* in this case, as a variable, but you do not want your program to change the value.

You must initialize a constant variable when you declare it. You cannot simply declare the variable and later assign it a value. The compiler will not let you do that, and it will generate and display an error if you attempt to declare a variable with the *const* keyword and do not initialize the variable.

As with literal constants, you should take care to give the *const* variable a descriptive name.

The advantage of using *const* variables is that you may use pointers and references to the variable, which you cannot do with literal constants.

It is possible to override the compiler and successfully compile a program file that attempts to modify the value of a *const* variable. The result of such an operation, however, may be unpredictable. The following program, *PiWhat.cpp,* compiles successfully but probably will crash when you attempt to run it:

```
#include    <iostream.h>

const double Pi = 3.14159;

void main (void)
{
    cout << "The value of pi is " << Pi << endl;
    double &dPi = (double) Pi;
    dPi = 6.28318;
    cout << "The value of pi is " << Pi << endl;
}
```

The program casts *Pi* from a const double to an ordinary double and assigns its address to a reference variable. Your program then uses the reference variable to attempt to change the value of *Pi*. Such bugs are very hard to find, and you should attempt to avoid constructions such as this.

What You Must Know

In this lesson, you learned how to declare constant values in your program using two methods. First, you learn how to use to the *#define* preprocessor directive to declare a literal constant. The preprocessor replaces all occurrences of the symbol with the literal constant value before the compiler begins compiling your program. In the second method, you learned how to declare "constant variables" that you may use as ordinary variables but which your program may not modify. In Lesson 19, "Writing a Windows Program," you will begin applying what you have learned and begin writing programs for Windows. Before you continue with Lesson 19, however, make sure you have learned the following key points:

◆ When you need a value that does not change throughout your program, you may use a *constant.*

◆ Literal constants are values that express themselves. You may create a literal constant using the *#define* preprocessor directive.

◆ A *const* variable is an ordinary variable declared using the *const* keyword. The compiler will not let you change the value of a *const* variable.

Lesson 19

Writing a Windows Program

You have learned how to declare and use variables in your program. In Lesson 18, "Declaring Constants," you learned how to define constants and how to declare constant variables. You have learned how to use arrays, how to break your program down into functions, and how to pass variables and values to your functions. Soon you will begin applying these concepts to write Windows programs. In this lesson, you will learn how Windows program differ from "standard" C++ programs, how to *register* windows with the operating system, and how intercept and use Windows *messages*. You also will learn how to build the framework for a basic Windows program. By the time you finish this lesson, you will understand the following key concepts:

♦ The operating system draws your window when you call functions to interact with the operating system. It is your job to draw the *contents* of your window.

♦ Window programs substitute a function named *WinMain* for the standard C++ *main* function.

♦ The operating system passes important information for your program through the *WinMain* function.

♦ Windows programs do not use standard input and output functions, so you need to include special Windows header files to declare the functions you need and to define the constants Windows programs use.

♦ Before you can create a window, you first must *register* the window with the operating system. When you register a window, you give the operating system some basic information about the window.

♦ Windows communicates with your program through a series of *messages*. By capturing and responding to these messages, your program can adjust to changes and keep your window up to date.

Understanding How Windows Programs Differ

Up to now, most of your programs have been *console* programs. That is, you compiled and ran the programs from the command line using the Windows console window. Console programs have the advantage that you may move them from one operating system to another and compile them. The programs do not create windows or perform other operations that are dependent upon one particular operating system. The programs are *portable.*

Ultimately, however, the purpose of Visual C++ is to let you write programs for Windows. Microsoft has included with Visual C++ a number of libraries that make up a very large Windows *application programming interface* (API). When you use the Windows API, you can take advantage of many of the peculiar features of Windows. In the process, however, you lose portability. You cannot, at this time, take a program that uses the Windows API and compile it on another operating system such as Linux.

Although Windows programs stick to the basic concepts of C++ programming, there are a number of differences between a Windows program and a standard C++ program. Early in your lessons, you learned that C++ programs enter through a function called *main,* but Windows programs enter through a *WinMain* function. With *main,* you could pass your own command line arguments to the function, as shown here:

```
void main (int argc, char *argv[])
{
    // Program statements
}
```

The *argc* parameter contains a value representing the number of arguments to *main,* and *argv* is an array of strings containing those arguments.

WinMain, however, has a fixed set of parameters. Although they may contain different values from one program to the next, the arguments always are the same:

```
int APIENTRY WinMain(HINSTANCE hInstance,
                     HINSTANCE hPrevInstance,
                     LPSTR     lpCmdLine,
                     int       nCmdShow)
{
    // Program statements
}
```

You still may pass command-line arguments, but you must handle them differently, as you will soon learn. Whereas *main* separated the arguments for you and placed them in an array, Windows passes the command-line arguments for *WinMain* in a single parameter, *lpCmdLine,* and you must separate them yourself. Separating the arguments is not always an easy task.

In a command-line program, you can write to the screen directly using standard input and output streams, as in the following simple program, *HelloCPP.cpp:*

```cpp
#include    <iostream.h>

void main (void)
{
    cout << "Hello, Visual C++ World!" << endl;
}
```

Windows programs, however, do not use standard input and output schemes. Instead, you must write any text you want to display to a window. The window may be a full text-editing window, or it may be nothing more than a *message box,* as shown in the following program:

```cpp
#include    <windows.h>

int APIENTRY WinMain(HINSTANCE hInstance,
                     HINSTANCE hPrevInstance,
                     LPSTR     lpCmdLine,
                     int       nCmdShow)
{
    MessageBox (0, "Hello, Windows!", "Hello", MB_OK);
    return (0);
}
```

To compile *HelloWin.cpp,* you must link it with the Windows API library functions using the following command line:

```
C:>cl hellowin.cpp user32.lib
```

In this simple program, Windows takes care of drawing the text in the *MessageBox* function. However, notice that the program uses *windows.h* instead of *iostream.h* or *stdio.h*. The *windows.h* header file contains the prototype for the *MessageBox* function. In addition, you must add the library that contains *MessageBox* to your program. That library is *user32.lib*. Later in this lesson, you will learn how to locate the name of the library file.

To interact with users, Windows programs use *controls* such as buttons, menus, and edit boxes. Sometimes you will need to create *dialog boxes* to hold these controls. You will learn more about dialog boxes in Lesson 30, "Creating Dialog Boxes" and controls in Lesson 31, "Using Windows Controls."

Windows programs necessarily are more complex than many standard C++ programs. There is a lot of "housekeeping" that you must perform to create a window, keep it up to date, and destroy it when your program no longer needs the window.

Creating a Windows Skeleton Program

Despite the fact that Windows programs are more complex than standard C++ programs, many of the tasks you must perform from one program to another are the same. Except for the simplest of programs, you must always write a *WinMain* function, you must always *register* your window class, you must always create your window, and you must always provide a function to handle messages from the operating system.

Obviously, retyping all this information each time you wanted to create a Windows program was tedious. Early in the history of Windows, programmers began writing *skeleton* programs containing the basic functions and code they needed to start writing Windows programs.

The skeleton program often included the code to register and create the program's main window and to respond to Windows Messages. It also included basic *resources* (menus, icons, and so on) such as an "about" dialog box and the code to create and display the about box. Programmers simply copied the skeleton program files to another directory when they began a new Windows project. The skeleton program creates the basic window, but little else, as shown in Figure 19.1.

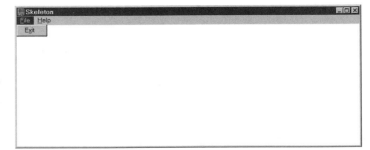

Figure 19.1

The skeleton window is the starting point for many Windows programs.

Using Visual C++, however, you do not have to maintain your own skeleton programs. Visual C++ contains the code for a number of basic programs—skeleton programs—for different types of projects. When you select a project type from the New dialog box, you are selecting a skeleton program from the Visual Studio's library. The Visual Studio will create the basic code for your project, saving you a lot of work.

Beginning with Lesson 20, "Using Structures in Visual C++ to Group Related Data," most of your programs will be Windows programs. You will create these programs as Visual C++ *projects* using the Visual Studio, but you should be aware of the basic blocks you need to build a Windows program.

The companion Web site *(http://www.primat-tech.com/books/books/5536/903)* contains a skeleton Windows program that you may modify as necessary for your own practice. To build the program, use the following command line:

```
C:>nmake -f skeleton.mak CFG="Skeleton - Win32 Debug"
```

The text following "CFG" will make the compiler write the intermediate and executable files to a *DEBUG* subdirectory.

Understanding the *WinMain()* Function

The *WinMain* function is the entry point for Windows programs. When you run a Windows program, the operating system loads the program code into memory and transfers control to the first statement in *WinMain*. This is much the same as for the standard *main* function, but *WinMain* can never have a *void* return type and handles the parameters differently.

The following is the *WinMain* function generated by the Visual Studio wizard and shows the general form of the *WinMain* function:

```
int APIENTRY WinMain(HINSTANCE hInstance,
                     HINSTANCE hPrevInstance,
                     LPSTR     lpCmdLine,
                     int       nCmdShow)
{
    // TODO: Place code here.
    MSG msg;
    HACCEL hAccelTable;

    // Initialize global strings
    LoadString(hInstance, IDS_APP_TITLE, szTitle,
            MAX_LOADSTRING);
    LoadString(hInstance, IDC_SKELETON, szWindowClass,
            MAX_LOADSTRING);
    MyRegisterClass(hInstance);
```

```
    // Perform application initialization:
    if (!InitInstance (hInstance, nCmdShow))
    {
        return FALSE;
    }


    hAccelTable = LoadAccelerators(hInstance,
                            (LPCTSTR)IDC_SKELETON);


    // Main message loop:
    while (GetMessage(&msg, NULL, 0, 0))
    {
        if (!TranslateAccelerator(msg.hwnd, hAccelTable,
                            &msg))
        {
            TranslateMessage(&msg);
            DispatchMessage(&msg);
        }
    }


    return msg.wParam;
}
```

The first thing you should notice is that the return type is never *void*, as can be the case with *main*. The return type for *WinMain* always is *int APIENTRY*. The *APIENTRY* gives the compiler some information about the format of the function call, including the order in which the operating system will pass parameters.

Throughout this version of *WinMain*, you will see several data types that may be unfamiliar to you, particularly a number that begin with a capital "H." These are data types defined in the Windows header files. The "H" types are *handles*. A handle is an indirect pointer to a memory location. In early versions of Windows, when computers had limited memory, Windows had to manage memory a little more carefully. Sometimes memory management involved moving objects around in memory, which meant any pointer to this memory in the program might become invalid. To get around this, Microsoft came up with handles. The operating system maintains the memory and lets the program access it through an identifier, the handle, regardless of the exact location in memory. When your program needs the exact memory address, it may obtain the address from the operating system using the handle. You will run across handles often as you write program for Windows.

After setting up some variables that the program will use, *WinMain* calls another function to *register* the window class. You should not confuse the window class with the C++ class, which you will study later. The window class concept was around long before the C++ class.

Next, *WinMain* calls another function, *InitInstance,* where your program may initialize other variables, open files that it will need, or perform any other initialization. Typically, *InitInstance* will create your window and make the window visible on the screen.

Having performed the initialization, *WinMain* then enters a *message loop* with the statement *while (GetMessage(&msg, NULL, 0, 0)).* As you will learn shortly, your program will communicate with the operating system through messages, and the operating system will send your program a series of messages.

When your program exits the message loop, usually because of a message to terminate, your program will end.

Using Windows Header Files

You have learned that your program can write to your screen and accept characters from the keyboard using standard input and output functions through C++ *streams.* These functions are defined in *stdio.h* and *iostream.h.* However, you also learned that Windows programs do not use standard input and output functions, so including files such as *stdio.h* or *iostream.h* is not enough. That is not to say that you will not need these files; in addition to standard input and output, these files also contain prototypes for functions that let you read and write from files.

To use the functions your program will need to accept keyboard input and to write to a window, you must include the file *windows.h.* The Windows API is very large, however, and many header files are necessary for your program to use the API. For example, the *winuser.h* file, which your Windows program will need, is 237,169 bytes just by itself. The *windows.h* file serves as a "wrapper" for all of these files and contains *#include* directives to add the files. When you add the *windows.h* file to your program using the following directive, you include most of these other files that you will need:

```
#include    <windows.h>
```

Obviously, you need some way of knowing which header files you must add to your program in case they are not in *windows.h.* The Visual Studio help files will tell you which header file you need for a particular function. For example, suppose you want to know which header file declares the *MessageBox* function. You can follow these steps:

1. Select the Visual Studio Help menu.

2. From the Help menu, select the Index item.

3. After a few seconds, the Microsoft Developers Network library window will appear, as shown in Figure 19.2.

4. Type **MessageBox** in the field marked "Type in the keyword to find." The list below this box will scroll to the "MessageBox" entry. Make sure the proper entry (the one with the upper-case "M" and "B") is highlighted in the list and press the Enter key.

5. When the Topics Found dialog box appears, again select the "MessageBox" item and click on the Display button.

6. Scroll down the large display window on the right side of the MSDN window until you find "QuickInfo" in large letters. The "Header" item in the QuickInfo block will tell you the header file you need to include in your program.

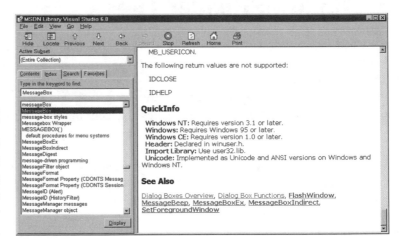

Figure 19.2

The QuickInfo block of the MSDN Help page for the MessageBox *function shows the* winuser.h *header file contains the declaration for the function.*

As part of a Visual C++ project, the Visual Studio creates a file called *stdafx.h* to include the Windows header files.

Success HINT: Finding the Modules to Link with Your Windows Program

In Lesson 14, "Getting Started with Visual C++ Functions," you learned that Visual C++ automatically adds the library functions your program needs when you include the proper header file. That is not always true with the Windows API, however. Sometimes you have to add specific library modules to your program.

The QuickInfo block of the MSDN Help page for a Windows function also lists the library module you need to link with your program. From the line in the QuickInfo block marked "Import Library," you can see that you must add the user32.lib module to your program to use the MessageBox function.

When you build a program from the command line, you simply add the library file name to the command line when you compile your program, as in the following:

```
C:>cl MyProgram.cpp user32.lib
```

Microsoft designed the Visual Studio to make many programming tasks easier. When you create a Windows-based project using one of the Visual Studio wizards, the Visual Studio will add the proper library files to your program.

Registering Window Classes

Before your program can create a window, it first must *register* the window's *class* with the operating system. When you register the window class, you are giving the operating system some basic information about the window, such as what color the background will be, which Windows cursor to use when the mouse enters the window, and what menu to attach to the window.

To register a window class, you must group the information together in a *WNDCLASSEX* structure. (A *structure* is a mechanism that lets you group related variables together in a single *object*. You will learn about structures in Lesson 20). The following function, *MyRegisterClass,* from the Visual Studio skeleton program, shows how your program registers a window class:

```
ATOM MyRegisterClass(HINSTANCE hInstance)
{
    WNDCLASSEX wcex;

    wcex.cbSize = sizeof(WNDCLASSEX);

    wcex.style          = CS_HREDRAW | CS_VREDRAW;
```

```
wcex.lpfnWndProc     = (WNDPROC)WndProc;
wcex.cbClsExtra      = 0;
wcex.cbWndExtra      = 0;
wcex.hInstance       = hInstance;
wcex.hIcon           = LoadIcon(hInstance,
                             (LPCTSTR)IDI_MYEDIT);
wcex.hCursor         = LoadCursor(NULL, IDC_ARROW);
wcex.hbrBackground   = (HBRUSH)(COLOR_WINDOW+1);
wcex.lpszMenuName    = (LPCSTR)IDC_MYEDIT;
wcex.lpszClassName   = szWindowClass;
wcex.hIconSm         = LoadIcon(wcex.hInstance,
                             (LPCTSTR)IDI_SMALL);


    return RegisterClassEx(&wcex);
}
```

The *MyRegisterClass* function first declares an *object* of *WNDCLASSEX*. The function then uses the object name, *wcex,* to set the individual *members* of the structure using the *member* operator, a period.

You should pay attention to the *lpfnWndProc* member. This member is the name of the function that will handle *messages* from the operating system. When you press a key on the keyboard, for example, Windows calls this function with information about the key press. When Windows calls this function, it is "sending a message" to your program. It is your program's responsibility to process the information or to ignore the message. In the next section, you will learn how to handle these messages.

Next you should notice the *lpszClassName* member. Your window class *must* have a name. In addition, the class should not be a name that another program already has registered with the operating system. Normally, you can use the program name for the name of your window class.

As you learned earlier, Windows programs often are more complex than command-line programs. You must provide the operating system with a lot of details about your program. Fortunately, the Visual Studio wizards handle much of this detail for you. However, as you continue writing Windows programs, you should familiarize yourself with the process in case you need to make adjustments to the wizard-generated code.

Responding to Windows Messages

You learned in this lesson that Windows communicates with your program by sending a series of *messages* to the program. To send messages, Windows calls the function in your program that you registered as the program's *window procedure*. The message system lets many programs share system resources and hardware.

For example, when you press a key on your keyboard, Windows sends a *WM_CHAR* message to the window procedure of the *window* that has the *focus*. Notice the emphasis on window rather than program. It is possible for a program to have multiple windows displayed, but only one of them can have the focus. (Technically, by definition, the window with the focus is the window currently receiving keyboard input; more practically, it usually is the topmost window on your screen.) Without this message, your program would never know that the user had pressed a key.

Windows procedures usually handle many messages, and so tend to be long. A lot happens when a Windows program executes. The user can move the mouse or click a mouse button, press a key on the keyboard, resize the window or select a menu or toolbar item. You program must be prepared to handle these "events." In the following function, *WndProc,* from a skeleton program, the first parameter is a handle to the window (HWND) to which the operating system is sending the messages. The second parameter is an *unsigned integer* (UINT) that identifies the message. The last two parameters (WPARAM and LPARAM) are additional numbers the operating system may need to send your program:

```
//
//   FUNCTION: WndProc(HWND, unsigned, WORD, LONG)
//
//   PURPOSE:  Processes messages for the main window.
//
//   WM_COMMAND  - process the application menu
//   WM_PAINT    - Paint the main window
//   WM_DESTROY  - post a quit message and return
//
//
LRESULT CALLBACK WndProc(HWND hWnd, UINT message, WPARAM wParam, LPARAM
lParam)
{
    int wmId, wmEvent;
    PAINTSTRUCT ps;
    HDC hdc;

    switch (message)
```

```
    {
        case WM_COMMAND:
            wmId    = LOWORD(wParam);
            wmEvent = HIWORD(wParam);
            // Parse the menu selections:
            switch (wmId)
            {
                case IDM_ABOUT:
                    DialogBox(hInst, (LPCTSTR)IDD_ABOUTBOX,
                                     hWnd, (DLGPROC)About);
                    break;
                case IDM_EXIT:
                    DestroyWindow(hWnd);
                    break;
                default:
                    return DefWindowProc(hWnd, message,
                                         wParam, lParam);
            }
            break;
        case WM_PAINT:
            hdc = BeginPaint(hWnd, &ps);
            // TODO: Add any drawing code here...
            RECT rt;
            GetClientRect(hWnd, &rt);
//
// Code to draw contents of window goes here
//
            EndPaint(hWnd, &ps);
            break;
        case WM_DESTROY:
            PostQuitMessage(0);
            break;
        default:
            return DefWindowProc(hWnd, message, wParam,
                                 lParam);
    }
    return 0;
}
```

The *message* parameter is an integer number, and *WndProc* uses a *switch* statement to select the statements to perform for each message number. In the Windows header files, Microsoft has used the *#define* directive to give names to these numbers to make them easier to remember and use. *WM_PAINT,* for example, is 15 and *WM_DESTROY* is 2. You can get a list of most of the Windows messages from the MSDN Help system. Select the Visual Studio Help menu, then select the Index item. In the Keyword field, type **WM_**. The list below the Keyword field will move to the first message entry, as shown in Figure 19.3. Select a message from the list and press the Enter key to display information about the messages.

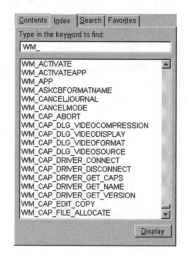

Figure 19.3

Typing WM_ in the MSDN Help window's keyword field moves the list to the section containing Windows messages.

You should notice that in the *switch* statement, the *WM_COMMAND* message case contains a nested *switch* statement. The *WM_COMMAND* message value is 273. Windows sends this message when the user selects a menu item, types an *accelerator key* (a shortcut keystroke such as Control+O to open a file), or presses a toolbar button on the window. Each menu item, accelerator, or button has a number called its *resource ID*. Windows "packs" this resource ID and another number representing the user action into a single number and passes it to your program in the *wParam* parameter. Your program must separate these numbers using Windows *macros*. The *wParam* value is 32 bits. The *LOWORD* macro returns the number contained in the lower 32 bits (the resource ID), and the *HIWORD* macro returns the value in the highest 16 bits (the user action).

The nested *switch* statement then uses the resource ID to determine which menu item, accelerator key, or button the user selected.

You also should notice the *default* case in each *switch* statement. If your program does not handle a message in the *switch* statement, *WinProc* calls *DefWindowProc*, a Windows API function, to process the message.

What You Must Know

In this lesson you learned about the basic building blocks to construct a Windows program and how to set up a skeleton Windows program. In addition, you learned that you must register your window class with the operating system before you create the window in your program. You also learned that Windows communicates with your program using a series of *messages*. Your program may intercept these messages and perform statements. If your program does not process a message, you should let the program call the Windows API default function to process the message. In Lesson 20, you will begin learning about Visual C++ objects, starting with the *structure*. You also will begin writing more programs for Windows rather than the command line. Before you continue with Lesson 20, however, make sure you have learned the following key points:

◆ To create a window, you first must register the window class (a name) with the operating system. The operating system draws your window, but your program is responsible for drawing the *contents* of the window.

◆ Windows programs use a function named *WinMain* as the entry point rather than *main*.

◆ Windows programs do not use standard input and output. You need to include *windows.h* to declare and use the Windows API functions to write to a window and read from the keyboard.

◆ Windows communicates with your program using *messages* to a special *window procedure* function. Your program may capture the messages in a *switch* statement and perform statements to process the messages.

Part 2

Intermediate
Visual C++

Lesson 20

Using Structures in Visual C++ to Group Related Data

Variables, as you have learned, are memory locations where your program can store information. You have learned how to declare and use variables in your program. You also have learned how to declare arrays to hold more than one value in a single variable name and how to use pointers and reference variables. Sometimes you need to group related pieces of information together to make it easier to pass the information to functions. Visual C++ contains a mechanism called a *structure* that lets you define related variables—even variables of different types—in a group. The structure becomes a new C++ data type, and you may declare all variables in the group by declaring a variable of the structure. By the time you finish this lesson, you will understand the following key concepts:

- ◆ A structure is a programming mechanism that lets you group several values into a single variable.

- ◆ Unlike arrays, the members of a structure do not have to be the same data type.

- ◆ A *union* is a structure-like object that stores only one value. That value, however, may be any of several data types.

- ◆ A structure is an object, and you may pass an entire structure, or the address of a structure, to a function as an argument.

- ◆ Structures may contain pointers to other structures of the same type. This makes structures useful for building *linked lists* in memory.

- ◆ In Visual C++, structures may contain functions and pointers to functions.

Defining Structures

Long before object-oriented programming became popular, the C language contained the seed of an early object, the *structure*. The founders of C determined that it would be convenient to package related variables of different types into a single mechanism. The structure was not an object according to modern definitions, but when it entered the C++ language, it took on all the characteristics of an object.

A structure lets you group related variables, even variables of different data types, into a single variable. You then may use the structure variable as you would any other variable, and pass it to functions as a single item. For example, suppose you need to store some information about an employee. The information might include the employee's first and last names, the middle initial, the employee's ID number, the rate of pay, and the number of hours worked this week. To declare a structure, use the *struct* keyword, as shown here:

```
struct EMPLOYEE
{
    char    szLastName[20];
    char    szFirstName[20];
    char    cMiddleInitial;
    int     iID;
    double  fHours;
    double  fPayRate;
};
```

You should notice that the structure definition includes the member variables enclosed in a set of braces. This is not a compound statement, and even if you have only one member, you still must include the braces. Also notice that the definition ends with a semicolon after the closing brace. The semicolon notifies the compiler that the structure definition is complete.

Defining a structure does not create a structure object. It simply creates a new data type. The compiler uses the definition as a template for this new data type. To create an object, you must declare a structure variable, the same as you would for any other data type such as *int*, *double*, or *char*. To access a member of the object, you write the variable name, the *member* operator (a period), and the member name. The following program, *Employee.cpp*, uses a structure to hold information about an employee:

```
#include    <iostream.h>

struct EMPLOYEE
{
    char    szLastName[20];
```

```
    char    szFirstName[20];
    char    cMiddleInitial;
    int     iID;
    double  fHours;
    double  fPayRate;
};

void main (void)
{
    EMPLOYEE   Worker;
    char       szString[20];

    cout << "Enter employee's last name and press Enter: ";
    cin  >> Worker.szLastName;

    cout << "Enter employee's first name and press Enter: ";
    cin  >> Worker.szFirstName;

    cout << "Enter employee's middle initial and "
         << "press Enter: ";
    cin  >> szString;
    Worker.cMiddleInitial = szString[0];

    cout << "Enter employee's ID number and press Enter: ";
    cin  >> Worker.iID;

    cout << "Enter number of hours the employee worked "
         << "and press Enter: ";
    cin  >> Worker.fHours;

    cout << "Enter employee's hourly wage and press Enter: ";
    cin  >> Worker.fPayRate;

    cout << endl << "Employee " << Worker.szFirstName << ' '
         << Worker.cMiddleInitial << ". "
         << Worker.szLastName
```

```
        << " (ID " << Worker.iID << ')'
        << " earned $" << Worker.fHours * Worker.fPayRate;
}
```

In *main*, the program first declares a variable of type *EMPLOYEE* called *Worker*, then uses *Worker* to store information in the members. To access members of the structure, you use the members the same as any other variable, except you must add the variable name, *Worker*, and the *member* operator.

 ## Objects versus Variables

A structure lets you declare related variables as a group. The structure also is the first object you have encountered in your Visual C++ lessons. In object-oriented programming, objects are similar to ordinary variables but have special properties. Variables contain only values, such as the number you assign to an int variable or the string that you assign to a char pointer variable.

Objects, on the other hand, may contain state information. This is information that describes how you set the values of the members of the object. Usually this information is in the form of a member function that sets the value of a variable.

In Visual C++, structures may contain functions, and it is this characteristic that puts C++ structures in the domain of objects rather than ordinary variables. (If you have studied the C language, you may remember that C structures may not contain functions.) The following short program, SetSpeed.cpp, shows one way to add a function to a Visual C++ structure:

```
#include  <iostream.h>
#include  <stdio.h>

struct BAUDRATE
{
    char    szRate[8];
    long    lRate;
    void    SetSpeed (long lSpeed)
            {
                sprintf (szRate, "%ld", lSpeed);
```

```
                        lRate = lSpeed;
                }
        };


        void main (void)
        {
            BAUDRATE   Baud;
            Baud.SetSpeed (9600);
            cout << "The string is " << Baud.szRate << endl;
            cout << "The long variable is " << Baud.lRate << endl;
        }
```

Later in this lesson, you will learn more about how to add functions to Visual C++ structures.

Declaring Structure Members

Structures let you group related variables in a single variable. The data types of the member variables may be different. As you learned, simply writing the *definition* of a structure only creates a new data type in Visual C++. To declare the variables, you must declare a variable of the structure first. In the following, you use the structure to store the baud rate for your modem as a string, which you may display on your screen, and as a number:

```
struct BAUDRATE
{
    char    szRate[8];
    long    lRate;
};


BAUDRATE B9600;
strcpy (B9600.szRate, "9,600");
B9600.lRate = 9600;
```

Earlier, you learned that you may initialize a variable when you declare the variable, as in the following statement:

```
int iVar = 42;
```

When you define a structure and declare its member variables, however, you may not initialize any of the members. The following structure definition would cause the compiler to generate and print error messages to your screen:

```
struct BAUDRATE
{
    char    *pszRate = "9,600";
    long    lRate = 9600;
};
```

The compiler issues a warning because the definition does not actually create any variables. The definition only tells the compiler what type of variables to include in the structure when you declare a structure variable.

In Lesson 13, "Using Array Variables to Store Multiple Values," you learned that you could initialize an array by adding the initial values between braces in the declaration. You may use the same technique to initialize structure members when you declare a structure variable. The following program, *BaudRate.cpp*, declares a *BAUDRATE* variable and initializes the member variables:

```
#include    <iostream.h>

struct BAUDRATE
{
    char    *pszRate;
    long    lRate;
};

void main (void)
{
    BAUDRATE B9600 = {"9,600", 9600};
    cout << "The " << B9600.pszRate << " baud rate value is "
        << B9600.lRate << endl;
}
```

Using Structures as Objects

As you have seen, structures let you declare multiple values, which may be of different types, using only one variable name. (In some languages such as Pascal, structures are called "records.") The ability to group different types of values into a single variable gives your program the ability to handle complex—and perhaps large—blocks of data more easily.

When you define a structure, you create a new C++ data type. Structures may include other structures as member variables. For example, if you need a structure to define a circle using the circle's center point and radius, you could first define a more general structure to hold a point, then include that structure in the circle structure, as in the following program, *CircleSt.cpp*:

```cpp
#include    <iostream.h>

struct POINT
{
    int     x;
    int     y;
};

struct CIRCLE
{
    POINT   Center;     // POINT is a new data type
    int     iRadius;
};

void main (void)
{
    CIRCLE Circle;
    Circle.Center.x = 20;
    Circle.Center.y = 42;
    Circle.iRadius = 300;

    cout << "The radius is " << Circle.iRadius << endl;
    cout << "The center is at (" << Circle.Center.x
        << ", " << Circle.Center.y << ")" << endl;
}
```

You may use structures as parameters to functions, and you may use pointers and references to structures the same as you do for any other variable. However, when you use a pointer to a structure, you must access the structure members using the *pointer to member* operator, which you write using a hyphen and a greater than symbol (—>) with no spaces between the symbols. The following program, *PointSt.cpp*, passes two structures as pointers to find the point on a circle:

```cpp
#include     <iostream.h>
#include     <math.h>

#define      RADIAN     57.29578

struct POINT
{
    int     x;
    int     y;
};

struct CIRCLE
{
    POINT    Center;      // POINT is a new data type
    int      iRadius;
};

void FindPoint (CIRCLE *Circle, int iAngle, POINT *Point);

void main (void)
{
    CIRCLE Circle;
    POINT  Point;
    Circle.Center.x = 30;
    Circle.Center.y = 42;
    Circle.iRadius = 300;

    FindPoint (&Circle, 60, &Point);

    cout << "The radius is " << Circle.iRadius << endl;
    cout << "The point on the circle is at (" << Point.x
        << ", " << Point.y << ")" << endl;
}
```

```
void FindPoint (CIRCLE *Circle, int iAngle, POINT *Point)
{
// Convert the angle from degrees to radians
    double fAngle = iAngle / RADIAN;
    Point->x = (int)((double)Circle->iRadius
                * cos (fAngle)) + Circle->Center.x;
    Point->y = (int)((double)Circle->iRadius
                * sin (fAngle)) + Circle->Center.y;
}
```

Examine the code in the *FindPoint* function. The *Circle* and *Point* parameters are pointers to structures, so you must access the member variables using the pointer to member operator (–>). However, notice how you access the variables in the *Center* member of the *Circle* structure pointer:

```
Circle->Center.x
```

To understand this, you need to look at the definition of the *CIRCLE* structure. In this structure, *POINT* is a structure, not a pointer to a structure. Thus, you need to use the pointer to member operator to access the *POINT* structure in *CIRCLE*, but then you use the member operator to access the individual members of the *POINT* structure.

Understanding Unions

You have learned how to store values of different types in a structure. You also learned that to use a variable, you must declare its type and name so the compiler knows how much memory to set aside for the variable's value. Sometimes, however, you will need to store just one value, but you may not know ahead of time what data type you will need to store.

The Visual C++ *union* lets you declare variables of different types in a single variable, much like a structure. Unlike a structure, however, a union may hold only one of those values at a time. A union is handy when you need to declare a variable but you do not know the data type. A union definition is similar to a structure definition except you use the *union* keyword:

```
union MyUnion
{
    int     iVal;      // An integer value
    double  fVal;      // A floating value
```

```
    char    *pszVal;   // A pointer to a string
};
```

As with a structure, just defining a union does not set aside any memory. When you declare a union variable, the compiler sets aside enough memory to hold only the member that needs the most memory. In Visual C++, both *int* and *char* pointer data types require four bytes of memory, but a *double* needs eight bytes. When you declare a variable of type *MyUnion*, the compiler sets aside eight bytes of memory:

```
MyUnion    var;
```

It is important that you understand that you may assign a value to only one of the union's members at any time. The member variables *share* the same memory location, and they all have the same address. If you first store a value in the *int* member of the preceding example and later store another value in the *double* member, you will overwrite the value in the *int* member.

In addition, if you use unions, you must remember that the compiler does not keep track of what kind of value you have stored in the union. If your program does not keep track of the last data type you stored, you could cause your program to crash. The following program, *UnionErr.cpp*, shows what can happen when you store an *int* value in a union, then store a *char* pointer in the union, and finally attempt to display the *int* value:

```
#include    <iostream.h>

union TestUnion
{
    int     iVar;
    char    *szVar;
};

void main (void)
{
    TestUnion test;
    test.iVar = 42;

    cout << "test.iVar = " << test.iVar << endl;
    test.szVar = "This is a test string";
    cout << "test.iVar = " << test.iVar << endl;
}
```

When you compile and run *UnionErr.cpp*, you will see the following output. The union contains the *char* pointer instead of the *int* value you attempt to print:

```
test.iVar = 42
test.iVar = 4227152
```

 Using Visual C++ Anonymous Unions

Visual C++ also lets you define anonymous unions *that do not have a name. Anonymous unions help your program save memory space by sharing the memory between two or more variables. Today, most personal computers have many megabytes of memory, so anonymous unions are not as important as they once were.*

Of course, you still may use only one member variable in an anonymous union at any one time. When you use an anonymous union, you do not have to declare a union variable, and you do not have to use the member *operator to access the variables, as in the following program,* Anon.cpp:

```
#include    <iostream.h>

void main (void)
{
    union
    {
        int    miles;
        long   meters;
    };

    miles = 10000;
    cout << "The value of miles is " << miles << endl;
    cout << "The value of meters is " <<
            (int) meters << endl;
    meters = 150000L;
    cout << "The value of meters is " << meters << endl;
    cout << "The value of miles is " <<
```

```
                    (long) miles << endl;
    }
```

As you can see when you compile and run this program, the anonymous union may store only one value at a time.

Understanding Structures That Reference Themselves

Many times in your programming, you may find that you need to give some order to structure variables. For example, you may have several structures that contain information about employees. Each structure variable has a different name, so you would have to construct statements to write each of them to your screen.

Fortunately, Visual C++ lets you include in a structure a pointer variable that points to another structure of the same type. You can use a structure pointer member to organize the structures, as in the following program, *List.cpp*:

```
#include    <iostream.h>
struct EMPLOYEE
{
    char    szName[40];
    int     iEmpNumber;
    double  fPayRate;
    EMPLOYEE  *pNext;
};

void main (void)
{
    EMPLOYEE Emp1 = {"John", 4820, 6.25};
    EMPLOYEE Emp2 = {"Kathy", 1621, 8.56};
    EMPLOYEE Emp3 = {"Bear", 2902, 9.12};
    Emp1.pNext = &Emp2;
    Emp2.pNext = &Emp3;
    Emp3.pNext = NULL;
```

```
    EMPLOYEE *current = &Emp1;
    while (current != NULL)
    {
        cout << "Employee " << current->szName << " (#"
             << current->iEmpNumber << ") earns $"
             << current->fPayRate << " per hour" << endl;
        current = current->pNext;
    }
}
```

By assigning the *pNext* variable a pointer to the next employee structure, you have organized the independent structures into a *linked list*. The first structure contains a pointer to the second structure, which contains a pointer to the third structure. The third structure, however, contains a *NULL* pointer, which the program uses as a signal that there are no more structures following.

To start the list, the program declares a structure pointer variable, *current,* and initializes it to point to the first structure in the list. The loop then prints the information about each employee, then sets the value of *current* to the *pNext* value of *current*. When the value of *current* is *NULL,* the loop exits.

You could change the order of the list simply by changing the value of the pointers in the *pNext* members.

Using Functions in Structures

Early in this lesson, you learned how to define a structure and how to include a function as part of a structure's definition. In addition, in Lesson 14, "Getting Started with Visual C++ Functions," you learned about *inline functions.* When you define a function within a structure definition, the function is an inline function. That means the compiler will substitute the function's code in your program each time you call it.

Structure functions do not have to be inline, however. To include a function that is not inline, simply prototype it in the structure definition, then include the code elsewhere in your program. To associate the function with the structure when you write the function's code, you use the structure name and the scope resolution operator, as in the following program, *SetSpeed2.cpp*:

```
#include  <iostream.h>
#include  <stdio.h>

struct BAUDRATE
{
```

```
    char    szRate[8];
    long    lRate;
    void    SetSpeed (long lSpeed);
};

void main (void)
{
    BAUDRATE  Baud;
    Baud.SetSpeed (9600);
    cout << "The string is " << Baud.szRate << endl;
    cout << "The long variable is " << Baud.lRate << endl;
}

void BAUDRATE::SetSpeed (long lSpeed)
{
    sprintf (szRate, "%ld", lSpeed);
    lRate = lSpeed;
}
```

Notice that the definition of the *BAUDRATE::SetSpeed* function is very similar to the way you defined a function in a *namespace* in Lesson 17, "Understanding Function and Variable Scope." Structures are not namespaces, but structures contain unique identifiers just as namespaces do.

Declaring Arrays of Structures

In Lesson 13, "Using Array Variables to Store Multiple Values," you learned that you could store multiple values in a single variable by declaring an array of values. In Visual C++, you may declare an array of a structure:

```
struct EMPLOYEE
{
    char    szName[40];
    int     iEmpNumber;
    double  fPayRate;
};
EMPLOYEE Employee[3];
```

As with arrays of variables of other types, you may initialize the members of an array of structures by writing the values inside a set of braces after you declare the array. However, with an array of structures, you must initialize the structure members in order, as shown in the following program, *StrucArr.cpp*:

```cpp
#include    <iostream.h>

struct EMPLOYEE
{
    char    szName[40];
    int     iEmpNumber;
    double  fPayRate;
};

void main (void)
{
    EMPLOYEE Employee[3] =
    {
        "John",  4820,  6.25,
        "Kathy", 1621,  8.56,
        "Bear",  2902,  9.12
    };

    for (int i = 0;
        i < sizeof (Employee) / sizeof (EMPLOYEE); ++i)
    {
        cout << "Employee " << Employee[i].szName << " (#"
            << Employee[i].iEmpNumber << ") earns $"
            << Employee[i].fPayRate << " per hour" << endl;
    }
}
```

In this example, the first line initializes *Employee[0]*, the second line initializes *Employee[1]*, and the third line initializes *Employee[2]*.

What You Must Know

In this lesson, you learned how to define and use *structures* and *unions*. A structure is a device that lets you combine more than one value, even values of different types, into a single variable. A union is a device that lets several variables share the same memory address. You also learned how to use a structure with a pointer to another structure of the same type to build a *linked list* in memory, an important concept in programming. Finally, you learned how to define and use arrays of structures. In Lesson 21, "Drawing in the Graphics Device Interface," you will use structures in writing Windows programs that draw text and graphics to your screen. Before you continue with Lesson 21, however, make sure you have learned the following key points:

◆ Structures let you group several values into a single variable. To access the member values, you use the *member* operator, a period.

◆ The member variables of a structure may have different data types.

◆ You may pass structures as arguments to functions. In addition, you may pass a pointer or a reference to a structure as an argument to a function.

◆ A *union* lets your program store values of different data types in the same memory location.

◆ Structures may contain pointers to other structures of the same type, making structures useful for building linked lists.

◆ You may include functions in the definition of a structure. The functions may be *inline* by defining them in the structure definition.

Lesson 21

Drawing in the Graphics Device Interface

Windows programs do not use the standard input and output devices that you have used in most previous programs. Instead, to write to a Windows program, you must "draw" the text in the window. To make this easier, the Windows API contains many functions for drawing text and shapes in a window. In addition, Windows provides a *device context*, a data device that lets you access the drawing capability of output devices such as your screen without knowing the technical details of how the device operates. In this lesson, you will learn how to write and draw to a window using the device context. You also will learn about the various graphics objects available to help you draw in a window. By the time you finish this lesson, you will understand the following key concepts:

◆ A window is an object on which you draw graphics. To a window, everything you add to the window is a graphic, even text.

◆ To help you draw on a window or to the printer. Windows creates a *device context* for your output device such as the screen. The same functions that draw to your screen may be used to draw to a printer.

◆ The Windows API contains a number of graphical objects to help you draw to a window, such as *fonts, brushes,* and *pens*.

◆ A font is a collection of images that represent the various characters, such as the alphabet, numbers, and symbols that you may draw to the screen. Different fonts may have different symbols.

◆ To write text to a window, you must draw it using a font. A device context contains a default font, but you may select another style of characters by selecting a different font.

◆ In addition to text, a window may contain lines and shapes such as squares, circles, and triangles of different colors.

◆ Graphic objects such as the *pen* and *brush* let you select the colors you will use to draw text and shapes.

Understanding Device Contexts

In Lesson 19, "Writing a Windows Program," you learned how to create a skeleton Windows program. You also learned that while Windows draws the window for you, your program is responsible for drawing the contents of the window, whether that is text or shapes.

With the myriad output devices on the market—display cards and monitors with different capabilities, printers, fax modems, and so on—drawing objects, even something so simple as text, can be a daunting task. To make it easier, Windows provides you with a device context that lets you draw text and shapes regardless of the output device.

The manufacturers of output devices provide you with a "device driver" program for Windows. This program contains all the code to draw text and lines on the device. From this driver, Windows builds a device context. Using the device context and the Windows API function, your program "draws" on the device. The same drawing functions work the same whether the output device is your screen or a printer.

To alert you that your program needs to draw the contents of the window, Windows sends your program a *WM_PAINT* message. To demonstrate the drawing operation, start the Visual Studio and follow these steps:

1. Select New from the File menu. When the New dialog appears, select the "Projects" page, then select the "Win32 Application" item.

2. Enter the directory where you keep your program files in the Location field.

3. Type **HelloWin** in the Project Name field and press the OK button. (You will change the name in this field throughout this lesson to create projects).

4. When the wizard page appears, select the third button next to the line that reads "A Typical 'Hello, World' application."

5. Press the Finish button. When the New Project Information dialog box appears, press the OK button.

The Visual Studio will respond by creating a Visual C++ project for Windows. Refer to Lesson 3, "Exploring the Visual Studio," if you need to refresh your memory about the location of the various windows in the Visual Studio.

Select the FileView page of the Workspace Window. Expand the files by clicking the mouse on the "+" sign next to the line that reads "HelloWin files." Next, expand the source files by clicking the mouse on the "+" sign next to the line that reads "Source Files." Double-click the mouse on the *HelloWin.cpp* file name.

The Visual Studio will open the *HelloWin.cpp* file in an editing window. Using the Page Down key, scroll to line 157. This is the section of code where your program handles the *WM_PAINT* message:

```
case WM_PAINT:
    hdc = BeginPaint(hWnd, &ps);
    // TODO: Add any drawing code here...
    RECT rt;
    GetClientRect(hWnd, &rt);
    DrawText(hdc, szHello, strlen(szHello), &rt, DT_CENTER);
    EndPaint(hWnd, &ps);
    break;
```

To begin the drawing process, your program must call the *BeginPaint()* Windows API function. This function returns a *handle* to the device context. The *GetClientRect()* function passes a pointer to a *RECT* structure to get the area in your window where you may draw your text and graphics. In this rectangle, the point (0,0) is the upper-left corner of the window. The *x* coordinate increases as you move to the right, and the y-coordinate increases as you move down. Then the *DrawText()* function passes the text to the driver program, which will write the text to the screen.

After your program has done its drawing, it must call the *EndPaint()* function to inform Windows that it is finished. If your program returns from the *WM_PAINT* handler code without calling *EndPaint()*, Windows again will send the *WM_PAINT* message, causing your program to repeat the drawing over and again.

Using Graphics Objects

Because your program is responsible for drawing the contents of your window, the Windows API provides a number of graphics objects to help you perform the drawing operation. The *pen* object, for example, determines the width and color of lines you draw in the window. The *font* determines the style of text. Table 21.1 summarizes the graphics objects.

Table 21.1. Windows Graphics Drawing Objects

Graphics Object	Purpose
font	Determines the style of text drawn in the window.
pen	Determines the color and width of lines.
brush	Determines the background color and the color used to fill shapes.
bitmap	Usually used to display graphics in the window.
palette	An array of the colors available on the output device.
path	The figure described by drawing operations.
region	A shape that describes an area in the window.

In this lesson, you will be concerned with the font, pen, and brush. The device context contains a default font, pen, and brush, which you may use to draw, or you may create your own. If you create objects, you should remember to delete the objects. In 32-bit Windows such as Window 95 or Windows 98, when your program exits, the operating system will delete any graphics object you create. However, you should practice deleting objects when you are finished to avoid using too much memory.

In addition, an unwritten rule of programming is "Leave it like you found it." When you use an object other than the default, you should restore the default object. If you practice this rule, you will always start from a known condition. Always save the value of the default object in a variable, then select the default object before deleting a new object. Deleting an object while you have it selected in the device context leaves the device context in an unknown state.

Using the same sequence you used in the last section, create a new Win32 project, except name the project *Frst-Graf.cpp*. Again, locate the paint code beginning at line 157 and modify the code so it looks like the following:

```
case WM_PAINT:
    hdc = BeginPaint(hWnd, &ps);
    // TODO: Add any drawing code here...
    RECT rt;
    HBRUSH hBrush, hOldBrush;
    GetClientRect(hWnd, &rt);
    hBrush = CreateSolidBrush (RGB(0, 255, 255));
    hOldBrush = (HBRUSH) SelectObject (hdc, hBrush);
    Ellipse (hdc, rt.left, rt.top, rt.right, rt.bottom);
    SelectObject (hdc, hOldBrush);
    EndPaint(hWnd, &ps);
```

```
// Delete the brush we created
   DeleteObject (hBrush);
   break;
```

When you compile and run *FrstGraf.cpp,* you will see the window shown in Figure 21.1.

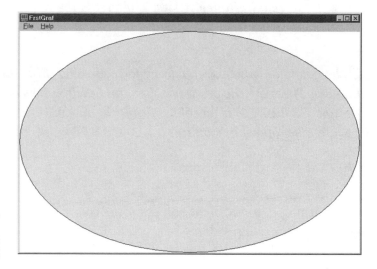

Figure 21.1

Your first graphic program draws a large ellipse filled with cyan.

This code declares the variable to hold the values of (or handles to) the default brush, *hOldBrush,* and the brush you will create, *hBrush.* The *CreateSolidBrush()* function creates the new brush using a color value of cyan. Next, you select your new brush using the *SelectObject(),* specifying the device context and the new brush. *SelectObject()* returns the handle of the current brush (which, at this point, is the default brush) as a *void* pointer, so you need to cast the function to *HBRUSH.*

Next, your program draws an ellipse. The device context fills the ellipse with the brush you selected. The *Ellipse()* function arguments are the device context in which you are drawing and the corners of the rectangle that will contain the ellipse.

Finally, *FrstGraf.cpp* selects the original brush, again using *SelectObject(),* then notifies Windows that it has finished drawing by calling the *EndPaint()* function.

Success HINT: Creating Colors

Functions that use a color value such as CreateSolidBrush() *require a* COLOR-REF *value.* COLORREF *is a 32-bit value containing the red, green, and blue components in the lowest three bytes. You can construct this value using the* RGB *macro.* RGB *requires three values. The first is the red component, the second is the green component, and the third is the blue component.*

All the colors on your screen can be formed using different values of red, green, and blue. These are the primary *colors, and their values range from 0 to 255. For example,* RGB(0,0,0) *is no colors, or black, and* RGB(255,255,255) *is all colors, or white. The following produces a* COLORREF *value for yellow:*

```
RGB(255, 255, 0);
```

In FrstGraf.cpp, *try different values for the colors to see what effect different values have on the ellipse color.*

Drawing Text in a Window

To write text to a window, you need to select a *font,* a collection of images that represent characters such as the uppercase and lowercase alphabet, the numbers, and the punctuation marks. Some fonts, such as WingDings, contain no letters, but instead contain various shapes such as a telephone, an envelope, and the signs of the Zodiac. When you installed Windows, you also installed some basic fonts, but the fonts installed on your computer will depend upon many factors. Many applications install their own fonts. To get a list of the fonts on your system, use the following steps:

1. Select the Start button from the task bar at the bottom of your screen.

2. About halfway up the Start menu is an item labeled "Settings." Move the cursor to "Settings" and a submenu will appear.

3. Select "Control Panel" from the submenu under "Settings."

4. When the Control Panel window appears, double-click the mouse on the item labeled "Fonts."

The list shows all the fonts available to your programs. To see a sample of a font, double-click the mouse on the font name.

Before your program can use a font, you must load it into memory using one of the Windows API functions. In this lesson, you will use the *CreateFontIndirect()* function, but first you need to learn how to set the size of a font to make the text size appear the same regardless of your display screen.

Printers measure the size of a font in *points*, which is about $\frac{1}{72}$ inch, which does not vary according to your display screen. Windows, however, measures fonts in terms of pixels, which will vary according to your display. You need to convert the size in points to the size in pixels. To do this, you need to know how many pixels there are per inch on your screen. The formula for converting pixels to points is shown here:

```
-MulDiv(PointSize, GetDeviceCaps(hdc, LOGPIXELSY), 72);
```

The *GetDeviceCaps()* function returns the number of pixels per inch for the output device (in this case, your screen). If you want your text to be $\frac{1}{4}$ inch high, you would use a value of 18 for *PointSize* (72 times $\frac{1}{4}$ inch is 18). To load a font into memory using *CreateFontIndirect()*, you need to enter this value in a *LOGFONT* structure (in Lesson 20, "Using Structures in Visual C++ to Group Related Data," you learned that a *structure* is a mechanism that lets you group related values into a single variable).

In the Visual Studio, create another Win32 Application project using the steps at the beginning of this lesson. Make the project name *Font*. Open the *Font.cpp* file and again locate the drawing code at line 157 and modify it to look like the following code:

```
case WM_PAINT:
    hdc = BeginPaint(hWnd, &ps);
    // TODO: Add any drawing code here...
    RECT rt;
    LOGFONT lf;
    HFONT hFont, hOldFont;
    memset (&lf, '\0', sizeof (LOGFONT));
    lf.lfHeight = -MulDiv(18, GetDeviceCaps(hdc,
                          LOGPIXELSY), 72);
    strcpy (lf.lfFaceName, "Times New Roman");
    hFont = CreateFontIndirect (&lf);
    hOldFont = (HFONT) SelectObject (hdc, hFont);
    GetClientRect(hWnd, &rt);
    DrawText(hdc, szHello, strlen(szHello), &rt, DT_CENTER);
    EndPaint(hWnd, &ps);
```

```
    DeleteObject (hFont);
    break;
```

When you compile and run *Font.cpp*, the window will display "Hello World" in large characters using the Times New Roman font. Try varying the point size and select a different font from your font list to see the result.

Of course, you program will need to display more than one line of text. The *DrawText()* function uses the rectangle *rt* to draw the text, so if you write more than one line, the new text will just overwrite the previous text. To write multiple lines, you need to adjust the position of the rectangle. To do this, modify the code, as shown in the following code. Notice that you are adding two new variables:

```
case WM_PAINT:
    hdc = BeginPaint(hWnd, &ps);
    // TODO: Add any drawing code here...
    RECT rt;
    int iBottom, iStep;
    LOGFONT lf;
    HFONT hFont, hOldFont;
    memset (&lf, '\0', sizeof (LOGFONT));
    lf.lfHeight = -MulDiv(18, GetDeviceCaps(hdc,
                            LOGPIXELSY), 72);
    strcpy (lf.lfFaceName, "Times New Roman");
    hFont = CreateFontIndirect (&lf);
    hOldFont = (HFONT) SelectObject (hdc, hFont);
    GetClientRect(hWnd, &rt);
    iBottom = rt.bottom;
    if (lf.lfHeight < 0)
        iStep = -lf.lfHeight;
    else
        iStep = lf.lfHeight;
    rt.bottom = iStep;
    while (rt.top < iBottom)
    {
        DrawText(hdc, szHello, strlen(szHello),
                &rt, DT_CENTER);
        rt.top += iStep;
        rt.bottom += iStep;
```

```
    }
    SelectObject (hdc, hOldFont);
    EndPaint(hWnd, &ps);
    DeleteObject (hFont);
    break;
```

Recompile and run the program. You will get a window similar to Figure 21.2.

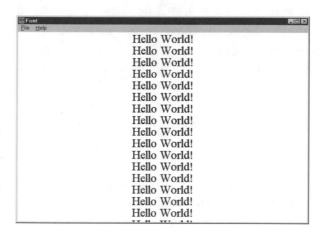

Figure 21.2

By changing the size and position of the rectangle, you can write multiple lines to your window.

In the *DrawText()* function, the *DT_CENTER* value tells the driver to draw the text horizontally centered in the window. Some other values you may want to try are *DT_LEFT* to set the text at the left side of the rectangle and *DT_RIGHT* to set the text on the right side of the rectangle.

Drawing Lines and Shapes

Earlier, you drew an ellipse in your window using the Windows API function *Ellipse()*. To draw the ellipse, you used the default *pen* in the device context. The default pen draws a black line one pixel wide. By changing the pen, you may draw the line forming the ellipse using different colors and widths.

In Windows, the selection of a pen can be very complex, offering many different drawing styles. In this lesson, you will use the *CreatePen()* Windows API function to create a pen. Using the steps provided earlier in this lesson, create a new Win32 Application project called *Pen*. Open the *Pen.cpp* and locate line 157 where the drawing code begins. Modify the code as shown here:

```
case WM_PAINT:
    hdc = BeginPaint(hWnd, &ps);
    // TODO: Add any drawing code here...
    RECT rt;
    HPEN hRedPen, hOldPen;
    hRedPen = CreatePen (PS_SOLID, 4, RGB (255, 0, 0));
    hOldPen = (HPEN) SelectObject (hdc, hRedPen);
    GetClientRect(hWnd, &rt);
    Ellipse (hdc, rt.left, rt.top, rt.right, rt.bottom);
    SelectObject (hdc, hOldPen);
    EndPaint(hWnd, &ps);
    DeleteObject (hRedPen);
    break;
```

When you compile and run *Pen.cpp*, you will see an ellipse drawn with a red line that is four pixels wide. The rectangle (the *bounding* rectangle) determines the size of the ellipse. You can change the sides of the rectangle to adjust the size and position of the ellipse. In the following code, you create two pens, then adjust the size and position of the ellipse so it appears in the middle of your window. In addition, you will draw the bounding rectangle around the ellipse using a green pen that is two pixels wide. Modify the drawing code in *Pen.cpp* so it looks like the following:

```
case WM_PAINT:
    hdc = BeginPaint(hWnd, &ps);
    // TODO: Add any drawing code here...
    RECT rt;
    HPEN hRedPen, hGreenPen, hOldPen;
// Create red and green pens
    hRedPen = CreatePen (PS_SOLID, 4, RGB (255, 0, 0));
    hGreenPen = CreatePen (PS_SOLID, 2, RGB (0, 255, 0));
    GetClientRect(hWnd, &rt);
    rt.left = rt.right / 4;
    rt.right = 3 * rt.left;
    rt.top = rt.bottom / 4;
    rt.bottom = 3 * rt.top;
```

```
    hOldPen = (HPEN) SelectObject (hdc, hGreenPen);
    Rectangle (hdc, rt.left, rt.top, rt.right, rt.bottom);
    SelectObject (hdc, hRedPen);
    Ellipse (hdc, rt.left, rt.top, rt.right, rt.bottom);
    SelectObject (hdc, hOldPen);
    EndPaint(hWnd, &ps);
// Delete the objects
    DeleteObject (hRedPen);
    DeleteObject (hGreenPen);
    break;
```

Recompile the *Pen* project and run the program. You will see a window similar to Figure 21.3.

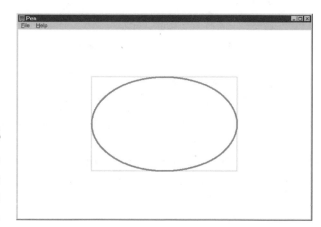

Figure 21.3

Using two pens, you can draw the bounding rectangle in one color and the ellipse in another color.

Notice that the lines for the green rectangle and the red ellipse overlap so that the ellipse writes on top of the rectangle. To correct this, try adding *PS_INSIDEFRAME* to the pen style:

```
hRedPen = CreatePen (PS_SOLID | PS_INSIDEFRAME, 4,
                RGB (255, 0, 0));
```

As an experiment, try changing the drawing order. Draw the ellipse first, then the square. You'll notice that the ellipse does not show up. When you draw the rectangle, the driver program fills the inside of the rectangle with the default brush, white, and erases the ellipse. The order in which you draw the shapes is important. You can change the *raster* mode by using the *SetROP2()* Windows API function to make the ellipse visible, as in the following code:

```
case WM_PAINT:
    hdc = BeginPaint(hWnd, &ps);
    // TODO: Add any drawing code here...
    RECT rt;
    HPEN hRedPen, hGreenPen, hOldPen;
    int iOldROP;
    hRedPen = CreatePen (PS_SOLID, 4, RGB (255, 0, 0));
    hGreenPen = CreatePen (PS_SOLID, 2, RGB (0, 255, 0));
    GetClientRect(hWnd, &rt);
    rt.left = rt.right / 4;
    rt.right = 3 * rt.left;
    rt.top = rt.bottom / 4;
    rt.bottom = 3 * rt.top;
// Set the raster mode to combine the pen and brush colors
iOldROP = SetROP2 (hdc, R2_MASKPEN);
    hOldPen = (HPEN) SelectObject (hdc, hGreenPen);
    Ellipse (hdc, rt.left, rt.top, rt.right, rt.bottom);
    SelectObject (hdc, hRedPen);
    Rectangle (hdc, rt.left, rt.top, rt.right, rt.bottom);
    SelectObject (hdc, hOldPen);
    EndPaint (hWnd, &ps);
    DeleteObject (hRedPen);
    DeleteObject (hGreenPen);
// Restore the old raster mode
    SetROP2 (hdc, iOldROP);
    break;
```

The *R2_MASKPEN* value causes the device driver to use only the colors that are common to the pen and the brush. The background brush is white, so the resulting color is simply the pen color.

As a final experiment, try changing the styles for the red and green pens using values from Table 21.2 to see the results.

Table 21.1 Windows Pen Styles

Pen Style	Description
PS_SOLID	Used to draw a solid line.
PS_DASH	Used to draw a dashed line.
PS_DOT	Used to draw a dotted line.
PS_DASHDOT	Draws a line with alternating dashes and dots.
PS_DASHDOTDOT	Draws a line with a dash alternating with two dots.
PS_NULL	An invisible pen.
PS_USERSTYLE	Used only with the extended pen. See text.
PS_INSIDEFRAME	A solid pen used to shrink a figure so that it fits into a bounding rectangle. Use this style along with one of the other styles.

The Windows API also contains a function for drawing lines. To draw a line, however, you first must set the *current position*. The device context maintains a drawing position where you last performed a drawing operation. At the beginning, the current position is at the upper-left corner of the window, at position (0,0). Not all drawing functions change this position. For example, the *Rectangle()* and *Ellipse()* functions drew the lines from the position you specified in the call to the function and do not change the current position.

A line, however, starts at the current position and extends to the point you specify. Afterward, the new value of the current position is the point you specified as the end of the line. You may change the current position using the *MoveToEx()* function, then draw the line using the *LineTo()* function.

Create a new Win32 Application project called *Line*. After the Visual Studio creates the project files, open the *Line.cpp* file and scroll to line 157. Change the drawing code as shown here:

```
case WM_PAINT:
    hdc = BeginPaint(hWnd, &ps);
    // TODO: Add any drawing code here...
    RECT rt;
    int cx1, cx2, cy1, cy2;
    HPEN hBluePen, hOrangePen, hGreenPen, hOldPen;
    hOrangePen = CreatePen (PS_SOLID, 2, RGB (255, 128, 0));
    hBluePen = CreatePen (PS_SOLID, 2, RGB (0, 0, 255));
    hGreenPen = CreatePen (PS_SOLID, 2, RGB (0, 255, 0));
    GetClientRect(hWnd, &rt);
    cx1 = rt.right / 4;
```

```
cx2 = 3 * cx1;
cy1 = rt.bottom / 4;
cy2 = 3 * cy1;
hOldPen = (HPEN) SelectObject (hdc, hOrangePen);
MoveToEx (hdc, cx1, cy1, NULL);
LineTo (hdc, cx2, cy2);
SelectObject (hdc, hBluePen);
LineTo (hdc, cx1, cy2);
SelectObject (hdc, hGreenPen);
LineTo (hdc, cx1, cy1);
SelectObject (hdc, hOldPen);
EndPaint (hWnd, &ps);
DeleteObject (hOrangePen);
DeleteObject (hBluePen);
DeleteObject (hGreenPen);
break;
```

The *Line.cpp* program draws a triangle using a different color for each leg of the triangle, as shown in Figure 21.4.

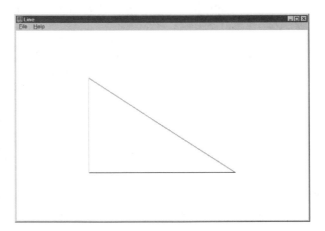

Figure 21.4

The LineTo() *function draws from the current position to the point you specify. Afterward, the new current position is the end point you specified.*

Notice that the last argument to the *MoveToEx()* function is *NULL*. You can pass a pointer to a *POINT* structure, and the function will fill in the values of the current position before you move to the new position, as in the following:

```
RECT rc;
MoveToEx (hdc, cx1, cy1, &rc);
```

This allows you to return to the original position instead of using a line's end point as the new starting position.

What You Must Know

In this lesson, you learned the basics of using the Windows *graphics device interface* and how to use the device context to draw text and shapes in a window. You learned how to create objects such as pens, fonts, and brushes and how to select these objects in the device context to draw to a window. You also learned how to draw text and lines in your window by responding to the Windows *WM_PAINT* message. In Lesson 22, "Getting Started with Classes," you will begin learning about Visual C++ *classes*. The class is the basic building block for object-oriented programming in Visual C++. You also will learn how to write classes for text and graphics and how to use these classes to draw on your screen. Before you continue with Lesson 22, however, make sure you have learned the following key points:

- A window is like an artist's canvas. Anything you add to the window is a graphic, even text.

- The device context provides an interface between your program and the output device, such as your screen.

- The font, brush, and pen are graphics objects you create to help you draw to a window.

- To draw text on the screen, you use a font object. To draw lines and shapes, you use a pen object. To fill an area in the window, you use a brush object.

- You should always delete a graphics object when you no longer need to use the object.

Lesson 22

Getting Started with Classes

The *class* is the primary tool for Visual C++ object-oriented programming. The class shares many properties with the *structure*, which you learned about in Lesson 20, "Using Structures In Visual C++ to Group Related Data." Structures may, but generally do not, contain functions. Classes, on the other hand, almost always contain functions to set, retrieve, and manipulate the information in the class. Visual C++ lets your program define an object's properties. For example, in the previous lesson, you drew a triangle using discrete lines in three function calls. With a C++ class, you could define the triangle using its three vertices and then let a class member function perform the drawing using a single function call. In this lesson, you will learn how to define and use C++ classes. By the time you finish this lesson, you will understand the following key concepts:

♦ A class definition provides the compiler with a template. The compiler then uses that template when your program creates objects of the class, much the same as you create variables of *int*, *double, char,* and so on.

♦ To define a class, you specify the name of the class using the *class* keyword. You then include the class variables (properties) and function (methods) inside a set of braces, much like a structure.

♦ To access a class variable or function, you use the *member* operator, a period, using the class object name and the class member name.

♦ Your program may declare pointers to class objects. Each class object has a special pointer called *this* that points to itself, making class objects aware of their own variables and functions and the class object's own location in memory.

Introducing the C++ Class

Object-oriented programming focuses on the properties of a system and the methods used to manipulate those properties. A property is a value or characteristic of an object, essentially a variable. A method basically is a function that lets you set or retrieve a property or perform an operation on an object. The Visual C++ class is the primary building block for object-oriented programming in C++. In Lesson 20, you learned how to define a *structure*. Classes share many characteristics with structures, and you declare classes in very much the same way you declare a structure:

```
class CClassName
{
    int    m_iDataMember;   // A data member
    void   ShowData ();     // A function member prototype
};
```

A common practice is to prefix member variable names with *m_* to indicate "a member of" the class. This helps to distinguish them from other variables in your program.

When you define a class, you create a new data type. After you have defined a class, you may declare variables—objects—of the class as you would any other variable of any other data type, as shown here:

```
CClassName  ObjectOne, ObjectTwo;
```

Each instance of a class—each object you declare—has its own variables. In the preceding declaration, *ObjectOne* has its own *m_iDataMember* variable that is distinct from the *m_iDataMember* variable of *ObjectTwo*. The variables in each instance may have different values.

Class member variables and functions may be given an *access specifier*. You will learn more about access specifiers and how to use them in Lesson 24, "Understanding Class Scope and Access Control." However, you need to be aware of access specifiers to begin your study of classes. In this lesson, you will need to use *public* access, which makes the variables and functions available to the entire program, and *private* access, which makes the variables and functions available only to statements in member functions.

The default access for class members is *private*, so to access them using non-member functions, you will have to change their access to *public*. (Structures also use access specifiers, but the default for structure members is *public*.) The following program, *FrstClas.cpp*, uses a structure to define a point, then uses an object of the structure to store the coordinates of a point:

```
#include    <iostream.h>
#include    <math.h>
```

```
class CPoint
{
public:
    int    x;
    int    y;
};

void main (void)
{
    CPoint point;
    int iAngle = 60;
    int iRadius = 300;

    double fAngle = iAngle / 57.29578;
    point.x =  int (iRadius * cos (fAngle));

    point.y = int (iRadius * sin (fAngle));
    cout << "The point on the circle is at ("
         << point.x << ", " << point.y
         << ")" << endl;
}
```

Notice that the member variables are *public*. Without the *public* label, the access for the variables would default to *private*, and the statements in *main* would not be able to access the values. In the next section, you will set the variables to *private* and then use *public* functions to set and retrieve the values.

Understanding the Similarity between Classes and Structures

In Lesson 20, you learned about structures, which let your program store values of different types in a single variable. Structures and classes have many characteristics in common. Classes also let your program store values of different types. For example, you learned that a structure may contain functions. These functions may be *inline* when you define them within the structure definition, or ordinary member functions when you define them outside the structure definition.

Visual C++ classes are much like structures. You may store variables in classes. In addition, classes may contain member functions. You declare variables and functions as members of a class in the same way you declared members of a structure.

In the previous section, you defined and used your first class, one that you used to hold the coordinates of a point. You could have defined a structure to perform the same task:

```
struct POINT
{
    int    x;
    int    y;
};
```

Notice that in defining the structure, you did not need to use the *public* keyword. In a structure, the member variables and functions are *public* by default. You do not need to use the keyword if you want the members to be public. In a class, all the member variables and functions are *private* by default, and to make them public, you must use the *public* keyword. This is one of the major differences between structures and keywords.

Using structures, you defined an external function by declaring the function as a member of the structure, then writing its definition using the *scope resolution operator,* the double colon (::):

```
struct BAUDRATE
{
    char    szRate[8];
    long    lRate;
    void    SetSpeed (long lSpeed);
};
void BAUDRATE::SetSpeed (long lSpeed)
{
    sprintf (szRate, "%ld", lSpeed);
    lRate = lSpeed;
}
```

You could just as easily have defined a class to hold the member variables and functions, and defined the class and member function in much the same way, by using the *public* keyword to make the members public:

```
class CBaudRate
{
```

```
public:
    char    m_szRate[8];
    long    m_lRate;
    void    SetSpeed (long lSpeed);
};
void CBaudRate::SetSpeed (long lSpeed)
{
    sprintf (m_szRate, "%ld", lSpeed);
    m_lRate = lSpeed;
}
```

You may use structures and classes interchangeably in many circumstances. However, as you will learn as you continue your lessons, classes have many properties beyond the properties of structures.

Defining Classes

When you define a class in Visual C++, you give the compiler a template. The definition creates a new data type in your program, but it does not set aside any memory for the class. Once defined, you may declare variables using the class name. The compiler then uses this definition when you declare an *instance* of a class by creating a variable of the new data type.

You define a class in Visual C++ using the *class* keyword followed by an open brace. You then declare the variables and functions you want as members of the class. You then end the definition with a closing brace followed by a semicolon.

It is common practice to keep variable members of classes *private* and access and set the values through *public* functions, as in the following program, *Class2.cpp*:

```
#include    <iostream.h>

class CPoint
{
private:
    int    x;
    int    y;

public:
```

```
    void  SetX (int cx);
    void  SetY (int cy);

    int   GetX ();
    int   GetY ();
};

void CPoint::SetX (int cx)
{
    x = cx;
}

void CPoint::SetY (int cy)
{
    y = cy;
}

int CPoint::GetX ()
{
    return (x);
}

int CPoint::GetY ()
{
    return (y);
}

void main (void)
{
    CPoint point;
    int iAngle = 60;
    int iRadius = 300;

    double fAngle = iAngle / 57.29578;
    point.SetX (int (iRadius * cos (fAngle)));
    point.SetY (int (iRadius * sin (fAngle)));
```

```
        cout << "The point on the circle is at ("
             << point.GetX() << ", " << point.GetY() << ")"
             << endl;
}
```

Notice that the member variables are *private*. This limits access to the variables to the member functions. As a general rule, you should try to keep member variables *private*. This isolates them from accidental modification by statements in functions outside the class. Instead, define member functions to set and retrieve the values. In this way, you can provide error-checking on the values. For example, suppose you wanted the values always to be positive. You could modify the *SetX()* function as follows:

```
void SetX (int cx)
{
    x = abs(cx);
};
```

If an expression in your program passes a negative value to the *SetX()*, the function will convert it to a positive value using the *abs()* library function.

Notice that in the class definition, you used the *public* and *private* keywords to set the *access level* of the class members. When you use one of the access keywords, all functions and variable members from that point inherit that level of access. You may change the access level at any point using one of the other keywords. In the preceding program, you used the *private* keyword to limit access to the variables *x* and *y*. Then you used the *public* keyword to declare the functions to access and set these member variables.

You may use the access keywords as often as you need them. For example, you could have two, three, or even more sections of your class definition declared *public*.

Using the Visual C++ ClassView Pane

The Visual C++ development environment, Visual Studio, contains several tools to help you declare and manage the classes in your programs. One of these that you will get to know very well is the ClassView pane of the Workspace Window. This tool normally is at the far left of the Visual Studio. Click your mouse on the ClassView tab at the bottom of the window to select the ClassView pane. Depending upon the settings for your computer, only the first few characters of the name may be visible on the tab, as in Figure 22.1.

Figure 22.1

The figure at left shows where you will find the Workspace window in the Visual Studio. The figure at right shows the ClassView pane with a list of classes in a project. Clicking the mouse on the "+" sign next to a class name expands the list to show members of the class.

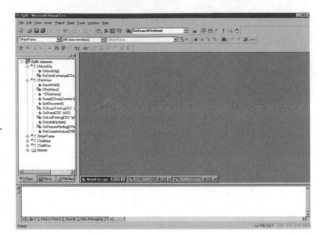

The ClassView pane lists all the classes and structures in your Visual C++ project in a *tree control*. (The tree control is one of the Windows controls mentioned in Lesson 19, "Writing a Windows Program." You will learn more about this control in Lesson 30, "Using Windows Controls.") In the tree control structure in the ClassView pane, your classes are the main branches of the tree (a special branch at the very bottom is for *global* variables you declare in your program). You can expand these branches to see the members of the individual classes.

In this control, if you double-click your mouse on a class name, the Visual Studio will open and display the file containing the class definition in an editing window. If you double-click the mouse on a variable name, the Visual Studio will move the caret to the point where you declared the variable. Finally, if you double-click the mouse on a member function name, Visual Studio will open the source code file and display the function definition.

Create a Windows program project using the following steps. Then you will add a class to the program using the ClassView pane. Next, you will add a member variable and function to the class.

1. Select New from the File menu of the Visual Studio. When the New dialog box appears, click your mouse on the Projects tab to select the page containing a list of project types.

2. Select the "Win32 Application" item from the list of project types. In the Project Name box at the upper-right, enter **Draw**. Click your mouse on the OK button to start the project wizard.

3. When the wizard starts, select A Typical "Hello, World" Application, then click the mouse on the Finish button.

3. Finally, to create the project, select the OK button on the New Project Information dialog box that appears.

Select the ClassView pane of the Workspace window, then click your mouse on the "+" sign next to the "Draw classes" item. Right now, your project should have no classes, and the only item branch should be the Globals item. *Right-click* the mouse on the "Draw Classes" item. On the menu that pops up, select the New Class item. You will get the New Class dialog box, as shown in Figure 22.2.

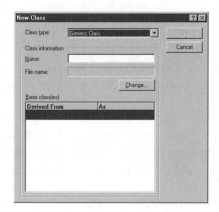

Figure 22.2

Using the New Class dialog box, you can easily add classes to your Visual C++ project.

The Class Type box of the New Class dialog box should have "Generic Class" selected. In the Name field, type **CCircle** (yes, two capital Cs; in Visual C++, programmers usually start all class names with a capital C). Notice that the Visual C++ program fills in the File name box with *Circle.cpp* as the name of the file that will hold your class. Windows projects tend to be large, and it is a good idea to keep each class in a file by itself. At the bottom of the dialog box is a large area labeled "Base class(es)." Later, when you learn about derived classes, you will use this box to *derive* new classes from other classes. For now, leave this area blank.

Click your mouse on the OK button to create the new class. Notice in the ClassView pane that Visual Studio has added *CCircle* to the class list. Click your mouse on the "+" sign next to *CCircle* to expand the branch. You should see two functions. The first, *CCircle()*, is the class *constructor,* and the second, *~CCircle(),* is the class destructor. You will learn about these functions in Lesson 23, "Understanding Constructors and Destructors."

Next, right-click the mouse on the *CCircle* class name in the ClassView pane. From the menu that pops up, select Add Member Variable. A dialog box like that at the left in Figure 22.3 will appear.

Figure 22.3

Use the Add Member Variable dialog box at the left to add variables to your class. The Add Member Function dialog box at the right will help you to add functions to your class.

In the Variable Type field of the Add Member Variable dialog box, type **POINT**. Then in the Variable Name field, type **m_ptCenter**. Select Private in the section labeled "Access," then click your mouse on the OK button. Notice that Visual Studio has added *m_ptCenter* to your *CCircle* class. The cyan box next to *m_ptCenter* indicates it is a *member* variable, and the small lock symbol indicates it is a *private* variable.

Next, again right-click the mouse on the *CCircle* class name in the ClassView pane. From the menu that pops up, select Add Member function. A dialog box like that at the right in Figure 22.3 will appear. In the Function Type field, type **void**. In the Function Declaration field, type **SetCenter (POINT& point)**. Select the Public box for the Access. For now, leave the Static and Virtual boxes *unchecked*. Click the mouse on the OK button.

The Visual Studio has added the function to your *CCircle* class. It has added the declaration to the *Circle.h* file and the function definition to the *Circle.cpp* file. Notice that a function has a magenta box next to it in the ClassView pane as opposed to a cyan box for a variable. Double-click the mouse on the *m_ptCenter* item. The Visual Studio will display the file containing the class definition, and the caret will be on the line where you declared the variable *m_ptPoint*.

Next, double-click the mouse on the *SetCenter()* function item in the ClassView pane. The Visual Studio will open and display the source file with the caret placed at the definition of the *SetCenter()* function.

Use the same technique to add another private variable, *m_iRadius,* to the class. Then add the functions *void SetRadius (int radius)* and *Draw (HDC hdc)* to your class. When you finish, your class definition in *Circle.h* should look like the following:

```
class CCircle
{
public:
    void Draw (HDC hdc);
    void SetRadius (int radius);
    void SetCenter (POINT& point);
    CCircle();
```

```
    virtual ~CCircle();

private:
    int m_iRadius;
    POINT m_ptCenter;
};
```

Next, add code to your *Circle.cpp* file that looks like the following code:

```
// Circle.cpp: implementation of the CCircle class.
//
//////////////////////////////////////////////////////////

#include "stdafx.h"
#include "Circle.h"


//////////////////////////////////////////////////////////
// Construction/Destruction
//////////////////////////////////////////////////////////

CCircle::CCircle()
{

}

CCircle::~CCircle()
{

}

void CCircle::SetCenter(POINT &point)
{
    m_ptCenter = point;
}

void CCircle::SetRadius(int radius)
```

```
{
    m_iRadius = radius;
}


void CCircle::Draw(HDC hdc)
{
    RECT rc;
    rc.left = m_ptCenter.x - m_iRadius;
    rc.right = m_ptCenter.x + m_iRadius;
    rc.top = m_ptCenter.y - m_iRadius;
    rc.bottom = m_ptCenter.y + m_iRadius;
    HPEN hPen = CreatePen (PS_SOLID, 2, RGB(255, 0, 255));
    HPEN hOldPen = (HPEN) SelectObject (hdc, hPen);
    Ellipse (hdc, rc.left, rc.top, rc.right, rc.bottom);
    SelectObject (hdc, hOldPen);
    DeleteObject (hPen);
 }
```

At the top of the *Draw.cpp* file, add the following line to include the *Circle.h* file:

```
#include "Circle.h"
```

Finally, in the *Draw.cpp* source file, move to the *WndProc()* function and change the *WM_PAINT* case of the *switch* statement to look like the following. (Notice that you enclose all the code in a set of braces to make it a compound statement. You need the braces because the *circle* object initializes itself using its *constructor*. Without the braces, you would get an error from the compiler.):

```
case WM_PAINT:
{
    hdc = BeginPaint(hWnd, &ps);
    // TODO: Add any drawing code here...
    RECT rt;
    CCircle circle;
    GetClientRect(hWnd, &rt);
    POINT point;
    point.x = 150;
    point.y = 150;
```

```
    circle.SetCenter (point);
    circle.SetRadius (100);
    circle.Draw (hdc);
    EndPaint(hWnd, &ps);
    break;
}
```

Compile and run this program. You now have a *CCircle* class that can draw itself. You need only change the center and radius to draw the circle in different locations and sizes in your window. Practice using different values for the center and radius. Try adding a *CSquare* class to your project using the same techniques. Compare your code with the project on the companion Web site *(http://www.prima-tech.com/books/book/5536/903).*

Understanding the *this* Pointer

In Lesson 16, "Changing Parameter Values within a Function," you learned that you can get the pointer to a variable by using the *address operator,* the ampersand symbol (&). When you declare an instance of a class as a variable, you also may get a pointer to the class variable and use it the same way you would use other pointer variables. You can pass the pointer as an argument to a function call.

Sometimes a class needs to refer to itself. To do this, it needs to know its own address. In C++, classes and structures have a special pointer variable called *this.* You don't need to declare a *this* variable; it is a part of the class itself, and you cannot change its value. In addition, *this* may be used only within member functions, but you may use it in calls to other functions where you need to identify the class *instance.* Each instance of a class has its own *this* pointer.

To show that the *this* pointer is unique to each instance, add a second circle to the *Draw* project code. Change the *WM_PAINT* portion of the *Draw.cpp* code to look like the following:

```
case WM_PAINT:
{
    hdc = BeginPaint(hWnd, &ps);
    // TODO: Add any drawing code here...
    RECT rt;
    CCircle circle1, circle2;
    CCircle *pCircle;
    GetClientRect(hWnd, &rt);
    POINT point;
```

```
      point.x = 150;
      point.y = 150;
// Get the pointer to circle1 and set its variables
    pCircle = &circle1;
    pCircle->SetCenter (point);
    pCircle->SetRadius (100);
// Now get the pointer to circle2 and set its variables.
// Use the same center, but make the radius smaller.
    pCircle = &circle2;
    pCircle->SetCenter (point);
    pCircle->SetRadius (50);
    circle1.Draw (hdc);
    circle2.Draw (hdc);
    EndPaint(hWnd, &ps);
    break;
}
```

Compile and run the program, and you will see one circle drawn inside the other.

Now, using the ClassView pane of the Workspace window, add a function to the *CCircle* class. The function type is *CCircle**, and the function name will be *GetCircle()*. Next, add a line to the function in *Circle.cpp* so that the function looks like the following:

```
CCircle* CCircle::GetCircle ()
{
    return (this);
}
```

You did not have to declare the *this* variable, and you did not have to assign it a value. Now change the code in the *WM_PAINT* portion of *Draw.cpp*, as shown here:

Change

```
    pCircle = &circle1;
```

to

```
    pCircle = circle1.GetCircle();
```

Change

```
pCircle = &circle2;
```

to

```
pCircle = circle2.GetCircle();
```

Compile and run the program once again. You should see the same result, a smaller circle drawn inside a larger circle. Returning the *this* pointer from a function is the same as taking the address of the class instance and assigning it to a pointer variable.

You will use the *this* pointer in Lesson 36, "Overloading Functions and Operators."

Understanding the *static* Modifier for Class Members

Earlier in this lesson, when you added variables and functions to a class using the ClassView pane of the Workspace window, you might have noticed a check box on the dialog boxes to declare the variable or function as *static*. In a Visual C++ class, *static* variables and functions have special properties, and some special limitations.

Also, in the first part of this lesson, you learned that each instance of a class has its own set of variables, and the variables in each instance may have their own values. When you declare a variable *static*, however, there is only one copy of the variable, and all instances of the class must share the value it contains. If one instance of a class changes the value of a *static* variable, it changes the value for all instances of the class.

In addition, you may assign a value to a *static* member variable even before you declare an instance of the class. To declare a *static* member variable, you must declare it twice, once as a member of the class and a second time as a global variable. Using the *Draw* project you created earlier, add a member variable for the color of the circle. Use the ClassView pane to summon the Add Member Variable dialog box. In the Variable Type field, type **static COLORREF**. In the Variable Name field, type **m_clrCircle**, and select the Public radio button. Click the mouse on the OK button, then examine the declaration in the *Circle.h* file:

```
static COLORREF m_clrCircle;
```

Next, near the top of the *Circle.cpp* source file, add the following line to declare the variable a second time and assign it a default variable:

```
COLORREF CCircle::m_clrCircle = RGB(255, 0, 255);
```

Notice that you identified it as a member of the class using the scope resolution operator, "::" but this time you did not declare it *static*. The *static* portion of the declaration is in the *Circle.h* file.

In the *Draw()* function, change the *CreatePen()* function call to use this color:

```
HPEN hPen = CreatePen (PS_SOLID, 2, m_clrCircle);
```

Compile and run the program. You will see that the *Draw()* function draws both circles in the same color.

Next, add the following line as the first line in the *WM_PAINT* section of *Draw.cpp*:

```
CCircle::m_clrCircle = RGB (0, 255, 0);
```

Notice that you are setting the color even before you declare an instance of the *CCircle* class. Recompile and run the program, and you should see both circles drawn in green, the new value of the *m_clrCircle* static variable.

You may declare functions *static* as well. You may call a *static* member function even before you declare an instance of a class. However, you should be aware that a *static* member function may not use the *this* pointer that you learned about in the last section. In addition, *static* member functions may access only *static* member variables and other *static* member functions.

Use the ClassView pane to add another function to the *CCircle* class. Enter **void** in the Function Type field and type **SetColor(COLORREF clr)** in the Function Declaration field. Select Public access, but this time check the Static box. Click the mouse on the OK button, and the Visual Studio will add the function to the class.

In the *Circle.cpp* file, change the function to the following:

```
void CCircle::SetColor(COLORREF clr)
{
    m_clrCircle = clr;
}
```

Finally, change the *WM_PAINT* code, as shown in the following code. Again, notice that you are calling the function *before* you declare an instance of the class.

Change

```
CCircle::m_clrCircle = RGB(0, 255, 0);
```

to

```
CCircle::SetColor (RGB(0, 0, 255);
```

Compile the program again and run it. You now should see both circles drawn in blue.

Once you declare an instance of the class, you can use the *member* operator to call the function as well:

```
CCircle circle;
circle.SetColor RGB(0, 255, 0);
```

What You Must Know

In this lesson, you learned how to declare and use classes in your Visual C++ programs. You also learned how to use the ClassView pane of the Workspace window to examine the classes and to access the class members by double-clicking the mouse on a member. You also learned how to use the ClassView pane to add member variables and functions to your class definitions. In addition, you learned about the *this* pointer that a class instance uses to refer to itself, and how to declare and use *static* member variables and functions. In Lesson 23, "Understanding Constructors and Destructors," you will learn how to use constructors and destructors in your classes. Before you continue with Lesson 23, however, make sure you understand the following key points about classes:

◆ A class definition is a template the compiler uses when you declare a variable using the class name (an *instance* of the class).

◆ Each instance of a class has its own set of variables that contain values that do not depend upon other instances of the class.

◆ To access a class member variable or function, you use the *member* operator. To access a member using a pointer, you use the *member pointer* operator.

◆ Each instance of a class contains a special pointer variable, *this*, that contains the address of the class instance. This pointer is different for each class instance, and you may not modify it.

◆ A class definition may contain *static* data members. You must declare these members both in the class definition and again as global variables. You may declare *static* functions as well, but these functions may access only *static* member variables and other *static* member functions.

Lesson 23

Understanding Constructors and Destructors

Y ou have learned that *objects* in Visual C++ may contain "state" information that describes how you set the values of the members of the object. The *class* is the primary tool for Visual C++ object-oriented programming. Each class contains at least two special functions called the *constructor* and the *destructor*. When you declare an instance of a class, the constructor executes automatically without you having to call it from your program. You may use the constructor to initialize member variables and to create other objects your class may need. When a variable containing an instance of a class goes out of scope, the class object is destroyed, and the destructor executes automatically. You may use the destructor to "clean up" a class instance, such as destroying any other objects your class may have created. In this lesson, you will learn how to use constructors and destructors and how to declare multiple constructors. By the time you finish this lesson, you will understand the following key concepts:

◆ To declare a constructor function, you declare a function using the same name as the class. Visual C++ recognizes functions with this name as constructors.

◆ A constructor function runs automatically when you declare an instance of a class. You may use a constructor to initialize member variables and to create other objects your class may need.

◆ You may have multiple constructor functions, but each must have a different argument list to make the constructors unique.

◆ To declare a destructor function, you declare a function using the same name as the class, but precede the name with a tilde (~); Visual C++ recognizes functions with this name as destructors.

◆ You may have one and only one destructor in a class. This function will execute automatically when a variable containing an instance of the class goes out of scope and is destroyed.

◆ Constructors and destructors may not return values, and you may not declare these functions using return types.

Understanding Constructors

When you define a class, you create a new data type in Visual C++. You then may declare an instance of the class by declaring a variable of the new data type. You may declare this variable in a function or as a global variable. You also may create an instance of a class on the *heap* using the *new* operator. You will learn how to use the heap in Lesson 32, "Using Memory Management."

When you create an instance of a class, your program executes a special function called a *constructor*. Every class has at least one constructor. If you do not include one in your class definition, the Visual C++ compiler will create a *default constructor,* which will have no parameters and no initialization code.

You declare a constructor by giving the function the same name as the class. A constructor cannot return a value, and you cannot assign it a return type. If you intend to declare instances of the class, the constructor must be *public*. (As you will see later, some classes may serve as *base class* from which you will *inherit* other classes. In these base classes, you may have a *protected* constructor). The following snippet declares a constructor for the *CCircle* class:

```
class CCircle
{
    CCircle();
};
CCircle::CCircle()
{
}
```

Notice that the constructor does not have a return type such as *void* or *int*. If you attempt to return a value from the constructor or assign the constructor a return type, the compiler will generate and print an error message.

When you added the *CCircle* class to the *Draw* project in Lesson 22, "Getting Started with Classes," using the ClassView pane of the Workspace window, the Visual Studio declared such a constructor for you when it created the class. Even if you delete the declaration and definition of the constructor, the compiler will create a default constructor when you compile your code.

Using Constructors

A constructor executes automatically whenever you declare an instance of a class. You may add statements to the constructor to initialize member variables or perform any other operations that need to be performed when your class initializes.

Using the steps from Lesson 22, create a new Win32 application named *Draw2*. Create the *CCircle* class just as you did for the *Draw* application in Lesson 22. Add the following variables to the *CCircle* class using the ClassView pane of the Workspace window:

```
POINT m_ptCenter;
int m_iRadius;
COLORREF m_clrCircle;
```

Add the *Draw()* function to *CCircle*, as follows:

```
void Draw(HDC hdc);
```

Open the *Circle.cpp* file and add code to the *Circle()* constructor and the *Draw()* function so that the file looks as follows:

```
// Circle.cpp: implementation of the CCircle class.
//
//////////////////////////////////////////////////////////////

#include "stdafx.h"
#include "Circle.h"


//////////////////////////////////////////////////////////////
// Construction/Destruction
//////////////////////////////////////////////////////////////

CCircle::CCircle()
{
    m_ptCenter.x = 200;
    m_ptCenter.y = 200;
    m_iRadius = 100;
```

```
    m_clrCircle = RGB(255, 0x0, 0x0);
}


CCircle::~CCircle()
{

}


void CCircle::Draw(HDC hdc)
{
    RECT rc;
    rc.left = m_ptCenter.x - m_iRadius;
    rc.right = m_ptCenter.x + m_iRadius;
    rc.top = m_ptCenter.y - m_iRadius;
    rc.bottom = m_ptCenter.y + m_iRadius;
    HPEN hPen = CreatePen (PS_SOLID, 2, m_clrCircle);
    HPEN hOldPen = (HPEN) SelectObject (hdc, hPen);
    Ellipse (hdc, rc.left, rc.top, rc.right, rc.bottom);
    SelectObject (hdc, hOldPen);
    DeleteObject (hPen);
}
```

Open the *Draw2.cpp* file and add *Circle.h* to the list of include files near the top of the file. Locate the *WM_PAINT* case statement in the *WinProc()* function and change the code so that it looks like the following (notice the set of braces to enclose the code):

```
case WM_PAINT:
{
    hdc = BeginPaint(hWnd, &ps);
    CCircle circle1;
    circle1.Draw (hdc);
    EndPaint(hWnd, &ps);
    break;
}
```

Click the mouse on the Build button to compile the program. When you run the program, you should see a red circle drawn with the center at (200,200) with a radius of 100 pixels.

In Lesson 15, "Passing Variables and Values to Functions," you learned that you may pass arguments to a function by writing a parameter list in the function declaration and definition. Even though you do not call a constructor explicitly, you may pass arguments to it. When you write a constructor with parameters, you pass the values when you declare the class object.

For example, modify the constructor in *Circle.h* to look like the following:

```
CCircle(int cx, int cy, int radius, COLORREF clr);
```

In the *Circle.cpp* file, change the definition of the constructor to look as shown below:

```
CCircle::CCircle(int cx, int cy, int radius, COLORREF clr)
{
    m_ptCenter.x = cx;
    m_ptCenter.y = cy;
    m_iRadius = radius;
    m_clrCircle = clr;
}
```

Return to the *WM_PAINT* code in the *Draw2.cpp* file and change the declaration for the *circle* variable to look like the following:

```
CCircle circle (450, 150, 50, RGB(0, 255, 0));
```

Compile the program again. When you run the program, you should see a smaller green circle drawn to the right of where the first circle appeared.

In Lesson 15, you also learned how to pass default arguments to a function by writing default values in the declaration statement. You can use default arguments for a constructor as well. When you use default arguments for a constructor, you pass only a partial argument list.

To use default arguments, modify the prototype for the constructor in *Circle.h* to look like the following:

```
CCircle(int cx = 200, int cy = 200, int radius = 100,
        COLORREF clr = RGB(255, 0x0, 0x0));
```

In the *WM_PAINT* code, add a second circle. Make the code look like the following:

```
case WM_PAINT:
{
```

```
    hdc = BeginPaint(hWnd, &ps);
    CCircle circle1;
    CCircle circle2 (450, 150, 50, RGB(0, 255, 0));
    circle1.Draw (hdc);
    circle2.Draw (hdc);
    EndPaint(hWnd, &ps);
    break;
}
```

The first circle, *circle1*, uses the default parameters. However, *circle2* passes arguments to the constructor, and these values override the default values. Compile and run the program. You should see two circles, one in red and a smaller green circle to the right, as shown in Figure 23.1.

Figure 23.1

The circle to the left uses the default values in the constructor. The circle to the right uses arguments passed when you declared the object.

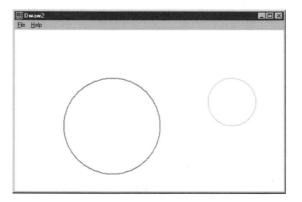

Using Multiple Constructors

You have learned how to write constructors and how to pass values to them. There are times when you might want to be able to pass values of different types to a constructor. You can do this by providing a class with multiple constructors through *overloading*.

In Lesson 35, "Overloading Functions and Operators," you will learn more about overloading, how to write more than one function using the same name, and how to redefine operators for a class. Overloading constructors to provide different variables to initialize a class is common and very easy to do.

When you overload a constructor, each function has the same name, which is the name of the class. However, you must make sure each constructor function is unique. To make a constructor unique, you must give it a parameter list that differs in the number or parameters or the data types of the parameters.

For example, suppose in your circle example, you might want to pass a *POINT* structure that contains the center point of the circle instead of specifying the coordinates as individual arguments. You could declare multiple constructors as follows:

```
CCircle();
CCircle(int cx, int cy, int radius, COLORREF clr);
CCircle(POINT& ptCenter, int radius, COLORREF clr);
```

This class will have three constructors. First, it will have the default constructor, which takes no arguments. Second, you may declare the center in terms of the *x* and *y* coordinates, followed by the radius and the color of the circle. Third, you may pass the constructor a *POINT* structure, followed by the radius and color. The compiler will select the proper constructor to call when you compile your program.

You should be aware that your program calls only one constructor for each class object you create. Just because you have multiple constructors does not mean that your program will call all of them. Because of this, you need to put any initialization code in all of the constructors.

Create a new Win32 Application called *Draw3*. Refer to the *Draw* application in the ClassView section of Lesson 22 and the *CCircle* class. Then add the same variables and functions you included there.

Next, add the following two constructors to the class. You can right-click on the class name in the ClassView pane of the Workspace window to add the constructors. Just remember to leave the Function Type field blank. (The Add Member Function dialog box will let you add a constructor with a return type, but you will get an error when you attempt to compile your project.)

```
CCircle(int cx, int cy, int radius, COLORREF clr);
CCircle(POINT& ptCenter, int radius, COLORREF clr);
```

Open the *Draw3.cpp* file (remember to add the *#include "circle.h"* at the top of the file). Locate the *WM_PAINT* portion of the *WndProc()* function and change the code to look like the following:

```
case WM_PAINT:
{
    hdc = BeginPaint(hWnd, &ps);
    // TODO: Add any drawing code here...
    POINT point;
```

```
    point.x = 350;
    point.y = 350;
    CCircle circle1;
    CCircle circle2 (400, 150, 50, RGB(0, 255, 0));
    CCircle circle3 (point, 75, RGB(0,0,255));
    circle1.Draw (hdc);
    circle2.Draw (hdc);
    circle3.Draw (hdc);
    EndPaint(hWnd, &ps);
    break;
}
```

The first circle, *circle1*, uses the default values you included in the default constructor, so you do not pass any values. The declaration for *circle2* passes the center as two integers along with the radius and color in the constructor. For *circle3*, you pass only three arguments, a *POINT* structure and the radius and color. For each declaration, the compiler picks the constructor whose parameter list matches the argument list.

Understanding Destructors

A class constructor, you have learned, executes automatically when you declare an instance of a class, which is to say, an object of the class data type. You can perform any variable initialization you need in a constructor, and you may pass arguments to a constructor.

The *destructor* operates in much the same way, except it executes automatically when the class object goes out of scope and your program destroys the instance. Unlike a constructor, you may have only *one* destructor in a class, and you may not pass it any arguments.

You declare a destructor by using the class name, the same as a constructor, but you precede the name with a tilde (~).

You use the destructor to provide any cleanup code that you might need to perform when your program destroys the class object. For example, in the previous projects, you created a pen object each time you drew the circle. However, as you learned in Lesson 21, "Drawing in the Graphics Device Interface," you should delete any resource object you create. So the *Draw()* function deletes the pen at the end of the *Draw()* function. You could create the pen in the constructors, then delete it in the constructor, making it available each time you call the *Draw()* function.

To do this, add a pen object as the member of the *CCircle* class. Right-click the mouse on the class name in the ClassView pane, then select Add Member Variable. In the Variable Type box, type **HPEN**. In the Variable Name box type **m_hPen**. Select Private access and click the mouse on the OK button.

Open the *Circle.cpp* file and add a line to create the pen to *each* constructor. Remove the call to *CreatePen()* and the *DeleteObject()* statement in the *Draw()* function. Change the argument in the call to *Ellipse()* to use the *m_hPen* member variable instead of *hPen*. Finally, add the *DeleteObject()* statement to the destructor, the *CCircle::~CCircle()* function. When you finish, *Circle.cpp* should look like the following code:

```cpp
// Circle.cpp: implementation of the CCircle class.
//
//////////////////////////////////////////////////////////

#include "stdafx.h"
#include "Circle.h"


//////////////////////////////////////////////////////////
// Construction/Destruction
//////////////////////////////////////////////////////////

CCircle::CCircle()
{
    m_ptCenter.x = 200;
    m_ptCenter.y = 200;
    m_iRadius = 100;
    m_clrCircle = RGB(255, 0x0, 0x0);
    m_hPen = CreatePen (PS_SOLID, 2, m_clrCircle);
}

CCircle::CCircle(int cx, int cy, int radius, COLORREF clr)
{
    m_ptCenter.x = cx;
    m_ptCenter.y = cy;
    m_iRadius = radius;
    m_clrCircle = clr;
    m_hPen = CreatePen (PS_SOLID, 2, m_clrCircle);
}
```

```
CCircle::CCircle(POINT &ptCenter, int radius, COLORREF clr)
{
    m_ptCenter = ptCenter;
    m_iRadius = radius;
    m_clrCircle = clr;
    m_hPen = CreatePen (PS_SOLID, 2, m_clrCircle);
}


CCircle::~CCircle()
{
    DeleteObject (m_hPen);
}


void CCircle::SetCenter(POINT &point)
{
    m_ptCenter = point;
}


void CCircle::SetRadius(int radius)
{
    m_iRadius = radius;
}


void CCircle::Draw(HDC hdc)
{
    RECT rc;
    rc.left = m_ptCenter.x - m_iRadius;
    rc.right = m_ptCenter.x + m_iRadius;
    rc.top = m_ptCenter.y - m_iRadius;
    rc.bottom = m_ptCenter.y + m_iRadius;
    HPEN hOldPen = (HPEN) SelectObject (hdc, m_hPen);
    Ellipse (hdc, rc.left, rc.top, rc.right, rc.bottom);
    SelectObject (hdc, hOldPen);
}
```

The *m_hPen* object will persist as a member of the class for as long as the class object persists. You need to create it only once. When your code destroys the class object, the destructor will delete the pen object.

What You Must Know

In this lesson, you continued your study of the Visual C++ class. You learned how to declare and use constructor functions in a class definition, how to pass arguments to constructors, and how to use the constructor functions to initialize class member variables. You also learned how to overload the constructor to provide for multiple constructors. You also learned about destructors and how to declare and use them in your classes. In Lesson 24, "Understanding Class Scope and Access Control," you will learn how to use the access keywords and examine class scope. You also will learn how to protect the data members of your class from outside manipulation. Before you continue with Lesson 23, however, make sure you understand the following key points about constructors and destructors:

◆ You declare a constructor function using the same name as the class for the name of the function. You may not assign return types to constructor functions.

◆ A constructor runs automatically when you declare or create an object of the class. You may provide initialization code in a constructor.

◆ You may have multiple constructors by giving them different parameter lists. The parameter lists must differ in the number or data type of the individual parameters.

◆ When you declare an instance of a class that has multiple constructors, one and only one constructor will execute. The compiler will select the proper constructor based upon your argument list when you declare the class object.

◆ Destructors execute automatically when a class object goes out of scope or you destroy the class object. You may include cleanup code in a destructor to remove any other objects your code may have created.

Lesson 24

Understanding Class Scope and Access Control

D uring your study of Visual C++ classes, you have learned how to define classes, which serve as templates for the compiler, and how to declare a variable to create an instance of a class. You have learned how to use constructors and destructors. In addition to declaring variables of a class, you may declare arrays of a class or you may create objects on the heap using the *new* operator. In Lesson 17, "Understanding Function and Variable Scope," you learned about the scope and visibility of variables in your program. In this lesson, you will learn about the scope of classes and the variables and functions in a class. You also will learn about the access keywords and how to limit access to functions and variables in a class. By the time you finish this lesson, you will understand the following key concepts:

◆ When you define a class, you create a *user defined* data type, and you may declare variables of this data type. Because a class definition becomes a data type, you also may declare arrays of a class.

◆ To limit access to the member functions and variables of a class, Visual C++ lets you declare members *public, protected*, or *private*.

◆ The *public* keyword exposes the members of a class to all statement in your program within the class object's *scope*. The *private* and *protected* keywords limit access to members of the class and certain other classes and functions.

◆ To allow access to *private* data members, your class can provide *public* member functions.

◆ Members of a class object have *class scope*. That is, they exist only within the class object that created the members.

Declaring Class Objects

You have learned how to define a class and to declare variables using the class name. You also learned how to use constructors and to pass variables to the constructor functions when you declare a class variable.

As you have seen, when you define a class, you are defining a new data type. This data type is what the C++ language calls as a *user defined* data type. Because a class becomes a data type, you may declare instances of a class the same as you would any other data type. To declare an instance of a class, you use the class name as the data type followed by the identifier you want to use as the variable name:

```
ClassName  Var;
```

In Lesson 13, "Using Array Variables to Store Multiple Values," you learned how to declare arrays of variables. You also may declare *arrays* of class objects using the array operator in your declaration. The following line declares an array of five class objects:

```
ClassName  Var[5];
```

This declaration passes no values to the class constructors, so you must have a constructor in your class that requires no parameters. The code in your class must do any initialization without any parameters. If your constructor requires only one parameter, you may initialize the array of class objects the same as you would an array of another variable type by placing the values inside a set of braces and separating the values with commas. The following short command-line program defines a class *CEmployee*. The constructor requires a single parameter, and the declaration in *main()* provides the values:

```
#include     <iostream.h>

class CEmployee
{
public:
    CEmployee (int ID) {m_EmployeeID = ID;}
    ~CEmployee () { };
    int GetID () {return (m_EmployeeID);}
private:
    int     m_EmployeeID;
};

void main (void)
{
```

```
CEmployee emp[] = {1641, 1802, 1732, 1752, 2401};

    for (int x = 0; x < sizeof(emp)/sizeof (CEmployee); ++x)
    {
        cout << "Employee ID No. " << x << " is "

                << emp[x].GetID() << endl;
    }
}
```

If, however, your constructor requires more than one parameter, things get, well, a little complicated. In this case, you must provide a call to the constructor, including the required parameters, in the initialization statement. The following program, *Employ2.cpp,* defines class *CEmployee,* which requires three parameters for the constructor. Pay particular attention to the initialization statement in the *main()* function:

```
//
//    Employ2.cpp
//
#include    <iostream.h>
#include    <string.h>

class CEmployee
{
public:
    CEmployee (int ID, char *First, char *Last);
    ~CEmployee ();

    int GetID () {return (m_EmployeeID);}
    char *GetFirstName () {return (m_EmployeeFirst);}
    char *GetLastName () {return (m_EmployeeLast);}
private:
    int      m_EmployeeID;
    char     m_EmployeeFirst[20];
    char     m_EmployeeLast[20];
};


void main (void)
```

```
{
CEmployee emp[] =  {
                CEmployee (1641, "Thomas", "Jefferson"),
                CEmployee (1802, "George", "Washington"),
                CEmployee (1732, "John", "Adams"),
                CEmployee (1752, "Andrew", "Jackson"),
                CEmployee (2401, "Elsie", "Smith")
                };

    for (int x = 0;
        x < (sizeof (emp) / sizeof (CEmployee));
        ++x)
    {
        cout << emp[x].GetFirstName() << " "
            << emp[x].GetLastName()
            << " employee ID is " << emp[x].GetID()
            << endl;
    }
}


CEmployee::CEmployee (int ID, char *First, char *Last)
{
    m_EmployeeID = ID;
    strcpy (m_EmployeeFirst, First);
    strcpy (m_EmployeeLast, Last);
}


CEmployee::~CEmployee ()
{

}
```

The concept of passing a function call as a single parameter where several parameters are required sometimes can be confusing to newcomers to C++. Fortunately, this situation does not arise often, but when it does, you should remember this special syntax.

Establishing Function Access

To protect the members of a class from accidental modification by statements outside the class, Visual C++ lets you set an *access specifier* in your class definition. The access specifier limits the scope of functions and statements that may access members of a class. The access keywords are summarized in Table 24.1.

Table 24.1 Visual C++ Access Keywords and the Type of Access They Permit

Keyword	Access
public	Allows access by any statement within the scope of the class object.
protected	Allows access by statements within class functions, or within *derived* or *friend* classes or *friend* functions.
private	Allows access only to statements within class functions, or within *friend* classes or *friend* functions.

The access keywords are a primary part of the C++ concept of *encapsulation*. A class is able to limit what statements may access its member variables and functions.

You set the access level of class members by specifying one of the security keywords followed by a colon. After you specify an access level, all members declared after that point have that access. You may change it at any point and even have several blocks with the same access level. It is common practice among some programmers to declare their functions in one part of the definition and their variables separately. In this case, they would use multiple declarations of the access keywords.

The *public access* level grants unrestricted access to a function or variable. Any member or non-member function that has access to the object's instance, or scope, may modify *public* member variables or call a *public* member function.

Protected access is stricter. Only member functions of the class, those of *derived* classes and those of special classes called *friends,* may access *protected* variables or execute *protected* functions. The *protected* status allows you to nestle your functions and variables behind a wall of safety, yet open them up for special classes. You will learn about derived classes in Lesson 26, "Letting a New Class Inherit the Attributes of an Existing Class."

The *private access* level gives the greatest protection for variables and functions. Only member functions may modify *private* variables or execute *private* functions. In addition, external functions and classes that you declare as *friend* may access *private* variables and execute *private* functions.

Your Class May Have Friends

The access keywords enforce the object-oriented programming concept of encapsulation. There are times, however, when you may want to make member functions or member variables protected or private, yet still allow access to them from external statements. To permit this, Visual C++ lets you declare these external classes and functions as friends *of the class.*

You declare a friend class using the keyword friend *and identifying the class by name. This, in effect, makes the friend a member of the class with all the privileges associated with that honor. A function in a friend class may access data members without regard to their access level.*

Outside functions, even individual member functions in a class that you do not declare as a friend, may be declared friend. *The following program,* Employ3.cpp, *defines a class that will be used as a* friend *class in* CEmployee. *It also declares* main() *a friend of* CEmployee. *Although the* m_EmployeeID *member is private to* CEmployee, *both the friend class and the friend function may access it directly.*

```
#include    <iostream.h>

class CEmployee;      // Forward reference
class CEmployeeFriend
{
public:
    CEmployeeFriend () { }
    ~CEmployeeFriend () { }
    int GetEmployeeID (CEmployee& emp);
};

class CEmployee
{
public:
    CEmployee (int ID) {m_EmployeeID = ID;}
    ~CEmployee () { };
```

```
    int GetID () {return (m_EmployeeID);}
private:
    int      m_EmployeeID;
    friend class CEmployeeFriend;
    friend void main (void);
};


void main (void)
{
CEmployee emp[] = {1641, 1802, 1732, 1752, 2401};

    cout << "Employee numbers from class member:" << endl;
    for (int x = 0; x < sizeof(emp)/sizeof (CEmployee); ++x)
    {
        cout << "Employee ID No. " << x << " is "
             << emp[x].GetID() << endl;
    }
    CEmployeeFriend MyFriend;
    cout << endl << "Employee numbers from friend class:"
         << endl;
    for (x = 0; x < sizeof(emp)/sizeof (CEmployee); ++x)
    {
        cout << "Employee ID No. " << x << " is "
             << MyFriend.GetEmployeeID(emp[x]) << endl;
    }
    cout << endl << "Employee numbers from friend function:"
         << endl;
    for (x = 0; x < sizeof(emp)/sizeof (CEmployee); ++x)
    {
        cout << "Employee ID No. " << x << " is "
             << emp[x].m_EmployeeID << endl;
    }
}


int CEmployeeFriend:: GetEmployeeID (CEmployee& emp)
{
```

```
        return (emp.m_EmployeeID);
    }
```

Many programmers attempt to avoid the use of the friend *keyword because it breaks the object-oriented programming concept of encapsulation.*

Accessing Data Members

Programmers usually prefer to keep the member variables of a class *private* and provide *public* member functions to set and access the values of the variables. Not only does this enforce the encapsulation of data, but also the member functions can provide some error-checking code before allowing access to the variables.

The following class may be used to keep track of a couple of events, *m_iEvent1* and *m_iEvent2* in *private* variables. Your program retrieves the average of *m_iEvent* by calling the *public* member function *GetEvent1Average ()*:

```
class CStat
{
public:
    CStat () {m_iEvent1 = m_iEvent2 = m_iTotal = 0;}
    void SetEvent1 ()
    {
        ++m_iEvent1;
        ++m_iTotal;
    }
    void SetEvent2 ()
    {
        ++m_iEvent2;
        ++m_iTotal;
    }
    int GetEvent1Average ()
    {
        return (((double) m_iEvent1/(double) m_iTotal)*100);
    }
private:
    int  m_iEvent1;
```

```
    int  m_iEvent2;
    int  m_iTotal;
};
```

Examine what happens when your code innocuously calls *GetEvent1Average ()* before an event has occurred at least once. In that case, the value of *m_iTotal* has a value of 0. When you divide *m_iEvent1* by *m_iTotal*, you get a divide by zero error and your program comes to an abrupt halt.

You can protect against such an error by having your member function first check to see whether *m_iTotal* contains a non-zero value first, and return an error code if the value is equal to zero.

```
int GetEvent1Average ()
{
    if (m_iTotal == 0)
        return (-1);
    return (int ((double) m_iEvent1/(double) m_iTotal) * 100);
}
```

Understanding Class Scope

In Lesson 17, "Understanding Function and Variable Scope," you learned that a variable has *scope,* the range of statements from which statements may access the variable. Objects that you creat from a class are variables and have the same scope as other variables. Depending upon where you declare a class object, only a limited number of statements within your program may access the object.

Members of a class, however, have *class scope.* Class members are *local* to the object that created them. The class members exist only within the class object itself. Declaring a class object creates the class members, and when the class object goes out of scope, your program destroys the class members.

Statements outside a class must use one of the *member* operators, a period or the "—>" symbol, to access members of a class, using the name of the class object on the left and the class member on the right, as in the following example:

```
CEmployee emp(1641);
emp.GetID();
```

The reason for this is that you may have more than one instance of a class in scope at any given time, and the compiler needs the object name to resolve which instance to use to access the member.

Statements in member functions may access member variables as ordinary variables. The members of a class are not aware of any other instances of the class and, thus, do not need the *member* operator. For example, in the last section, the *GetID()* function of the *CEmployee* class may access the *m_EmployeeID* variable that holds the ID number without using the *member* operator.

What You Must Know

In this lesson, you learned how to declare and use class objects and how to declare and use arrays of class objects. You also learned how to use the access keywords, *public* and *private*. The examples showed you how to keep the data members of a class definition *private* and to permit access to them only through *public* member functions. This allows your class to provide some error checking. In Lesson 25, "Using an Existing Class to Derive a New Class," you will learn how to use your class definitions to derive new classes that inherit the properties (variables) and methods (functions) of an existing class. Before you continue with Lesson 25, however, make sure you understand the following key points:

◆ A class definition creates a new data type that you may treat as any other data type. You may declare variables of this data type, and you may create arrays of class objects.

◆ The Visual C++ access specifiers let you limit access to the member variables and functions of a class.

◆ The *public* access specifier is the most permissive type of access and exposes members declared *public* to all statements within the class object's scope. The *private* access specifier is the most restrictive and protects class members from accidental modification. The *protected* specifier allows access to certain other classes.

◆ To allow access to *protected* or *private* class members, you may declare another class or an external function a *friend* of the class.

◆ Members of a class exist only within the class object that created the member. They have *class scope*. To access them from outside the class, you must use one of the *member* operators.

Lesson 25

Using an Existing Class to Derive a New Class

Thus far, you have learned how to define and use classes and how to declare variables and arrays of a class. You also have learned the meaning of the access keywords, *public, protected,* and *private.* You learned how the access keywords help to support the object-oriented concept of *encapsulation.* Classes also support the concepts of *inheritance* and *polymorphism.* Inheritance is the ability of a class to use another class as a base and to assume the properties and methods of the base class. The new class becomes a *derived* class. Polymorphism is the ability of a derived class to alter the properties of a base class. In this lesson, you will learn how to derive new classes from existing classes and how to inherit and modify the properties and methods of the existing class. By the time you finish this lesson, you will understand the following key concepts:

◆ *Inheritance* lets you define new classes based on existing classes. The new class is a *derived* class, and the existing class is the *base* or *ancestor* class.

◆ A derived class takes on, or inherits, the member variables and functions of its ancestor class.

◆ A derived class may inherit the variables and functions of an ancestor class as *public, protected,* or *private* by using the access keyword as part of the inheritance declaration.

◆ *Polymorphism* lets the functions in a derived class change the behavior of functions in a base class.

◆ Classes support polymorphism by letting similarly named functions in derived classes override *virtual* functions in base classes.

Understanding Inheritance

Inheritance is a fundamental principle in object-oriented programming. Using inheritance, you may use an existing class as a *base* class to derive a new class. This new class then will inherit the member variables and functions of the base class.

To derive a new class from an existing class, write the new class definition as you normally would. However, after the class name, write a colon followed by the name of the base class, as shown here:

```
class NewClassName : BaseClassName
{
// New class members
}
```

You also may specify an access keyword for the base class. You will learn how to do that and how it affects the inheritance later in this lesson. Suppose you define a class to hold information about an employee in your company, as shown here:

```
class CEmployee
{
public:
    CEmployee(char *EmpName, char *Position, float Salary);
    void ShowEmployeeData();
private:
    char m_szEmployeeName[64];
    char m_szPosition[32];
    float m_fSalary;
};
```

Not all employees in the company are the same, however. Some employees may be managers, and the class that contains information about them might need additional information, such as the departments they oversee and the amount of annual bonuses they might receive. They will need the same information as in *CEmployee*, so you can *derive* a new class, *CManager*, from *CEmployee*:

```
class CManager : public CEmployee
{
public:
    CManager (char *Name, char *Position, float Salary,
```

```
              char *Dept, float Bonus);
     void ShowManagerData ();
private:
     char m_szDepartment[32];
     float m_fBonus;
};
```

The *CManager* class inherits all of the functions and variables of *CEmployee,* but adds the variables needed to hold information specific to managers. The constructor contains the same parameters as the *CEmployee* class, but adds two more for the department name and the annual bonus. The constructor for *CManager* passes the first three parameters as arguments to the constructor for *CEmployee.* The following program, *Employ4.cpp,* shows how you would use these classes in a program:

```
#include   <iostream.h>
#include   <string.h>

class CEmployee
{
public:
     CEmployee(char *EmpName, char *Position, float Salary);
     void ShowEmployeeData();
private:
     char m_szEmployeeName[64];
     char m_szPosition[32];
     float m_fSalary;
};

class CManager : CEmployee
{
public:
     CManager (char *Name, char *Position, float Salary,
               char *Dept, float Bonus);
     void ShowManagerData ();
private:
     char m_szDepartment[32];
     float m_fBonus;
};
```

```
void main (void)
{
    CManager ToyMan ("Santa Clause", "Manager", 327.65,
"Toys", 1500.00);

    cout << "Information for ToyMan:" << endl;
    ToyMan.ShowManagerData ();
}


CEmployee::CEmployee(char *EmpName, char *Position,
                    float Salary)
{
    strcpy (m_szEmployeeName, EmpName);
    strcpy (m_szPosition, Position);
    m_fSalary = Salary;
}


void CEmployee::ShowEmployeeData()
{
    cout << "Employee data:" << endl;
    cout << "\tName: " << m_szEmployeeName << endl;
    cout << "\tPosition: " << m_szPosition << endl;
    cout << "\tSalary: " << m_fSalary << endl;
}


CManager::CManager (char *Name, char *Position,
                    float Salary, char *Dept, float Bonus)
        : CEmployee (Name, Position, Salary)
{
    strcpy (m_szDepartment, Dept);
    m_fBonus = Bonus;
}


void CManager::ShowManagerData ()
{
```

```
    ShowEmployeeData ();
    cout << "Manager data:" << endl;
    cout << "\tDepartment: " << m_szDepartment << endl;
    cout << "\tBonus: " << m_fBonus << endl;
}
```

The *CManager* class inherits the members of the *CEmployee* class. You did not have to include any of the members of *CEmployee* specifically in *CManager*. The inheritance takes care of that. For example, the *main()* function calls only the *ShowManagerData()* function, which in turn calls the *ShowEmployeeData()* function as though it were a member of *CManager*.

You should notice the definition of the *CManager::CManager()* constructor:

```
CManager::CManager (char *Name, char *Position,
                    float Salary, char *Dept, float Bonus)
        : CEmployee (Name, Position, Salary)
```

This constructor has five parameters, but the constructor for *CEmployee* needs only three parameters. When you derive a new class from a base class, the derived class's constructor must invoke the base class's constructor, passing the parameters required by the base class. To do this, write a colon after you finish the parameter list for the derived class constructor, then write the call to the base class constructor.

Using Access Keywords for Base Classes

Derived classes inherit the properties and functions of base classes in different ways. A base class cannot lower the access level for members of a base class. For example, if a variable in a base class is declared *private,* it still will be private when you derive a new class from the base class, and the derived class will not be able to access the variable.

By default, all the members of a base class become *private* members of a derived class. In the last section, the *CEmployee* class declared the *GetEmployeeData()* function as *public*. But when the *CManager* class inherited the function, the function became a private member of *CManager*. To show this, try inserting the following line in the *main()* function:

```
ToyMan.ShowEmployeeData ();
```

When you compile the program, the compiler will issue the following error:

```
Employ4.cpp(31) : error C2248: 'ShowEmployeeData' : cannot
 access public member declared in class 'CEmployee'
      Employ4.cpp(8) : see declaration of 'ShowEmployeeData'
```

Leave the call to *ToyMan.ShowEmployeeData()* in the main function for now.

A derived class may specify how it wants to inherit members of a base class by using one of the access specifiers. To do this, write the access specifier before the name of the base class when you write the definition for the base class. In the preceding example, change the definition as follows:

```
class CManager : public CEmployee
```

Now recompile the program and the compiler will not issue an error. *ShowEmployeeData()* now is a *public* member of *CManager*.

Inheriting a base class with the *public* access specifier leaves the access for the base class members unchanged. All *public* members are still *public,* and *private* members still are *private* in the base class.

If you specify *protected* as the access specifier, then the derived class inherits all *public* members of the base class as *protected* members of itself. *Protected* members remain *protected* in the base class, and *private* members remain *private.* Remember from Lesson 24, "Understanding Class Scope and Access Control," that a derived class may access *protected* members of a base class.

If you specify *private* access, then the derived class inherits all the *public* and *protected* members of the base class as *private* members. *Private* members of the base class remain *private* to the base class. A derived class may not access *private* members of a base class.

Hiding Class Members

You have learned that variables have a certain *scope* depending upon where you declare them within your program. The scope is from the point in your program where you declare a variable until the end of the block in which you declare the variable. The block may be a compound statement or a function, or even the entire source file if you declare the variable as *global.*

In Lesson 17, "Understanding Function and Variable Scope," you also learned that you can "hide" the name of a variable by declaring a variable by the same name in smaller scope. In a class, a member variable exists in *class scope.*

In a derived class, your definition may hide a variable in the base class by declaring another variable by the same name in the derived class. For example, if a base class contains a variable named *m_iVar* and you declare another variable by the same name in the derived class, the new variable will hide the base class variable:

```
class CEmployee
{
public:
    CEmployee(char *Name, float Salary);
protected:
    char m_szName[64];
    float m_fSalary;
};

class CManager : public CEmployee
{
public:
    CManager (char *Name, float Salary);
    void ShowData(void);
protected:
    float m_fSalary;
};
```

In this sample, the *m_fSalary* variable in *CManager* hides the *m_fSalary* variable in *CEmployee*. In Lesson 17, you also learned that you may access a hidden variable by using the *scope resolution operator,* a double colon (::), as part of the variable's name. In a class, you may reference a hidden variable in the base class using the base class name, the scope resolution operator, and the variable's name. The following short command-line program, *Employ5.cpp,* shows an example of this:

```
#include   <iostream.h>
#include   <string.h>

class CEmployee
{
public:
    CEmployee(char *Name, float Salary);
protected:
    char m_szName[64];
    float m_fSalary;
```

```
};

class CManager : public CEmployee
{
public:
    CManager (char *Name, float Salary);
    void ShowData(void);
protected:
    float m_fSalary;
};
void main (void)
{
    CManager mgr ("Kris Kringle",  327.65);
    mgr.ShowData ();
}


CEmployee::CEmployee (char *Name, float Salary)
{
    strcpy (m_szName, Name);
    m_fSalary = Salary;
}


CManager::CManager (char *Name, float Salary)
                    : CEmployee (Name, 0)
{
    m_fSalary = Salary;
}


void CManager::ShowData ()
{
    cout << "Manager information:" << endl;
    cout << "\tName: " << m_szName << endl;
    cout << "\tSalary: $" << m_fSalary << endl;
    cout << "\tCEmployee::m_fSalary = $"
        << CEmployee::m_fSalary << endl;
}
```

In this program, the constructor for *CManager* passes *0* as the salary to the constructor for *CEmployee,* then stores the real salary in the class object's own *m_fSalary* variable. When you run the program, you will see the following output:

```
Manager information:
    Name: Kris Kringle
    Salary: $327.65
    CEmployee::m_fSalary = $0
```

More often than not, you will not need to hide variable names in base classes. However, you should be aware that C++ does not consider it an error when you declare identical variable names in base and derived classes.

You also may hide a function name in the same way. However, hiding function names may present some other problems, as you will see in "Using Virtual Functions," later in this lesson.

Understanding the Order of Constructors and Destructors

Your program calls constructor functions automatically when you create an object from a class definition. In addition, your program calls destructor functions automatically when it destroys a class object. As you have learned in this lesson, the constructor for a derived class passes the variables needed by a base class when the derived class constructor executes. Even if you do not call the base class constructor specifically, your program will perform the call using the same parameters you passed to the derived class.

You may derive other classes from a derived class. You may often hear the term "ancestor" to refer to a base class when there are multiple base classes. In this case, the first base class is the "most distant ancestor" class.

When you use multiple classes in an ancestry chain and declare an instance of the derived class, your program will call the constructor for the most distant ancestor first. Then your program will call the next most distant ancestor, working its way down the chain until the constructor for the most recent class executes. In this way, the ancestor classes will create any objects that might be needed by the derived classes before the constructor for the derived class executes.

When the class instance goes out of scope and your program destroys it, your program calls the destructors in the reverse order that it called the constructors. The program calls the most recently derived class first and works its way up the chain until it executes the destructor for the most distant ancestor class.

The following program, *Ancestor.cpp*, defines a base class, *CFirstClass*, from which it derives a new class, *CSecondClass*. After that, *CThirdClass* uses *CSecondClass* as a base class, inheriting all the properties of *CSecondClass* and *CFirstClass*. Each constructor and destructor prints a message when it executes.

```cpp
#include <iostream.h>

class CFirstClass
{
public:
    CFirstClass()
    {
        cout << "CFirstClass constructor" << endl;
    }
    ~CFirstClass()
    {
        cout << "CFirstClass destructor" << endl;
    }
};
class CSecondClass : public CFirstClass
{
public:
    CSecondClass()
    {
        cout << "CSecondClass constructor" << endl;
    }
    ~CSecondClass()
    {
        cout << "CSecondClass destructor" << endl;
    }
};
class CThirdClass : public CSecondClass
{
public:
    CThirdClass()
    {
        cout << "CThirdClass constructor" << endl;
```

```
    }
    ~CThirdClass()
    {
        cout << "CThirdClass destructor" << endl;
    }
};

void main (void)
{
    CThirdClass MyClass;
}
```

When you compile and run the program, you will see the following output, showing the order in which your program calls constructors and destructors:

```
CFirstClass constructor
CSecondClass constructor
CThirdClass constructor
CThirdClass destructor
CSecondClass destructor
CFirstClass destructor
```

Using Virtual Functions

You have learned how Visual C++ classes use *encapsulation* to keep values in member variables. You also have learned how classes use *inheritance* to let a derived class assume the properties and functions of a base class.

The third primary concept of object-oriented programming is *polymorphism*, the idea that a class not only can assume the properties and variables of an ancestor class, but may modify the behavior of the parent class as well.

The primary mechanism through which Visual C++ classes use polymorphism is the *virtual function*. You declare a function virtual by preceding its declaration with the keyword *virtual:*

```
virtual void ShowData ();
```

When you declare a function in a class as *virtual*, the compiler looks for a function by the same name in any derived classes. If the derived class has a function by the same name, your program will execute it instead of the base class function. You may use the *virtual* keyword only on class member functions. Functions in global scope may not use the *virtual* modifier.

The following program, *Employ4.cpp*, shows two classes, *CManager* and *CSalesman*, derived from *CEmployee*. Notice that all three classes have a function named *ShowData()*. However, in *CEmployee*, the function declaration uses the *virtual* modifier:

```
#include   <iostream.h>
#include   <string.h>

class CEmployee
{
public:
    CEmployee(char *EmpName, char *Position, float Salary);
    ~CEmployee () { }
    virtual void ShowData();
protected:
    char m_szEmployeeName[64];
    char m_szPosition[32];
    float m_fSalary;
};

class CManager : public CEmployee
{
public:
    CManager (char *Name, char *Position, float Salary,
             char *Dept, float Bonus);
    ~CManager () { }
    void ShowData ();
protected:
    char m_szDepartment[32];
    float m_fBonus;
};

class CSalesman : public CEmployee
```

```
{
public:
    CSalesman (char *Name, char *Position, float Salary,
              char *Dept, float Bonus);
    ~CSalesman () { }
    void ShowData ();
protected:
    char m_szDepartment[32];
    float m_fCommission;
};


void ShowIt (CEmployee *emp);

void main (void)
{
CManager ToyMan ("Santa Clause", "Manager", 327.65,
                 "Toys", 1500.00);
    CSalesman Elf ("Judy Smith", "Salesman", 315.25,
                   "Toys", .15);

    cout << "Information for ToyMan:" << endl;
    ShowIt (&ToyMan);
    cout << endl << "Information for Elf:" << endl;
    ShowIt (&Elf);
}


void ShowIt (CEmployee *emp)
{
    emp->ShowData ();
}


CEmployee::CEmployee(char *EmpName, char *Position,
                     float Salary)
{
    strcpy (m_szEmployeeName, EmpName);
    strcpy (m_szPosition, Position);
```

```cpp
    m_fSalary = Salary;
}


void CEmployee::ShowData()
{
    cout << "Employee data:" << endl;
    cout << "\tName: " << m_szEmployeeName << endl;
    cout << "\tPosition: " << m_szPosition << endl;
    cout << "\tSalary: $" << m_fSalary << endl;
}


CManager::CManager (char *Name, char *Position,
                    float Salary, char *Dept, float Bonus)
        : CEmployee (Name, Position, Salary)
{
    strcpy (m_szDepartment, Dept);
    m_fBonus = Bonus;
}


void CManager::ShowData ()
{
    CEmployee::ShowData ();
    cout << "Manager data:" << endl;
    cout << "\tDepartment: " << m_szDepartment << endl;
    cout << "\tBonus: $" << m_fBonus << endl;
}


CSalesman::CSalesman (char *Name, char *Position,
                      float Salary, char *Dept,
                      float Commission)
        : CEmployee (Name, Position, Salary)
{
    strcpy (m_szDepartment, Dept);
    m_fCommission = Commission;
}
```

```
void CSalesman::ShowData ()
{
    CEmployee::ShowData ();
    cout << "Salesman data:" << endl;
    cout << "\tDepartment: " << m_szDepartment << endl;
    cout << "\tCommission: " << m_fCommission * 100
        << "%" << endl;
}
```

In this program, you should notice that the *ShowIt()* function takes as a parameter a reference to a *CEmployee* class, but the two calls to the function in *main()* use *CManager* and *CSalesman* as parameters. In C++, it is legal to cast a pointer to a derived class to a pointer to a base class. Also notice that the *ShowData()* functions in *CManager* and *CSalesman* call the base class function by using the scope resolution operator, *CEmployee::ShowData()*.

When you compile and run *Employ4.cpp*, you will see the following output. Although the parameter to *ShowIt()* is a pointer to *CEmployee*, the statement *emp->ShowIt()* actually calls the functions in the derived classes:

```
Information for ToyMan:
Employee data:
    Name: Santa Clause
    Position: Manager
    Salary: $327.65
Manager data:
    Department: Toys
    Bonus: $1500

Information for Elf:
Employee data:
    Name: Judy Smith
    Position: Salesman
    Salary: $315.25
Salesman data:
    Department: Toys
    Commission: 15%
```

What You Must Know

In this lesson, you learned about the object-oriented concepts of *inheritance* and *polymorphism*. In the code in this lesson, you used base classes to build new classes, and you used a virtual function to override a function in a base class. In Lesson 26, "Letting a New Class Inherit the Attributes of an Existing Class," you will develop a Windows program that contains a class hierarchy beginning with a point and working down to specific shapes such as a circle and rectangle. Before you continue with Lesson 26, however, make sure you understand the following key points:

◆ *Inheritance* lets a derived class include all the variables and functions of a base class in a new class definition.

◆ Using *protected* access for variables and functions in a base class lets a derived class access the variables and functions in the base class.

◆ If a derived class uses a variable or function of the same name as a member of a base class, the base class variable or function is "hidden" by the base class. You may access hidden elements by using the scope resolution operator.

◆ When you declare an instance of a derived class, your program executes the ancestor constructor first, then the derived class constructor. Your program executes destructor functions in the reverse order. The derived class destructor executes first, then the base class destructor.

◆ Classes support *polymorphism* by using *virtual* function declarations in the base class. When you declare a function *virtual*, the compiler looks for a function with the same name in a derived class.

Lesson 26

Letting a New Class Inherit the Attributes of an Existing Class

You have learned about the three basic concepts of object-oriented programming, *encapsulation, inheritance,* and *polymorphism.* As you use these principles, you will become more familiar with them. In this lesson, you will develop a series of classes to draw shapes in your Windows program. The classes will use encapsulation because you will place all the information needed to draw the shapes in the class objects. After you create a base class, all the other classes will be derived from the one base class, thus showing the principle of inheritance. Each class that draws a shape will contain its own drawing code, but derived classes will override the function to draw particular shapes to demonstrate polymorphism. By the time you finish this lesson, you will understand the following key concepts:

◆ To develop a tree of classes, examine what properties and methods the derived classes will have in common and place them in a *base* class.

◆ A new class derived from a base class may use code and variables you already have placed in the base class.

◆ You may declare a base class *virtual* when you derive a new class from it. This helps you to avoid some of the problems of *multiple inheritance.*

◆ When a derived class inherits a base class through two or more branches of inheritance, the functions and variables in the base class may be ambiguous.

Using Base Classes

Throughout your Visual C++ programming experience, you will have the opportunity to develop new classes. Often in a single program, some of these classes will have properties and functions in common. When this happens, you don't have to duplicate code or repeat variable declarations in each class. You can define the common elements in a base class or ancestor class and reuse the variables and functions in your derived classes.

You have learned how to use a *virtual function* in a class definition to let a derived class override the function, even when it is called from the base class. In this lesson, you will create a *CShape* class that will contain two functions—one that your derived classes will override to draw their shapes and a second that all the derived classes will use to rotate the shapes.

The Windows Application Programming Interface (API) contains functions to draw the shapes you will create, but there are some aspects you might not like about the API functions.

First, the functions that draw closed shapes such as an ellipse or rectangle fill the enclosed area with the default brush, erasing whatever already is there. You can create a *NULL* brush or set the background drawing mode to overcome this, but these are extra steps you do not need to take. The classes you develop in this lesson will draw the shapes using line segments and *cubic Bezier curves*. Now, before you close the book, you will not have to calculate any Bezier points. Instead, you will use the graphics device interface (GDI) to transform the lines into Bezier points.

(A Bezier—pronounced "bay-zee-ay"—curve uses four points to describe a curved line. Two of the points are the end points of the line. The other two are "control" points that push and pull the line into the proper shape.)

Second, the Windows API functions draw shapes that are aligned with the edges of your window. The shapes are drawn left to right or top to bottom. In real life, geometric shapes do not appear that way. If you want an ellipse that is slightly slanted, you have to use some other *transformation* functions that work only on Windows NT and 2000. You cannot use these transformation functions on Windows 95 and 98.

In addition, suppose you want to draw a line 300 pixels long starting at a given point and sloping upward at a 12.6-degree angle. You would have to use trigonometric functions to find that point, or waste time with a calculator. Then, if you were to change the angle, you would have to redo your calculations. Wouldn't it be easier to say simply, "I want a line that starts here, is this long, and slants at that angle; so draw it"? Your *CLine* class in the following program will do just that.

Create a new Win32 Application project using the steps you performed in Lesson 21, "Drawing in the Graphics Device Interface." Call this application "Shapes." First, you will want to add a class to the project called *CShape*. From this base class, you will derive the other classes you will use to draw to your window, as shown in the tree in Figure 26.1.

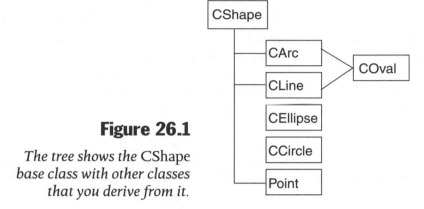

Figure 26.1

The tree shows the CShape *base class with other classes that you derive from it.*

Using the ClassView pane of the Workspace window, add the *CShape* class to the project. Then add the functions and variables, as shown in the following listing:

```
class CShape
{
public:
    virtual void Show (HDC hdc);
    CShape();
    virtual ~CShape();

protected:
    void Rotate (int iAngle, const POINT& ptCenter,
                 POINT* ptControl, int Count);
    virtual void Draw();
    HDC        m_hdc;
    COLORREF     m_clrPen;
    HPEN       m_hPen;
    int      m_cx1;
    int      m_cy1;
int      m_iPenWidth
};
```

In *CShape,* the *Show()* function prepares the device contexts for drawing and then calls the *Draw()* function. The function uses a default pen width of two points, but you could add another member variable to the class to hold a new pen width. After the drawing is complete, the function deletes the pen object, so you do not have to worry about it in your code.

You should notice in the following code that the *Draw()* does not contain any code. The *CShape* class will not do any actual drawing to your window, and your derived classes must override the function to provide specific drawing code. In Lesson 27, "Understanding Abstract Classes," you will learn how to declare the *Draw()* function so that you do not have to write the empty function. *CShape* will hold the variables such as the handle to the device context and the drawing pen. The data members are *protected*, which lets derived classes access them.

The *Rotate()* function, shown next, uses elementary math analysis formulas to translate the center point and rotate the points in an array around the center point. You may use this function with any set of points that you need to rotate on the screen:

```cpp
// Shape.cpp: implementation of the CShape class.
//
/////////////////////////////////////////////////////////

#include "stdafx.h"
#include "Shape.h"
#include <math.h>


/////////////////////////////////////////////////////////
// Construction/Destruction
/////////////////////////////////////////////////////////

CShape::CShape()
{
m_cx1 = 0;
    m_cy1 = 0;
    m_clrPen = 0;
    m_iPenWidth = 2;
}

CShape::~CShape()
{

}
```

```
//
//   Rotate a set of points about a central point.
//
void CShape::Rotate(int iAngle, const POINT &ptCenter,
                    POINT *ptControl, int iSize)
{
//
//   If the angle is 0, there's no need to
//   do anything
     if (!iAngle)
         return;
//
//   Translate the angle from tenths of a degree
//   to radians. That's what the trig functions use.
     double fAngle = (iAngle / 10.0) / 57.29578;
//
//   Get the sine and cosine of the rotation angle.
     double fSine = sin(fAngle);
     double fCosine = cos(fAngle);
//
//   Translate the center point so it will be the point of
//   rotation.
     double fRotateX = ptCenter.x - ptCenter.x * fCosine
                       - ptCenter.y * fSine;
     double fRotateY = ptCenter.y + ptCenter.x * fSine
                       - ptCenter.y * fCosine;


//
//   Rotate the control points, then add the
//   translation for the center point. Rebuild
//   the control points.
     for (int i = 0; i < iSize; ++i)
     {
         double fNewX = ptControl[i].x * fCosine
                        + ptControl[i].y * fSine + fRotateX;
```

```
        double fNewY = -ptControl[i].x * fSine
                        + ptControl[i].y * fCosine + fRotateY;
        ptControl[i].x = (long) (fNewX + .5);
        ptControl[i].y = (long) (fNewY + .5);
    }
}
//
//  Create the pen to draw the lines, select it
//  into the device context. Then call the Draw()
//  function. Use the R2_NOTXORPEN mode, which will
//  let you erase the shape simply by drawing it a
//  second time.
//
void CShape::Show(HDC hdc)
{
    m_hdc = hdc;
    m_hPen = CreatePen (PS_SOLID, m_iPenWidth, m_clrPen);
    HPEN hOldPen = (HPEN) SelectObject (m_hdc, m_hPen);
    int iOldROP = SetROP2 (hdc, R2_NOTXORPEN);
Draw ();
SetROP2 (hdc, iOldROP);
    SelectObject (m_hdc, hOldPen);
    DeleteObject (m_hPen);
}


void CShape::Draw()
{
}
```

You cannot use the *CShape* class directly. In the next section, you will use *CShape* as a base class to derive new classes that actually will draw objects on your screen.

Using Pure Virtual Functions

When you declare a class that you intend to use only with a base class, you may have one or more functions that your base class will not use. You do not need to provide a body of code for these functions. Instead, you may declare a function as a pure virtual function. To do this, declare it virtual *in your class definition and set the address of the function to 0:*

```
virtual void Draw() = 0;
```

Declaring one or more pure virtual functions in a class makes the class an abstract class, *and you may not declare any instances of the class. To use an abstract class, you will have to derive a new class using it as a base class, override the pure virtual function, and provide a definition for the function. You will learn more about abstract classes in Lesson 27.*

Understanding Ancestor Classes

Once you declare a new class using another class as a base class, the base class becomes an *ancestor* for the new class. This means the new class may use the *public* and *protected* variables and functions in the ancestor class. If you derive yet another class from the derived class, then this new class will inherit both the base class and the derived class as ancestor classes.

To show how a class may use the variables and functions in an ancestor class, add a new class to the *Shapes* project you created in the last section using the ClassView pane of the Workspace window. Call this new class "Point." (Normally in this book, you would precede a class name with a *C* to indicate it is a class. However, when you start learning about the Microsoft Foundation Class library, you will find there already is a *CPoint* class.)

After you name the class in the New Class dialog box, however, click the mouse on the Derived From column of the highlighted line in the Base Class(es) list at the bottom of the dialog box. The dialog box will respond by opening an editable field in this column. Type **Cshape** as the name of the base class. To the right of this edit field is a box that lets you select Public, Protected, or Private access. Set the access level set to Public, then click the mouse on the OK button.

The Visual Studio will respond by adding to files, *point.cpp* and *point.h,* to your project and list your new class in the ClassView pane. Add a *Draw()* function to the *Point* class. Right-click the *Point* class in the ClassView pane and select Add Member Function from the menu. In the Add Member Function dialog box, the function type is *void*. Check the Protected box and also check the Virtual box, then click the mouse on the OK button. Open the *point.h* file and modify the constructor so that the class definition looks like the following code:

```
class Point : public CShape
{
public:
    Point(int cx, int cy, COLORREF clr = 0);
    virtual ~Point();

protected:
    virtual void Draw();
};
```

Open the *Point.cpp* file and change the constructor to match the constructor in the class definition, as shown in the following code:

```
// Point.cpp: implementation of the Point class.
//
//////////////////////////////////////////////////////////

#include "stdafx.h"
#include "Point.h"


//////////////////////////////////////////////////////////
// Construction/Destruction
//////////////////////////////////////////////////////////

Point::Point(int cx, int cy, COLORREF clr)
{
    m_cx1 = cx;
    m_cy1 = cy;
    m_clrPen = clr;
}

Point::~Point()
{
}
```

```
void Point::Draw()
{
    SetPixel (m_hdc, m_cx1, m_cy1, m_clrPen);
/*  Remove this comment line to draw "+" for the point
    POINT pt;
    MoveToEx (m_hdc, m_cx1 - 5, m_cy1, &pt);
    LineTo (m_hdc, m_cx1 + 5, m_cy1);
    MoveToEx (m_hdc, m_cx1, m_cy1 - 5, NULL);
    LineTo (m_hdc, m_cx1, m_cy1 + 5);
    MoveToEx (m_hdc, pt.x, pt.y, NULL);
 */ //Remove this comment line to draw "+" for the point
}
```

Notice that your constructor is setting member variables, but your *Point* class does not contain any variables. The variables are *protected* members of the base class, *CShape,* and your new class has inherited all the members of the base class.

The *Draw()* function simply sets a point on the screen in the color you specified in the constructor. On most screens, a single point is difficult to see. In your experimenting, you may make the function draw a large "+" sign where the point should appear by uncommenting the code in the *Draw()* function.

Use the same process to add another class called "CLine" to your project. Add the *virtual void Draw()* function as a protected member of the class. Remember to keep the *Draw()* function *virtual.* This will let you derive yet another class from *CLine.* Add the *protected* member variables as shown in the code below and modify the constructor to accept the variables shown:

```
class CLine : virtual public CShape
{
public:
    CLine(int cx1, int cy1, int iLength,
          int iAngle = 0, COLORREF clr = 0);
    virtual ~CLine();

protected:
    int m_iLength;
    int m_iAngle;
    virtual void Draw();
};
```

Remember to add the *virtual* keyword to the first line where you derive your class from *CShape*. You will have to type this keyword in yourself because the New Class dialog box does not provide any way to enter it when you create the new class. You will see the reason for this when you derive a *COval* class in the next section. The code for the *CLine* class is shown here:

```cpp
// Line.cpp: implementation of the CLine class.
//
//////////////////////////////////////////////////////

#include "stdafx.h"
#include "Line.h"


//////////////////////////////////////////////////////
// Construction/Destruction
//////////////////////////////////////////////////////
//
//   The anchor point for a line is the first point
//   entered.
//
CLine::CLine(int cx1, int cy1, int iLength,
             int iAngle, COLORREF clr)
{
    m_cx1 = cx1;
    m_cy1 = cy1;
    m_iLength = iLength;
    m_iAngle = iAngle;
    m_clrPen = clr;
}

CLine::~CLine()
{
}

void CLine::Draw()
{
    POINT ptOld;
```

```
        POINT pt[2]  = {m_cx1, m_cy1,
                        m_cx1 + m_iLength, m_cy1};
        Rotate (m_iAngle, pt[0], pt, 2);
        MoveToEx (m_hdc, pt[0].x, pt[0].y, &ptOld);
        LineTo (m_hdc, pt[1].x, pt[1].y);
        MoveToEx (m_hdc, ptOld.x, ptOld.y, NULL);
}
```

Add yet another class to your project. Call this new class *CArc* and derive it from *CShape*. Also make the inheritance *virtual*, as you did for *CLine*. In the next section, you will use *multiple* inheritance to create a racetrack shape from *CArc* and *CLine* by drawing just one line and one arc. Add the member variables and change the constructor, as shown in the following class definition:

```
class CArc : virtual public CShape
{
public:
    CArc(int cx1, int cy1, int StartAngle, int EndAngle,
        int radius, COLORREF clr = 0);
    virtual ~CArc();

protected:
    POINT   m_ptCenter;
    int     m_cx2;  // Starting point for arc
    int     m_cy2;
    int     m_cx3;  // Ending point for arc
    int     m_cy3;
    int     m_iRadius;
    RECT    m_rc;   // Bounding box for arc
    virtual void Draw();
int     m_iStartAngle;
    int     m_iEndAngle;
private:
    void CalculateArc(int StartAngle, int EndAngle);
};
```

Open the *Arc.cpp* file and add the code, as shown here:

```cpp
// Arc.cpp: implementation of the CArc class.
//
//////////////////////////////////////////////////////////

#include "stdafx.h"
#include "Arc.h"
#include "math.h"
#include "stdio.h"


//////////////////////////////////////////////////////////
// Construction/Destruction
//////////////////////////////////////////////////////////


//
//   The anchor point for an arc is the center
//   of rotation.
//
CArc::CArc(int cx1, int cy1, int StartAngle, int EndAngle,
           int radius, COLORREF clr)
{
    m_iRadius = radius;
    m_cx1 = m_ptCenter.x = cx1;
    m_cy1 = m_ptCenter.y =cy1;
    CalculateArc(StartAngle, EndAngle);
    m_clrPen = clr;
m_iStartAngle = StartAngle;
    m_iEndAngle = EndAngle;
}

CArc::CArc(int cx1, int cy1, int depth, int radius,
           COLORREF clr)
{
    if ((2 * radius) > depth)
        depth = 2 * radius;
```

```
    m_iRadius = radius;
    m_cx1 = cx1;
    m_cy1 = cy1;
    m_clrPen = clr;
    m_ptCenter.y = cy1 + depth / 2;
    double fSine = ((double) depth / 2.0) / (double) radius;
    m_iStartAngle = (int)(asin (fSine) * 57.29578 * 10.0
                    + .5) + 900;
    m_iEndAngle = 3600 - m_iStartAngle;
    m_ptCenter.x = (int) (sqrt(radius * radius - (depth / 2)
                    * (depth / 2)) + cx1 + .5);
    m_cx2 = m_cx3 = cx1;
    m_cy2 = cy1;
    m_cy3 = cy1 + depth;
    m_rc.right = m_ptCenter.x + m_iRadius;
    m_rc.left = m_ptCenter.x - m_iRadius;
    m_rc.top = m_ptCenter.y - m_iRadius;
    m_rc.bottom = m_ptCenter.y + m_iRadius;
}


CArc::~CArc()
{

}


void CArc::Draw()
{
    RECT rcArc;
    rcArc.left = m_cx1 - m_iRadius;
    rcArc.right = m_cx1 + m_iRadius;
    rcArc.top = m_cy1 - m_iRadius;
    rcArc.bottom = m_cy1 + m_iRadius;

    double fStartAngle = (m_iStartAngle / 57.29578) / 10.0;
    double fEndAngle = (m_iEndAngle / 57.29578) / 10.0;
```

```
        int iStartX = m_cx1 + (int) (m_iRadius
                     * cos (fStartAngle));
        int iStartY = m_cy1 + (int) (-m_iRadius
                     * sin (fStartAngle));

        int iEndX = m_cx1 + (int)(m_iRadius * cos(fEndAngle));
        int iEndY = m_cy1 + (int)(-m_iRadius * sin(fEndAngle));

        Arc (m_hdc, rcArc.left, rcArc.top,
            rcArc.right, rcArc.bottom,
            iStartX, iStartY, iEndX, iEndY);

        return;
}


void CArc::CalculateArc(int StartAngle, int EndAngle)
{
    m_rc.right = m_ptCenter.x + m_iRadius;
    m_rc.left = m_ptCenter.x - m_iRadius;
    m_rc.top = m_ptCenter.y - m_iRadius;
    m_rc.bottom = m_ptCenter.y + m_iRadius;
    double fAngle = ((double) StartAngle) / 10.0;
    fAngle /= 57.29578;
    m_cx2 = m_ptCenter.x + (int)((double) m_iRadius
            * cos (fAngle) + .5);
    m_cy2 = m_cy1 + (int)((double) -m_iRadius
            * sin (fAngle) + .5);
    fAngle = ((double) EndAngle) / 10.0;
    fAngle /= 57.29578;
    m_cx3 = m_ptCenter.x + (int)((double) m_iRadius
            * cos (fAngle) + .5);
    m_cy3 = m_ptCenter.y + (int)((double) -m_iRadius
            * sin (fAngle) + .5);
}


void CArc::SetArcPoints(int cx1, int cy1, int StartAngle,
```

```
                        int EndAngle, int radius)
{
    m_iRadius = radius;
    m_cx1 = m_ptCenter.x = cx1;
    m_cy1 = m_ptCenter.y = cy1;
    CalculateArc(StartAngle, EndAngle);
    m_iStartAngle = StartAngle;
    m_iEndAngle = EndAngle;
}
```

Compile and run your program. You should see an orange line intersecting a red arc. If you uncommented the code to draw the "+" symbol for a point, you should see two crossed lines at the location for the point. More importantly, you have specified these objects in terms that are easier to use. The *line* object has a starting point, a length, and an angle. The *arc* object has a center point and starting and ending angles.

Deriving a New Class from a Derived Class

The properties of a Visual C++ class make it possible to derive a new class from any existing class. Even if the existing class already is derived from another class, it may serve as a base class for a new, derived class.

When you derive a new class from a derived class, the new class inherits the properties of the derived class, plus all the properties and functions of any ancestor classes.

To show how this works, add a new class called *CEllipse* to the *Shapes* project in the last section. Use the same steps that you used in the previous section to create a derived class. This time, however, type **CLine** in the Derived From column to derive the *CEllipse* class from *CLine* instead of directly from *CShape*. You will store the drawing information in the *CShape* base class and the rotation angle in the *CLine* class. The class definition needs only to store the lengths of the major and minor axes and override the *Draw()* function:

```
class CEllipse : public CLine
{
public:
    CEllipse (int x1, int y1, int iMajor, int iMinor,
             int iAngle = 0, COLORREF clr = 0);
    virtual ~CEllipse();
protected:
    virtual void Draw();
    int m_iMajor;
```

```
        int m_iMinor;
};
```

In the source file, notice that the constructor passes some of the parameters to the *CLine* constructor function. *CLine* takes care of storing these variables. The class overrides the *Draw()* function to provide code specific to drawing an ellipse:

```
// Ellipse.cpp: implementation of the CEllipse class.
//
//////////////////////////////////////////////////////////////


#include "stdafx.h"
#include "Ellipse.h"
#include <math.h>


//////////////////////////////////////////////////////////////
// Construction/Destruction
//////////////////////////////////////////////////////////////
//
//   The anchor point for an ellipse is the center
//   of the ellipse.
//
CEllipse::CEllipse(int x1, int y1, int iMajor, int iMinor,
int iAngle, COLORREF clr)
                : CLine (x1, y1, 0, iAngle, clr)
{
    m_iMajor = iMajor;
    m_iMinor = iMinor;
}

CEllipse::~CEllipse()
{

}


void CEllipse::Draw()
```

```
{
    //
//  Calculate the offsets for the Bezier points for
//  the ellipse
    int OffsetX = (int) (2 * m_iMajor * (2 * (sqrt(2) - 1)
                 / 3) + 0.5);
    int OffsetY = (int) (2 * m_iMinor * (2 * (sqrt(2) - 1)
                 / 3) + 0.5);
    POINT ptEllipse[13] =
    {
        m_cx1 + m_iMajor, m_cy1,
        m_cx1 + m_iMajor, m_cy1 - OffsetY,
        m_cx1 + OffsetX,  m_cy1 - m_iMinor,
        m_cx1,            m_cy1 - m_iMinor,
        m_cx1 - OffsetX,  m_cy1 - m_iMinor,
        m_cx1 - m_iMajor, m_cy1 - OffsetY,
        m_cx1 - m_iMajor, m_cy1,
        m_cx1 - m_iMajor, m_cy1 + OffsetY,
        m_cx1 - OffsetX,  m_cy1 + m_iMinor,
        m_cx1,            m_cy1 + m_iMinor,
        m_cx1 + OffsetX,  m_cy1 + m_iMinor,
        m_cx1 + m_iMajor, m_cy1 + OffsetY,
        m_cx1 + m_iMajor, m_cy1
    };
//
//  Initialize a point for the center of the ellipse
    POINT ptCenter = {m_cx1, m_cy1};
//  Rotate the ellipse about the center
    Rotate(m_iAngle, ptCenter, ptEllipse, 13);
//  Draw the rotated ellipse using Bezier points
    PolyBezier (m_hdc, ptEllipse, 13);
}
```

An ellipse requires 13 points to draw using Bezier curves. You need five for the start and end points of each quadrant of the ellipse (the begin point for a segment is the end point for the previous segment). Then you need eight control points to push and pull the curve into the shape of an ellipse. You pass these 13 points to the

Rotate() function in *CShape* and then call the API function *PolyBezier()* to actually draw the rotated ellipse. Closed shapes drawn with *PolyBezier()* do not fill the center and, thus, do not erase anything underneath.

Next, add a *CCircle* class to the project and derive it from *CEllipse*. By this time, your work is very simple. The ancestor classes *CEllipse*, *CLine*, and *CShape* already store all the information you need. The entire class definition is shown here:

```
class CCircle : public CEllipse
{
public:
    CCircle(int cx1, int cy1, int radius, COLORREF clr = 0);
    virtual ~CCircle();
};
```

The *CCircle* class does not even have to provide a *Draw()* function. You can reuse the code in *CEllipse* to draw the circle. After all, a circle is nothing but an ellipse with equal major and minor axes, so that's all you need to send the *CEllipse* constructor:

```
// Circle.cpp: implementation of the CCircle class.
//
/////////////////////////////////////////////////////////

#include "stdafx.h"
#include "Circle.h"


/////////////////////////////////////////////////////////
// Construction/Destruction
/////////////////////////////////////////////////////////
//
//   The anchor point for a circle is the center
//   of the circle. It is an ellipse with equal major
//   and minor axes.
//

CCircle::CCircle(int cx1, int cy1, int radius, COLORREF clr)
            : CEllipse (cx1, cy1, radius, radius, 0, clr)
{
```

```
}

CCircle::~CCircle()
{
}
```

That's all there is to a circle. You send the *radius* parameter as both the major and minor axes to the *CEllipse* constructor. By reusing the variables and code in ancestor classes, you have created a new class that requires no more work.

Return to the *Shapes.cpp* source file and add the following *#include* statement near the top of the file (*circle.h* includes the *ellipse.h* file, so you do not have to include it again):

```
#include "Circle.h"
```

Modify the *WM_PAINT* code in the *Shapes.cpp* file so the code looks like the following:

```
case WM_PAINT:
{
    hdc = BeginPaint(hWnd, &ps);
    RECT rc;
    GetClientRect (hWnd, &rc);
    Point point (304, 304, RGB(255, 0, 0));
    CLine line (300, 300, 300, 1350, RGB(255, 128, 0));
    CArc arc (300, 300, 1050, 1700, 200, RGB(255,0,0));
    CCircle circle (300, 300, 150, RGB(0, 0, 255));
    CEllipse ellipse (3 * rc.right / 4 - 50,
              rc.bottom / 4, 100, 50, 450, RGB(0,255,0));
    point.Show (hdc);
    line.Show (hdc);
    arc.Show (hdc);
    circle.Show (hdc);
    ellipse.Show (hdc);
    EndPaint(hWnd, &ps);
    break;
}
```

Build the project and run the program. Your screen should look similar to Figure 26.2.

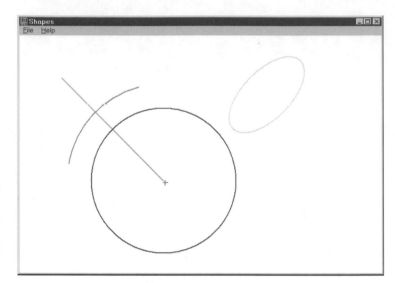

Figure 26.2

Your Shapes.exe *program now contains classes to draw and rotate lines, arcs, ellipses, and circles easily.*

Experiment with the code. Try moving the shapes around and giving them different rotation angles. Try giving the ellipse different values for the major and minor axes.

Understanding Multiple Inheritance of a Class

Sometimes you may find that you need more than one base class to build a new derived class. In the previous examples, each derived class included only a single base class. That base class itself might inherit properties from its ancestor classes as well, but there still is only a single base class.

To inherit from more than one base class, simply add the name of the second base class in your derived class definition, separating the names of the base classes with a comma. When using the New Class dialog box from the ClassView pane, after you enter **CLine** as a base class in the Derived From column, press the Enter key and use the down arrow key on your keyboard to open up a place to enter a second base class, as shown in Figure 26.3.

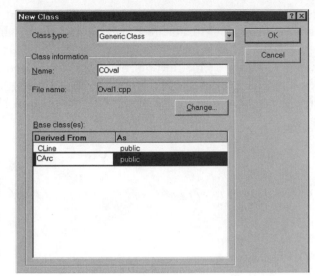

Figure 26.3

To add more than one base class, use the cursor down key to open a line to enter the second base class name.

The following class, *COval*, is derived from both *CLine* and *CArc* and draws a race track shape by drawing a single line and a single arc:

```
class COval : public CLine, public CArc
{
public:
    COval(int cx1, int cy1, int width, int depth,
          int iRotate = 0, COLORREF clr = 0);
    virtual ~COval();

protected:
    int m_iWidth;
    int m_iDepth;
    int m_iAngle;
    void Draw();
};
```

The information for the line is stored in the *CLine* ancestor class, and the information for the arc is stored in the *CArc* ancestor class. Notice also that *COval* defines a new *m_iAngle* variable, the same as a variable name in *CLine,* thus overriding a variable name in the derived class. The *Draw()* function will call the *CLine::Draw()* and the *CArc::Draw()* functions to draw each element of the shape. In the code that follows, notice that the constructor always passes 0 as the rotation angle for the line. The *Draw()* function in *COval* will handle the rotation. Also notice how the constructor calls the constructors for the base classes by separating the calls with a comma:

```cpp
// Oval.cpp: implementation of the COval class.
//
/////////////////////////////////////////////////////////////

#include "stdafx.h"
#include "Oval.h"


/////////////////////////////////////////////////////////////
// Construction/Destruction
/////////////////////////////////////////////////////////////
//
//   The anchor point for an oval is the center
//   of the oval.
//
COval::COval(int cx1, int cy1, int width, int depth,
             int iRotate, COLORREF clr)
        : CArc (cx1, cy1, 0, 900, clr),
          CLine (cx1, cy1, width, 0, clr)
{
    m_iWidth = width;
    m_iDepth = depth;
    m_iAngle = iRotate;
}

COval::~COval()
{
}

void COval::Draw()
```

```
{
//
//    Get the center of the universe
//
    POINT ptCenter;
    ptCenter.x = m_cx1 + m_iWidth / 2;
    ptCenter.y = m_cy1 + m_iDepth / 2;
//
//    Get the line path
//
    BeginPath (m_hdc);
    CLine::Draw ();
    EndPath (m_hdc);
    POINT *ptLine;
    BYTE *byteTypes;
    int iLineCount = GetPath (m_hdc, NULL, NULL, 0);
    if (!iLineCount)
        return;
    ptLine = new POINT[iLineCount];
    byteTypes = new BYTE[iLineCount];
    GetPath (m_hdc, ptLine, byteTypes, iLineCount);
//
//    Rotate the line about the center point if needed
//
    Rotate (m_iAngle, ptCenter, ptLine, iLineCount);
    Polyline (m_hdc, ptLine, iLineCount);
//
//    Now rotate 180 degrees and redraw to get the
//    other side of the racetrack.
//
    Rotate (1800, ptCenter, ptLine, iLineCount);
    Polyline (m_hdc, ptLine, iLineCount);
    delete [] byteTypes;
    delete [] ptLine;
//
//    Draw the arcs at the end. On Windows 95/98 you
```

```
//   cannot simply use BeginPath() because arcs are
//   not stored. Calculate the arc center, then reset
//   the CArc component. Then do it for the other end.
//
//   First, save the old center points. This code will
//   change m_cx1 and m_cy1, so we want to restore the
//   old values.
//

     int cxOld = m_cx1;
     int cyOld = m_cy1;
//   Draw the arc on the left end
     POINT ptArcCenter;
     ptArcCenter.x = m_cx1;
     ptArcCenter.y = m_cy1 + m_iDepth / 2;
     Rotate (m_iAngle, ptCenter, &ptArcCenter, 1);
     int iAngle = m_iAngle;
     iAngle += 900;
     CArc::SetArcPoints (ptArcCenter.x, ptArcCenter.y,
                    iAngle, iAngle + 1800, m_iDepth / 2);
     CArc::Draw ();
     //   Draw the arc on the other end
     ptArcCenter.x = cxOld + m_iWidth;
     ptArcCenter.y = cyOld + m_iDepth / 2;
     iAngle -= 1800;
     Rotate (m_iAngle, ptCenter, &ptArcCenter, 1);
     CArc::SetArcPoints (ptArcCenter.x, ptArcCenter.y,
                    iAngle, iAngle + 1800, m_iDepth / 2);
     CArc::Draw ();

     m_cx1 = cxOld;
     m_cy1 = cyOld;
}
```

After finding the center of the oval, the *Draw()* function uses the *StartPath(), EndPath(),* and *GetPath()* functions to save the line in the device context. It then rotates the line according to the angle you specified in the constructor. Then it draws the line using the *Polyline()* Windows API function. This function works much the same as the *PolyBezier()* function, except it operates on straight lines rather than curves.

Rather than call the *CLine* draw code again, you rotate the line around the center 180 degrees and repeat the call to *PolyLine()*. This draws the second straight side of the racetrack figure. To draw the arc on both ends, you use a similar technique, drawing the arc at one end, then rotating it and drawing it on the other end. The *BeginPath()* and *EndPath()* statements do not store arcs on Windows 98.

Open the *Shapes.cpp* file and change the list of include files to look like the following:

```
#include "stdafx.h"
#include "resource.h"
#include "point.h"
#include "circle.h"
#include "oval.h"
```

Now return to the *WM_PAINT* code in the *Shapes.cpp* source file and add an oval to your drawing code. Add the following two lines:

```
COval oval (3 * rc.right / 4, rc.bottom / 3, 200, 100,
            750, RGB(255, 0, 255));
oval.Show(hdc);
```

Build your project again and run the program. You should see a racetrack figure on the right side of your window rotated at an angle of 75 degrees, as shown in Figure 26.4.

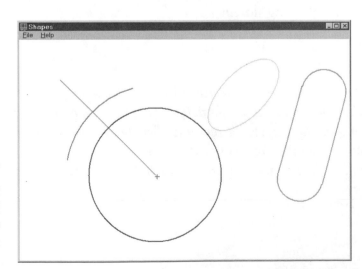

Figure 26.4

The COval class uses the drawing code in CArc and CLine as well as its own code to draw a figure shaped like a racetrack.

Experiment with the code by changing the position, size, and angle of the oval. Also, using the information you have learned in this lesson, try adding *CRectangle* and *CSquare* classes to your project. The code on the companion Web site (*http://www.prima-tech.com/books/book/5536/903*) contains these classes.

 Using The *new* And *delete* Operators

To retrieve the points to draw the line portion of the oval, you called the GetPath() Windows API function with an array of points as one of the arguments. However, you have no way of knowing ahead of time how many points the function will return, so you cannot declare an array variable to hold the points.

If you call GetPath() using 0 as the last argument, the function will return the number of elements you need in the array of POINT structures. You then may use that value to dynamically allocate an array on the heap, an area of memory set aside for temporary storage. To do this, you use the new operator: This operator returns a pointer to the newly allocated memory block. The following sets aside memory and returns a pointer to a POINT structure:

```
POINT *ptArc;
ptArc = new POINT;
```

To dynamically allocate an array, you enclose the number of elements you want inside square brackets. To allocate an array of five POINT structures, you would use the following statement:

```
ptArc = new POINT[5];
```

You may use the new operator with any Visual C++ data type, including structures and classes that you define. You must remember that memory you allocate using the new operator remains allocated even after your program ends, so you must remember to deallocate the memory after you are finished using it. To remove the memory allocation, you use the delete operator:

```
delete ptArc
```

To remove the allocation for an array, you need to follow the delete *operator with a set of square brackets, but you do not need to include the size:*

```
delete [] ptArc
```

You will learn more about the new *and* delete *operators in Lesson 32, "Using Memory Management."*

Resolving Ambiguity

In the last section, you learned how to derive a new class using more than one base class. When the base classes themselves are derived from the same base class, however, it is possible your new class will inherit two instances of an ancestor. This is the case with *COval*.

Both the *CLine* and *CArc* classes are derived from *CShape* and, thus, each inherits the functions and variables in *CShape*. When you derived *COval* from *CLine* and *CArc*, the compiler has no way of knowing which *CShape* ancestor to use. The call to the function *Show()* then becomes ambiguous because it might be the *Show()* function in *CLine* or the *Show()* function in *CArc*.

To prevent this from happening, you declare the inheritance of the *CShape* class in your base classes as *virtual:*

```
class CLine : virtual public CShape
class CArc : virtual public CShape
```

This tells the compiler to allow only one instance of the *CShape* class when both *CLine* and *CArc* are used as base classes to derive a new class, which in this program is *COval*.

To show you the confusion faced by the compiler, try removing the *virtual* keyword from the definition of, say, the *CLine* class definition:

```
class CLine : public CShape
```

Recompile your program, and you will get many errors from the compiler telling you that function and variable references are ambiguous. When you see these types of errors, trace the ancestry of your base classes to determine whether you are inheriting more than one copy of a class. Declare each inheritance of the ambiguous class *virtual* to remove the ambiguity.

What You Must Know

In this lesson, you applied what you knew about the basic concepts of object-oriented *programming—encapsulation, inheritance,* and *polymorphism*—to derive classes to draw shapes in your Windows program. You learned how to place common variables and functions in a base class so that they may be used by derived classes. In addition, you learned how to use more than one base class when you create a new derived class and how to avoid ambiguous references. In Lesson 27, "Understanding Abstract Classes," you will learn more about base classes and how to declare a class that *must* be used only as a base class. Before you continue with Lesson 27, make sure you understand the following key points:

◆ When you design and create a class that you intend to use as a base class, examine the variables and functions that might be needed by derived class. Place these variables and functions in your base class.

◆ Declare any functions that your derived classes might have to modify as *virtual* functions. When your program calls a *virtual* function, it will call the function in the derived class. The *virtual* keyword is the mechanism through which Visual C++ supports polymorphism.

◆ Derived classes may have more than one base class. In this case, it will inherit the properties and functions of all the base classes, and all the ancestors of the base classes. This is *multiple inheritance.*

◆ If base classes are derived from the same ancestor class, it is possible that a derived class that uses multiple inheritance will inherit more than one copy of an ancestor, resulting in *ambiguity.*

◆ To avoid ambiguity in multiple inheritance, use the *virtual* keyword for the ancestor class when you derive your base classes.

Lesson 27

Understanding Abstract Classes

Sometimes you will want to create a class simply to hold the variables and declare the functions that will be used by derived classes. In this case, you will not want to declare an instance of the class. To prevent this, Visual C++ lets you define *abstract* classes. You cannot declare an instance of an abstract class, and you must use it as the base class to create new class definitions. You create an abstract class by declaring one or more of its member functions as *pure virtual functions*. In this lesson, you will learn how to declare and use pure virtual functions and abstract classes. By the time you finish this lesson, you will understand the following key concepts:

◆ A *pure virtual function* is a function that you declare as part of a class but for which you do not write a body of code.

◆ To declare a pure virtual function, you declare the function as a *virtual* member of a class using the *pure specifier,* that is, you set the function equal to *NULL*.

◆ If a class contains one or more pure virtual functions, the class becomes an *abstract* class. You cannot declare a variable to create an instance of an abstract class.

◆ An abstract class serves as a base class only. To use an abstract class, you must derive a new class from it and provide a body of code for the pure virtual function.

Using an Abstract Base Class

In Lesson 26, "Letting a New Class Inherit the Attributes of an Existing Class," you developed a set of classes that drew shapes in a window. To do this, you first created an ancestor class, *CShape*, that all of your derived classes used to store common information and function. The *Show()* function in *CShape* prepared the information in member variables, then called the virtual function *Draw()* to actually draw the shapes on the screen.

In terms of output to your window, however, *CShape* does nothing. In fact, you declared the *Draw()* member function *virtual* because you never intended to call the function; instead, your derived classes provided the drawing code. Thus, you did not have to include any actual drawing code for *Draw()*.

It would do you no good to declare an instance of *CShape*. In the *Shapes* project from Lesson 26, try adding the following code to the *WM_PAINT* message section of the *WndProc()* function in the *Shapes.cpp* file:

```
CShape shape;
shape.Show(hdc);
```

This code does nothing except occupy space in your program. It doesn't do any damage, but for speed and code size, you do not want to have any unnecessary statements in your program.

To prevent this from happening, you can declare a base class as an *abstract* class. You may use abstract classes only as base classes. The compiler will issue errors when you attempt to declare an instance of an abstract class.

To create an abstract class, you use the *pure specifier* for at least one function in the class. The pure specifier is nothing more than "= 0". In effect, you set the function equal to zero:

```
virtual void Draw() = 0;
```

You may use the pure specifier only on virtual functions inside a class definition. When you declare a function this way, it is a *pure virtual function*.

Defining an Abstract Class

To define an abstract class, you must use the pure specifier on one or more virtual functions declared in the class definition. Declaring a function with the pure specifier makes it a pure virtual function. This tells the compiler that you do not intend to provide a definition—the actual code—for the function. Instead, you will leave it up to classes that you derive from the abstract class to provide code for the pure virtual function.

When you declare a pure virtual function, you do not have to provide a body for the function's definition. The compiler will not generate an error if you do write the code for a pure virtual function, but programs using the abstract class never will execute the function.

If you do not provide code for a pure virtual function in a derived class, then the derived class itself becomes an abstract class.

In the last section, you added two lines to the *WM_PAINT* code in the *Shapes.cpp* source file. Now open the *Shape.h* file where you defined the *CShape* class. Modify the declaration for *Draw()* as follows:

```
virtual void Draw() = 0;
```

This now makes *CShape* an abstract class. Recompile your program. The compiler will not let you declare an instance of an abstract class. Instead, the compiler generates and prints error messages:

```
Shapes.cpp(177) : error C2259: 'CShape' : cannot
instantiate abstract class due to following members:
        shape.h(13) : see declaration of 'CShape'
Shapes.cpp(177) : warning C4259: 'void __thiscall
CShape::Draw(void)' : pure virtual function was not defined
        shape.h(21) : see declaration of 'Draw'
```

To make the code compile again, you will have to remove the lines from the *WM_PAINT* code where you attempted to declare and use the *CShape* class directly.

You may declare as many pure virtual functions in an abstract class as you need, but it only takes one to change an ordinary class into and abstract class. Derived classes must provide code for *all* of the pure virtual functions you declare, or those classes, too, will become abstract classes.

 ## Using a *protected* Constructor in a Base Class

You do not have to use an abstract class to prevent your code from creating an instance of the class. If your class is a container for variables only or you do not have functions that your derived classes need to override, you can provide your base class with a protected constructor.

Only derived classes and friend classes may call a protected constructor for a base class, so you cannot create a direct instance of such a class. In the Shapes project, change the definition for the CShape class so that the constructor is protected (be sure to change the pure virtual function Draw() back to a virtual function):

```
class CShape
{
protected:
    CShape ();
public:
    virtual void Show (HDC hdc);
    virtual ~CShape();

protected:
    void Rotate (int iAngle, const POINT& ptCenter,
                POINT* ptControl, int Count);
    virtual void Draw();
    HDC       m_hdc;
    COLORREF     m_clrPen;
    HPEN      m_hPen;
    int       m_cx1;
    int       m_cy1;
};
```

Add the lines in the WM_PAINT code to declare an instance of CShape:

```
CShape shape;
shape.Show(hdc);
```

Recompile your program. The compiler will complain that it cannot access the protected *constructor. However, the* protected *constructor has no effect on the derived classes:*

```
Shapes.cpp(177) : error C2248: 'CShape::CShape' : cannot
access protected member declared in class 'CShape'
        n:\cfiles\gsvc\lesson26\shapes\shape.h(15) : see
declaration of 'CShape::CShape'
```

You do not need to override any functions in your derived classes, but you have protected CShape so that your code cannot create an instance of it.

Deriving a Class from an Abstract Class

When you define an abstract class, your code cannot create an instance of the class. Instead, you may use such a class only as a base class for derived classes. In an abstract class, at least one function is a pure virtual function, and your derived class *must* override any pure virtual functions and provide code for the functions.

If the derived class does not provide code for all the pure virtual functions in a base class, then the derived class itself is an abstract class as well. You cannot create an instance of a derived class in your code until you have provided functions to override the pure virtual functions.

In the last section, you modified *CShape* to be an abstract class by declaring the *Draw()* function as a pure virtual function:

```
virtual void Draw() = 0;
```

In a class definition derived from *CShape*, such as *CLine*, you declared the *Draw()* function as virtual, leaving off the pure specifier ("= 0"):

```
class CLine : virtual public CShape
{
public:
    CLine(int cx1, int cy1, int iLength,
          int iAngle = 0, COLORREF clr = 0);
    virtual ~CLine();

protected:
    int m_iLength;
    int m_iAngle;
    virtual void Draw();
};
```

In your derived class, *CLine* in this case, you do not need to declare the *Draw()* function *virtual* unless you intend to derive additional classes from the derived class. In the classes you created in Lesson 26, you later derived *COval* from *CLine*.

To override a pure virtual function, the new function must have the same return type (*void* in the case of *Draw()*), and the parameter list must have the same number of parameters of the same data types as the pure virtual function.

What You Must Know

In this lesson, you learned about *abstract classes* and how to use such classes to derive other classes. You learned about the *pure specifier* and how to declare *pure virtual functions*. You learned how to override pure virtual functions in a derived class to provide code for the new function. In Lesson 28, "Using the Microsoft Foundation Class Library," you will begin to learn about the Microsoft Foundation Class (MFC) library. The Visual Studio contains a lot of support for MFC, including application wizards to help you build programs based on MFC. Before you continue with Lesson 28, however, make sure you understand the following key points:

◆ You may use an abstract class only as a base class from which you derive new classes.

◆ To create an abstract class, declare one or more member functions using the *pure specifier*, which is "= 0". Functions that you declare this way are *pure virtual functions*.

◆ You do not need to provide a body of code for a pure virtual function. If you do, however, the compiler will ignore the code.

◆ Virtual functions have meaning only in class definitions. You cannot declare or create a *virtual* or a pure virtual function outside a class definition.

◆ To derive a new class from an abstract class, you must override all pure virtual functions and provide code to implement the new functions.

Lesson 28

Using the Microsoft Foundation Class Library

You have learned about classes in Visual C++ and how to use classes to encapsulate variables and code. You have learned how to use base classes and how to derive new classes that inherit the properties of ancestor classes. In addition, you have learned how to use a derived class to change the behavior or a base class using polymorphism. In this lesson, you will learn the basics of the Microsoft Foundation Class library. By the time you finish this lesson, you will understand the following key concepts:

◆ The Microsoft Foundation Class (MFC) is a class library to help you program for Windows.

◆ MFC contains several *view* classes, many of which contain Windows controls, to speed your project development.

◆ The *document/view architecture* separates the responsibility for handling your window and the data contained in your client area among several different classes. With MFC, you may easily create a project using the document/view architecture.

◆ The *ClassWizard* tool helps you manage the classes in your program that are derived from MFC base classes.

◆ MFC-derived classes use macros in a *message map* to map Windows messages to functions that will handle the messages.

Using MFC in a Windows Program

A *class library* is a collection of C++ classes designed to implement a particular task. Usually, they encapsulate the objects and code that are particular to the task at hand.

The Microsoft Foundation Class library is an example of a class library that was designed to help you to program for Windows. Among its classes, you find the code to create windows, classes for device contexts, and other objects peculiar to Windows. In your non-MFC applications from earlier lessons, you had to go through the process of registering your window classes and creating the windows in your own code. This is all encapsulated in the MFC functions.

A class library can make some programming tasks much easier, but an extensive library such as MFC can require much additional learning. If you've mastered your basic Windows applications and the use of the device context, you should have no problems learning MFC; many of the encapsulated functions have the same names as the API functions.

The Visual Studio supports MFC through class wizards to create MFC-based projects. In addition, a new tool you will learn about in this lesson, the ClassWizard, helps you to maintain and expand classes derived from MFC base classes.

To use MFC in a program, create a new project. Use the following steps:

1. Select New from the File menu. When the New dialog box appears, select the Projects page, then select the "MFC AppWizard (exe)" item.

2. Enter the directory where you keep your program files in the Location field.

3. Type **HelloMFC** in the Project Name field and press the OK button. (You will change the name in this field throughout this lesson to create projects.)

4. When the wizard page appears, select Single Document and *uncheck* the box next to the line that reads "Document/View Architecture." You will look at the document/view architecture in the next section.

5. Accept the defaults in Steps 2 and 3, but stop at Step 4. In Step 4, click the mouse on the Advanced button. This button will display another dialog box, where you will see options that determine how your application's window will appear. The Thick Frame option gives your program a main window that you may resize using the mouse. The Minimize Box, Maximize Box, and, System Menu option determine the options for the window title bar, as

shown in Figure 28.1. The wizard always adds the Close button. The last two options, Minimized and Maximized, determine how your window will appear when you first run your program. Minimized will reduce it to an icon on your Windows task bar. Maximized will make it occupy the full screen. The default is to run as a normal window with neither checked.

Figure 28.1

The window title bar shows some of the options you may add.

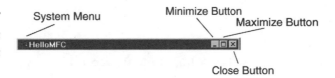

6. Close the Advanced dialog box without changing any settings. Accept the defaults in Steps 4 and 5 by clicking on the Next button. In Step 6, examine the list of classes the wizard will create for you. The *CMainFrame* class will create the window frame with a toolbar. The *CHelloMFCApp* class will handle setting up your application and creating the *CMainFrame* object. The *CChildView* class will provide you with a client window in which you may draw text and objects.

7. Accept the defaults in Step 6 by clicking the mouse on the Finish button. When the New Project Information dialog box appears, press the OK button.

Build the project and run the program. You now have a window similar to those you created in past lessons. However, notice that the wizard has added a more extensive menu and a toolbar at the top of the window frame. In addition, the wizard has placed a status bar at the bottom of the window frame.

Open the *ChildView.cpp* file. Scroll down a few lines until you find the section shown here:

```
BEGIN_MESSAGE_MAP(CChildView,CWnd )
    //{{AFX_MSG_MAP(CChildView)
    ON_WM_PAINT()
    //}}AFX_MSG_MAP
END_MESSAGE_MAP()
```

This is the message map, which takes care of many of the functions of the *WndProc()* function you used in previous lessons. However, instead of a *switch* statement with many cases, you will add separate functions to handle the Windows messages.

Particularly notice the two commented lines inside the message map (the lines beginning with "//"). *Do not* add or delete anything between these lines. The Visual Studio reserves this area for a tool called the ClassWizard, which you will learn about in this lesson. If you must add your own message handlers to this map, add them outside block marked by the commented lines:

```
BEGIN_MESSAGE_MAP(CChildView,CWnd )
    //{{AFX_MSG_MAP(CChildView)
    ON_WM_PAINT()
    //}}AFX_MSG_MAP
// The following entry was added manually
    ON_BN_CLICKED(IDC_RADIOTOOL1, OnRadiotool)
END_MESSAGE_MAP()
```

The wizard has added a handler for the *WM_PAINT* message to the map already. Instead of case statements, the wizard uses *macros*, which the compiler translates into calls to the proper message function.

Scroll farther down to the *OnPaint()* function. This is the function that handles the *WM_PAINT* Windows message. There is only one line of code in this function, plus some instructions the wizard left for you:

```
CPaintDC dc(this); // device context for painting
```

The line creates a device context using one of the MFC classes, *CPaintDC*. Remember in past projects you had to call the *BeginPaint()* function in your drawing code, then call *EndPaint()* when you finished drawing. *CPaintDC* handles this for you. When you create the *CPaintDC* object, the constructor calls *BeginPaint()* for you. When the *OnPaint()* function ends, the object is destroyed, and the destructor calls *EndPaint()* for you. The *this* pointer, remember, is a pointer to the current class object. The class object includes another MFC class, *CWnd,* which handles all the details of registering and creating the window that contains the client area of your project.

Modify the code in the *OnPaint()* function so that it looks like the following:

```
void CChildView::OnPaint()
{
    CPaintDC dc(this); // device context for painting

    // TODO: Add your message handler code here

    CRect rc;
    GetClientRect (rc);
```

```
    CFont font;
    font.CreatePointFont (240, "Times New Roman");
    CFont *OldFont = dc.SelectObject (&font);
    rc.top = rc.Height() / 2;
    CString strText = _T("Hello, MFC!");
    dc.DrawText (strText, rc, DT_CENTER);
    dc.SelectObject (OldFont);
    font.DeleteObject ();

    // Do not call CWnd::OnPaint() for painting messages
}
```

Build your project again and run the program. The client area of your program now should display text near the center, as shown in Figure 28.2.

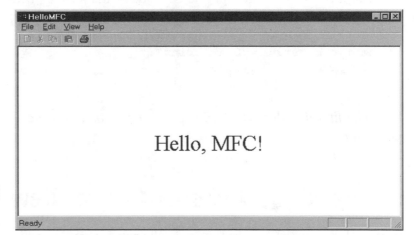

Figure 28.2

Your first MFC project.

The code you added uses MFC classes to create the objects it uses. You may use *CRect* just as you used the *RECT* structure in previous programs. The *CRect* class contains functions to manipulate the data it contains. For example, to get the height of a rectangle using a *RECT* structure, you had to subtract the top from the bottom. With *CRect,* you simply call the *Height()* member function. There also is a *Width()* member function.

The *CFont* class encapsulates all the information and functions needed by the graphics device interface to create and manipulate a font. It contains a handle to the font. It contains a function, *CreatePointFont(),* that lets you create a font by passing only the size in tenths of a point and the font name. MFC contains other classes to encapsulate GDI objects. For example, there is a *CPen* class for the pen, a *CBrush* class for the brush, and so on.

CString contains several functions that make string handling far easier than the standard C++ functions. Notice the string you place in the CString object, _T("Hello, MFC"). The CString class supports Unicode character sets. You simply could have written CString strText = "Hello, MFC!". However, enclosing the text translates the text to and from Unicode as necessary.

 Using Unicode Characters

The Unicode character set uses 16 bits to hold the value of a character. The ASCII character set uses only eight, so the Unicode character set can contain up to 65,538 characters, and the ASCII character set can contain only 256 characters. When you deal with some languages, such as some Asian or Middle Eastern languages, the ASCII character set cannot contain all the characters needed, so you need to resort to Unicode.

Standard C++ also supports Unicode in the form of wide *characters. The data type is* wchar_t, *and you must prefix the string or character with a capital* L:

```
wchar_t *str1 = L"A string";
wchar_t ch = L'A';
```

The first line declares a wide character string, and the second declares a single wide character.

Understanding Documents and Views

You might not have noticed, but the last section introduced you to a new concept—the view. The application class—which your program created when you ran the program—created the *CMainFrame* object, which holds the contents of your window. The *CMainFrame* object then created a client window, *CChildView,* to hold the client area where you draw text and graphics in your program. For the project in the last section, which did not use the document/view architecture, the wizard derived *CChildView* directly from MFC's window class, *CWnd.*

The document/view architecture adds more elements to this process. First, a new class derived from *CDocument* is responsible for reading and storing the files you will display in your project windows. A class derived from *CView* will create and display the contents of the document in your window area, and accept any new data you enter into the document. The view object provides a means of scrolling through the document when it cannot display the entire document in the client window. *CView* uses *CWnd* as a base class, and classes derived from *CView* usually incorporate a control object such as *CEdit* for an editing window.

In the document/view architecture, the application class—derived from *CApplication*—creates a document template, which will be *CSingleDocTemplate* in this project. The document template creates the *CMainFrame* object for the main window and the document object. The *CMainFrame* object creates the view object. The sequence of events is shown in Figure 28.3.

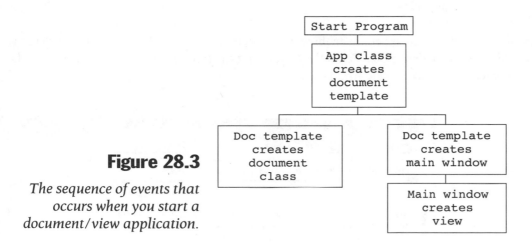

Figure 28.3

The sequence of events that occurs when you start a document/view application.

After the document template creates the document class and the main window object, the main window creates the view. The program is ready to open or create a file.

Creating a Document/View Program

When you use the document/view architecture, the application wizard performs a lot more work when it creates your program. With document/view, you may select a view class that incorporates a control so that you may start using it right away. In this section, you will create a project based on the *CEditView* class, which contains a multiline edit control.

To create a document/view application, repeat the steps in the previous section. Call this project "DocView." On the first page of the wizard, leave the check mark in the box next to the line that reads "Document/View Architecture Box." Remember to select the Single Document item. (The Multiple Document item uses the more complex "multiple document interface" [MDI]. You will not cover MDI in this book. When you finish this book, however, look at a copy of *1001 Visual C++ Programming Tips* [Prima Publishing, ISBN 0-7615-2761-3], which contains a description of the MDI system and tips on how to use it.)

In Step 6 of the wizard, notice that you have more options available for the view class. Here you may select one of the MFC view classes as the base class for your view (in the previous section, the view class used *CWnd* as the base class, and you could not change it). Select the arrow on the Base Class box and select *CEditView* as the base class. The wizard builds your view class name by prefixing the name of the project with a "C" and adding "View" at the end, so your view class now has the strange name of "CDocViewView." You may change it to "CDocView" or leave it as is.

Click on the Finish button. Then click on the OK button when the New Project Information dialog box appears. The wizard will create your new application.

Build your project and run the program. When the main window appears, select the File menu, then select the Open item to summon the File Open dialog box. Select the *Readme.txt* file from the dialog box and click on the Open button. Your window should look like Figure 28.4.

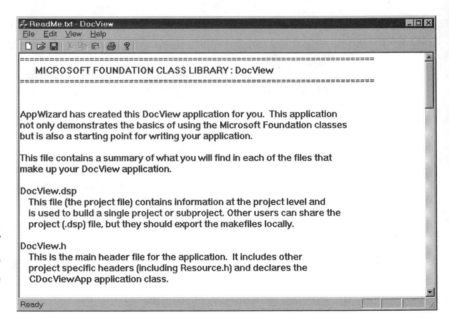

Figure 28.4

Using the CEditView base class, your program is ready to edit text documents.

You have a good start on an application. The MFC document/view classes, which the MSDN documentation refers to as the *framework*, handle much of the work you had to do in your basic Windows programs.

Adding Variables with the ClassWizard

If you are not convinced that a class library such as the Microsoft Foundation Class can save you a lot of work, you are about to meet a very handy tool, the ClassWizard. Unfortunately, for whatever reason, Microsoft has chosen to limit this tool to classes derived from MFC base classes. You cannot use ClassWizard to manipulate classes that do not use MFC classes as base classes.

Using the ClassWizard, you may add variables for objects on dialog boxes and message handlers for the messages that are available to a particular class object. You also may override virtual functions in MFC base classes using the ClassWizard. To start the ClassWizard, press Ctrl+W. You also may select the View menu, then the ClassWizard item. A third way to start the ClassWizard is to right-click the mouse on an open file and select ClassWizard from the menu that pops up. For example, in the *DocView* application from the last section, open the *DocView.cpp* source code file. Right-click the mouse on any area in the editing window that contains the *DocView.cpp* file. Select ClassWizard. Using any of the three methods, the ClassWizard dialog box will appear, as shown in Figure 28.5. This is not a true wizard in the programming sense, but it contains a tabbed dialog box with five pages.

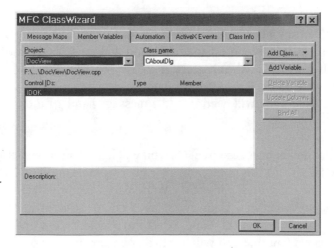

Figure 28.5

The Visual Studio ClassWizard is a tabbed dialog box containing five pages of information about classes you derive from MFC base classes.

To select a page in the ClassWizard, click the mouse on one of the tabs at the top of the dialog box. If the Member Variables page is not already selected, click the mouse on the Member Variables tab.

At the upper-center, you will see a box labeled "Class name." Click on the arrow to display the MFC-based classes in your project. Select the item that reads "CAboutDlg." This is the class that displays the About dialog box for your project when you select the About item on the Help menu. Notice there is a large list area labeled "Control IDs." There should be one item in the list called *IDOK*. This is the *resource ID* of the OK button on your about box. Select the item and click on the Add Variable button. (A resource ID is a number that the resource compiler associates with an object such as a Windows control. You will learn more about resources in Lesson 29, "Understanding Program Resources.") The Add Member Variable dialog box should appear, as shown in Figure 28.6.

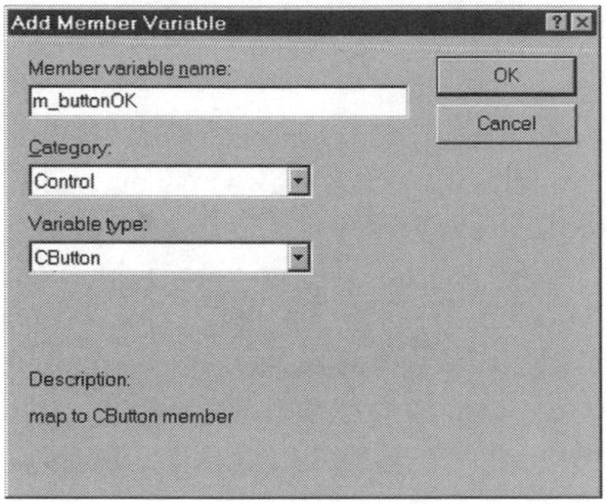

Figure 28.6

The Add Member Variable dialog box lets you create class member variables for objects that have a resource ID.

Type **m_buttonOK** in the Member variable name box. Leave the Category and Variable type boxes as they are and click on the OK button. The ClassWizard will respond by adding the variable information to the list on the Member Variables page. It is important to understand that the ClassWizard does not add the variable to your class immediately. If you click on the Cancel button, the wizard will not add the variable to your class. To complete the operation, click on the OK button. You now have a variable that gives you access to the OK button on your dialog box. To use it, you will need to add a message hander function, which you will learn to do in the next section.

To add variables that do not have resource IDs, you will have to use the method you learned in Lesson 22,"Getting Started with Classes." At this point, add a member variable that will let you create a font for your project's view class. Click on the ClassView pane of the Workspace window and right-click on the *CDocViewView* class (or whatever you named your view class in the last section). Select Add Member Variable. Make the Variable Type **CFont** and the variable name **m_Font**. Select the Private access and click on the OK button. In the next section, you will create a font that you will use to display text in your project.

Using the Message Map

You have added two variables to your project. One variable gives you access to the OK button on the program's About box, and the other is a variable to hold a font object for your view class. To use these variables, you need to add *message handler functions* to your MFC classes. Earlier in this lesson, you learned about the message map, which you may use only with MFC-based projects.

Press Ctrl+W to start the ClassWizard again or use one of the other methods from the last section. Click on the Message Maps to select the Messages page. From this page, you may add handler functions for Windows messages or override virtual functions in the MFC base classes. Select *CAboutDlg* in the Class Name box. Also select *CAboutDlg* in the Object IDs box. In the Messages box, you will see a list of virtual functions and messages available to the *CAboutDlg* class. Scroll through the list until you find the *WM_INITDIALOG* entry. Click on it with the mouse and then click on the Add Function. The ClassWizard will add the *OnInitDialog()* function to the Member Functions box. In the Member Functions box, items with a "V" are virtual function overrides, and items with a "W" are Windows message handlers.

Click the Edit Code button and the Visual Studio will move to the source file containing the *OnInitDialog()* function. Add code so the function looks like the following:

```
BOOL CAboutDlg::OnInitDialog()
{
    CDialog::OnInitDialog();
    m_buttonOK.SetWindowText (_T("This is Good"));
    // TODO: Add extra initialization here

    return TRUE;   // return TRUE unless you set the focus
                   // to a control
                   // EXCEPTION: OCX Property Pages should
                   // return FALSE
}
```

Build your project and run the program. Select the Help menu and then select the About DocView item. The dialog box will appear with the text "This is Good" instead of "OK" on the OK button. You have not changed the purpose or how you use the OK button; you have just changed the text it displays. Click on the This is Good button to close the About box.

Select the File menu and then select Exit to close the program. Start the ClassWizard again by pressing Ctrl+W. Select the Message Maps page again, but this time select the *CDocViewView* class in the Class Name box. In the Object IDs box, select *CDocViewView*. The Message box will show a list of virtual functions and messages for the view class.

Scroll through the list in the Message box until you find the *WM_CREATE* message. This message serves much the same purpose for a view object as the *WM_INITDIALOG* function serves for a dialog box. Add the message handler using the steps you just learned. Click on the Edit Code button, and the Visual Studio will take you to the newly created message handler function. Modify the code so it looks line the following:

```
int CDocViewView::OnCreate(LPCREATESTRUCT lpCreateStruct)
{
    if (CEditView::OnCreate(lpCreateStruct) == -1)
        return -1;

    m_Font.CreatePointFont (100, "Courier New Bold");
    CEdit& edit = GetEditCtrl ();
    edit.SetFont (&m_Font);

    return 0;
}
```

Now scroll back through the code until you find the class destructor. Remember that you need to delete the GDI object in the *m_Font* object after you have finished using the object. Add a line to delete the object:

```
CDocViewView::~CDocViewView()
{
    m_Font.DeleteObject();
}
```

Build your project again and run the program. Open the *Readme.txt* file to display text in the window. You should see the text displayed in the Times New Roman font rather than the, well . . . not-so-pretty, system font.

Remember that the program now is capable of editing and saving text files, so if you make any changes to the *Readme.txt* file, when you exit your program will ask you if you want to save the changes.

Adding Functions to an MFC-Derived Class

Of course, as you develop an application, you will need to add functions to it other than Windows message handlers and virtual function overrides. Unfortunately, these are the only types of functions the ClassWizard will handle. To add other functions, you will have to use the method you learned in Lesson 22. Alternatively, you may use the WizardBar shown in Figure 28.7. The WizardBar is a toolbar near the top of the Visual Studio.

At the far left of the Wizard Bar you will find an arrow pointing down. Next to that arrow (MSDN calls it the "Action" arrow) is the Wizard Action button. If you click on the down arrow, you will cause the Wizard Bar Action menu to appear. From the menu, select the Add Member Function. You will get the same dialog box you get when you use the ClassView pane of the Workspace window. Fill in the information about your new function and click the OK button.

Figure 28.7

*The WizardBar offers an
alternate means of adding
functions to your class.*

| CDocViewView | ▾ | (All class members) | ▾ | ◈ CDocViewView | ▾ | 🔍 ▾ |

What You Must Know

You have had your first introduction to a class library, the Microsoft Foundation Class library. As you learned, a class library is a set of classes that help you to perform a particular programming task. The Microsoft Foundation Class library helps you to write programs for Windows. There are about 200 classes in MFC, so a complete explanation of them is not possible in this book. In this lesson, you learned how to use the Visual Studio's MFC AppWizard to create projects based on MFC and how to create a project using the document/view architecture. In later lessons, you will learn more about MFC classes. In Lesson 29, "Understanding Program Resources," you will learn about *resources* and how to use the Visual Studio resource editor. Before you continue with Lesson 29, however, make sure you understand the following key points:

♦ The Microsoft Foundation Class library is a *class library* that makes it easier for you to write programs for Windows.

♦ The MFC classes contain many virtual functions that you may override to change the behavior of the base classes.

♦ The document/view architecture divides your program into distinct parts that perform specific operations, thus making your programming tasks easier.

♦ When using MFC, you use a *message map* to direct your program to message handler functions.

♦ The ClassWizard tool lets you add message handler functions and override MFC virtual functions. The ClassWizard works only with MFC-based classes.

Lesson 29

Understanding Program Resources

You have had your first introduction to the Microsoft Foundation Class, a library of classes that helps you to program for Windows. You have learned how to create programs using the wizards in the Visual Studio. You learned how to use the ClassWizard to add message handling functions to your MFC-based classes, and how to override virtual functions in MFC. Programming the main window, however, is only part of writing a Windows project. To develop a Windows program, eventually you will have to deal with *resources*. Resources are the menus, icons, toolbars, buttons, and other objects that you find in Windows programs. The Visual Studio includes a very capable resource editor and resource compiler. In this lesson, you will learn how to use the resource editor, and in the next two lessons, you will learn about Windows controls and how to use resources and controls to create a dialog box. By the time you finish this lesson, you will understand the following key concepts:

♦ Users interact with your program through *resources,* the menus, toolbars, and other items located on the window frame and in dialog boxes.

♦ You create and prepare resources using the Visual Studio *resource editor.* You access the resource editor through the ResourceView pane of the Workspace window.

♦ Visual Studio compiles resources using a *resource compiler* rather than the Visual C++ compiler.

♦ Your program accesses the resources using *resource IDs*. The resource editor assigns numbers to the resource IDs.

♦ The Visual C++ linker joins the compile resource file with the C++ modules in your program.

Using the ResourceView

You have explored two panes on the Workspace window—the FileView pane, which lists all of the files in your program, and the ClassView pane, which lists all of the classes along with member variables and functions of the classes. The third pane on the Workspace window is the ResourceView pane, which lists all the resources in your program and is your entry point into the Visual Studio *resource editor*.

Resources are the means through which users interact with your program. Resources include the menus, the toolbars, the accelerator keys, and other Windows *controls* that you place on your window's frame or on dialog boxes.

You create resources for your program using the Visual Studio's resource editor. You enter the resource editor through the ResourceView pane of the Workspace window. In the Visual Studio, open the *HelloMFC* project from Lesson 28, "Using the Microsoft Foundation Class Library." Click the mouse on the tab labeled "ResourceView." The entire label may not be visible, but it is the middle tab at the bottom of the Workspace Window. Click on the "+" symbol next to the items to expand the list until the ResourceView pane looks like Figure 29.1.

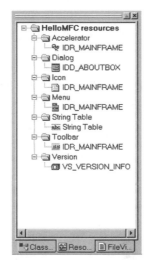

Figure 29.1

The ResourceView pane is the entry point to the Visual Studio resource editor.

The item listed in the Accelerator branch contains the "shortcut" keys your program uses. The Dialog item contains the About box for your program. The Icon, Menu, and Toolbar items contain the icon that Windows uses to represent your program, the menu that displays on the main window frame, and the toolbar that appears below the menu. The String Table item contains text items that you may reference using a resource ID. The Version item lets you maintain the name and revision level of your program, such as "HelloMFC Version 1.4."

The resource editor actually contains many components that the editor invokes as needed. For example, if you open the Toolbar item, the resource editor will invoke the toolbar editor. If you open the Icon item, the resource editor will invoke the icon editor.

Notice that there is at least one item under each resource type. For example, the Accelerator, Icon, Menu, and Toolbar items all have an entry "IDR_MAINFRAME." This is a symbol the Visual C++ *resource compiler* associates with a number (the "resource ID") that identifies with the resource entry. You can view these numbers and their symbols by right-clicking the mouse on the top item (the line that reads "HelloMFC Resources" for this project), then select Resource Symbols from the menu that pops up. For this project, the Resource Symbols dialog box should look similar to Figure 29.2.

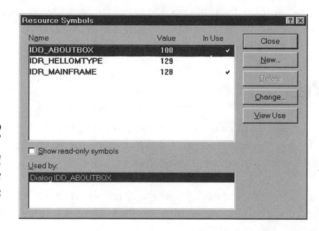

Figure 29.2

The Resource Symbols dialog box lists the symbols and the number the resource editor has assigned the symbol.

The symbol is the resource ID associated with a resource object. In a project you create using the MFC App-Wizard, the Visual Studio places the resource IDs in the *resource.h* file.

To open an item, double-click the mouse on the entry. You also may right-click the mouse on the entry and select Open from the pop-up menu. Double-click on the *IDR_MAINFRAME* item under the Icon resource type, and the resource editor will open the icon editor and display the icon in a window where you may edit the icon, as shown in Figure 29.3. Notice that the resource editor also has displayed two toolbars for you to use while editing the icon—a Graphics toolbar containing drawing tools and a Colors toolbar to let you set the color for the drawing objects.

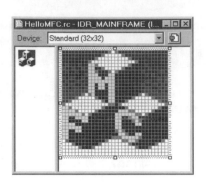

Figure 29.3

The icon editor uses the Graphics and Colors toolbars so you may edit the icon.

With a resource item open in the resource editor, you can get a brief description of the Visual Studio tool by pressing the F1 key. For example, if you have a dialog box open and you press the F1 key, a small help window will appear at the upper right of your screen describing the dialog box editor.

Creating Resources

The items you saw in the ResourceView in the last section are "stock" objects the Visual Studio uses for many programs. For example, if you create another, similar project, the MFC AppWizard will include the same icon, the same toolbar, and the same menus in your project.

Programs, however, are different, and each project may require resource items beyond the stock items the MFC AppWizard creates for you. You may want to create your own icon, menu or dialog box (you will learn about dialog boxes in Lesson 30, "Creating Dialog Boxes").

To add a resource, you need to use the Insert Resource dialog box, shown in Figure 29.4. You may display this dialog box in several ways, including the following:

◆ From the ResourceView pane, right-click the mouse on any item, then select the Insert item from the menu that pops up.

◆ Select the Insert menu on the Visual Studio main window, then select the Resource item.

◆ From anywhere in the Visual Studio, press Ctrl+R.

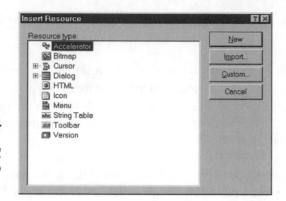

Figure 29.4

Use the Insert Resource dialog box to add new resources to your project.

Select the resource type you want to add, then click on the New button. The resource editor will create a blank resource of the type you selected and display the resource in a window.

You will learn about the menu editor later in this lesson and about the dialog box editor in Lesson 30. It is not possible to cover all of the various components of the resource editor, but you can find plenty of help in the MSDN documentation. Select the Help menu from Visual Studio, then select Index. Type in the name of the editor for which you want to find the documentation (for example, "icon editor"), then press Enter. The display window will take you to the first help page.

Editing Resources

After you have created your resources and tested them in your program, you likely will have to go back and modify them until they are to your liking. Resources are like any other code in your program. Any time you make changes to resources, you must recompile your program so the Visual C++ compiler will add the changes to your executable file. The Visual C++ compiler starts the resource compiler automatically for resource files, so you do not have to compile the resources separately. Just click the mouse on the Build button or press the F7 key. The compiler will do the rest.

To edit a resource, click on the ResourceView tab of the Workspace Window. If the resource list is compressed, expand the list by clicking on the "+" symbol on the bold line at the top of the ResourceView pane. Expand the list again by clicking on the "+" next to the resource type you want to edit. For example, if you want to edit a toolbar, expand the list to show the available toolbars by clicking on the "+" symbol next to Toolbar.

Double-click the mouse on the resource ID of the item you want to edit. The Visual Studio will respond by launching the proper component and opening the item in an editing window. For example, if you double-click on the resource ID in the Toolbar list, the resource editor will launch the toolbar editor component and display the toolbar you selected. Alternatively, you may select the item by clicking on it once, then pressing the Enter key.

The icon editor and the toolbar editor are "bitmap" editors. A bitmap is a method of representing points on your screen by setting individual pixels. In the icon and toolbar editors, each of the small squares on the resource represents a pixel. You can set the color of individual pixels by clicking on the Pencil item in the Graphics toolbar, then selecting a color in the Colors toolbar. Then move to the bitmap image and click on the square for which you want to change the color.

You may have multiple resources open in the resource editor at the same time. For example, using the *HelloMFC* project from Lesson 28, open the Icon list and double-click on the resource ID *IDR_MAINFRAME* to display the icon in an editing window. Then open the Toolbar list and click on the *IDR_MAINFRAME* to display the toolbar in another editing window.

On the Colors tool window for the icon editor, notice that in the third column, two small display screen images have replaced the color boxes. The colors in these images are special colors for icons. The color at the top (sort of a dark cyan) is a *transparent* color for icons. When Windows displays the icon for your program, for example in a directory window, the pixels you have painted with this color will disappear and any image under the pixels, say another icon, will be visible through the pixel. Just below the transparent color in the Color tool window is the *inverse* color (sort of a dark pink). When Windows displays an icon containing this color, the pixels drawn in the inverse color will appear black until the item is selected. When you select the icon, the inverse color will disappear, and images below these pixels will be visible.

Adding New Items to Menus

The menu is the one most important resource to users of your program. Users may overlook the fact that your program does not have a toolbar, or at most a minimum toolbar, and they may ignore the fact that you used a stock icon. But users have come to expect *all* Windows programs to have a menu.

With this in mind, you should carefully design the menu for your project. The default menu contains only basic items because, obviously, the MFC AppWizard does not know what type of project you want to create. However, the Visual Studio contains an excellent menu editor that lets you easily add menu items and move menu items around.

Using the steps you learned in Lesson 28, create a new project using the MFC AppWizard (exe). Name this project "Menu." Be sure to select Single Document on the first page of the wizard. This time, however, stop at Step 3 of the wizard and select Container for the Compound Document Support. Continue to Step 6 and use *CEditView* as the base class.

Select the ResourceView pane of the Workshop window and open the resource list by clicking on the "+" symbol. Click again on the "+" symbol next to the Menu entry to open the list of menus. Double-click the mouse on the *IDR_MAINFRAME* resource ID to open the menu in the Visual Studio menu editor. You should see a menu with four items across the top plus a blank box, as shown in Figure 29.5.

Figure 29.5

The Menu project's menu as the MFC AppWizard created it.

The four items on the menu are the main menu items and are *pop up-menus* (some programmers call these items *drop-down* menus to distinguish them from the type of menu that you see when you right-click on items in the Visual Studio). If you click the mouse on one of the main menu items in the menu editor, the menu list will appear with the items on the drop-down menu.

Notice the blank box to the right of the main menu items. This box lets you add your own drop-down menu to the main menu bar. You may drag it with the mouse to place it anywhere on the menu bar you like. For example, click and hold the left mouse button on the blank box, then drag the mouse to the left. An insert line will jump between the menu items as you move the mouse. When the insert line is between the Edit and View items, release the mouse button, and the box will move to that location. Type **My &Menu**. When you press the first key, a Main Menu Properties dialog box will appear, and the characters you type will display simultaneously in the dialog box and in the menu item in the menu editor.

The ampersand (&) before a character causes the menu editor to underscore the character. This character now becomes the *mnemonic* character for the menu item. When the person using your program presses the Alt+M key (because you typed **&M**), your program will select this menu automatically. If you want to add a real ampersand to your menu item, you must double type the ampersand. For example, to make the text "Sign & Sound" appear in a menu item, you would have to type **Sight && Sound**.

Notice that the menu editor has added a blank box below your drop-down menu item. This is for the first item in your drop-down menu. As you add items, the menu editor will continue moving the blank box down one. Click the mouse on the blank box to select it, then type **&Set Font**. As you begin typing, the Menu Items Properties dialog box appears. Now click the mouse on another menu item and then click again on the Set Font item you just added. Press Alt+Enter to display the Properties dialog box again (to keep the Properties dialog box visible, click on the push pin in the upper-left corner of the Properties dialog box). The dialog editor has assigned your menu item a resource ID of *ID_MYMENU_SETFONT*. The editor builds this name from the name of your drop-down menu (My Menu) plus the name of the menu item (Set Font), removing any spaces and capitalizing the characters. You may assign it any other resource ID you want, but the default name usually is descriptive of how the item will be used. (If the dialog editor did not enter the *ID_MYMENU_SETFONT* resource ID, change it now). Finally, in the Prompt field of the Properties dialog box, type **Set window font and text color\nFont and text color**. Your program will display the text up to the "\n" on your program's main window status bar when you move the mouse cursor over the menu item. If you later add a toolbar button for this menu item, the program will display the text after the "\n" when you move the mouse cursor over the toolbar button.

Using the procedures in the previous paragraph, add a second item to the menu called "&Window Color." For the prompt text, enter **Set window background text color\nBackground color**. The menu editor will assign this item a resource ID of *ID_MYMENU_WINDOWCOLOR*. (If the editor did not assign this ID, change it now in the ID box of the Properties dialog box). When you are finished, your menu should look like Figure 29.6a.

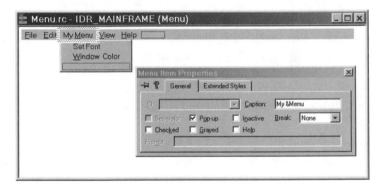

Figure 29.6a

Your main menu should look like this after adding items to set the font and background color of your application's window.

Build the project and run your program. Select My Menu with the mouse or press Alt+M. Notice that both of your new menu items are inactive or "grayed out." Menu items are inactive until you create a message handler function for the item. That will be your next step.

Exit your program and open the *MenuView.cpp* file from the FileView pane of the Workshop window. Press Ctrl+W to start the ClassWizard. When the ClassWizard dialog box appears, click on the Message Maps tab. Scroll through the Object IDs list until you find the entry for your first menu item, *ID_MYMENU_SETFONT,* and click the mouse on it. In the Messages box, you should have two items, *COMMAND* and *UPDATE_COM-MAND_UI.* Click on *COMMAND* to select it. Selecting an item also enables the Add Function button. Click on the Add Function button. Instead of adding a function directly for a menu item, the ClassWizard asks you for a name for the function. The default name usually is descriptive, so click the OK button to accept the default. Repeat this process to add a function for *ID_MYMENU_WINDOWCOLOR.* After you have added the second function, click on the Edit Code button. The ClassWizard will open the *MenuView.cpp* file and place the caret at the position where it added the functions.

Using the ClassView pane of the Workspace window, add member variables to the *CMenuView* class, as shown next. Set the Access for all the variables to *private*:

```
CFont m_Font;
COLORREF m_clrCustom[16];
COLORREF m_clrText;
COLORREF m_clrBack;
CBrush m_Brush;
```

Now add code to the functions you just added to the *CMenuView* class, as shown here:

```
void CMenuView::OnMymenuSetfont()
{
    CFontDialog cf;
    LOGFONT lf;
    CFont *font = GetEditCtrl().GetFont ();
//
//    The first time through, the font will be
//    NULL. Set up some defaults
    if (font == NULL)
    {
        font = new CFont;
        font->CreatePointFont (100, "System");
        font->GetLogFont (&lf);
        delete font;
    }
    else
    {
        font->GetLogFont (&lf);
    }

    cf.m_cf.lpLogFont = &lf;
    cf.m_cf.rgbColors = m_clrText;
    cf.m_cf.Flags |= CF_INITTOLOGFONTSTRUCT;
    if (cf.DoModal () == IDCANCEL)
        return;
//
```

```
//    If m_Font has been created already, delete it
//    then create a new font from the LOGFONT in
//    the dialog box.
    if (m_Font.m_hObject != NULL)
        m_Font.DeleteObject ();
    m_Font.CreateFontIndirect (&lf);
    GetEditCtrl ().SetFont (&m_Font);
//
//    Set the new text color
    m_clrText = cf.m_cf.rgbColors;
}


void CMenuView::OnMymenuWindowcolor()
{
    CColorDialog cc;
//
//  Set the default color to the current color
    cc.m_cc.Flags |= CC_RGBINIT;
    cc.m_cc.rgbResult = m_clrBack;
//
//  A pointer to our custom colors
    cc.m_cc.lpCustColors = m_clrCustom;
    if (cc.DoModal () == IDCANCEL)
        return;
//
//  Delete any old brush
    if (m_Brush.m_hObject != NULL)
        m_Brush.DeleteObject ();
//
//  Create a new brush with the selected color
    m_clrBack = cc.GetColor ();
    m_Brush.CreateSolidBrush (m_clrBack);
//
//  Force the window to redraw
    Invalidate ();
}
```

This code will let you set the window's font using the menu item. There are a couple of more steps you need to take to make everything work. First, add the following code to the *CMenuView* constructor and destructor:

```
CMenuView::CMenuView()
{
    m_clrText = 0;                       // Text color is black
    m_clrBack = RGB(255, 255, 255); // Background is white
    m_Brush.CreateSolidBrush (m_clrBack);
}


CMenuView::~CMenuView()
{
    if (m_Brush.m_hObject != NULL)
        m_Brush.DeleteObject ();
    if (m_Font.m_hObject != NULL)
        m_Font.DeleteObject ();
}
```

Start the ClassWizard again by pressing Ctrl+W. On the Message Maps page, search through the Messages list for an item named =*WM_CTLCOLOR* (note the equals sign in front of the name). When some Windows controls such as the edit control embedded in the *CEditView* class needs to redraw itself, it sends a message, *WM_CTLCOLOR*, to its parent asking for color information. The "=" sign means the message is "reflected." When you use MFC, a reflected message may be handled by the control itself, or the parent window, or by both. Make the code in the message handler look like the following:

```
// If CtlColor returns a NULL brush, no colors will change
HBRUSH CMenuView::CtlColor(CDC* pDC, UINT nCtlColor)
{
    pDC->SetTextColor (m_clrText);
    pDC->SetBkColor (m_clrBack);
    return ((HBRUSH) m_Brush);
}
```

Compile your project again and run the program. Using your new menu items, try changing the font and text color by selecting the Set Font item on My Menu. Set the background color using the Window Color item. Move the mouse cursor over a menu item to make sure the text appears on the status bar at the bottom of the window.

Success HINT: Using Common Dialogs

The CColorDialog *and* CFontDialog *classes that you used in this lesson are the MFC classes for two of the* Windows *common dialog boxes. Windows includes these dialog boxes as part of the operating system program files, and you do not have to create them for your projects.*

In addition to the font and color dialog boxes, Windows provides common dialog boxes to open and save a file, to search and replace text in a file, and to print a file from your program. The Microsoft Foundation Class contains classes for all of these dialog boxes. The CFileDialog *class encapsulates the open and save file dialog boxes, the* CFindReplaceDialog *provides a class for the find and replace dialog boxes, and the* CPrintDialog *gives you access to the print and printer setup dialog boxes from your MFC-based program.*

Using these dialog classes can be involved. 1001 Visual C++ Programming Tips *(published by Prima-Tech) contains detailed information on how to construct and use the common dialog boxes both in an MFC-based program and in a Windows API program.*

What You Must Know

In this lesson, you learned how your program uses *resources*. You learned how to use the ResourceView pane of the Workspace window to edit resources and to add new resources to your program. You learned how the resource editor invokes its various components when you add or edit resources. You learned how to use the menu editor to add new drop-down menus to your program and new items to your drop-down menus. Then you learned how to add message handler functions for these menu items. In the next lesson, you will learn how to create and edit dialog boxes for your program. Before you continue with Lesson 30, "Creating Dialog Boxes," however, make sure you understand the following key points:

◆ Resources are the menus, toolbars, and other items on the window frame and in dialog boxes that let a user interact with your program.

◆ The Visual Studio contains a resource editor that has various components to edit different resource types.

◆ Visual Studio compiles the resources in your program using a resource compiler, then adds the compiled resources to your program file.

◆ Your program accesses resource items using resource IDs assigned by the resource editor or by yourself.

◆ The resource editor places the resource IDs in a file named *resource.h*.

Lesson 30

Creating Dialog Boxes

You have learned how your Windows programs use resources and how resource IDs identify resources within your program. You also learned how to create and edit resources using the ResourceView pane of the Workspace window and how to add new items to menus using the resource editor. In addition to the control objects on the main window frame, you will use the resource editor to create and edit *dialog boxes* in your program. A dialog box is a window that holds controls to display information or to accept input from users. You create dialog boxes to perform auxiliary tasks in your program, such as asking the user to enter the name of a file to open. Windows programs frequently communicate with users through dialog boxes. The Message Box is an example of a simple dialog box. In this lesson, you will learn how to create and edit dialog boxes using the Visual Studio dialog box editor. By the time you finish this lesson, you will understand the following key concepts:

◆ Dialog boxes are temporary windows that you display to show information to a user or to get information from the user that your program needs.

◆ To create a dialog box in your program, you first must create a *dialog box template* in your program's resource file.

◆ Your program identifies a dialog box through its resource ID. When you derive a class for your dialog using the Microsoft Foundation Class library, you must use the dialog box's resource ID.

◆ You set the options for your dialog box, including the font, using the Dialog Properties dialog box in the resource editor.

◆ Dialog boxes contain *controls,* which are small, special-purpose windows that you may use to display text and graphics and to accept input from a user.

Using the Dialog Box Editor

At some point in developing a Windows program, you will need to prompt the user with some information and get a response from the user. In pre-WIndows days, a program could use the command line to inform a user of status information or to accept input from a user. Windows programs, however, commonly use a *dialog box* to display information for a user or accept a user response. A dialog box is a temporary window your program uses to interact with a user, display text and graphics, and accept a response from the user. Typically, a dialog box uses *controls* such as text boxes, lists, and check boxes to display information and let the user select an option.

It is a rare Windows program that does not use dialog boxes. Even the skeleton programs created by the Visual C++ application wizards provide an About box, which is a simple dialog box dedicated to providing the user with information about your program.

In Visual C++, you create and edit dialog boxes using the dialog box editor, which you access through the ResourceView pane of the Workspace window. In the next section, you will create a dialog box in a Windows program, but for now, you need to learn the basics of the dialog box editor.

Open the *HelloMFC* project from Lesson 29, "Understanding Program Resources." Use the following steps to edit the About dialog box:

1. Click your mouse on the ResourceView tab of the Workspace window to get a list of resources in your program.

2. Click on the "+" symbol next to the line that reads "HelloMFC resources." Normally, when you first open a project in Visual C++, only this top line will be visible in the Resource-View pane.

3. Click on the "+" symbol next to the Dialog item. The list should expand to show a single entry with the resource ID of *IDD_ABOUTBOX*.

4. Open the About box in the dialog editor by double-clicking the mouse on the IDD_ABOUTBOX item. You also may open the dialog box by clicking the mouse once on the item, then pressing the Enter key.

After following the preceding steps, the dialog box editor will display the About box in an editing window, as shown in Figure 30.1.

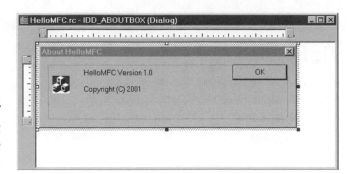

Figure 30.1

The HelloMFC project's About box as it appears in the dialog box editor.

Click on the OK button on the About box. Instead of closing the dialog box as the OK button would do in your program, the button appears with a highlight line, or *selection border,* around it, as shown in Figure 30.2. The button is an example of a control. While the OK button shows the selection border, you may drag it to a new location using the mouse or by pressing the cursor movement keys on your keyboard.

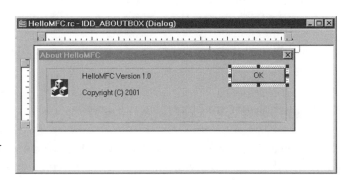

Figure 30.2

The OK button in the About box has a selection border around it when you select the button using the mouse. The small boxes around the edge of the button are resize handles.

Notice also that the selection border around the OK button has several small boxes, one at each corner and one in the middle of each side. These are *resize* handles. You may change the size of the button by clicking and holding the mouse on one of these resize handles and dragging the mouse cursor until the button is the size you want.

In Lesson 28, "Using the Microsoft Foundation Class Library," you used a variable in your program to set the text. You may permanently change the text on a button in the dialog box editor. With the OK button selected, press the Enter key to display the properties for a push button control, as shown in Figure 30.3.

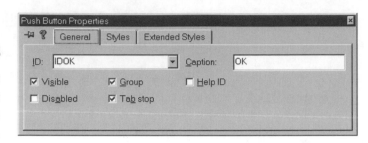

Figure 30.3

The Push Button Properties dialog box is where you set the styles and text for a control on a dialog box.

The ID field contains the resource ID of the button control, and the Caption field contains the text that appears on the button. Click on the "OK" text in the Caption field and type something else, say, **This is good**. As you type, the text on the button will change to display your new text.

Click on another item such as the line that reads "HelloMFC Version 1.0" (refer to Figure 30.2). The selection border will move to this line, which is a *static text* control. Press the Enter key to display the Push Button Properties dialog box. (You can keep this dialog box from disappearing by pressing the "push pin" at the upper-left of the dialog box. To hide the Push Button Properties dialog box, press the "X" at the upper-right.)

Later in this lesson, you will learn how to set options for a dialog box and how to add controls to a dialog box.

Creating Your First Dialog Box

Although the Visual Studio application wizards add an About box to your program, you often will find that you need to create your own dialog boxes to handle special tasks. You create new dialog boxes using the dialog box editor, which you access through the ResourceView pane of the Workshop window.

In this section, you will create a dialog box in a Win32 project and add a menu item to show your dialog box. Then you will add an accelerator key that also will display your dialog box. By learning how to handle a dialog box in a Win32 project, you will better understand how the Microsoft Foundation Class library helps you to deal with dialog boxes.

Use the application wizard to create a new Win32 application named "HelloDialog." This can be a "Hello, World" type of application. When the wizard finishes creating the project files, click on the ResourceView pane of the Workspace window, then click on the "+" symbol on the first line to expand the resource list.

Right-click on the Dialog item on the resource list and select Insert Dialog from the menu that pops up. You also may press Ctrl+R to display the New Resource dialog box, then select "Dialog" as the resource type, and then click on the New button.

Notice that the dialog box editor has given the new dialog box a default resource ID of *IDD_DIALOG1* and placed two buttons on the dialog box template, an OK button and a Cancel button. From the window containing your new dialog box, press Alt+Enter to get the Dialog Properties dialog box. Enter **IDD_FIRSTDIALOG** in the ID box. Now type **First Dialog** in the Caption box. As you type, notice in the dialog box editor that the text in the title bar of the dialog box changed.

There are small solid boxes on the right and bottom sides and on the lower-right corner of your dialog box. These are resizing points. You can make your dialog box as large or as small as you need by grabbing one of the resizing points with your mouse and moving the box to resize the dialog box. Take a few minutes to practice changing the size of the dialog box. More often than not, you will need to change the size of a dialog box to fit your own needs. As you change the size of the dialog box, the Visual Studio status bar shows the size of the dialog box in the lower-right corner of your screen.

For now, that is all you will need to do with your dialog box. Now you need to provide some method to access the dialog box from your program. In this program, you will provide a menu item and an accelerator key.

In the ResourceView pane of the Workspace window, click on the "+" symbol next to the Menu item to expand the list to show your program's menus. There should be only one, *IDC_HELLODIALOG*. Open this menu for editing using one of the methods you have learned.

Add a new drop-down menu named "My Dialog." Drag the empty box to the right of the menu to a point between File and Help. Type **My Dialog**, then add a single item to the menu named "First." Give the menu item a resource ID of *ID_MYDIALOG_FIRST*.

You now have created a dialog box and provided a menu item to display the dialog box. The next step is to add code to your program to use the new resources. In a Win32 application, each dialog box should have its own window procedure to handle the messages Windows sends to the dialog box. Open the *HelloDialog.cpp* source code file and look for the following line near the top of the file:

```
// Forward declarations of functions included in this code module:
```

The next few lines contain prototypes for the functions in your program. Add the following prototype to the list:

```
LRESULT CALLBACK    FirstDlg(HWND, UINT, WPARAM, LPARAM);
```

Your dialog box procedure will need to handle at least two messages. First, you should return *TRUE* when Windows sends the *WM_INITDIALOG* message. Eventually, you will use this message to initialize the controls on your dialog box to give the controls default values. You also will need to handle the *WM_COMMAND* message. The controls on your dialog box, including the OK and Cancel buttons, will send this message when they need to notify your program of an event, such as a mouse click. Add the following function at the bottom of the *HelloDialog.cpp* source code file:

```cpp
// Message handler for First Dialog.
LRESULT CALLBACK FirstDlg(HWND hDlg, UINT message,
                          WPARAM wParam, LPARAM lParam)
{
    switch (message)
    {
        case WM_INITDIALOG:
            return TRUE;

        case WM_COMMAND:
            switch (LOWORD (wParam))
            {
                case IDOK:
                    EndDialog(hDlg, IDOK);
                    return TRUE;
                case IDCANCEL:
                    EndDialog(hDlg, IDCANCEL);
                    return TRUE;
                default:
                    break;
            }
            break;
    }
    return FALSE;
}
```

For now, your dialog box contains only the OK and Cancel buttons. When you use other controls, you will use the *IDOK* section to retrieve information and values from these other controls when the user presses the OK button on your dialog box.

Finally, you need to add code to the window procedure for your main window to call the dialog message handler. In the *WndProc()* function, locate the section that handles the *WM_COMMAND* message. This is the message that will be sent when you select the First item from the My Dialog menu. Add code to make the message section look like the following code. The entire *WM_COMMAND* handler is shown, but you need to add only the code for *ID_MYDIALOG_FIRST*:

```
case WM_COMMAND:
    wmId     = LOWORD(wParam);
    wmEvent  = HIWORD(wParam);
    // Parse the menu selections:
    switch (wmId)
    {
        case IDM_ABOUT:
            DialogBox(hInst, (LPCTSTR)IDD_ABOUTBOX,
                        hWnd, (DLGPROC)About);
            break;
        case IDM_EXIT:
            DestroyWindow(hWnd);
            break;
//
//  Add the following case statement to the code
        case ID_MYDIALOG_FIRST:
            DialogBox(hInst, (LPCTSTR)IDD_FIRSTDIALOG,
                        hWnd, (DLGPROC)FirstDlg);
            break;
        default:
            return DefWindowProc(hWnd, message,
                                    wParam, lParam);
    }
    break;
```

Build the *HelloDialog* application and run the program. Select the My Dialog drop-down menu and then select the First item. Your dialog box will appear in the upper-left corner of your program's main window. In the next section, you will learn how to change the position where your dialog box appears.

Before leaving this section, however, you will add an accelerator key to bypass the menu item and display your dialog box when you press the Ctrl+D key. Return to the ResourceView pane of the Workspace window. This time, click on the "+" symbol next to Accelerator to expand the list. Under Accelerator, double-click the mouse on the *IDC_HELLODIALOG* item. The list of accelerator keys—the *accelerator table*—will appear in an editing window.

The only two items in the accelerator table are two items to display the About box when you press Alt+/ or Alt+? Press the Ins or Insert key to create a new accelerator item. Type **ID_MYDIALOG_FIRST** in the ID field. Now click the mouse on the large button labeled "Next Key Typed." The accelerator editor will accept the next key you press as the key to use for the accelerator item. Press Ctrl+D. The accelerator editor places "D" in the Key field, then checks the Ctrl modifier box and VirtKey as the type.

Build your project again and run the program. This time, instead of selecting the menu item, simply press Ctrl+D to display your dialog box.

Setting Dialog Box Options

The Properties dialog box for the dialog box editor is one of the most involved of the Properties dialogs, and contains more options than any other resource object. In addition to the General page of the property sheet, there are Styles, More Styles, and Extended Styles pages, each filled with options you may select for your dialog boxes. Any time you need to review the purpose of any of the options, select the page that contains the option, then press the large question mark in the upper-left corner of the Properties dialog box.

On the General page, you can set the font and size of the text for your dialog box. Click your mouse on the Font button to display the Select Dialog Font dialog box. Select a new font or point size for your dialog font. If you select a different font, you should select one that will be installed on any computer on which you will run your program. If the font is not available on a computer, the font will default to the System font. The dialog box editor uses MS Sans Serif as the default font, which is not a particularly attractive font but which is available on all computers running Windows. For now, at least change the size of the font from 8 to 10, then click on the OK button. Notice that the dialog editor has made your dialog box larger to accommodate the larger type size.

Next, remember that your dialog box appeared in the upper-left corner of your program's main window when you selected it by using the menu item or by pressing Ctrl+D. There are three methods of changing the initial position of the dialog box. Try changing the position using the following options listed to see the effects on your dialog box. Each time you change a dialog box option, you must recompile your program before the changes take effect.

- ◆ On the General page of the Properties dialog box, enter the coordinates where you want the upper-left corner of the dialog to appear. Enter the horizontal position in the X Pos field and the vertical position in the Y Pos field. The 0,0 position is the upper-left corner of the client area of your program's main window.

- ◆ On the More Styles page of the Properties dialog box, check the Center check box. This will make the center of the dialog box appear in the center or your program's main window.

◆ Also on the More Styles page, check the Center Mouse check box. This will make the center of your dialog appear at the mouse cursor position. Remember to uncheck the Center check box. (If you leave both boxes checked, your program will use the Center Mouse option).

In addition, on the More Styles page, checking the Absolute Position check box will cause your program to use the upper-left corner of the screen as the 0,0 point rather than the upper-left corner of your program's client area.

On the More Styles page, there are some options you should know about. The System Modal box causes the dialog box to appear always on the top of all windows that are displayed on your screen, even windows created by other applications. This makes it the Dialog Box That Ate Chicago. Use this style very sparingly, and only when there is a critical situation that requires the user to intervene immediately.

The No Fail Create is an important option, particularly when debugging. When you later add controls to your dialog box and you give a control an illegal option, it may fail to create. If this happens, you dialog box also may fail to create. Setting the No Fail Create option causes the dialog box to appear anyway, and you can look for a missing control to see which control caused the problem.

Adding Controls to Your Dialog Box

A dialog box with nothing but OK and Cancel buttons is not of much use to your program. All you can do is display the dialog box and then dispatch it by selecting one of the buttons. Even if the dialog box only displays a message, the primary purpose of a dialog box is to serve as a place for you to place Windows controls.

When you created your dialog box or when you opened a dialog box in the dialog box editor, the Visual Studio displayed a Controls toolbar. Initially, this toolbar is on the right side of your screen, but you may move it to wherever you want. (Be careful when moving the Controls toolbar. It is a *dockable* toolbar, and it has a nasty habit of attaching itself to odd places around the frame when you least expect it.) The toolbar is shown in Figure 30.4.

Figure 30.4

The Controls toolbar appears when you create or edit a dialog box template.

The Controls toolbar contains buttons for many of the Windows *common controls,* which are available on all systems running Windows 95, 98, NT, 2000, and ME. Not all of the common controls are represented on the Controls toolbar. Some of them, such as the *image list* and the *header control,* are support controls that you use with other common controls.

You will learn more about the common controls in the next lesson. In this lesson, you will learn how to place the controls on your dialog boxes.

To add a control to your dialog box, move the mouse cursor so that it is over the image representing the control you want to add. If you let the mouse cursor hover over an image for about half a second, a small tool tip window will appear telling you the name of the control. Click on the image to select the button. If you change your mind, simply select another control or click on the selection arrow at the upper-left of the toolbar.

Move the mouse cursor to the place on the dialog box template where you want the control to appear. Click and hold the left mouse button to begin drawing the control. Move the mouse cursor to the position where you want the opposite corner of the control to be. Notice that the dialog box editor draws an outline of the control as you move the mouse. Release the left mouse button and the dialog editor will place the control on your dialog box.

For now, practice with the Static Text and Edit Box controls. First, select the Static Text control as just described (the Static Text control is the second control in the first column of the toolbar, just below the selection arrow). Move to your dialog box template and draw the control on the template. The control is the top control in Figure 30.5 with the word "Static." (Figure 30.5 has a border around the Static Text control to show you where to draw it, but you will not have to add the border.) Press Alt+Enter to display the Text Properties dialog box. Type **Enter new text** in the Caption field.

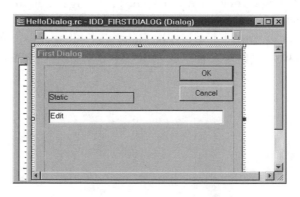

Figure 30.5

Your first dialog box as it should appear after you have drawn Static Text and Edit Box controls on the dialog box template.

Use the same process to draw the Edit Box control. The button to select an Edit Box control is next to the Static Text on the Controls toolbar. Draw the control as shown in Figure 30.5. You will not have to change the text in the Edit Box control. You will do that from your program.

Open the *HelloDialog.cpp* source file. Near the top of the file you will find a comment line that says "Global Variables." Add the following declaration after this line:

```
// Global Variables:
TCHAR szDialogText [MAX_LOADSTRING];
```

You will have to make several changes to the *WndProc()* function. Change the code so that it looks like the following code. Notice that you are adding a *case* statement to handle the *WM_CREATE* message and changing the *WM_PAINT* code to draw the *szDialogText* string. You also will make some changes in the *ID_MYDIALOG_FIRST* code:

```
LRESULT CALLBACK WndProc(HWND hWnd, UINT message,
                    WPARAM wParam, LPARAM lParam)
{
    int wmId, wmEvent;
    PAINTSTRUCT ps;
    HDC hdc;
    TCHAR szHello[MAX_LOADSTRING];
    LoadString(hInst, IDS_HELLO, szHello, MAX_LOADSTRING);

    switch (message)
    {
// Add the following case for the WM_CREATE message
        case WM_CREATE:
            LoadString(hInst, IDS_HELLO, szDialogText,
                    MAX_LOADSTRING);
            break;
        case WM_COMMAND:
            wmId    = LOWORD(wParam);
            wmEvent = HIWORD(wParam);
            // Parse the menu selections:
            switch (wmId)
            {
                case IDM_ABOUT:
                    DialogBox(hInst, (LPCTSTR)IDD_ABOUTBOX,
                            hWnd, (DLGPROC)About);
                    break;
```

```
                    case IDM_EXIT:
                        DestroyWindow(hWnd);
                        break;
                    case IDD_FIRSTDIALOG:
                         break;
                    case ID_MYDIALOG_FIRST:
//   Do the following only if the user clicks on OK
                        if (DialogBox(hInst,
                                    (LPCTSTR)IDD_FIRSTDIALOG,
                                     hWnd, (DLGPROC)FirstDlg)
                                     == IDOK)
                        {
// Force the window to redraw using the new text
                            RECT rc;
                            GetClientRect (hWnd, &rc);
                            InvalidateRect (hWnd, &rc, TRUE);
                        }
                        break;
                    default:
                        return DefWindowProc(hWnd, message,
                                            wParam, lParam);
                }
                break;
            case WM_PAINT:
                hdc = BeginPaint(hWnd, &ps);
                // TODO: Add any drawing code here...
                RECT rt;
                GetClientRect(hWnd, &rt);
//   Change the following line to use szDialogText instead
//   of the szHello string.
                DrawText(hdc, szDialogText,
                        strlen(szDialogText), &rt, DT_CENTER);
                EndPaint(hWnd, &ps);
                break;
            case WM_DESTROY:
                PostQuitMessage(0);
```

```
            break;
        default:
            return DefWindowProc(hWnd, message,
                                    wParam, lParam);
    }
    return 0;
}
```

Finally, you will need to modify the *FirstDlg()* function to place the old text in the Edit Box control. You will add a *case* statement to handle the *WM_INITDIALOG* message. Then you will need to retrieve any new text when the user clicks on the OK button. You will retrieve the text in the *IDOK* portion of the *WM_COMMAND* message case. When you are finished, the *FirstDlg()* function should look as shown here:

```
// Message handler for First Dialog.

LRESULT CALLBACK FirstDlg(HWND hDlg, UINT message,
                          WPARAM wParam, LPARAM lParam)
{
    switch (message)
    {
        case WM_INITDIALOG:
            SetDlgItemText (hDlg, IDC_EDIT1, szDialogText);
            return TRUE;
        case WM_COMMAND:
            switch (LOWORD (wParam))
            {
                case IDOK:
                    GetDlgItemText (hDlg, IDC_EDIT1,
                        szDialogText, sizeof (szDialogText));
                    EndDialog(hDlg, IDOK);
                    return TRUE;
                case IDCANCEL:
                    EndDialog(hDlg, IDCANCEL);
                    return TRUE;
                default:
                    break;
            }
```

```
        break;
    }
    return FALSE;
}
```

Build your project again and run the program. Display your dialog box. The text in the program's main window should appear in the Edit Box control. Type some new text in the Edit Box control and then click on the OK button. The new text should appear in the main window. Try it again, but this time click on the Cancel button instead of the OK button. The text in your main window should not change.

Creating a Dialog Box Class

Now that you have created and used a dialog box in a Win32 application, you will appreciate all the work the MFC AppWizard and the ClassWizard will do for you when you want to write a program using a dialog box.

You will create your dialog box using the same method that you used to create a dialog box for the Win32 application. The difference will be the method you use to write code to handle the dialog box.

Create another application named "MFCDialog." This time, select MFC AppWizard (exe). On the first page of the wizard, select Single Document, and on Page 6 use the *CEditView* class as the base class for your view. These are the same steps you used in Lesson 28.

Create a new dialog box using the method you learned in this lesson for the Windows API program. You may use the same resource IDs. Remember to add the drop-down menu and the First item to the menu and the accelerator key.

Select your dialog box template in the dialog box editor. Press Ctrl+W to summon the ClassWizard. Instead of going directly into the ClassWizard dialog box, you will get the Adding a Class dialog box first, asking you whether you want to create a new class for your dialog box. Click on the OK button, and the ClassWizard will display the New Class dialog box. Notice that the wizard already has selected *CDialog* as the base class and entered the resource ID of your dialog box template. In the Name field, type **CMyDialog**. As you type, the wizard will create a file name for you. Click the OK button to accept the file name and start the ClassWizard.

For now, leave your new class as it is. Instead, select the *CMFCDialogView* class in the Class Name box. In the Object IDs box, find and click your mouse on the resource ID for the menu item that you added (that should be *ID_MYDIALOG_FIRST*). Next, click on the *COMMAND* entry in the Messages box, then on the Add Function button, and then on the OK button on the Add Member Function dialog box to accept the function name the wizard created for you. Click on the Edit Code button, and the wizard will open the *MFCDialogView.cpp* and take you to the function definition. Make the function read as shown here:

```
void CMFCDialogView::OnMydialogFirst()
{
    CMyDialog dlg;
    dlg.DoModal ();
}
```

This function creates an object of the *CMyDialog* class, then calls the *DoModal()* member function, which creates and displays the dialog box. When the function exits, the object goes out of scope, and the *CMyDialog* destructor destroys the dialog box and any controls on the dialog box.

At the top of the *MFCDialogView.cpp* file, add the following to the list of include files:

```
#include "MyDialog.h"
```

Build the project and run the program. Summon your dialog box using both the menu item and the accelerator key, Ctrl+D. It does not do anything yet. That is the next step, so exit your program.

Enter the ClassWizard again by pressing Ctrl+W. Select the *CMyDialog* class in the Class Name box. Now click on the Member Variables tab at the top of the ClassWizard. Select the resource ID for the Edit Box control you added to your dialog box (it is *IDC_EDIT1* because you accepted the default ID). Click on the Add Variable button to get the Add Member Variable dialog box. Type **m_Edit** as the name of the variable. Leave the Category as Value and the type as CString. Click the OK button on the Add Member Variable dialog box, then click the OK button on the ClassWizard dialog box (do *not* close the ClassWizard with the Cancel button, or it will not add your member variable).

Using the ClassView pane of the Workspace window, add the following two functions to the *CMyDialog* class. Set the access for both functions to *public:*

```
void CMyDialog::GetText(CString &strText)
{
    strText = m_Edit;
}


void CMyDialog::SetText(CString &strText)
{
    m_Edit = strText;
}
```

Now return to the *CMFCDialogView.cpp* file and modify the *OnMydialogFirst()* function, as shown here:

```
void CMFCDialogView::OnMydialogFirst()
{
    CString strEdit;
    GetSelectedText (strEdit);
    CMyDialog dlg;
    dlg.SetText (strEdit);
    if (dlg.DoModal () == IDCANCEL)
        return;
    dlg.GetText (strEdit);
    GetEditCtrl().ReplaceSel ((LPCSTR) strEdit);
}
```

Build your project again and run the program. Open the *ReadMe.txt* file to display some text on the screen. Select some text in the file by dragging the mouse across the text, then summon your dialog box. The selected text should appear in the Edit Box control of the dialog box. When you type some text in the box and press the OK button, the new text will replace the selected text in your program's view window.

 Enabling and Disabling Dialog Controls

You may have noticed that on the main window frame, some of the toolbar controls are enabled or disabled depending upon whether you are displaying the contents of a file in your view window. The enabling and disabling is achived using the MFC command enabler class, CCmdUI. From time to time, you may want to enable or disable controls in your code to keep the user from making an improper selection. This can be an important feature in building a well-designed dialog box, but the CDialog class that you use as the base for your dialog classes does not support command enablers directly. However, you may roll your own code to enable and disable controls.

Using the ClassView pane of the Workspace window, add the following functions to the CMyDialog class:

```
LRESULT CMyDialog::OnKickIdle(WPARAM wParam, LPARAM lParam)
{
```

```
        CWnd::UpdateDialogControls (this, FALSE);
        return (0);
}


void CMyDialog::OnUpdateOK(CCmdUI *pCmdUI)
{
        pCmdUI->Enable (m_bModified);
}
```

Using the ClassWizard, select the Message Map page, then click on the IDC_EDIT1 entry in the Object IDs box. In the Messages box, select EN_CHANGE, then click on the Add Function button to add a handler for this message. Whenever the user changes the text in the Edit Box control, Windows will send this message.

Add a member variable, m_bModified, to the CMyDialog class and set the variable equal to false in the class constructor. At the top of the file, add afxpriv.h to the list of include files (this file defines the WM_KICKIDLE message). Finally, manually add entries to the message map to handle the WM_KICKIDLE message and to enable IDOK. When you are finished, the message map should look as shown here:

```
BEGIN_MESSAGE_MAP(CMyDialog, CDialog)
    //{{AFX_MSG_MAP(CMyDialog)
    ON_EN_CHANGE(IDC_EDIT1, OnChangeEdit1)
    //}}AFX_MSG_MAP
    ON_MESSAGE(WM_KICKIDLE, OnKickIdle)
    ON_UPDATE_COMMAND_UI(IDOK, OnUpdateOK)
END_MESSAGE_MAP()
```

Note particularly that the ON_EN_CHANGE message, which you added using the ClassWizard, is within the area reserved for the ClassWizard. However, you added the WM_KICKIDLE and IDOK messages outside this area.

In the OnChangeEdit1() *function, add code to set the* m_bModified *variable to* true *as shown here:*

```
void CMyDialog::OnChangeEdit1()
{
    m_bModified = true;
}
```

Build the application once again and run the program. When the dialog box first appears, the OK button will be disabled. Once you type something in the Edit Box control, the OK button will become enabled.

What You Must Know

In this lesson, you learned how to create and edit dialog boxes in your Win32- and MFC-based applications and how to add items to the menu and accelerator tables to access the dialog box. For MFC-based applications, you learned how to add a class for the dialog box and how to add member variables and message handlers for the controls on the dialog box. You learned how to create an object of a dialog box class, then call the *DoModal()* function to create and display the dialog box. In Lesson 31, "Using Windows Controls," you will learn more about using the Windows common controls. Before you continue with Lesson 31, however, make sure you understand the following key points:

◆ A *dialog* box is a temporary window that contains controls through which you display and accept information from a user.

◆ You design a dialog box and determine the appearance using a dialog box template in the Visual Studio's dialog box editor.

◆ Every dialog box template has a resource ID. Your program identifies the dialog box template using the ID.

◆ The Dialog Box Properties dialog box in the dialog box editor lets you set options, including the font and type size, for your dialog box.

◆ When you use a dialog box in an MFC-based application, you create a class for your dialog box. Then you create the dialog box by creating an instance of the class and calling the *DoModal()* member function.

Lesson 31

Using Windows Controls

In the last two lessons, you learned about program resources and how your program uses resource IDs. You learned how to access the Visual Studio resource editor and how to edit resources in your program. You also learned how to create and edit dialog boxes. Dialog boxes are temporary windows that you use to present information to users and to accept information from users. Dialog boxes use *controls* to display information in different forms such as a line of text in an Edit Box control or several lines of information in a List Box control. Controls are special purpose windows that perform specific tasks such as presenting text or graphics, providing a scroll interface, or listing related items. The Windows operating system provides a set of *common controls* to help you write your Windows program. In this lesson, you will learn about several of the common controls and how to use them. By the time you finish this lesson, you will understand the following key concepts:

◆ Controls are special purpose windows that may be manipulated by the user or by your program to perform specific tasks.

◆ Dialog boxes use controls to display information to the user and to accept information from the user that your program needs.

◆ You add controls to your dialog box using the dialog box editor and the Controls toolbar.

◆ A control may appear in many different ways according to the styles you give the control. Some styles may affect the way the control functions.

◆ Controls communicate with your program by using Windows messages. Your program also may send messages to controls.

Understanding the Purpose of Controls

A control is a window with a purpose. That purpose may be to convey information to the user in the form of text or graphics or to accept input from the user as keystrokes or a mouse action. A control may be as small as an icon or pushbutton, or it might be as large as the client area of your program's window.

Controls relieve the programmer of many chores in creating an application. The Edit Box control, for example, contains all the programming to accept keyboard input, inserting characters into a string, deleting characters, and displaying the resulting text. The MFC *CEditView* class, for example, contains an Edit Box control.

You will find controls in virtually every Windows program that displays a window. Even menu items are controls. The individual buttons of a toolbar that you find on most Windows applications actually are pushbutton controls.

Controls communicate with your program through Windows messages. Your program also may send messages to controls to command them to perform specific tasks. The Edit Box control, for example, accepts keyboard input. When the user presses a key and the Edit Box control processes the key, it sends your program an *EN_CHANGE* message.

Examining Common Controls

Windows has provided programmers with a set of basic controls since it was first introduced. Over the years, these controls have been refined, and their number has grown. These are the Windows *common controls*. Many new controls were introduced with Windows 95 and later and may be used only in program that run under 32-bit versions of Windows.

One of the advantages of common controls is that they present the user with a consistent interface. Although the programmer may customize the common controls to some extent, the common controls function the same in every program that uses them. The user does not need to learn new keyboard commands to use a control in every program.

The Microsoft Foundation Class library contains classes that encapsulate the common controls. In the MFC classes, you usually use member functions instead of messages to communicate with the controls; the member functions, in turn, handle the process of sending the messages.

Originally, Windows contained six basic controls, as summarized in Table 31.1 along with the MFC class that supports them.

Table 31.1 **The Basic Windows Common Controls Showing Their Associated MFC Classes**

Control	MFC Class	Description
Static Text	CStatic	A text control for labeling other controls.
Edit Box	CEdit	Boxes for entering text. Often used as the underlying control in a document window.
Button	CButton	Buttons such as OK or Cancel.
List Box	CListBox	Contains a list of strings.
Combo Box	CComboBox	Edit box and list box combination.
Scroll Bar	CScrollBar	Scroll bar used inside a dialog box.

Another common control, the Radio Button control, is a special case of the Button control. When used in a group, the Radio Button control allows the user to select only one button in the group.

To explore the basic common controls, create a new MFC AppWizard project named "Controls." Add a dialog box to the project using the resource ID of *IDD_CONTROLSDLG*. The controls you will need to add to it are shown in the left image of Figure 31.1. First, you will have to drag the OK and Cancel buttons from the right side of the dialog box to the bottom.

Figure 31.1

The left image shows the dialog box with controls on it. The image at the right shows the tab order *of the controls.*

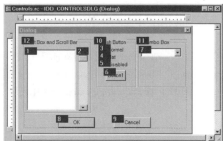

Add controls to the dialog box in the order shown in the following list. You can use the default resource IDs for the controls. To draw a control, select the item in the Controls toolbar, then move the mouse to the dialog box template and left-click and hold the mouse button where you want the upper-left corner to appear. Drag the mouse to where you want the lower-right corner of the control to appear. Release the mouse button. Refer to Figure 30.4 in Lesson 30 for the location of the various controls on the Controls toolbar. Place the controls according to the numbers in the tab order shown in the right image of Figure 31.1. (You also may refer to the code on the companion Web site: *http://www.prima-tech.com/books/book/5536/903*.)

1. Draw the list box (the button is the fifth one down in the second column of the Controls toolbar) in Position 1. Display the Properties dialog box for this control and *uncheck* the Sort

option on the Styles page. For this project, you will fill the list box with the files in a directory, so you do not want to sort the names.

2. Draw a vertical scroll bar in Position 2. The vertical scroll bar button is just below the list box button on the Controls toolbar.

3. Draw three radio button controls in Positions 3, 4, and 5. The radio button on the toolbar is just above the list box button. In the Properties dialog box, set the captions for the radio buttons to "Normal," "Flat," and "Disabled." Check the Group box on the General page for the first radio button only. The Group box for the second and third radio buttons should be unchecked.

4. Draw a push button control in Position 6. The push button on the toolbar is just above the radio buttons. On the Properties dialog box, check the Group button on the General page. This will end the group you started for the radio buttons.

5. Add a combo box control in Position 7. The combo box button on the toolbar is just to the left of the list box button.

To finish off the dialog box, you can draw group boxes around the three areas shown in Figure 31.1. The group box is nothing but a static control that also draws a border around itself. Its button on the toolbar is the third from the top in the first column.

If you draw the controls in a different order, they will have an incorrect tab order. The tab order is the sequence of controls that will receive the focus (the caret) when the user presses the Tab key. In the case of the Radio Button control, this order is critical to make the single-selection process work.

Press Ctrl+D to display the *tab order*. The numbers should be the same as in Figure 31.1. If they are not, you can reset the tab order by clicking on the items one by one, starting with the list box control. It is important that you realize that the radio buttons should be numbered one after another and that the push button should be the next in the tab order after the last radio button. This establishes the three radio buttons as a *group*. When radio buttons are in a group, the user may check only one of the buttons at any time. Selecting another radio button in the group will uncheck the button that is checked.

When you have finished examining or resetting the tab order, press the Enter key or click the mouse on any blank area of the dialog box template. The dialog editor will respond by setting the new tab order and removing the numbers. If you make a mistake, end the tab order display and start again.

Next press Ctrl+W to start the ClassWizard. The Adding a Class dialog box should appear. Click the OK button to display the New Class dialog box to add a class for your dialog box. On the New Class dialog box, name the class *CControlsDlg* and click the OK button. You will be taken to the ClassWizard.

Click on the Member Variable tab in the ClassWizard. Add member variables for the controls, as shown in Table 31.2. For the Button, Combo Box, Scroll Bar, and List Box controls, select Control as the category in the Add Member Variable dialog box. Leave the category for the Radio Button controls as Value. Notice that there is only one entry for the three radio buttons. This is because you created them as a group of controls. The Class-Wizard is astute enough that it knows you need only one variable for a group of Radio Button controls.

Table 31.2 The Resource IDs and Types of the Variable to Add to the CControlsDlg Class

Resource ID	Type	Variable Name
IDC_BUTTON1	CButton	m_ButtonCtl
IDC_COMBO1	CComboBox	m_ComboCtl
IDC_LIST1	CListBox	m_ListCtl
IDC_RADIO1	int	m_Radio
IDC_SCROLLBAR1	CScrollBar	m_ScrollCtl

Click on the Message Maps tab of the ClassWizard. Add message handlers for the controls, as shown in Table 31.3. Notice that on the Message Maps page, all three of the radio buttons appear in the Object ID list. You will need to add functions to handle each radio button.

Table 31.3 Adding Message Handlers for the Button Control and the Three Radio Button Controls

Resource ID	Message	Function Name
IDC_BUTTON1	BN_CLICKED	OnButton1()
IDC_COMBO1	CBN_SELCHANGE	OnSelchangeCombo1()
IDC_RADIO1	BN_CLICKED	OnRadio1()
IDC_RADIO2	BN_CLICKED	OnRadio2()
IDC_RADIO3	BN_CLICKED	OnRadio3()

After adding the message handlers for the controls, scroll to the top of the Object IDs box and select the *CControlsDlg* item. Scroll through the Messages box and add message handlers for the *WM_INITDIALOG* and *WM_VSCROLL* messages. You will not have a choice on function names for these messages. For most of your dialog box classes, you will need to add the *WM_INITDIALOG* message handler; this is where you will initialize your controls and give them initial values and settings.

Now add a menu item to the projects menu using the same method that you used in Lesson 30, "Creating Dialog Boxes." Add a message handler to the *CControlsView* class for the menu item to create the dialog box class object and call its *DoModal()* member function, as shown here:

```
void CControlsView::OnMydialogControls()
{
    CControlsDlg cd;
    cd.DoModal ();
}
```

All the preparatory work is done. Now you need to add code to the *ControlsDlg.cpp* source code file. Before you begin, the Scroll Bar control probably is the most arithmetic-intensive of the basic common controls. Calculating scroll positions can be a chore because the Scroll Bar control deals in logical points on the screen, while most controls deal with larger units such as text lines. Fortunately, most of the MFC view classes handle scrolling for you, but this example will show you how much work is involved.

The code for the *ControlsDlg.cpp* source code file is shown here:

```
// ControlsDlg.cpp : implementation file
//

#include "stdafx.h"
#include "Controls.h"
#include "ControlsDlg.h"

#ifdef _DEBUG
#define new DEBUG_NEW
#undef THIS_FILE
static char THIS_FILE[] = __FILE__;
#endif


/////////////////////////////////////////////////////////
// CControlsDlg dialog
```

```
CControlsDlg::CControlsDlg(CWnd* pParent /*=NULL*/)
    : CDialog(CControlsDlg::IDD, pParent)
{
    //{{AFX_DATA_INIT(CControlsDlg)
    m_Radio = 0;
    //}}AFX_DATA_INIT
}


void CControlsDlg::DoDataExchange(CDataExchange* pDX)
{
    CDialog::DoDataExchange(pDX);
    //{{AFX_DATA_MAP(CControlsDlg)
    DDX_Control(pDX, IDC_BUTTON1, m_ButtonCtl);
    DDX_Control(pDX, IDC_COMBO1, m_ComboCtl);
    DDX_Control(pDX, IDC_SCROLLBAR1, m_ScrollCtl);
    DDX_Control(pDX, IDC_LIST1, m_ListCtl);
    DDX_Radio(pDX, IDC_RADIO1, m_Radio);
    //}}AFX_DATA_MAP
}


BEGIN_MESSAGE_MAP(CControlsDlg, CDialog)
    //{{AFX_MSG_MAP(CControlsDlg)
    ON_BN_CLICKED(IDC_RADIO1, OnRadio1)
    ON_BN_CLICKED(IDC_RADIO2, OnRadio2)
    ON_BN_CLICKED(IDC_RADIO3, OnRadio3)
    ON_BN_CLICKED(IDC_BUTTON1, OnButton1)
    ON_WM_VSCROLL()
    //}}AFX_MSG_MAP
END_MESSAGE_MAP()

/////////////////////////////////////////////////////////////
// CControlsDlg message handlers

BOOL CControlsDlg::OnInitDialog()
```

```
{
    CDialog::OnInitDialog();

    const char *szColors [] =
        {
        "Red",
        "Blue",
        "Green",
        "Magenta",
        "Cyan",
        "Yellow"
    };

    m_ListCtl.Dir (0x4000 | 0x8000, "");
    m_ListCtl.Dir (0x0010 | 0x8000, ".\\*.*");
    m_ListCtl.Dir (0x0007, ".\\*.*");

    m_iHeight = m_ListCtl.GetItemHeight (0);
    CRect rc;
    m_ListCtl.GetWindowRect (rc);
    int iNum = rc.Height() / m_iHeight;
    memset (&m_siVert, '\0', sizeof (SCROLLINFO));
    m_siVert.cbSize = sizeof (SCROLLINFO);
    m_siVert.nMin = 0;
    m_siVert.nMax = m_ListCtl.GetCount ()
                * m_ListCtl.GetItemHeight (0)
                - rc.Height() + m_iHeight * 2;
    m_siVert.nPage = m_siVert.nMax / 10;
    m_siVert.nPos = 0;
    m_siVert.fMask = SIF_ALL;
    m_ScrollCtl.SetScrollInfo (&m_siVert);

    for (int i = 0;
        i < sizeof (szColors) / sizeof (char *);
        ++i)
    {
```

```
            m_ComboCtl.AddString (szColors[i]);
        }
    m_ComboCtl.SelectString (-1, szColors[0]);

    return TRUE;
}

void CControlsDlg::OnRadio1()
{
    m_ButtonCtl.EnableWindow (TRUE);
    m_ButtonCtl.ModifyStyle (BS_FLAT, 0, TRUE);
    m_ButtonCtl.Invalidate ();
}

void CControlsDlg::OnRadio2()
{
    m_ButtonCtl.EnableWindow (TRUE);
    m_ButtonCtl.ModifyStyle (0, BS_FLAT, TRUE);
    m_ButtonCtl.Invalidate ();
}

void CControlsDlg::OnRadio3()
{
    m_ButtonCtl.EnableWindow (FALSE);
}

void CControlsDlg::OnButton1()
{
    MessageBeep (IDOK);
}

void CControlsDlg::OnVScroll(UINT nSBCode, UINT nPos,
                            CScrollBar* pScrollBar)
{
//
//  The scroll bar isn't the only control that sends
```

```
//   scroll messages. On a dialog box, always test for
//   the identity of a scroll bar.
//
    CRect rc;
    if (pScrollBar != &m_ScrollCtl)
    {
        return;
    }
    switch (nSBCode)
    {
        case SB_TOP:                // Scroll to far left/top.
            m_siVert.nPos = m_siVert.nMin;
            m_ListCtl.SetTopIndex (0);
            break;
        case SB_ENDSCROLL:      // End scroll.
            m_ListCtl.SetTopIndex (m_ListCtl.GetTopIndex());
            return;
        case SB_LINEUP:      // Scroll left/up.
            m_siVert.nPos -= m_ListCtl.GetItemHeight (0);
            m_ListCtl.SetTopIndex(m_ListCtl.GetTopIndex()
                                    -1);
            if (m_ListCtl.GetTopIndex() == 0)
                m_siVert.nPos = m_siVert.nMin;
            if (m_siVert.nPos < m_siVert.nMin)
                m_siVert.nPos = m_siVert.nMin;
            break;
        case SB_LINEDOWN:       // Scroll right/down.
            m_siVert.nPos += m_ListCtl.GetItemHeight (0);
            m_ListCtl.SetTopIndex (m_ListCtl.GetTopIndex ()
                                    + 1);
            if (m_siVert.nPos > m_siVert.nMax)
                m_siVert.nPos = m_siVert.nMax;
            break;
        case SB_PAGEUP:      // Scroll one page left/up.
            m_ListCtl.GetWindowRect (rc);
            m_ListCtl.SetTopIndex (m_ListCtl.GetTopIndex ()
```

```
                        - rc.Height()
                        / m_ListCtl.GetItemHeight(0));
        m_siVert.nPos -= rc.Height();
        if (m_siVert.nPos < m_siVert.nMin)
            m_siVert.nPos = m_siVert.nMin;
        break;
    case SB_PAGEDOWN:    //  Scroll one page right/down.
        m_ListCtl.GetWindowRect (rc);
        m_ListCtl.SetTopIndex (m_ListCtl.GetTopIndex ()
                        + rc.Height()
                        / m_ListCtl.GetItemHeight(0));
        m_siVert.nPos += rc.Height();
        if (m_siVert.nPos > m_siVert.nMax)
            m_siVert.nPos = m_siVert.nMax;
        break;
    case SB_BOTTOM:      //  Scroll to far right/bottom.
        m_siVert.nPos = m_siVert.nMax;
        break;
    case SB_THUMBPOSITION:  //  Scroll to absolute
                            //  position. The current
                            //  position is specified by
                            //  the nPos parameter.
        m_siVert.nPos = nPos;
        break;
    case SB_THUMBTRACK:    //  Drag scroll box to
                            //  specified position. The
                            //  current position is
                            //  specified by the nPos
                            //  parameter
        m_siVert.nPos = nPos;
        break;
    }
    m_siVert.fMask = SIF_ALL;
    m_ScrollCtl.SetScrollInfo (&m_siVert);
}
```

```
void CControlsDlg::OnSelchangeCombo1()
{
    CString strMessage = _T("You chose ");
    int iIndex = m_ComboCtl.GetCurSel ();
    CString strSel;
    m_ComboCtl.GetLBText (iIndex, strSel);
    strMessage += strSel;
    MessageBox (strMessage);
}
```

Notice that the first line of *OnInitDialog()* calls *CDialog::OnInitDialog()*. Do not attempt to initialize or set any values for controls before this function call. The *CDialog* function actually creates the controls. Until the call to *CDialog::OnInitDialog()* returns, there are no controls to initialize.

Build the project and run the program. Clicking on the Button control should make your computer beep. Selecting one of the Radio Button controls should change the appearance of the Button control. Clicking on one of the up or down arrows on the Scroll Bar control should cause the contents of the List Box control to scroll. Finally, selecting an item in the Combo Box control should display a message box informing you of the color you selected.

Eventually, as computers became more powerful and Windows developed into a 32-bit operating system, these six controls were not enough to handle the needs of programmers, and Windows itself needed some additional controls. For example, when you open a "folder" in Windows 95 and higher, the operating system displays the contents of the folder using the new List control (do not confuse the List control with the basic List Box control).

Some of the controls could not have been developed using the older 16-bit Windows. For example, the Animation control requires its own *thread* to produce the moving picture effect such as the flying sheet of paper you see when you copy a file from one folder to another. (A *thread* is an execution point in a program. The 16-bit version of Windows had only a single execution point, but 32-bit Windows programs may have multiple threads executing in the same program at the same time.)

The controls that are available only when your program is running under 32-bit versions of Windows are summarized in Table 31.4 along with the MFC classes that encapsulate them.

Table 31.4 The Windows Advanced Common Controls and Their Associated MFC Classes

Control	MFC Class	Description
Animation	*CAnimate*	Displays successive frames of an AVI video clip.
Calendar	*CMonthCalCtrl*	Displays a simple calendar from which a date may be selected.
Date/Time Picker	*CDateTimeCtrl*	Interface to display and enter date and time information.
Extended Combo Box	*CComboBoxEx*	Extended version of the combo box that may use an image list to include icons in the list box.
Header	*CHeaderCtrl*	Buttons above a column of text, such as in a list control in report mode.
Hot Key	*CHotKeyCtrl*	Enables user to create a "hot key" to perform an action quickly.
Image List	*CImageList*	Is used to manage large sets of icons or bitmaps. (This is not a true control, but it supports lists used by other controls.)
IP Address	*CIPAddressCtrl*	Enables the user to enter and display a number in Internet Protocol format.
List	*CListCtrl*	Displays a list of text with icons.
Progress	*CProgressCtrl*	A bar that indicates the progress of an operation.
ReBar	*CReBarCtrl*	A control bar that provides layout, persistence, and state information for its controls.
Rich Edit	*CRichEditCtrl*	Edit control that allows multiple character, paragraph, and color formatting. Often used as the underlying control for a document window.
Slider	*CSliderCtrl*	Similar to a sliding control used as volume control on audio equipment.
Spin Button	*CSpinButtonCtrl*	A pair of arrow buttons to increment or decrement a value.
Status Bar	*CStatusBarCtrl*	A bar to display information, such as the state of the insert or NumLock keys, or to write status or help messages.
Tab	*CTabCtrl*	Is used in property sheets. Similar to notebook tabs.
Toolbar	*CToolBarCtrl*	Contains buttons to generate command messages.
ToolTip	*CToolTipCtrl*	A small pop-up window that describes the use of a button or tool.
Tree	*CTreeCtrl*	Displays a hierarchical list.

You should be aware of these controls so you may recognize when they are used in other programs. For example, in the Visual Studio, the three Workspace window panes contain Tree controls to list the files, resources, and classes in your program. A detailed description of the advanced controls and how to use them is an advanced topic and could easily take hundreds of pages. *1001 Visual C++ Programming Tips* contains explanations and samples for each of these controls.

Setting Control Styles

As you experiment with the different common controls, you will notice that each control has different styles that you may select. The styles on the General page of the Properties dialog box and many of the styles on the Extended Styles page are common to all of the controls, but the pages in between differ for each control.

As you did with the dialog box styles in the last lesson, try experimenting with the various styles for the controls to see how the appearance and function of the controls change.

For each page on a control's Properties dialog box, you can get extensive help from the Visual Studio by clicking on the large question mark in the upper-left corner of the Properties dialog box.

What You Must Know

In this lesson, you learned the basics of Windows controls. You learned how to add controls to a dialog box and how to add message handlers to your dialog box class to manipulate the controls. In addition, you learned how to access the Properties dialog box to set the styles and appearance for your dialog box and controls. You also learned about the Windows common controls, which are available on all Windows systems and which your program may use. In Lesson 32, "Using Memory Management," you will learn about allocating objects and variables dynamically on the program's heap or free store. Before you continue with Lesson 32, however, make sure you understand the following key points:

- *Controls* are special purpose windows that are intended to perform a specific task.

- The Windows operating system contains a collection of controls called *common controls* that you may use in your program.

- You can modify the appearance and behavior of controls by setting styles for the control.

- You use the Control toolbar in the Visual Studio to select the control you want to draw on a dialog box.

- Controls notify your program of significant events by sending Windows messages to your program.

Part 3

Advanced
Visual C++

Lesson 32

Using Memory Management

You have learned how to declare variables to store values in your program and how to declare arrays to store multiple values in a single variable. There will be times, however, when you will need to declare variables *dynamically*, meaning that instead of declaring a variable directly, you declare a pointer to the variable and then allocate the memory for the variable in your program using the *heap* or *free store*. For example, you might want to build a list in your program, but you do not know until your program runs just how many items you will have in the list. Or you may need to declare an array, but you do not know how many elements the array needs to hold. Visual C++ provides two methods to dynamically allocate memory. In this lesson, you will learn how to use both methods to allocate memory as you need it and free it when you no longer need the memory. By the time you finish this lesson, you will understand the following key concepts:

♦ The heap, sometimes called the *free store*, is a section of memory your program may use to temporarily store variables whose size or use cannot be determined when you write your program.

♦ You can access variables you create on the heap only through pointers.

♦ Visual C++ provides two methods to allocate memory on the heap, the *malloc()* function and the *new* operator.

♦ Variables you create in the heap remain until you destroy the variables. You must destroy the variables before your program exits to avoid *memory leaks*.

♦ When you allocate memory using *new*, you must release it using the *delete* operator. When you use *malloc()* to allocate memory, you must use the *free()* function.

Understanding the Heap or Free Store

When you run a program on your computer, the operating system assigns several blocks of memory for your program. First your program gets a segment for the program code where your program's functions are loaded. Then it gets a segment for data, where your program sets up any global variables you have declared. Then it gets a stack segment, which is where your program stores function return addresses and where your program creates automatic variables, those variables you declare within functions or variables with *block* scope.

Your program also has access to a portion of memory that is not assigned for any particular purpose. This is the *heap,* which programmers sometimes call the *free store.* You may declare variables, blocks of memory, or objects on the heap. Memory you allocate from the heap is never initialized, but instead contains whatever data was there before you requested the memory. You must assign the new variable or object a value before you use it.

Unlike other variables and objects in your program, your program does not automatically destroy those on the heap when a function exits, or even when your program ends. You are responsible for freeing the memory when you are finished using it. If you do not free the memory before your program ends, the memory remains allocated and no other program, not even another instance of your program, may access it. The memory remains lost to the operating system. Programmers call this situation a *memory leak.*

If programs leave too much memory in the heap, your computer might run out of memory space prematurely. The only way to recover memory lost to memory leaks is to reboot your computer.

The heap can be useful for allocating memory for arrays when you do not know beforehand how many elements your array will need. Remember from Lesson 13, "Using Array Variables to Store Multiple Values," that when you declared an array, you had to give the compiler a *constant* value as the number of elements so that the compiler knew the size of the array. You could not use a variable or an expression to define the size of the array. When the compiler is converting your program to object code, it does not evaluate variables and expressions, and so has no way to determine the size of the array. The following is an invalid statement in Visual C++:

```
int iSize = 10;
int MyArray[iSize];
```

When you create an array on the heap, however, you may use a variable or expression for the array size. When your program is running, it evaluates variables and expressions, so your program knows what value to use for the new array.

Visual C++ provides two mechanisms for allocating memory on the heap. The first, the *malloc()* function, is a carryover from the older C language. You should learn how to use *malloc(),* however, because some of the Windows API functions still use this function for allocating memory.

Using the *malloc()* and *free()* functions

The *malloc()* function is the method C and C++ programs originally used to allocate memory on the heap. The name is a contraction for *memory allocate*. The *malloc()* function requires a size as its only parameter. The size argument is in bytes, and your program must provide an expression to calculate the number of bytes your program needs. For example, if you program needs to allocate memory for an array of type *int* containing 10 elements, you would write the following statement:

```
int *iArray;
iArray = (int *) malloc (sizeof (int) * 10);
```

You should notice the explicit cast to a pointer to *int* to assign the new memory to an integer pointer. The C language lets you do a direct assignment, but C++ performs much stricter data type checking, and you must cast the return value to the proper data type.

The *malloc()* function does not initialize the new block of memory. The contents of the memory will be whatever values were already there when the function allocated the memory. However, the *calloc()* function assigns memory in the same way as the *malloc()* function, but initializes all the memory to zeroes (0). You should note in the following snippet that *calloc()* requires two parameters. The first is the number of elements (this differs from *malloc()* where you had to pass the size in bytes), and the second is the size of each element:

```
int *iArray;
// Allocate and initialize a block of 10 integers
iArray = (int *) calloc (10, sizeof (int));
```

One advantage of *malloc()* and *calloc()* is that you may reallocate a memory block to change the size of the block. Assuming your original block contained enough memory for an array of 10 integers and you later find that you need space for 12 integers, you could change the size by calling the *realloc()* function:

```
int *iArray;
iArray = (int *) malloc (sizeof (int) * 10);
// Some statements to initialize the 10 elements
// You now find that you need 12 elements
int *iNewArray = (int *) realloc(iArray, sizeof (int) * 12);
if (iNewArray != NULL)
    iArray = iNewArray;
```

If the *realloc()* function succeeds, it will return a pointer to a new block of memory. It will copy the old block into the new block and then release the old memory block. If *realloc()* fails—perhaps there is not enough free memory available—then the function will return a *NULL* pointer and will leave the old memory block unchanged. Thus, you should always check the return value before reassigning your original array variable to the new block.

If you create an object such as a structure or class object on the heap, you must access its member functions and variables using the *pointer to member* operator (–>):

```
struct MYSTRUCT
{
    int      iIntMember;
    double   fDoubleMember;
};


MYSTRUCT *pMyStruct = (MYSTRUCT *) malloc(sizeof(MYSTRUCT));
pMyStruct->iIntMember = 42;
pMyStruct->fDoubleMember = 3.14159;
```

When you allocate memory using the *malloc()*, *calloc()*, or *realloc()* functions, you must release the memory with a subsequent call to the *free()* function, passing a pointer to the memory to be freed as an argument:

```
free (iArray);
```

You need to be aware that you should *never* call *free()* on any memory block that you did not allocate using *malloc()*, *calloc()*, or *realloc()*. Attempting to do so may affect future allocation requests and cause errors.

These older C functions appear less and less often in new C++ programs. However, to remain compatible with C and C++, many of the Windows API functions, particularly those that return handles to globally allocated memory, use these functions, and you should be aware of them.

You need to be aware of the fact that the *malloc()* family of functions only sets aside memory for objects and does not actually create any objects. These functions are C functions and are not aware of C++ objects. If you allocate memory for a class object using *malloc()*, the class constructor *will not* be called.

Using the *new* Operator

Dynamically allocating memory is such a common practice in programming that C++ provides a special operator for that purpose, the *new* operator. The *new* operator works much the same way as *malloc()* except more intelligently. Instead of writing an expression to pass the size in bytes of the memory segment you want, you simply pass *new* the type of object you want. The operator will calculate the size of the memory and return a pointer to the newly allocated memory:

```
struct MYSTRUCT
{
    int      iIntMember;
    double   fDoubleMember;
};


MYSTRUCT *pMyStruct = new MYSTRUCT;
pMyStruct->iIntMember = 42;
pMyStruct->fDoubleMember = 3.14159;
```

To declare an array, you use the array version of new, *new[]*. You only need to pass *new[]* the data type of the array and the number of elements in the new array:

```
int *pInt = new int [10];
```

Notice that you do not need to cast the return pointer to pointer to *int*. The operator is astute enough to know that you want an array of type *int* and returns a pointer to that data type.

The *new* operator never initializes memory, and there is no equivalent to the *calloc()* function. You must initialize any newly allocated memory before using the values.

However, the *new* and *new[]* operators are designed to work with C++ objects. These operators not only reserve memory for an object, but also create the object in memory. Unlike the *malloc()* functions, if you allocate a class object using the *new* operator, the class constructor will be called automatically when *new* creates the object:

```
class MyClass
{
    MyClass();
};


MyClass *pClass = new MyClass;
```

Although the *new* operator will not initialize the data when it allocates memory, the constructor for your class may perform any initialization you need.

The *new* and *new[]* operators return a pointer to the newly allocated memory when they succeed. In Visual C++, the operators return *NULL* when they fail to allocate memory for any reason. Usually, the only reason the operators will fail is if there is not enough memory to allocate a block of the size you requested. With the virtual memory scheme used by Windows, this situation is not likely. However, it is a good idea to check for a *NULL* pointer any time you attempt to allocate memory.

Using the *delete* Operator

As with the *malloc()* functions, when you allocate memory on the heap with the *new* and *new[]* operators, you must remember to release the memory before your program ends. However, you may not use the *free* function to release memory allocated with *new*. For that, you must use one of the matching *delete* operators.

To release memory for a variable or object you created using the *new* operator, you must use the *delete* operator:

```
class MyClass
{
    MyClass();
};


MyClass *pClass = new MyClass;
//
// Some statements that use pClass
delete pClass;
```

If you declare an array using the *new[]* operator, you must use the *delete []* operator to release the memory allocation:

```
int *pArray = new int [10];
//
// some statements that use pArray
delete [] pArray;
```

Notice that you do not have to pass the *delete[]* operator the size of the array. The *new[]* operator stores that information as part of the memory block that it sets aside.

It is important that you realize that the *malloc()* function and the *new* operator perform very differently. You may use both *malloc()* and *new* in your program, but you must remember that you cannot release memory allocated with the *new* operator using the *free()* function. That would cause unpredictable errors in your program. Similarly, you may not use *delete* to release memory that you reserved using one of the *malloc()* functions.

Unless you have a good reason to use *malloc()*, you should try to use the *new* or *new[]* operators in your C++ programs. When your skills advance, you will recognize there are some situations in which you must use *malloc()* to make your program code compatible with other systems.

Declaring Pointer Variables

In Lesson 16, "Changing Parameter Values within a Function," you learned that you declare pointer variables by prefixing the name of the variable with the indirection operator, an asterisk (*). When you allocate memory using the *new* operator, you must store the returned address in a pointer variable.

Unlike variables declared in a function or in global space, you cannot directly access the values in variables stored on the heap. The only way to set or retrieve the value of a variable on the heap is through the pointer to the variable. This means that you must use the indirection operator to store or read the information:

```
void Func()
{
    int *pInt = new int;
    *pInt = 42;
    int iInt = *pInt;
}
```

You should realize in the preceding code that the variable in which your program stores the address is local to the function. When the function exits, the local variable will be destroyed, and you no longer will have access to the variable you created in the heap. You will not be able to delete the variable, and when your program exits, you will have a memory leak.

To guard against this, remember to delete the variable you created using the *new* operator in the same function in which you created the variable. You must do this *before* the pointer variable holding the address goes out of scope:

```
void Func()
{
    int *pInt = new int;
    *pInt = 42;
    int iInt = *pInt;
    delete pInt;
}
```

Dynamically Creating Variables

Of course, creating a variable of a simple data type using the *new* operator as you did in the last section doesn't make much sense. It complicates your program more than anything. Dynamic variables are best used when you do not know the type or size of the variable at the time you write your program. You can use dynamically allocated objects to control the order in which the objects are created as well.

For example, in Lesson 28, "Using the Microsoft Foundation Class Library," you learned that a document/view program using the Microsoft Foundation Class creates a document template in the application class, which in turn creates the main window object and the document object. However, the application class must perform a lot of preparation before it can create the document template. It must register the window class name and retrieve information from the Registry, among other things. If the document template or the main window object were declared as members of the application class, they would get created in the application class constructor long before the preparatory work has been performed.

To get around this, the application class instead declares a *pointer* to the main window frame. When the program is ready for the document template and the mainframe class object, MFC creates the document template using the new operator, as shown in the following code from the *DocView* application from Lesson 28:

```
CSingleDocTemplate* pDocTemplate;
    pDocTemplate = new CSingleDocTemplate(
        IDR_MAINFRAME,
        RUNTIME_CLASS(CDocViewDoc),
        RUNTIME_CLASS(CMainFrame), // main SDI frame window
        RUNTIME_CLASS(CDocViewView));
    AddDocTemplate(pDocTemplate);

    // Parse command line for standard shell commands,
    // DDE, file open
    CCommandLineInfo cmdInfo;
    ParseCommandLine(cmdInfo);

    // Dispatch commands specified on the command line
    if (!ProcessShellCommand(cmdInfo))
        return FALSE;

    // The one and only window has been initialized,
    // so show and update it.
```

```
    m_pMainWnd->ShowWindow(SW_SHOW);
    m_pMainWnd->UpdateWindow();
```

When the document template creates the main window class object, it sets the application class member variable *m_pMainWnd* to point to the object.

Sometimes you do not know the size of the variable when you write your program. When your program calculates the size, you can create the variable using the *new* operator. For example, suppose you have a program to reverse a string entered by a user. You do not know ahead of time how many characters the user will type. The following program, *Reverse.cpp*, shows how to handle such a situation using the *new* operator:

```cpp
#include     <iostream.h>
#include     <string.h>


void main (int argc, char *argv[])
{
// Check for input errors.
    if (argc < 2)
    {
        cerr << "Please enter a string" << endl;
        return;
    }
// Check that there is only one argument
    if (argc > 2)
    {
        cerr << "Please quote the string to be reversed"
            << endl;
        return;
    }
// Output the original string
    cout << argv[1] << endl;
// Get a new string. The size is the length of the original
// string plus 1 for the null terminator.
    char *szReverse = new char [strlen(argv[1]) + 1];
// Issue an error and exit if the allocation failed
    if (szReverse == NULL)
    {
```

```
        cerr << "Memory error" << endl;
        return;
    }
// Set a pointer to the end of the original string
    char *s = szReverse + strlen (argv[1]);
// And another pointer to the beginning of the string
    char *t = argv[1];
// Add the null terminator to the new string
    *s = '\0';
    —s;
// Copy the string character by character in reverse order
    while (*t)
    {
        *s = *t;
        —s, ++t;
    }
// Output the reversed string
    cout << szReverse << endl;
// Clean up after ourselves
    delete [] szReverse;
}
```

Compile the program from the command line. Run the program using a quoted string as the argument, and you should see the output shown here:

```
C:>reverse "Able was i ere I saw Elba"
Able was i ere I saw Elba
ablE was I ere i saw elbA
```

Dynamically Creating Arrays

Now it is time for you to apply your knowledge of the *new* operator to a Windows program. Remember from Lesson 13 that when you declare an array variable, the name of the variable itself is a pointer. You then apply a subscript to the variable name to access one of the elements in the array:

```
int iIntArray[10];
iIntArray[5] = 42;
```

Because the value returned by the *new* and *new[]* operators is a pointer, you may create arrays on the heap and access them the same way as you did with an array variable. But because you are creating the array on the heap, you may use a variable or an expression to specify the size:

```
int iVar = 10;
int *pIntArray = new int [iVar];
pIntArray[5] = 42;
delete [] pIntArray;
```

You can use this any time you do not know the exact size of an array in advance. For example, a property of the List Box control that you learned about in Lesson 31, "Using Windows Controls," allows the user to select more than one item in the list. If you are listing items from a directory, your program cannot know ahead of time how many items will be in the list, nor can it know ahead of time how many items the user will select.

Create a new MFC AppWizard project named "Dynamic." Add a dialog box to the project using the steps you learned in the last lesson. Add two List Box controls and two Button controls to the dialog box, as shown in Figure 32.1. Be sure to add a menu item so you can display the dialog box. Label the buttons by setting the caption to the text in Figure 32.1.

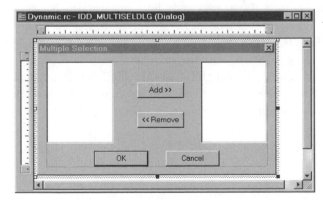

Figure 32.1

Using the buttons on this dialog box, you will be able to move items from one List Box to the other.

Change the resource ID of the dialog box from *IDD_DIALOG1* to *IDD_MULTISELDLG* by displaying the Properties dialog box and typing the new ID in the ID field. Select the List Box control on the left, display the Properties dialog box, and change the resource ID to *IDC_SOURCELIST*. Similarly, change the resource ID of the second List Box control to *IDC_DESTINATIONLIST*. Also on the Properties dialog for both List Box controls, uncheck the Sort box on the Styles page, then change the Selection from Single to Multiple.

Change the resource ID for the top button to *IDC_ADDBUTTON* and the resource ID for the bottom button to *IDC_REMOVEBUTTON*.

Press Ctrl+W to start the ClassWizard and add a class for the dialog box using the same steps you learned in the last lesson. Name the class *CListDlg*.

After making sure you have added the menu item, open the *DynamicView.cpp* file and add a message handler for your menu item. Also add *ListDlg.h* to the top of the file. Your new code in *DynamicView.cpp* should look like the following:

```
#include "ListDlg.h"


void CDynamicView::OnMymenuDialog()
{
    CListDlg dlg;
    dlg.DoModal ();
}
```

Build your project and run the program to make sure you can display the dialog box. Everything should be kosher, so you will need to add code to the *CListDlg* class. First, add a message handler for the *WM_INITDIALOG* Windows message. Then add handlers for the *BN_CLICKED* messages for the two buttons.

When you are finished adding the message handlers, click on the Member Variable tab and add variables for each of the list boxes. Name the variable for *IDC_SOURCELIST* control *m_SourceListCtrl* and the variable for the *IDC_DESTINATIONLIST* control *m_DestinationListCtrl*.

The following code also shows a handler for the *WM_KICKIDLE* message and functions to enable and disable the buttons, but you do not need to add them to make your program work. It does give the dialog box a more professional feel to have the buttons enable and disable themselves.

```
// ListDlg.cpp : implementation file
//

#include "stdafx.h"
#include "Dynamic.h"
#include "ListDlg.h"
#include <afxpriv.h>


#ifdef _DEBUG
```

```
#define new DEBUG_NEW
#undef THIS_FILE
static char THIS_FILE[] = __FILE__;
#endif


/////////////////////////////////////////////////////////
// CListDlg dialog

CListDlg::CListDlg(CWnd* pParent /*=NULL*/)
    : CDialog(CListDlg::IDD, pParent)
{
    //{{AFX_DATA_INIT(CListDlg)
        // NOTE: the ClassWizard will add member
        // initialization here
    //}}AFX_DATA_INIT
}


void CListDlg::DoDataExchange(CDataExchange* pDX)
{
    CDialog::DoDataExchange(pDX);
    //{{AFX_DATA_MAP(CListDlg)
    DDX_Control(pDX, IDC_DESTINATIONLIST,
                                m_DestinationListCtl);
    DDX_Control(pDX, IDC_SOURCELIST, m_SourceListCtl);
    //}}AFX_DATA_MAP
}


BEGIN_MESSAGE_MAP(CListDlg, CDialog)
    //{{AFX_MSG_MAP(CListDlg)
    ON_BN_CLICKED(IDC_ADDBUTTON, OnAddbutton)
    ON_BN_CLICKED(IDC_REMOVEBUTTON, OnRemovebutton)
    //}}AFX_MSG_MAP
    ON_MESSAGE(WM_KICKIDLE, OnKickIdle)
    ON_UPDATE_COMMAND_UI(IDC_ADDBUTTON, OnUpdateAddbutton)
    ON_UPDATE_COMMAND_UI(IDC_REMOVEBUTTON,
                        OnUpdateRemovebutton)
```

```
END_MESSAGE_MAP()

/////////////////////////////////////////////////////
// CListDlg message handlers

BOOL CListDlg::OnInitDialog()
{
    CDialog::OnInitDialog();
    m_SourceListCtl.Dir (0x0007, ".\\*.*");
    return TRUE;
}

void CListDlg::OnAddbutton()
{

    int Count = m_SourceListCtl.GetSelCount ();
    if (!Count)
        return;
    int *pSelItems = new int [Count];
    m_SourceListCtl.GetSelItems (Count, pSelItems);
//
//   Copy the selected items to the Destination list box
    for (int i = 0; i < Count; ++i)
    {
    CString strText;
    int iIndex;

        m_SourceListCtl.GetText (pSelItems[i], strText);
//
//   The item data is a user specified number. It usually is
//   a pointer to a structure containing detail information
//
        DWORD dwData = m_SourceListCtl.GetItemData
                                            (pSelItems[i]);
        iIndex = m_DestinationListCtl.AddString
                                        ((LPCSTR) strText);
```

```
            m_DestinationListCtl.SetItemData (iIndex, dwData);
    }
//
//   Delete the selected items from the highest
//   index to the lowest. Deleting the lowest
//   index first changes the relative index of the
//   higher index selected items.
//
    for (i = Count - 1; i >= 0; --i)
    {
        m_SourceListCtl.DeleteString (pSelItems[i]);
    }
    delete [] pSelItems;
    m_SourceListCtl.SetSel (-1, false);
}


void CListDlg::OnRemovebutton()
{

    int Count = m_DestinationListCtl.GetSelCount ();
    if (!Count)
        return;
    int *pSelItems = new int [Count];
    m_DestinationListCtl.GetSelItems (Count, pSelItems);
//
//   Copy the selected items to the Source list box
    for (int i = 0; i < Count; ++i)
    {
    CString strText;
    int iIndex;

        m_DestinationListCtl.GetText(pSelItems[i], strText);
        DWORD dwData = m_DestinationListCtl.GetItemData
                                          (pSelItems[i]);
        iIndex = m_SourceListCtl.AddString
                                      ((LPCSTR) strText);
```

```
        m_SourceListCtl.SetItemData (iIndex, dwData);
    }
//
//  Delete the selected items from the highest
//  index to the lowest. Deleting the lowest
//  index first changes the relative index of the
//  higher index selected items.
//
    for (i = Count - 1; i >= 0; —i)
        m_DestinationListCtl.DeleteString (pSelItems[i]);

    delete [] pSelItems;
    m_DestinationListCtl.SetSel (-1, false);
}


LRESULT CListDlg::OnKickIdle(WPARAM wParam, LPARAM lParam)
{
    CWnd::UpdateDialogControls (this, FALSE);
    return (0);
}


void CListDlg::OnUpdateAddbutton(CCmdUI *pCmdUI)
{
    pCmdUI->Enable (m_SourceListCtl.GetSelCount ());
}


void CListDlg::OnUpdateRemovebutton(CCmdUI *pCmdUI)
{
    pCmdUI->Enable (m_DestinationListCtl.GetSelCount ());
}
```

Your program cannot know in advance how many items the user will select in one of the List Box controls. However, by getting the count of the number of selected items, then dynamically allocating the *pSelItems* array, it was able to adjust to the conditions.

What You Must Know

In this lesson, you learned how to allocate memory dynamically using the *malloc()* function and the C++ *new* operator. You learned how to use variables and expressions to determine the size of dynamically allocated arrays. You also learned how to free memory using the *free()* function and the C++ *delete* operator. In addition, you learned how to apply that knowledge to create an array of unknown size based on variables in your program. In Lesson 33, "Using the Keyboard and Mouse in a Windows Program," you will learn how to make your program respond when the user presses a keyboard or mouse button or moves the mouse pointer on the screen. Before you continue with Lesson 33, however, make sure you understand the following key points:

◆ When you run a program, Windows assigns various segments of memory for your program to use.

◆ In addition to the memory assigned by Windows, your program may allocate memory in an unassigned section of memory called the *heap* or *free store*.

◆ The C *malloc()* function allocates memory for variable storage, but it does not create objects when you use it to allocate memory for a class. If you allocate memory for a class, the class constructor will not be called.

◆ The C++ *new* and *new[]* operators allocate memory as well, but are aware of C++ objects. When you create a class object using the *new* operator, the class constructor is called.

◆ You must release any memory you allocated on the heap before your program ends. You use the *free()* function for memory you allocated with *malloc()* and the *delete* operator for memory you allocated using the *new* operator.

◆ You cannot use the *delete* operator to release any memory you allocated using the *malloc()* function.

Lesson 33

Using the Keyboard and Mouse in a Windows Program

In the last few lessons, you have learned how to write Windows programs, both using the Windows API and using the Microsoft Foundation Class library to create document/view applications. You learned how to create a dialog box and how to add items to a menu so you could access and display your dialog box. Then you learned about Windows common controls and how to add controls to your application. Eventually, you are going to have to handle keyboard and mouse messages in your programs. The keyboard and mouse are the primary input devices in Windows. The MFC view classes handle most of the details for you when you write MFC-based programs, but with Windows API functions, you will have to do the work yourself. In this lesson, you will learn how to intercept and process messages from the keyboard and the mouse. By the time you finish this lesson, you will understand the following key concepts:

◆ All Windows programs that display a window share the keyboard and mouse inputs. Only one window may have the *input focus* at any given time, however.

◆ Windows sends keyboard messages only to the window that has the input focus.

◆ When the user presses a key on the keyboard, Windows sends a message to the window with the focus. Windows sends another message when the key is released.

◆ A window does not have to have the focus to receive mouse messages. When the mouse cursor enters a window, the operating system begins sending that window messages from the mouse.

Understanding Input Focus

Your computer has only one keyboard, but in the Windows operating system, many windows may be waiting for keyboard input at any time. Not all the windows can use the keyboard at the same time. For example, if you are writing a letter in a word processing program and have a spreadsheet program running in the background, it would not be acceptable for both programs to process the keyboard information. You would not want "Dear Sirs" to replace the formula in a spreadsheet cell.

In addition, a single application may have several windows displayed on the screen at the same time. The application may be displaying multiple documents in different windows, and it may have a dialog box displayed.

Windows must sort out all of the various windows that are waiting for keyboard input and decide which one will receive key presses from the keyboard. It does this by sending keyboard information in the form of messages. The messages are sent only to the program that has the *input focus*.

The window that has the input focus is not necessarily the active window. A window may give up the input focus to a child window such as a dialog box or one of the controls on a dialog box or toolbar. You may identify the active window in several ways. If the window has a title bar, Windows highlights the title bar in a system color, usually dark blue. In addition, the button on the system task bar will appear depressed.

A window can determine when it gets the input focus by capturing the *WM_SETFOCUS* Windows message. It can determine when it loses the input focus by capturing the *WM_KILLFOCUS* message. If your program is processing text and creates a caret, it must use these messages to create a caret when it receives the focus and to destroy the caret when it loses the focus. Remember that the caret is the point at which text will be inserted when the program processes a message from the keyboard.

Capturing Keyboard Input

Keyboard input in a Windows program is not nearly as simple as a command-line program. In a command-line program, you can simply accept text from *cin* or *stdin,* and let the command processor handle cursor movement. Windows programs, however, do not have the standard input and output that is available to command-line programs. In a Windows program, you will have to accept characters from the keyboard one by one and decide where in the window to display the characters. You also will have to save all the characters typed so you can display them on command. For example, if a user selects another application's window and that window covers your window, your code will have to redraw all of the characters when it becomes visible again.

You will learn most about keyboard input by processing characters in a Windows API program. In an MFC-based program using the document/view architecture, most of the view classes handle the details of keyboard input, such as showing and hiding the caret, determining the position in the window to place characters, and displaying the text.

The MSDN documentation contains a program to demonstrate keyboard input. To see it, select the Help menu in the Visual Studio, then select Search. When the MSDN help window appears, type **Processing Keyboard Input** in the search field, then at the bottom check the box that is labeled "Search titles only."

The program presented here will take a similar but more difficult approach to achieve the same result. In this program, in addition to learning how to process keyboard messages, you will learn how to allocate and use a two-dimensional array using the *new* operator. It will give you an appreciation of what the Edit Box control does in the next lesson. Also, you will process a mouse message to move the caret.

Create a new Win32 application using the Visual Studio wizard. Call the project "Kbd." On the first page of the wizard, select "Hello, World type application." In this application, you will create a two-dimensional character array to hold the characters you type from the keyboard, and the position of the character in the array will determine the position on the screen.

Open the *Kbd.cpp* source code and locate the *WndProc()* function. You will need the following variables to handle the keyboard and mouse messages. You do not have to add them now; the variable listing will appear in the listing for the *WndProc()* function that appears later in this section:

```
static char **pTextMatrix = NULL;
    static int nCharX,          // Width of character
              nCharY,           // Height of character
              nWindowCharsX,    // Screen width in characters
              nWindowCharsY,    // Screen depth in characters
              nCaretPosX,       // X position of caret
              nCaretPosY;       // Y position of caret
    static UINT uOldBlink;      // Save the old blink rate
```

Remember that a string is an array of type *char*. Your program will create an array of strings or an array of arrays. To declare the pointer for this array, you need to use two *indirection* operators, so the declaration is ***pTextMatrix*.

You will use the *TEXTMETRIC* structure to measure the size of the characters, and thus the number of characters that will fit across and down the window. The *static int* variables will let you keep track of the window size and character and caret positions.

Initially, you will need to process four Windows messages. To handle the *WM_CREATE* message, you will select a fixed-pitch font and measure the characters in it using the *TEXTMETRICS* structure. After Windows creates your window, it will send your program a *WM_SIZE* message informing your program of the window height and width. You will use this information to calculate how many characters will fit on the screen and create the character array to hold the text you type from the keyboard.

Then your program will have to handle the *WM_SETFOCUS* and *WM_KILLFOCUS*. In these message handlers, you will create and destroy the caret as required. As a well-behaved program, your code should restore any caret attributes that it changes when it receives the *WM_KILLFOCUS*.

The handler code for the *WM_SETFOCUS* messages creates the caret each time your window receives the focus. The *CreateCaret()* function creates a hidden caret, and you must call *ShowCaret()* to make the caret visible.

The *WM_CHAR* case in the following code will process the characters that can be displayed and ASCII control characters. The *WM_KEYDOWN* case will handle keys that cannot be displayed, such as the cursor keys.

Instead of displaying the "Hello, World!" message at the top of the screen, you will want to display the characters in your character array. Change the *WM_PAINT* message code, as shown in the code for the *WndProc()* function that follows shortly.

Prepare the *WndProc()* function for character processing by adding code so it looks like the following. This code adds the necessary variables at the top of the function, adds code to handle the *WM_CREATE*, *WM_SIZE*, *WM_SETFOCUS*, and *WM_KILLFOCUS*. It also modifies the *WM_PAINT* and *WM_DESTROY* message code.

```
LRESULT CALLBACK WndProc(HWND hWnd, UINT message,
                    WPARAM wParam, LPARAM lParam)
{
    static char **pTextMatrix = NULL;
    static int nCharX,          // Width of character
              nCharY,           // Height of character
              nWindowCharsX,    // Screen width in characters
              nWindowCharsY,    // Screen depth in characters
              nCaretPosX,       // X position of caret
              nCaretPosY;       // Y position of caret
    static UINT uOldBlink;      // Save the old blink rate

    int wmId, wmEvent;
    PAINTSTRUCT ps;
    HDC hdc;
```

```
switch (message)
{
    case WM_COMMAND:
        wmId    = LOWORD(wParam);
        wmEvent = HIWORD(wParam);
         // Parse the menu selections:
        switch (wmId)
        {
            case IDM_ABOUT:
                DialogBox(hInst, (LPCTSTR)IDD_ABOUTBOX,
                          hWnd, (DLGPROC)About);
                break;
            case IDM_EXIT:
                DestroyWindow(hWnd);
                break;
            default:
                return DefWindowProc(hWnd, message,
                                     wParam, lParam);
        }
        break;
    case WM_CREATE:
    {
        TEXTMETRIC tm;
        hdc = GetDC (hWnd);
        SelectObject (hdc,
                    GetStockObject(SYSTEM_FIXED_FONT));
        GetTextMetrics (hdc, &tm);
        ReleaseDC (hWnd, hdc);
        nCharX = tm.tmAveCharWidth;
        nCharY = tm.tmHeight;
        uOldBlink = GetCaretBlinkTime ();
        break;
    }
    case WM_SETFOCUS:
        CreateCaret (hWnd, NULL, 1, nCharY);
        SetCaretPos (nCaretPosX * nCharX,
```

```
                              nCaretPosY * nCharY);
            ShowCaret (hWnd);
            SetCaretBlinkTime (500);
            break;
        case WM_KILLFOCUS:    // Destroy the caret when we
                              // lose focus
            SetCaretBlinkTime (uOldBlink);
            DestroyCaret ();
            break;
//
//   The window size has changed.
        case WM_SIZE:
          {
//   Declare a temporary array of strings
            char **pNewTextMatrix = NULL;
//   The new width and height from the parameters
            int nWidth = LOWORD(lParam) / nCharX;
            int nHeight = HIWORD(lParam) / nCharY;
//   Make sure there is a least one usable line
            if (!nHeight)
                nHeight = 1;
//   Declare the first dimension, which is array of char
//   pointers large enough to hold one string for each
//   line on the screen.
            pNewTextMatrix = new char * [nHeight];
//   Declare the second dimension for each line on the screen
            for (int i = 0; i < nHeight; ++i)
            {
                pNewTextMatrix[i] = new char [nWidth + 1];
//  Initialize each char array to spaces with a null
                memset (pNewTextMatrix[i], ' ', nWidth);
                pNewTextMatrix[i][nWidth] = '\0';
            }
//   If the text matrix already exists, copy as much of it
//   as possible.
            if (pTextMatrix != NULL)
```

```
        {
            for (i = 0; i < nWindowCharsY; ++i)
            {
                if (i == nHeight)
                    break;
                int nLength = min (strlen
                            (pTextMatrix[i]),
                            strlen(pNewTextMatrix[i]));
                strncpy (pNewTextMatrix[i],
                        pTextMatrix[i], nLength);
                pNewTextMatrix[i][nLength] = ' ';
                pNewTextMatrix[i][nWidth] = '\0';
            }
//  Delete the old second dimension arrays in the array.
            for (i = 0; i < nWindowCharsY; ++i)
            {
                delete [] pTextMatrix[i];
                pTextMatrix[i] = NULL;
            }
//  Now delete the first dimension array
            delete [] pTextMatrix;
            pTextMatrix = NULL;
        }
//  Set the text matrix to the new array of arrays.
        pTextMatrix = pNewTextMatrix;
        nWindowCharsX = nWidth;
        nWindowCharsY = nHeight;
//  Make sure the caret stays in the window
        nCaretPosX = min(nWindowCharsX - 1, nCaretPosX);
        nCaretPosY = min(nWindowCharsY - 1, nCaretPosY);
        SetCaretPos (nCaretPosX * nCharX,
                    nCaretPosY * nCharY);
        break;
    }
    case WM_PAINT:
    {
```

```
            hdc = BeginPaint(hWnd, &ps);
            SelectObject (hdc,
                     GetStockObject(SYSTEM_FIXED_FONT));
            for (int cy = 0; cy < nWindowCharsY; ++cy)
            {
                TextOut (hdc, 0, cy * nCharY,
                         pTextMatrix[cy], nWindowCharsX);
            }
            EndPaint(hWnd, &ps);
            break;
        }
        case WM_DESTROY:
        {
// Clean up time. Delete the string arrays
            for (int i = 0; i < nWindowCharsY; ++i)
            {
                delete [] pTextMatrix[i];
                pTextMatrix[i] = NULL;
            }
// Delete the array of strings
            delete [] pTextMatrix;
            PostQuitMessage(0);
            break;
        }
        default:
            return DefWindowProc(hWnd, message,
                              wParam, lParam);
    }
    return 0;
}
```

Build the project and run the program. At this point, your code is not processing any characters, but it should show a blank screen with a blinking caret in the upper-left corner. It is ready to accept keyboard input, however. For now, try changing the caret blink rate in the *WM_SETFOCUS* message case. The time is in milliseconds, so a value of 500 makes the caret blink twice a second.

Processing Character Messages

When you press and release a key on the keyboard, Windows sends three messages. First, it sends you a *WM_KEYDOWN* message to inform you that a key has been pressed. This message contains various flags for the keyboard state and the actual character as a *virtual key*. A virtual key is the Windows representation of a key. Next, it sends you a *WM_CHAR* message containing the actual ASCII character translated from the virtual key. Finally, Windows sends you a *WM_KEYUP* message indicating the user released the key. Normally, you will process the *WM_CHAR* message to accept keyboard input.

To begin processing characters, add the following *case* statement to the *switch(message)* statement. This code will process ASCII characters using the *WM_CHAR* message and handles some of the basic control codes such as those sent by the Tab and Enter keys.

```
//   Process characters that can be displayed
     case WM_CHAR:
         switch (wParam)
         {
         case 8:    // Backspace key
             if (nCaretPosX > 0)
             {
                 —nCaretPosX;
                 SendMessage (hWnd, WM_KEYDOWN,
                             VK_DELETE, 1L);
             }
             break;
         case 9:    // Tab key
             do
             {
                 SendMessage (hWnd, WM_CHAR,
                             ' ', 1L);
             } while (nCaretPosX % 4);
             break;
         case 13:      // Carriage return
             nCaretPosX = 0;
             if (++nCaretPosY > nWindowCharsX)
                 nCaretPosY = nWindowCharsX;
             break;
```

```
            case 10:      // Line feed
            case 27:      // Escape
                break;    // Ignore these
            default:
//  Add the character to the array
                pTextMatrix[nCaretPosY][nCaretPosX] =
                                    (char) wParam;
                HideCaret(hWnd);
                hdc = GetDC(hWnd);
                SelectObject (hdc,
                    GetStockObject(SYSTEM_FIXED_FONT));
//  display just the one character
                TextOut (hdc, nCaretPosX * nCharX,
                  nCaretPosY * nCharY,
                  &pTextMatrix[nCaretPosY][nCaretPosX],
                  1);
                ReleaseDC(hWnd, hdc);
                ShowCaret (hWnd);
//  Move the caret to the next position. If necessary, place
//  the caret on the next line.
                if (++nCaretPosX == nWindowCharsX)
                {
                    nCaretPosX = 0;
                    if (++nCaretPosY == nWindowCharsY)
                    {
                        nCaretPosY = 0;
                    }
                }
                break;
        }
        SetCaretPos (nCaretPosX * nCharX,
                nCaretPosY * nCharY);
        break;
```

Notice that in the *default* case, your program hides the caret before drawing the individual characters. Anytime you draw on a window outside the *WM_PAINT* code, you should hide the caret or you likely will wind up with some ghost carets on your screen. After you hide the caret, you must call *ShowCaret()* again to show the caret.

Calls to the *HideCaret()* function are cumulative. When you call *HideCaret()*, you will have to call *ShowCaret()* an equal number of times for the caret to become visible. If you call *HideCaret()* twice, you will have to call *ShowCaret()* twice before the caret will reappear.

Build the project once again and run the program. Begin typing some text. As you type, the characters will appear on the screen, one after another. However, notice that the caret moves only when you type a character that causes text to appear on the screen. The cursor movement keys do nothing at this point. The reason is that the cursor keys do not produce ASCII characters, and so never cause Windows to send a *WM_CHAR* message. To handle these keys, you will need to process the *WM_KEYDOWN* message.

Processing Non-Character Keyboard Messages

Your keyboard processing program now processes Windows *WM_CHAR* messages, then stores and displays the characters as you press keys on the keyboard. However, not all keys on the keyboard produce characters that your program can display. The function keys, F1 through F12 (F10 on some keyboards), for example, do not have any meaning in the ASCII character set. The cursor movement keys also do not translate directly to ASCII characters. In these cases, Windows does not send your program a *WM_CHAR* message, and you will need to process the *WM_KEYDOWN* message.

Windows considers the non-character keys *virtual* keys and identifies them with macros beginning with *VK_*. For example, the F1 key is *VK_F1*, and the cursor up key is *VK_UP*. In fact, all the keys, even the character keys, have virtual key codes in Windows. In the *WM_KEYDOWN* message, the virtual key code is contained in the *wParam* parameter.

To process these keystrokes, add a *case* statement for the *WM_KEYDOWN* message to the *WndProc()* function as shown here:

```
//   Process other keystrokes that cannot be displayed
     case WM_KEYDOWN:
         switch (wParam)
         {
             case VK_HOME:      // Home key
                 nCaretPosX = 0;
                 break;
             case VK_END:       // End key
```

```
        nCaretPosX = nWindowCharsX - 1;
        break;
    case VK_PRIOR:      // Page Up key
        nCaretPosY = 0;
        break;
    case VK_NEXT:       // Page down key
        nCaretPosY = nWindowCharsY - 1;
        break;
    case VK_LEFT:       // Left arrow
        —nCaretPosX;
        if (nCaretPosX < 0)
        {
            nCaretPosX = nWindowCharsX - 1;
            —nCaretPosY;
            if (nCaretPosY < 0)
                nCaretPosY = nWindowCharsY - 1;
        }
        break;
    case VK_RIGHT: // Right arrow
        ++nCaretPosX;
        if (nCaretPosX == nWindowCharsX)
        {
            nCaretPosX = 0;
            ++nCaretPosY;
            if (nCaretPosY == nWindowCharsY)
                nCaretPosY = 0;
        }
        break;
    case VK_UP:     // Up arrow
        —nCaretPosY;
        if (nCaretPosY < 0)
            nCaretPosY = nWindowCharsY - 1;
        break;
    case VK_DOWN:  // Down arrow
        ++nCaretPosY;
        if (nCaretPosY == nWindowCharsY)
```

```
                          nCaretPosY = 0;
                     break;
                case VK_DELETE: // Delete key
                {
                     for (int cx = nCaretPosX;
                          cx < nWindowCharsX; ++cx)
                     {
                         pTextMatrix[nCaretPosY][cx] =
                             pTextMatrix[nCaretPosY][cx + 1];
                     }
                     pTextMatrix[nCaretPosY]
                                 [nWindowCharsX - 1] = ' ';
// Redraw the line
                     HideCaret (hWnd);
                     hdc = GetDC(hWnd);
                     SelectObject (hdc,
                         GetStockObject(SYSTEM_FIXED_FONT));
                     TextOut (hdc, nCaretPosX * nCharX,
                         nCaretPosY * nCharY,
                         &pTextMatrix[nCaretPosY][nCaretPosX],
                         nWindowCharsX - nCaretPosX);
                     ReleaseDC(hWnd, hdc);
                     ShowCaret (hWnd);
                     break;
                }
           }
           SetCaretPos (nCaretPosX * nCharX,
                        nCaretPosY * nCharY);
           break;
```

When you build the project again and run the program, the cursor keys—including the Home, End, Page Up, and Page Down keys—now will move the caret.

Using the Mouse

After the keyboard, the mouse is the most important input device on your computer. Unlike the keyboard, a window does not need to have the focus to receive Windows messages dealing with the mouse. Even if a window is only partially visible, as soon as the mouse cursor moves over the part of a window that is visible, the window starts receiving mouse messages.

Windows includes support for three-button mouse devices and for those with a "mouse wheel," although the great majority of mouse devices are two-button without wheels. Your program may support the third button on the mouse wheel, but it also should work with the simple, two-button mouse.

Each mouse message contains the current mouse position in the *lParam* parameter. The low-order 16 bits of this parameter contain the X position when the mouse event occurred, and the high-order 16 bits contains the Y position. In addition, for the mouse click events, the *wParam* parameter contains flags indicating whether the Ctrl or Shift keys, or any other mouse button, was down at the time of the event. Table 33.1 summarizes the mouse messages.

Table 33.1 Mouse Messages Sent to the Window Under the Cursor

Mouse message	Meaning
WM_MOUSEMOVE	The user has moved the mouse.
WM_LBUTTONDOWN	Left mouse button was pushed.
WM_MBUTTONDOWN	Middle mouse button was pushed.
WM_RBUTTONDOWN	Right mouse button was pushed.
WM_LBUTTONUP	Left mouse button was released.
WM_MBUTTONUP	Middle mouse button was released.
WM_RBUTTONUP	Right mouse button was released.
WM_LBUTTONDBLCLK	Left mouse button was double-clicked.
WM_MBUTTONDBLCLK	Middle mouse button was double-clicked.
WM_RBUTTONDBLCLK	Right mouse button was double-clicked.
WM_MOUSEWHEEL	The mouse wheel was moved. The high-order 16 bits of *lParam* contains the amount of movement. The low-order 16 bits of *lParam* contains the key flags.

You can finish the *Kbd* project from this lesson by making it possible to set the caret position by clicking the mouse anywhere in the client area of your program's window. Then in the next section, you will develop a program that uses the mouse more extensively. Add the following *case* statement to your program:

```
// When the user presses the left mouse button, move the
// caret to the position nearest the mouse click
case WM_LBUTTONDOWN:
    nCaretPosX = (LOWORD(lParam) + nCharX / 2) / nCharX;
    nCaretPosY = (HIWORD(lParam) + nCharY / 2) / nCharY;
    nCaretPosX = min(nCaretPosX, nWindowCharsX - 1);
    nCaretPosY = min(nCaretPosY, nWindowCharsY - 1);
    SetCaretPos (nCaretPosX * nCharX, nCaretPosY * nCharY);
    break;
```

Build the project and run the program once more. Click the left mouse button anywhere in the client area, and the caret should move to the character position closest to the mouse click.

Processing Mouse Messages

You probably have seen graphics drawing programs where you can grab a point on a line with the mouse and pull the line to one side to form a complex curve. When the curve has the shape you want, you release the mouse button.

This is an example of mouse message processing. You capture the button-down and button-up messages. As long as the mouse button is held down, you capture the mouse move messages and use the information to move a control point that determines the shape of the line.

It would appear that the program is performing some complex calculations to draw the complex curve, but the Graphics Device Interface really is doing most of the work. There are several methods of achieving curves, called *splines* after the curved splines used in drafting. The most common is the *Bezier spline,* and the GDI contains functions to draw Bezier curves.

Create a new Win 32 Application project called "Lines." As with the project earlier in this lesson, it can be a "Hello, World type application." After the wizard creates the project, you will need to add three classes to your project. First, add a class named *CShape* (it is the same *CShape* class you used in Lesson 26, "Letting a New Class Inherit the Attributes of an Existing Class.") The code for the header and source files is shown here. First, the class definition in *Shape.h*:

```
class CShape
{
public:
    void GetPen(int& Style, int& Width, COLORREF& clr);
```

```
    void SetPenWidth (int iPenWidth);
    virtual void Show (HDC hdc);
    CShape();
    virtual ~CShape();

protected:
    void Rotate (int iAngle, const POINT& ptCenter,
                 POINT* ptControl, int Count);
    virtual void Draw();
    HDC       m_hdc;
    COLORREF    m_clrPen;
    HPEN     m_hPen;
    int      m_cx1;
    int      m_cy1;
    int m_iPenWidth;
};
```

The following listing is for the *Shape.cpp* file where you implement the code for the *CShape* class:

```
// Shape.cpp: implementation of the CShape class.
//
//////////////////////////////////////////////////////

#include "stdafx.h"
#include "Shape.h"
#include <math.h>


//////////////////////////////////////////////////////
// Construction/Destruction
//////////////////////////////////////////////////////

CShape::CShape()
{
    m_cx1 = 0;
    m_cy1 = 0;
    m_clrPen = 0;
```

```
    m_iPenWidth = 2;
}


CShape::~CShape()
{
}


//
//  Rotate a set of points about a central point.
//
void CShape::Rotate(int iAngle, const POINT &ptCenter,
                    POINT *ptControl, int iSize)
{
//
//  If the angle is 0, there's no need to
//  do anything
    if (!iAngle)
        return;
//
//  Translate the angle from tenths of a degree
//  to radians. That's what the trig functions use.
    double fAngle = (iAngle / 10.0) / 57.29578;
//
//  Get the sine and cosine of the rotation angle.
    double fSine = sin(fAngle);
    double fCosine = cos(fAngle);
//
//  Translate the center point so it will be the point of
//  rotation.
    double fRotateX = ptCenter.x - ptCenter.x * fCosine
                        - ptCenter.y * fSine;
    double fRotateY = ptCenter.y + ptCenter.x * fSine
                        - ptCenter.y * fCosine;


//
//  Rotate the control points, then add the
```

```
//    translation for the center point. Rebuild
//    the control points.
    for (int i = 0; i < iSize; ++i)
    {
        double fNewX = ptControl[i].x * fCosine
                        + ptControl[i].y * fSine;
        double fNewY = -ptControl[i].x * fSine
                        + ptControl[i].y * fCosine;
        fNewX += fRotateX;
        fNewY += fRotateY;
        ptControl[i].x = (long) (fNewX + .5);
        ptControl[i].y = (long) (fNewY + .5);
    }
}
//
//    Create the pen to draw the lines, select it
//    into the device context. Then call the Draw()
//    function.
//
void CShape::Show(HDC hdc)
{
    m_hdc = hdc;
    m_hPen = CreatePen (PS_SOLID, m_iPenWidth, m_clrPen);
    HPEN hOldPen = (HPEN) SelectObject (m_hdc, m_hPen);
    int iOldROP = SetROP2 (hdc, R2_NOTXORPEN);
    Draw ();
    SelectObject (m_hdc, hOldPen);
    DeleteObject (m_hPen);
    SetROP2 (hdc, iOldROP);
}

void CShape::Draw()
{
}

void CShape::SetPenWidth(int iPenWidth)
```

```
{
    m_iPenWidth = iPenWidth;
}

void CShape::GetPen(int& Style, int& Width, COLORREF& clr)
{
    Style = PS_SOLID;
    Width = m_iPenWidth;
    clr = m_clrPen;
}
```

Next, derive two classes from *CShape*. Name one of them *CBezierPoint* and the other *CBezierLine*. The *CBezier-Point* class will draw a small square with a dot in the center to where it appears on your screen. The code for both classes is shown here.

The following code defines the *CBezierPoint* class in the *BezierPoint.h* file:

```
class CBezierPoint : public CShape
{
public:
    void SetPoint (HDC hdc, int cx, int cy);
    POINT& GetPoint();
    void RotatePoints (int iAngle, int cx, int cy);
    bool IsNearPoint (int cx, int cy, int Tolerance);
    CBezierPoint(int cx, int cy, COLORREF clr = 0);
    virtual ~CBezierPoint();

protected:
    POINT m_pt;
    virtual void Draw();
    friend class CBezierLine;
private:
    CBezierPoint ();
};
```

The following code implements the *CBezierPoint* class. The *Draw()* member function draws the point as a dot within a small square. The *IsNearPoint()* function determines whether a point is close to the center: The following code is for the *BezierPoint.cpp* file:

```
// BezierPoint.cpp: implementation of the
// CBezierPoint class.
//
//////////////////////////////////////////////////////////

#include "stdafx.h"
#include "BezierPoint.h"


//////////////////////////////////////////////////////////
// Construction/Destruction
//////////////////////////////////////////////////////////

CBezierPoint::CBezierPoint(int cx, int cy, COLORREF clr)
{
    m_cx1 = cx;
    m_cy1 = cy;
    m_clrPen = clr;
    m_iPenWidth = 1;
}

CBezierPoint::~CBezierPoint()
{

}

void CBezierPoint::Draw()
{
    Rectangle (m_hdc, m_cx1 - 5, m_cy1 - 5,
                      m_cx1 + 5, m_cy1 + 5);
    HBRUSH hBrush = CreateSolidBrush (m_clrPen);
    HBRUSH hOldBrush = (HBRUSH) SelectObject(m_hdc,hBrush);
    Ellipse (m_hdc, m_cx1 - 2, m_cy1 - 2,
```

```
                        m_cx1 + 2, m_cy1 + 2);
    SelectObject (m_hdc, hOldBrush);
    DeleteObject (hBrush);
}


CBezierPoint::CBezierPoint()
{
}


bool CBezierPoint::IsNearPoint(int cx,int cy,int Tolerance)
{
    if (cx < (m_cx1 - Tolerance + 1))
        return (false);
    if (cx > (m_cx1 + Tolerance - 1))
        return (false);
    if (cy < (m_cy1 - Tolerance + 1))
        return (false);
    if (cy > (m_cy1 + Tolerance - 1))
        return (false);
    return (true);
}


void CBezierPoint::RotatePoints(int iAngle, int cx, int cy)
{
    POINT pt = {m_cx1, m_cy1};
    POINT ptCenter = {cx, cy};
    Rotate (iAngle, ptCenter, &pt, 1);
    m_cx1 = pt.x;
    m_cy1 = pt.y;
}


POINT& CBezierPoint::GetPoint()
{
    m_pt.x = m_cx1;
    m_pt.y = m_cy1;
    return (m_pt);
```

```
}

void CBezierPoint::SetPoint(HDC hdc, int cx, int cy)
{
    Show (hdc);
    m_cx1 = cx;
    m_cy1 = cy;
    Show (hdc);
}
```

The *CBezierLine* class contains the end points of the line and the two control points. The listing that follows is for the class definition that you should place in the *BezierLine.h* file:

```
class CBezierLine : virtual public CShape
{
public:
    void ShowPoints (HDC hdc);
    void GetEndPoints (POINT &start, POINT &finish);
    void SetPoint (HDC hdc, int Index, int cx, int cy);
    int IsPoint (int cx, int cy);
    CBezierLine(int cx1, int cy1, int iLength,
                int iAngle = 0, COLORREF clr = 0);
    virtual ~CBezierLine();

protected:
    int m_iLength;
    int m_iAngle;
    virtual void Draw();
private:
    CBezierPoint    m_pt1;
    CBezierPoint    m_pt2;
    CBezierPoint    m_bpt1;
    CBezierPoint    m_bpt2;
}
```

Finally, you add the implementation code for the *CBezierLine* class to the *BezierLine.cpp* file:

```cpp
// BezierLine.cpp: implementation of the CBezierLine class.
//
//////////////////////////////////////////////////////////

#include "stdafx.h"
#include "BezierLine.h"


//////////////////////////////////////////////////////////
// Construction/Destruction
//////////////////////////////////////////////////////////
//
//   The anchor point for a line is the first point
//   entered.
//
CBezierLine::CBezierLine(int cx1, int cy1, int iLength,
                         int iAngle, COLORREF clr)
{
    m_cx1 = cx1;
    m_cy1 = cy1;
    m_pt1.m_cx1 = cx1;
    m_pt1.m_cy1 = cy1;
    m_pt2.m_cx1 = cx1 + iLength;
    m_pt2.m_cy1 = cy1;
    m_clrPen = clr;
    POINT pts[3] = {m_pt1.m_cx1, m_pt1.m_cy1,
                    m_pt2.m_cx1, m_pt2.m_cy1, cx1, cy1};
    Rotate (iAngle, pts[2], pts, 2);
    m_cx1 = m_pt1.m_cx1 = pts[0].x;
    m_cy1 = m_pt1.m_cy1 = pts[0].y;
    m_pt2.m_cx1 = pts[1].x;
    m_pt2.m_cy1 = pts[1].y;
    m_pt1.m_clrPen = m_pt2.m_clrPen = 0;
    m_pt1.m_iPenWidth = m_pt2.m_iPenWidth = 1;
```

```
    pts[0].x = m_cx1 + iLength / 2 - 10;
    pts[0].y = cy1;
    pts[1].x = m_cx1 + iLength / 2 + 10;
    pts[1].y = cy1;
    Rotate (iAngle, pts[2], pts, 2);
    m_bpt1.m_iPenWidth = m_bpt2.m_iPenWidth = 1;
    m_bpt1.m_cx1 = pts[0].x;
    m_bpt1.m_cy1 = pts[0].y;
    m_bpt2.m_cx1 = pts[1].x;
    m_bpt2.m_cy1 = pts[1].y;
}


CBezierLine::~CBezierLine()
{

}


void CBezierLine::Draw()
{
    POINT pt[4]  = {m_pt1.m_cx1, m_pt1.m_cy1,
                    m_bpt1.m_cx1, m_bpt1.m_cy1,
                    m_bpt2.m_cx1, m_bpt2.m_cy1,
                    m_pt2.m_cx1, m_pt2.m_cy1};
    PolyBezier (m_hdc, pt, 4);
}


int CBezierLine::IsPoint(int cx, int cy)
{
//  Start point
    if (m_pt1.IsNearPoint (cx, cy, 5))
        return (1);
//  End point
    if (m_pt2.IsNearPoint (cx, cy, 5))
        return (4);
//  Bezier point 1
    if (m_bpt1.IsNearPoint (cx, cy, 5))
```

```
            return (2);
//   Bezier point 2
        if (m_bpt2.IsNearPoint (cx, cy, 5))
            return (3);
        return (0);
}


void CBezierLine::SetPoint(HDC hdc, int Index,
                                    int cx, int cy)
{
        switch (Index)
        {
            case 1:
                m_pt1.SetPoint (hdc, cx, cy);
                break;
            case 4:
                m_pt2.SetPoint (hdc, cx, cy);
                break;
            case 2:
                m_bpt1.SetPoint (hdc, cx, cy);
                break;
            case 3:
                m_bpt2.SetPoint (hdc, cx, cy);
                break;
            default:
                return;
        }
}


void CBezierLine::GetEndPoints(POINT &start, POINT &finish)
{
        start.x = m_pt1.m_cx1;
        start.y = m_pt1.m_cy1;
        finish.x = m_pt2.m_cx1;
        finish.y = m_pt2.m_cy1;
}
```

```
void CBezierLine::ShowPoints(HDC hdc)
{
    m_pt1.Show (hdc);
    m_pt2.Show (hdc);
    m_bpt1.Show (hdc);
    m_bpt2.Show (hdc);
}
```

The hard work is done. Now you need to add code to the *Lines.cpp* source file to process the mouse messages. Add *BezierLine.h* to the list of header files in *Lines.cpp*. Then find the *WndProc()* function and add the following variables at the top of the function:

```
static bool bLButtonDown = false;
static CBezierLine bline(300,300,300,750,RGB(160,0, 255));
static int iPoint = 0;
```

Now you will need to add cases to the *switch(message)* statement to process the mouse messages. Then you will need to modify the *WM_PAINT* code slightly. The code is as follows:

```
case WM_LBUTTONDOWN:
    iPoint = bline.IsPoint (LOWORD(lParam), HIWORD(lParam));
    break;
case WM_LBUTTONUP:
    iPoint = 0;
    break;
case WM_MOUSEMOVE:
    if (!iPoint)
        break;
    hdc = GetDC (hWnd);
//
//   Showing the line in R2_NOTXORPEN mode will
//   erase the old line. The CShape class sets the
//   drawing mode to R2_NOTXORPEN in the Show() function.
    bline.Show (hdc);
//
//   Set the point to the new position
```

```
        bline.SetPoint (hdc, iPoint, (int) LOWORD(lParam),
                        (int) HIWORD(lParam));
//
//   Show the line again in R2_NOTXORPEN mode
        bline.Show (hdc);
        ReleaseDC (hWnd, hdc);
        break;
case WM_PAINT:
        hdc = BeginPaint(hWnd, &ps);
        bline.Show (hdc);
        bline.ShowPoints (hdc);
        EndPaint(hWnd, &ps);
        break;
```

Build and run the project. When the window appears, you should see a line drawn at an angle with four points represented by small boxes with a dot in the center, one point at each end of the line and two near the center. These are the *control points,* which are the objects of your mouse message processing. Move the mouse cursor to one of the points, then click and hold the left mouse button. Drag the point around the screen to see how the line changes into a curve, as shown in Figure 33.1.

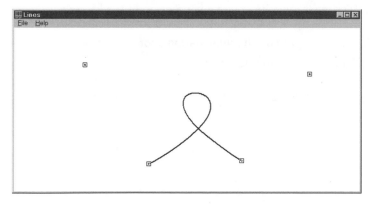

Figure 33.1

By dragging the control points around the window, your program easily can produce some complex curves.

Try grabbing other control points and drag them around the window as you watch the shape of the curve change.

What You Must Know

You have learned how all the programs running on your computer share the keyboard and mouse input devices and how only the window that has the input focus will receive Windows messages that give it information about keys the user has pressed. You have learned how to process keyboard messages and to add characters the user types to your Windows program. You also learned how to handle keyboard messages that do not have a character that can be displayed in your window. You also learned how to use mouse messages, including the mouse button-down and mouse button-up messages and the mouse move message. In Lesson 34, "Using C++ Streams," you will learn about C++ streams and how to use streams in your Windows programs. Before you continue with Lesson 34, however, make sure you understand the following key points:

◆ All programs running on your computer must share the keyboard and mouse devices.

◆ Windows notifies your program about keyboard and mouse activity by sending messages. Only the window that has the input focus receives keyboard messages. However, Windows sends mouse messages to the window under the mouse cursor even if it does not have the input focus.

◆ Windows sends a message when the user presses a key on the keyboard. If the key press results in a character that your window can display, Windows sends a second message containing information about that character. When the user releases the key, Windows sends another message informing your program of the key release.

◆ Mouse messages contain information about the location of the mouse cursor when the mouse event occurs and whether one of the mouse buttons was pressed or released.

◆ The *WM_MOUSEMOVE* message lets your program keep track of the location of the mouse cursor on the screen.

Lesson 34

Using C++ Streams

In your programs, you have used the C++ streams *cin, cout,* and *cerr.* Your use of the C++ streams, however, has been limited to outputting to the screen and getting input from the keyboard. The *cin, cout,* and *cerr* streams are distinctly C++. The Visual C++ compiler implements these standard input and output streams through classes. These base classes for these streams are capable of much more than just console I/O, as you have used them. Although you cannot use the standard I/O streams in a Windows program, you can use the same principles to write to and read from files and I/O devices on your computer. In this lesson, you will learn more about C++ streams and how to use them to read and write files. By the time you finish this lesson, you will understand the following key concepts:

◆ A *stream* is a sequence of data flowing from one part of your computer to another, whether it is from keyboard to screen, file to file, or file to hardware port.

◆ Visual C++ includes a library of stream classes that you may use to read and write files.

◆ The standard I/O streams *cin, cout,* and *cerr* are stream *objects* that use the streams classes.

◆ Using the streams classes, you may open and access a file in *binary* or *text* format. You may access some stream objects, such as those you create for files, randomly; but you must access other streams, such as the keyboard, sequentially.

◆ An *inserter* is a program-defined operator that reads characters and data from a stream. An *extractor* is a program-defined operator that writes characters and data to a stream.

◆ To read from or write to a file, you may use extractors and inserters or member functions in the streams class.

Using the C++ I/O Stream Library

In your command-line programs, you have been using the C++ standard I/O streams *cin, cout,* and *cerr.* The *cin* stream accepts keyboard input from the user, and the *cout* stream prints information from your program onto the display monitor. The *cerr* is similar to *cout,* but the designers of C++ provided a separate stream in case you want to direct error messages to a file or output device other than the screen.

A *stream* is a sequence of data flowing from one part of your computer to another. For example, when you use the *cin* stream in your program, information flows from the keyboard to your program. When you use the *cout* stream, information flows from your program to the screen. Data written by a program travel downstream to their destination, and data read by a program travel upstream from their source. These directions are relative, of course, because what is upstream at one end will be downstream at the other. The following statements direct keyboard input into a string and then output the string to the screen:

```
char szString[128];
cin >> szString;    // Upstream flow to your program
cout << szString;   // Downstream flow to the screen
```

From a practical standpoint, both ends of the streams are processes. Your program does not actually read directly from the keyboard. Instead, the stream connects with a *driver* program, which places the keystrokes into the stream. Visual C++ defines several stream types to handle various types of I/O. The *istream* class is used for input from *cin,* the standard input device. The *ifstream* is used to read from a file, and the *istrstream* is used to read buffered input from a string.

C++ is a *machine-independent* language. It does not contain any I/O capability. Visual C++ provides the ability to write to and read from streams under the various Windows operating systems using an object-oriented package that includes the standard streams. To use the Visual C++ stream classes, you must include the standard header file *iostream.h* in your program. The classes also contain functions to set the precision and field width of the streams and to output to memory strings.

Understanding the *stream* Classes

The C++ stream classes are built from a class hierarchy such as you created in Lesson 26, "Letting a New Class Inherit the Attributes of an Existing Class." The base class is *ios,* which is the ancestor class for *istream* for input streams and *ostream* for output streams. Another class, *iostream,* is derived from both *istream* and *ostream* and has two-way stream capability, that is, you can use a single stream based on *iostream* to read and write to a file or device.

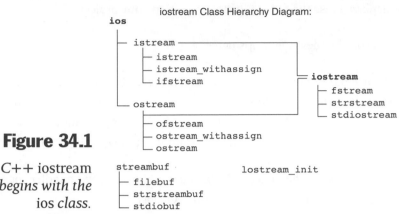

Figure 34.1

The Visual C++ iostream class hierarchy begins with the ios class.

The Microsoft Foundation Class library view classes read and write files using the *CArchive* class, which opens a stream object. You will learn more about streams by creating a project that does not use the document/view architecture. Create a new project using the MFC AppWizard (exe). Call the project "InStream" and click on the OK button to start the wizard. On the first page, select Single Document and *uncheck* the box labeled "Document/view architecture support?" Click the Next button and continue clicking on Next until you come to Page 6 of the wizard. Click on the Finish button and then click on OK when the New Project Information dialog box appears.

In Lesson 33, "Using the Keyboard and Mouse in a Windows Program," you created a window to accept keyboard input and display it on the screen. This time you will take an easier approach. By selecting MFC AppWizard, your project will have access to the Microsoft Foundation Class, and you will be able to use the ClassWizard to add message handlers to your window class, which is *CChildView* in this project. However, *CChildView* is derived directly from *CWnd* rather than one of the MFC view classes. In this class, you will attach an edit control, which will handle the keyboard and display tasks.

Using the ResourceView pane of the Workshop window, edit the *IDR_MAINFRAME* menu. Add an "Open" item to the File menu. Give this item a resource ID of *ID_FILE_OPEN,* then close the menu.

Start the ClassWizard by pressing Ctrl+W. Select *CChildView* in the Class Name box. Click your mouse on the Class Info tab (the tab on the far right). At the bottom left of the Class Info page is an Advanced Options area. In the left of this area is a box labeled "Message Filter." When you create a project using the MFC App-Wizard but without document/view support, the wizard selects "Not a Window" in the Message Filter box. Instead, you want to select "Child Window" in this box. This will make the ClassWizard display the messages available for a window.

With the ClassWizard displayed, use the following steps to set up your project:

1. Click the mouse on the Message Maps page.

2. Select *CChildView* in the Object IDs list, then add message handlers for the *WM_CREATE* (do not select the *Create* virtual function—the message handler is a separate item), the *WM_SETFOCUS*, and the *WM_SIZE* messages. These message handlers have predefined function names, so you may add the functions simply double-clicking on the items.

3. Select *ID_FILE_OPEN* in the Object IDs box and add a message handler for the *COMMAND* message. Make the function name *OnFileOpen()*.

4. Click on the OK button to close the ClassWizard.

5. Using the ClassView pane of the Workspace window, add the following private member variables to the CChildView class:

```
CEdit     m_Edit;
CFont     m_Font;
CString   m_strFileName
```

In this program, you will construct a *CEdit* object (an edit box control) in the *OnCreate()* message handler, then size the control to fit the client area in the *OnSize()* function. The edit control will handle the details of accepting input from the keyboard and displaying text on the screen.

The *OnFileOpen()* function has the job of reading the file into the edit control. First, *OnFileOpen()* will check whether edit control has changed and ask you if you want to save the old file first. Right now, this program will not save changes.

After adding the message handler functions and the member variables, you will need to add code to the *CChildView* class to handle the Windows messages. The following listing shows how the *ChildView.cpp* file should appear after you have added the code:

```
// ChildView.cpp : implementation of the CChildView class
//


#include "stdafx.h"
#include "InStream.h"
#include "ChildView.h"
```

```
#include      <fstream.h>

#ifdef _DEBUG
#define new DEBUG_NEW
#undef THIS_FILE
static char THIS_FILE[] = __FILE__;
#endif

/////////////////////////////////////////////////////////
// CChildView

CChildView::CChildView()
{
//   Use "Untitled" to show that no file has been selected
     m_strFileName = _T("Untitled");
}


CChildView::~CChildView()
{
     if (m_Font.m_hObject)
         m_Font.DeleteObject ();
}


BEGIN_MESSAGE_MAP(CChildView,CWnd )
     //{{AFX_MSG_MAP(CChildView)
     ON_WM_PAINT()
     ON_COMMAND(ID_FILE_OPEN, OnFileOpen)
     ON_WM_SIZE()
     ON_WM_SETFOCUS()
     ON_WM_CREATE()
     //}}AFX_MSG_MAP
END_MESSAGE_MAP()



/////////////////////////////////////////////////////////
// CChildView message handlers
```

```cpp
BOOL CChildView::PreCreateWindow(CREATESTRUCT& cs)
{
    if (!CWnd::PreCreateWindow(cs))
        return FALSE;
// Add the client edge style to the main window and
// remove the border style
    cs.dwExStyle |= WS_EX_CLIENTEDGE;
    cs.style &= ~WS_BORDER;
    cs.lpszClass = AfxRegisterWndClass
                        (CS_HREDRAW|CS_VREDRAW|CS_DBLCLKS,
                         ::LoadCursor(NULL, IDC_ARROW),
                         HBRUSH(COLOR_WINDOW+1), NULL);

    return TRUE;
}


void CChildView::OnPaint()
{
    CPaintDC dc(this); // device context for painting

    // TODO: Add your message handler code here

    // Do not call CWnd::OnPaint() for painting messages
}
//
// Create the edit control in the OnCreate message handler.
int CChildView::OnCreate(LPCREATESTRUCT lpCreateStruct)
{
    if (CWnd ::OnCreate(lpCreateStruct) == -1)
        return -1;
// Create the edit control using the styles needed
// for a multiline text editing window.
    m_Edit.Create (ES_WANTRETURN | ES_MULTILINE
                    | WS_VISIBLE | ES_AUTOHSCROLL
                    | ES_AUTOVSCROLL | WS_HSCROLL
```

```
                    | WS_VSCROLL, CRect (0, 0, 10, 10),
                     this, 0);
//  Create a font for the edit control
    m_Font.CreatePointFont (100, "Courier New Bold");
    m_Edit.SetFont (&m_Font);
//  Set the tab stops to four characters
    m_Edit.SetTabStops (16);

    return 0;
}
//
//  When this window gets the focus, change it to the edit
//  control. This will cause the keyboard messages to go to
//  the edit control
void CChildView::OnSetFocus(CWnd *pOldWnd)
{
    m_Edit.SetFocus ();
}
//
//  Resize the edit control to match the size of the
//  client window
void CChildView::OnSize(UINT nType, int cx, int cy)
{
    m_Edit.MoveWindow (0, 0, cx, cy, TRUE);
}
//
//  Open a file and read it into the edit control. Check
//  if the buffer has changed first.
void CChildView::OnFileOpen()
{
    if (m_Edit.GetModify ())
    {
        CString strMessage;
        strMessage.Format ("Save changes to %s?",
                        m_strFileName);
        switch (AfxMessageBox (strMessage, MB_YESNOCANCEL))
```

```
        {
            case IDCANCEL:
                return;
            case IDYES:
                break;
            case IDNO:
                break;
        }
    }
    CFileDialog cfd (TRUE);
    cfd.m_ofn.lpstrFilter = "Text files (*.txt)\0*.txt\0"
                            "All Files (*.*)\0*.*\0";
    cfd.m_ofn.lpstrTitle   = _T("Open Text File");
    cfd.m_ofn.nMaxFile  = MAX_PATH;
    if (cfd.DoModal () == IDCANCEL)
        return;
    m_Edit.SetWindowText ("");
    m_strFileName = cfd.m_ofn.lpstrFile;
    ifstream InStream ((LPCSTR)m_strFileName, ios::binary);
//
// Seek to the end to get the file size
    InStream.seekg (0, ios::end);
    long lSize = InStream.tellg ();
    InStream.seekg (0, ios::beg);
    TCHAR szBuffer[256];
//  Set redraw to false while adding text. This keeps the
//  edit control from redrawing itself each time a line of
//  text is added.
    m_Edit.SetRedraw (FALSE);
    while (InStream.tellg () < (lSize))
    {
        InStream.getline (szBuffer, 256);
// SetSel(-1,-1) sets the caret to the end of the
// text in the edit control
        m_Edit.SetSel (-1, -1);
        strcat (szBuffer, "\r\n");
```

```
        m_Edit.ReplaceSel (szBuffer, FALSE);
    }
//  Move the caret to the top of the edit control window
    m_Edit.SetSel (0, 0);
//  Set the redraw flag to TRUE. This will make the edit
//  control display the text just added.
    m_Edit.SetRedraw (TRUE);
// New file has been added. Set the modified flag to false
    m_Edit.SetModify (FALSE);
//  The ifstream destructor closes the file.
}
```

The *OnFileOpen()* function uses an *ifstream* object to read the file one line at a time, adding each line to the edit control. The *getline()* member function reads one line, but strips the line ender (the carriage return and line feed combination) from the text, so you must add it again.

Build the project and run your program. Open the *ReadMe.txt* file and make some changes. Then open the same file again. You should get a prompt asking if you want to save the changes first. At this point, your program will not actually save any changes. Your next step is to give the program the ability to save changes, so exit the program by selecting Exit from the File menu.

Open the *IDR_MAINFRAME* menu in the ResourceView pane. Add a Save item to the File menu. Make sure the resource ID is *ID_FILE_SAVE*. Close the menu. Using the ClassWizard, select *ID_FILE_SAVE* in the Object IDs box of the Message Maps page. Add a message handler for the *COMMAND* message. When the wizard asks you for a name for the message handler, name it *OnFileSave()*.

The message handler has a return type of *void*, but you will want to handle the actual saving of the file in a function that returns a *UINT* value. You will see why at the end of this section, when you handle the message to close the application. Using the ClassView pane, add a function to the *CChildView* class. Call the function *SaveFile()*. Make the function type *UINT* and check the Public box, then click the OK button. Code the *OnFile-Save()* and *SaveFile()* functions as shown in the following listing:

```
void CChildView::OnFileSave()
{
    SaveFile ();
}


UINT CChildView::SaveFile()
{
//  If the file does not have a name, display a
```

```
//   file save dialog box to get a name.
     if (m_strFileName == "Untitled")
     {
         CFileDialog cfd (FALSE);
//   Set the filter to display *.txt type files.
         cfd.m_ofn.lpstrFilter = "Text files "
                                    "(*.txt)\0*.txt\0"
                                    "All Files (*.*)\0*.*\0";
         cfd.m_ofn.lpstrTitle    = _T("Save Text File");
         cfd.m_ofn.nMaxFile  = MAX_PATH;
         if (cfd.DoModal () == IDCANCEL)
             return (IDCANCEL);
         m_strFileName = cfd.m_ofn.lpstrFile;
     }
     ofstream OutStream ((LPCSTR) m_strFileName,
                        ios::out | ios::binary);
     if (!OutStream.is_open ())
     {
         CString strMessage;
         strMessage.Format ("Cannot open %s",
                        (LPCSTR) m_strFileName);
         AfxMessageBox (strMessage, MB_OK);
         return (IDCANCEL);
     }
     char szLine[256];
     int iIndex = 0;
     memset (szLine, '\0', 256);
     while (m_Edit.GetLine (iIndex, szLine, 255))
     {
         strcat (szLine, "\n");
         OutStream << szLine;
         ++iIndex;
         memset (szLine, '\0', 256);
     }
     m_Edit.SetModify (FALSE);
     return (IDOK);
}
```

You now can open, edit, and save files using a "view" that you created yourself without the document/view architecture. Well, there needs to be some more work done—such as a Save As command—before your *CChild-View* class performs the same tasks as *CEditView,* but it is more useful than the project in Lesson 33.

You still have not handled the Close item on the File menu yet. To finish this project, add a message handler for the *ID_FILE_CLOSE* to the *CChildView* class. You will want to handle closing the file in a separate function as you did with the code to save a file. Using the ClassView pane, add another member function to the *CChild-View* class. Name the function *CloseFile( )*. Type **UINT** as the function type and check the Public box. The code for these two functions follows:

```
void CChildView::OnFileClose()
{
    switch (CloseFile())
    {
        case IDYES:
            if (SaveFile() == IDCANCEL)
                return;
        case IDCANCEL:
            return;
        default:
            break;
    }
    m_Edit.SetRedraw(FALSE);
    m_Edit.SetSel (0, -1);
    m_Edit.Clear ();
    m_Edit.SetRedraw(TRUE);
    m_Edit.SetModify (FALSE);
}


UINT CChildView::CloseFile()
{
    if (m_Edit.GetModify ())
    {
        CString strMessage;
        strMessage.Format ("Save changes to %s?",
                            m_strFileName);
        switch (AfxMessageBox (strMessage, MB_YESNOCANCEL))
```

```
        {
            case IDCANCEL:
                return (IDCANCEL);
            case IDYES:
                return (SaveFile ());
                break;
            case IDNO:
                break;
        }
    }
    return (IDOK);

}
```

Compile and run your program again. Open a text file and make some changes. Select the File menu and you will notice the Close item no longer is disabled. If you close the file, your program will ask you if you want to save the changes.

There is one last step to take care of before you have a usable text editing program. Run your program, open a text file, and make some changes. Exit the program either by selecting Exit from the File menu or by clicking on the Close button on the main window. Notice that the program just exited and did not offer you a chance to save your changes. Now that's pretty rude; some users might consider it downright mean.

The MFC function that handles the Exit menu option does nothing but send a *WM_CLOSE* message to the main window frame. You can add a handler for that function, then call the view class function to close a file. Open the *MainFrm.cpp* file. Type **Ctrl+W** to start the ClassWizard. Select the *CMainFrame* class in the Class Name field. Now search through the message list for the *WM_CLOSE* message. Double-click on this item to add the message handler, then click on the Edit Code button. All you need to do in this function is to call the *CloseFile()* function in *CChildView*. If the function returns *IDCANCEL*, you simply return to abort the termination. The code is shown in the following listing:

```
void CMainFrame::OnClose()
{
    if (m_wndView.CloseFile() == IDCANCEL)
        return;
    CFrameWnd::OnClose();
}
```

Now your program is more polite. If the contents of the edit control have changed, the user now can decide whether to save the file, ignore the changes, or stop the operations altogether.

Using Text and Binary I/O

As the Windows operating system evolved, it first was a program that you ran under PC-DOS. From this heritage, Windows came to have two methods of opening files. One, the *text* mode, wrote a carriage return and line feed at the end of each line. If your code just placed either a carriage return or a line feed at the end of the line, the operating system (DOS) would replace it with both characters. This still is the default method Windows uses to open files.

The other method, the *binary* mode, simply writes the characters you write to the file without replacing the end-of-line characters. This is the default method of most operating systems other than DOS or Windows. In fact, some operating systems such as UNIX do not support the text mode and always open files in binary mode.

In the preceding example, you used the *ios::binary* flag to signify that you wanted to open the files in binary format:

```
ofstream OutStream ((LPCSTR) m_strFileName,
                    ios::out | ios::binary);
```

If you omit this flag, Windows will open the file in text mode. You should be aware that if your program opens a file in text mode and you expect Windows to replace the end of line characters with carriage return and line feed combinations, your programs may not store text properly if you compile it on another operating system such as Linux.

The following code will store a carriage return and line feed at the end of each line even though you wrote only a line feed (\n) in the string:

```
ofstream OutStream ("File.txt", ios::out);
OutStream << "This is a test, eh\n";
```

However, by specifying binary output, the same output will write only a line feed to the file:

```
ofstream OutStream ("File.txt", ios::out | ios::binary);
OutStream << "This is a test, eh\n";
```

To write both a carriage return and line feed combination at the end of the line, you need to include them in the string you are writing:

```
ofstream OutStream ("File.txt", ios::out | ios::binary);
OutStream << "This is a test, eh\r\n";
```

Whenever possible, you should open files in binary mode so you may control the output.

Accessing Files Using Sequential I/O

Streams by their nature are *sequential*. That is, you access one piece of information after another. When you write to the screen using a stream, you write one line, and the next line you write will appear right below the first line. It would not make much sense if the lines appeared at random places on the screen.

When you use a stream to read or write a file, the stream maintains its current position in the file using a *file pointer*. When you first open a file using a stream, the initial value of the file pointer is 0, or the beginning of the file. Then, when you read information from a file, the stream moves the file pointer to the position immediately after the *end* of the information you read. Thus, the next time your program reads the file, it will get new information.

In the simple editor program in this lesson, you read an entire file line by line. Each time you read a line, the stream positioned the file pointer to the beginning of the next line. (The member function *getline()* removes the carriage return and line feed from your string after you read the line.)

Reading and writing a file in this way is an example of sequential I/O. You use sequential I/O when the file contains information of different sizes. In a text file, one line might be 80 characters, the next 65 characters, and the third 72 characters. It is like finding a song on a tape. Each song has a different length, so you start at the beginning of the tape and scan forward until you find the song you want.

You can move the file pointer yourself by using the *seekg()* member function. You can get the file pointer value by calling the *tellg()* member functions. You used those functions earlier to find the size of the file:

```
InStream.seekg (0, ios::end);
long lSize = InStream.tellg ();
InStream.seekg (0, ios::beg);
```

The first line moved the file pointer to the end of the file (0 bytes from *ios::end,* the end of the file). The second line retrieved the file pointer value and stored it in *lSize.* Then you positioned the file pointer back to the beginning of the file (0 bytes from *ios::beg,* the beginning of the file).

Accessing Files Using Random I/O

By using the *seekg()* member function, you can begin reading from or writing to a file at any point in the file. When you do this, you are accessing the file *randomly* and performing *random I/O* of the file.

Random file access is useful on *structured* files. When a file has structure, you know beforehand where to find the pieces of information. For example, suppose you are storing employee records in a file. Each record has the same size, so you know that to get to the third record, you need to move the file pointer from the beginning of the file to the beginning of the third record and then read the record:

```
Stream.seekg(2 * sizeof (EMPLOYEE), ios::beg);
Stream.read ((char *) &Employee, sizeof (EMPLOYEE));
```

To demonstrate random I/O, you can use a *dialog box–based* application. You have not use dialog boxes as the basis for an entire project before, but this type of project allows you to bypass the main window and create a dialog box directly. The following project also will show you how to display one dialog box from another. To create the dialog box–based application, use the following steps.

Select the New item on the File menu. When the New dialog box appears, click on the Projects tab, then click on MFC AppWizard (exe).

1. Give the project a name as you would for any other type of application. Enter **Random** for the name of this project. Click on the OK button to start the wizard.

2. On the wizard's first page, select "Dialog based" as the application type. Click on the Next button to go to Page 2.

3. On Page 2, uncheck the check box item labeled "About box." At the bottom of Page 2 is a box labeled "Please enter a title for your dialog." Type **Random File Access** in this box. Click your mouse on the Next button to move to Page 3.

4. On Pages 3 and 4, the defaults are OK. Click the Next button on Page 3 and the Finish button on Page 4. When the New Project Information dialog box appears, click OK to create the application.

The wizard will create the dialog box–based application and display a dialog box in the dialog box editor. This dialog box has only OK and Cancel buttons, but it will be the main window for your application. Add controls to the dialog box, as shown in Figure 34.2. You might have to resize the dialog box. (You can delete the Cancel button on this dialog box. Click your mouse on the Cancel button and press the Delete key.)

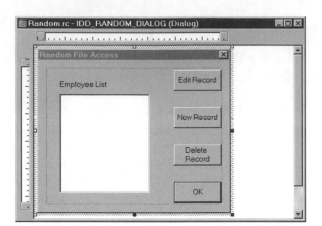

Figure 34.2

This dialog box will be the main window for your dialog box–based application.

The large window is a List Box control. Give this List Box control a resource ID of *IDC_LIST_EMPLOYEES*. Use the static text box for the label just above the List Box control. Add three new buttons: "Edit Record" with a resource ID of *IDC_EDITRECORD*, "New Record" with a resource ID of *IDC_NEWRECORD*, and "Delete Record" with a resource ID of *IDC_DELETERECORD*. Select the Delete Record button and press Alt+Enter to display the Properties dialog box. On the Styles page, check the Multiline box. Carefully size the Delete Record button to make sure all the text will fit on two lines. Now select all four buttons by holding the Shift key down and clicking the mouse on each button. Press Alt+Enter to display the Properties dialog box. On the Styles page of the Properties dialog box, check the Multiline box. With all four buttons still selected, click on the Layout menu at the top of the Visual Studio, then select the Make Same Size item. From the drop-down menu that appears, select Both, and the dialog box editor will make all four buttons the same size. (You may have to select Multiline for the other buttons as well).

Add a second dialog box to your project using the ResourceView pane of the Workspace window. The new dialog box is shown in Figure 34.3. This is where you will display the information from the file when you read the records into memory.

Use static text controls to label each of the Edit Box controls. Give each Edit Box control a resource ID as shown in Table 34.1. Give the dialog box a resource ID of *IDD_EMPLOYEEDLG*. Do not worry about a title for the dialog box; you will set that from your program.

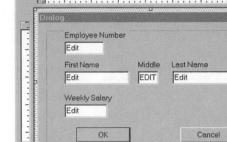

Figure 34.3

The employee record dialog box will display the information in the employee record when you read the data from the file.

Table 34.1 The Labels and Resource IDs for Controls on Your Application's Second Dialog Box

Label	Resource ID	Style Boxes to Change
Employee Number	IDC_EMPLOYEENUMBER	None
First Name	IDC_EMPLOYEEFIRST	None
Middle	IDC_EMPLOYEEMIDDLE	Uppercase
Last Name	IDC_EMPLOYEELAST	None
Weekly Salary	IDC_SALARY	None

Once you have prepared your dialog boxes, you will need to create a class for the second dialog box. As part of the project, the application wizard created a class, *CRandomDlg,* for your first dialog box. With the second dialog box selected in an editing window, press Ctrl+W to start the ClassWizard. You will be given the chance to create a new class for the dialog box, so click on the OK button to start the New Class dialog box. Name the class *CEmployeeDlg,* then click on the OK button.

When the ClassWizard appears, add a message handler for the *WM_INITDIALOG* Windows message. Also add a *BN_CLICKED* message handler for the OK button (select *IDOK* in the Object IDs box, then *BN_CLICKED* in the Messages box.)

Add a message handler for the *EN_CHANGE* message for each of the Edit Box controls. This message handler will set a flag that the user has changed the record so you can specify the same function, *OnFormChange(),* as the handler for each of these messages. When you add the message handler, the ClassWizard will suggest a default function name. Simply change each of these to *OnFormChange().*

Add variables for each of the Edit Box controls as shown in the following Table 34.2:

Table 34.2 Variables Used for the Employee Record Dialog Box

Resource ID of Control	Type	Variable Name
IDC_EMPLOYEENUMBER	int	m_iNumber
IDC_EMPLOYEEFIRST	CString	m_strFirst
IDC_EMPLOYEEMIDDLE	CString	m_strMiddle
IDC_EMPLOYEELAST	CString	m_strLast
IDC_SALARY	float	m_fSalary

When you add each of these variables, a box will appear at the bottom of the ClassWizard where you may declare the maximum number of characters the user may enter in the Edit Box controls. Enter **23** for the first and last name boxes and **1** for the middle initial box. This will prevent the user from typing a name longer than the size allowed in the employee record.

Select *CRandomDlg* in the Class Name box at the top of the ClassWizard. Add a message handler for the *WM_INITDIALOG* Windows message. Add message handlers for the *BN_CLICKED* message for all three buttons you added to the dialog box, *IDC_DELETERECORD*, *IDC_EDITRECORD*, and *IDC_NEWRECORD*.

Click the OK button on the ClassWizard to store the changes and close the ClassWizard dialog box. Using the ClassView pane of the Workspace window, add the *OnKickIdle()* function to *both* dialog box classes. It is type *void*, and the access level may be *protected* or *private*. In the *CRandomDlg* class, add the following function:

```
void OnUpdateButtons(CCmdUI *pCmdUI)
```

In the *CEmployeeDlg* class, add a *protected* member variable of type *bool* named *m_bModified* and a *CString* variable named *m_strTitle*. Then add the following function:

```
void OnUpdateOK(CCmdUI *pCmdUI)
```

You are almost finished with the preparatory work. Open the *stdafx.h* file and add the following to the list of include files:

```
#include    <afxpriv.h>
```

Now you need to add the code to your dialog box classes to make the program work. The header and source files for the *CRandomDlg* class is shown next (be sure to add the include files). The following listing shows the *RandomDlg.h* file:

```
////////////////////////////////////////////////////////
// CRandomDlg dialog

#include    <fstream.h>
#include    "EmployeeDlg.h"

class CRandomDlg : public CDialog
{
// Construction
public:
    CRandomDlg(CWnd* pParent = NULL);// standard constructor

// Dialog Data
    //{{AFX_DATA(CRandomDlg)
    enum { IDD = IDD_RANDOM_DIALOG };
    CListBox    m_EmployeeList;
    //}}AFX_DATA

    // ClassWizard generated virtual function overrides
    //{{AFX_VIRTUAL(CRandomDlg)
    protected:
    // DDX/DDV support
    virtual void DoDataExchange(CDataExchange* pDX);
    //}}AFX_VIRTUAL

// Implementation
protected:
    void OnUpdateButtons(CCmdUI *pCmdUI);
    void OnKickIdle();
    HICON m_hIcon;

    // Generated message map functions
```

```
    //{{AFX_MSG(CRandomDlg)
    virtual BOOL OnInitDialog();
    afx_msg void OnPaint();
    afx_msg HCURSOR OnQueryDragIcon();
    afx_msg void OnNewrecord();
    afx_msg void OnEditrecord();
    afx_msg void OnDeleterecord();
    //}}AFX_MSG
    DECLARE_MESSAGE_MAP()
private:
    bool m_bModified;
};
// RandomDlg.cpp : implementation file
//

#include "stdafx.h"
#include "Random.h"
#include "RandomDlg.h"

#ifdef _DEBUG
#define new DEBUG_NEW
#undef THIS_FILE
static char THIS_FILE[] = __FILE__;
#endif

/////////////////////////////////////////////////////////
// CRandomDlg dialog

CRandomDlg::CRandomDlg(CWnd* pParent /*=NULL*/)
    : CDialog(CRandomDlg::IDD, pParent)
{
    //{{AFX_DATA_INIT(CRandomDlg)
    //}}AFX_DATA_INIT
    // Note that LoadIcon does not require a subsequent
    // DestroyIcon in Win32
    m_hIcon = AfxGetApp()->LoadIcon(IDR_MAINFRAME);
```

```
        m_bModified = false;
    }

    void CRandomDlg::DoDataExchange(CDataExchange* pDX)
    {
        CDialog::DoDataExchange(pDX);
        //{{AFX_DATA_MAP(CRandomDlg)
        DDX_Control(pDX, IDC_LIST_EMPLOYEES, m_EmployeeList);
        //}}AFX_DATA_MAP
    }


    BEGIN_MESSAGE_MAP(CRandomDlg, CDialog)
        //{{AFX_MSG_MAP(CRandomDlg)
        ON_WM_PAINT()
        ON_WM_QUERYDRAGICON()
        ON_BN_CLICKED(IDC_EDITRECORD, OnEditrecord)
        ON_BN_CLICKED(IDC_DELETERECORD, OnDeleterecord)
        ON_BN_CLICKED(IDC_NEWRECORD, OnNewrecord)
        //}}AFX_MSG_MAP
        ON_MESSAGE(WM_KICKIDLE, OnKickIdle)
        ON_UPDATE_COMMAND_UI(IDC_EDITRECORD, OnUpdateButtons)
        ON_UPDATE_COMMAND_UI(IDC_DELETERECORD, OnUpdateButtons)
    END_MESSAGE_MAP()


    ///////////////////////////////////////////////////////////
    // CRandomDlg message handlers

    BOOL CRandomDlg::OnInitDialog()
    {
        CDialog::OnInitDialog();

        // Set the icon for this dialog.  The framework does
        // this automatically
        //  when the application's main window is not a dialog
        SetIcon(m_hIcon, TRUE);         // Set big icon
        SetIcon(m_hIcon, FALSE);        // Set small icon
```

```
        // TODO: Add extra initialization here
//  Open the employee file in binary mode
        fstream Stream ("Employee.dat", ios::in | ios::binary);
//  If we cannot open the file, display an error
        if (!Stream.is_open ())
        {
            AfxMessageBox ("Open failed for Employee.dat");
            return (FALSE);
        }
        int iNumber = 0;
//  Read the employee records in the file and place the
//  employee names in the list box.
        while (1)
        {
            EMPLOYEE Employee;
            Stream.read ((char *) &Employee, sizeof (EMPLOYEE));
            if (Stream.eof())
                break;
            if (!Employee.m_iNumber)
                continue;
//  Build a string containing the employees first name, the
//  middle initial followed by a period and the last name.
            CString strEmployee = _T(Employee.m_szFirstName);
//  Add a space
            strEmployee += ' ';
//  Add the middle initial only if there is one (some people
//  do not have middle names).
            if (isalpha(Employee.m_cMiddleInitial))
            {
                strEmployee += Employee.m_cMiddleInitial;
                strEmployee += ". ";
            }
//  Add the last name and place the string in the list box.
            strEmployee += Employee.m_szLastName;
            int iIndex = m_EmployeeList.AddString (strEmployee);
```

```
//   Set the item data to iNumber. You will use this number
//   to seek to the proper record when you edit an employee
//   record.
        m_EmployeeList.SetItemData (iIndex,(DWORD)iNumber);
        ++iNumber;
    }
    Stream.close();
    UpdateData (FALSE);

    return TRUE;
}


// If you add a minimize button to your dialog, you will
// need the code below to draw the icon.  For MFC
// applications using the document/view model, this is
// automatically done for you by the framework.

void CRandomDlg::OnPaint()
{
    if (IsIconic())
    {
        CPaintDC dc(this); // device context for painting

        SendMessage(WM_ICONERASEBKGND,
                    (WPARAM) dc.GetSafeHdc(), 0);

        // Center icon in client rectangle
        int cxIcon = GetSystemMetrics(SM_CXICON);
        int cyIcon = GetSystemMetrics(SM_CYICON);
        CRect rect;
        GetClientRect(&rect);
        int x = (rect.Width() - cxIcon + 1) / 2;
        int y = (rect.Height() - cyIcon + 1) / 2;

        // Draw the icon
        dc.DrawIcon(x, y, m_hIcon);
```

```
    }
    else
    {
        CDialog::OnPaint();
    }
}


// The system calls this to obtain the cursor to display
// while the user drags the minimized window.
HCURSOR CRandomDlg::OnQueryDragIcon()
{
    return (HCURSOR) m_hIcon;
}


void CRandomDlg::OnKickIdle()
{
    CWnd::UpdateDialogControls (this, FALSE);
}
//
//   OnUpdfateButtons is the command enabler function you
//   added to selectively enable the button. Enable a button
//   only if a item has been selected in the list box
void CRandomDlg::OnUpdateButtons(CCmdUI *pCmdUI)
{
    pCmdUI->Enable (m_EmployeeList.GetCurSel() < 0 ?
                                        FALSE : TRUE);
}
//
//   OnNewRecord is called when you press the New Record
//   button.
void CRandomDlg::OnNewrecord()
{
    EMPLOYEE Employee;
//   Open the employee data file as a stream
    fstream Stream ("Employee.dat", ios::out | ios::in
                                    | ios::binary);
```

```
    if (!Stream.is_open ())
        return;
    DWORD dwRecord;
    DWORD pos;
//  initialize the employee record to nothing
    memset (&Employee, '\0', sizeof (EMPLOYEE));
//  The following loop will search through the file for an
//  empty record (a record where the employee number is 0).
//  If there are no empty records, the pos variable will
//  point to the end of the file
    while (1)
    {
        pos = Stream.tellg();
        Stream.read((char *) &Employee, sizeof (EMPLOYEE));
//  Break if at the end of the file
        if (Stream.eof())
            break;
// If this is an empty record, break out of the loop
        if (!Employee.m_iNumber)
            break;
    }
    dwRecord = pos / sizeof (EMPLOYEE);
//  Create a dialog box to get the information about an
//  employee. Set the title to "New Record" and call
//  DoModal() to display the dialog box.
    CEmployeeDlg ed;
    memset (&ed.m_Employee, '\0', sizeof (EMPLOYEE));
    ed.m_strTitle = _T("New Record");
//  IF the user clicked the cancel button, do nothing
    if (ed.DoModal () == IDCANCEL)
        return;
//  Copy the employee record from the dialog box into
//  a local structure.
    memcpy (&Employee, &ed.m_Employee, sizeof (EMPLOYEE));
//  Clear the flags in the stream.
    Stream.clear ();
```

```
//   Seek to the empty record found earlier (or the end of
//   the file is there was no empty record).
     Stream.seekg(pos, ios::beg);
//   Write the employee record to the file
     Stream.write ((char *) &Employee, sizeof (EMPLOYEE));


//   Add the new employee name to the list box.
     CString strEmployee = _T(Employee.m_szFirstName);
     strEmployee += ' ';
     if (isalpha(Employee.m_cMiddleInitial))
     {
         strEmployee += Employee.m_cMiddleInitial;
         strEmployee += ". ";
     }
     strEmployee += Employee.m_szLastName;
     int iIndex = m_EmployeeList.AddString (strEmployee);
     m_EmployeeList.SetItemData (iIndex, dwRecord);
     Stream.close ();
}


//   OnEditrecord is called when the user press the Edit
//   Record button
void CRandomDlg::OnEditrecord()
{
//   Get the currently selected item in the list box
     int iIndex = m_EmployeeList.GetCurSel();
//   If none, do nothing (this should not happen).
     if (iIndex < 0)
         return;
//   Open the employee file as a stream
     fstream Stream;
     Stream.open ("Employee.dat", ios::out | ios::in
                                | ios::binary);
     if (!Stream.is_open ())
     {
         AfxMessageBox (_T("Could not open data file"));
```

```
            return;
        }


        EMPLOYEE Employee;
//  Get the index for the current record and seek to that
//  position in the file.
        DWORD dwRecord = m_EmployeeList.GetItemData (iIndex);
        Stream.seekg (dwRecord * sizeof (EMPLOYEE), ios::beg);
//  Read the employee record into memory
        Stream.read ((char *) &Employee, sizeof (EMPLOYEE));
//  Create a dialog box to edit the record. Copy the
//  employee record from local memory to the dialog box
//  and call DoModal() to display the dialog box
        CEmployeeDlg ed;
        memcpy (&ed.m_Employee, &Employee, sizeof (EMPLOYEE));
        ed.m_strTitle = _T("Editing Record");
        if (ed.DoModal() == IDCANCEL)
            return;
//  Write the modified changes to the stream.
        Stream.seekg (dwRecord * sizeof (EMPLOYEE), ios::beg);
        memcpy (&Employee, &ed.m_Employee, sizeof (EMPLOYEE));
        Stream.write ((char *) &Employee, sizeof (EMPLOYEE));
        Stream.close();
//  Delete the old entry in the list box. The employee name
//  might have change and you want the list box to refect
//  the new name.
        m_EmployeeList.DeleteString (iIndex);
//  Re-insert the employee name in the list box
        CString strEmployee = _T(Employee.m_szFirstName);
        strEmployee += ' ';
        if (isalpha(Employee.m_cMiddleInitial))
        {
            strEmployee += Employee.m_cMiddleInitial;
            strEmployee += ". ";
        }
        strEmployee += Employee.m_szLastName;
```

```
    iIndex = m_EmployeeList.AddString (strEmployee);
    m_EmployeeList.SetItemData (iIndex, dwRecord);
}


//  OnDeleterecord is called when the user clicks on the
//  Delete Record button.
void CRandomDlg::OnDeleterecord()
{
    int iIndex = m_EmployeeList.GetCurSel ();
    if (iIndex < 0)
        return;
    CString strName;
    m_EmployeeList.GetText (iIndex, strName);
    CString strText;
//  Ask first to make sure the button was not clicked
//  accidentally.
    strText.Format ("Are you sure you want to delete\n"
                    "employee %s", (LPCSTR) strName);
    if (AfxMessageBox (strText, MB_YESNO) == IDNO)
        return;
    DWORD dwRecord = m_EmployeeList.GetItemData (iIndex);
    if (dwRecord == LB_ERR)
        return;
    fstream Stream ("Employee.dat", ios::out | ios::in
                                    | ios::binary);

    EMPLOYEE Employee;
//  Zero out the employee record. This will allow the Add
//  Record reuse the file location later.
    memset (&Employee, '\0', sizeof (EMPLOYEE));
//  Seek to the record position in the file
    Stream.seekg (dwRecord * sizeof (EMPLOYEE), ios::beg);
    Stream.write ((char *) &Employee, sizeof (EMPLOYEE));
    Stream.close ();
//  Remove the string from the list box
    m_EmployeeList.DeleteString (iIndex);
}
```

The code in the *OnInitDialog()* function uses a stream to read a file named *Employee.dat*. It reads the information into a structure named *EMPLOYEE* (which you will define in the *CEmployeeDlg* class). It adds the name of the employee to the list box and keeps count of the record number. The code stores this number in the List Box data member for the item. When you edit or delete a record, the program retrieves this number using the *GetItemData()* member function of *CListBox*. Using the record number, your program seeks to the proper location in the file and reads the record.

When you delete a record, the program writes all zeroes (0) to the record. If you later add a record, the program will look for a "hole" such as this (the employee number is 0) and write the new record where you deleted the old record. This keeps the file from growing large with a lot of empty records.

The code for the *CEmployeeDlg* class is shown next. Notice the definition of the *EMPLOYEE* structure at the top of the header file. The following listing is for the *EmployeeDlg.h* file:

```
/////////////////////////////////////////////////////////
// CEmployeeDlg dialog

struct EMPLOYEE
{
    int     m_iNumber;
    char    m_szFirstName[24];
    char    m_cMiddleInitial;
    char    m_szLastName[24];
    float   m_fSalary;
};


class CEmployeeDlg : public CDialog
{
// Construction
public:
    CString m_strTitle;
    EMPLOYEE m_Employee;
    CEmployeeDlg(CWnd* pParent = NULL);   // standard
                                          // constructor

// Dialog Data
    //{{AFX_DATA(CEmployeeDlg)
    enum { IDD = IDD_EMPLOYEEDLG };
```

```
    CString m_strFirst;
    CString m_strLast;
    CString m_strMiddle;
    float   m_fSalary;
    int     m_iNumber;
    //}}AFX_DATA

// Overrides
    // ClassWizard generated virtual function overrides
    //{{AFX_VIRTUAL(CEmployeeDlg)
    protected:
    virtual void DoDataExchange(CDataExchange* pDX);
    //}}AFX_VIRTUAL

// Implementation
protected:
    void OnKickIdle();
    void OnUpdateOK (CCmdUI *pCmdUI);
    bool m_bModified;

    // Generated message map functions
    //{{AFX_MSG(CEmployeeDlg)
    virtual BOOL OnInitDialog();
    virtual void OnOK();
    afx_msg void OnFormChange();
    //}}AFX_MSG
    DECLARE_MESSAGE_MAP()
};
```

The implementation for the employee dialog is in the *EmployeeDlg.cpp* file, which is shown in the following listing:

```
// EmployeeDlg.cpp : implementation file
//


#include "stdafx.h"
```

```
#include "Random.h"
#include "EmployeeDlg.h"

#ifdef _DEBUG
#define new DEBUG_NEW
#undef THIS_FILE
static char THIS_FILE[] = __FILE__;
#endif

//////////////////////////////////////////////////////
// CEmployeeDlg dialog

CEmployeeDlg::CEmployeeDlg(CWnd* pParent /*=NULL*/)
    : CDialog(CEmployeeDlg::IDD, pParent)
{
    //{{AFX_DATA_INIT(CEmployeeDlg)
    m_strFirst = _T("");
    m_strLast = _T("");
    m_strMiddle = _T("");
    m_fSalary = 0.0f;
    m_iNumber = 0;
    //}}AFX_DATA_INIT
    m_bModified = false;
}

void CEmployeeDlg::DoDataExchange(CDataExchange* pDX)
{
    CDialog::DoDataExchange(pDX);
    //{{AFX_DATA_MAP(CEmployeeDlg)
    DDX_Text(pDX, IDC_EMPLOYEEFIRST, m_strFirst);
    DDV_MaxChars(pDX, m_strFirst, 23);
    DDX_Text(pDX, IDC_EMPLOYEELAST, m_strLast);
    DDV_MaxChars(pDX, m_strLast, 23);
    DDX_Text(pDX, IDC_EMPLOYEEMIDDLE, m_strMiddle);
    DDV_MaxChars(pDX, m_strMiddle, 1);
    DDX_Text(pDX, IDC_SALARY, m_fSalary);
```

```
    DDX_Text(pDX, IDC_EMPLOYEENUMBER, m_iNumber);
    //}}AFX_DATA_MAP
}



BEGIN_MESSAGE_MAP(CEmployeeDlg, CDialog)
    //{{AFX_MSG_MAP(CEmployeeDlg)
    ON_EN_CHANGE(IDC_EMPLOYEEFIRST, OnFormChange)
    ON_EN_CHANGE(IDC_EMPLOYEELAST, OnFormChange)
    ON_EN_CHANGE(IDC_EMPLOYEEMIDDLE, OnFormChange)
    ON_EN_CHANGE(IDC_EMPLOYEENUMBER, OnFormChange)
    ON_EN_CHANGE(IDC_SALARY, OnFormChange)
    //}}AFX_MSG_MAP
    ON_MESSAGE(WM_KICKIDLE, OnKickIdle)
    ON_UPDATE_COMMAND_UI(IDOK, OnUpdateOK)
END_MESSAGE_MAP()


/////////////////////////////////////////////////////
// CEmployeeDlg message handlers

BOOL CEmployeeDlg::OnInitDialog()
{
    CDialog::OnInitDialog();
//  Set the initial values of the controls according to
//  the information passed from the calling function.
    m_strFirst = _T(m_Employee.m_szFirstName);
    m_strLast = _T(m_Employee.m_szLastName);
    m_strMiddle = _T(m_Employee.m_cMiddleInitial);
    m_fSalary = m_Employee.m_fSalary;
    m_iNumber = m_Employee.m_iNumber;
    SetWindowText (m_strTitle);
//  UpdateData(FALSE) causes the dialog box to display the
//  new information.
    UpdateData (FALSE);
    return TRUE;
}
```

```
void CEmployeeDlg::OnOK()
{
//   UpdateData(TRUE) reads the information in the controls
//   and places it in the member variables.
    UpdateData (TRUE);
//   Check that there is a first name
    if (!m_strFirst.GetLength ())
    {
        AfxMessageBox ("Please enter a first name");
        return;
    }
//   Check that there is a last name
    if (!m_strLast.GetLength ())
    {
        AfxMessageBox ("Please enter a last name");
        return;
    }
//   Check that there is an employee number
    if (m_iNumber < 1)
    {
        AfxMessageBox("Please enter an employee ID number");
        return;
    }
//   Copy the information from the control to the employee
//   record structure
    strcpy (m_Employee.m_szFirstName, (LPCSTR) m_strFirst);
    strcpy (m_Employee.m_szLastName, (LPCSTR) m_strLast);
    m_Employee.m_cMiddleInitial = m_strMiddle.GetLength() ?
                            m_strMiddle.GetAt(0) : ' ';
    m_Employee.m_fSalary = m_fSalary;
    m_Employee.m_iNumber = m_iNumber;
//   End the dialog.
    CDialog::OnOK();
}
```

```
//  OnFormChange sets a flag when any of the information
//  in the Edit Boxes change. This flag will be used to
//  enable or disable the OK button.
void CEmployeeDlg::OnFormChange()
{
    m_bModified = true;
}


//  OnUpdateOK enables the OK button only if the information
//  in one of the Edit Box controls has changed
void CEmployeeDlg::OnUpdateOK(CCmdUI *pCmdUI)
{
    pCmdUI->Enable (m_bModified);
}


//  OnKickIdle forces the framework to send command enabler
//  messages.
void CEmployeeDlg::OnKickIdle()
{
    CWnd::UpdateDialogControls (this, FALSE);
}
```

Build the project and run the program. The sample code on the companion Web site *(http://www.prima-tech.com/books/book/5536/903)* contains a file named *Employee.dat* that you can use for testing. It already has a few records.

Using Inserters and Extractors

When you use streams, you can use *inserters* and *extractors* to place information in the stream and take information from the stream. You used these operations when you were reading from and writing to the console:

```
cin >> string;
cout << string;
```

The "<<" symbol is a stream inserter. The ">>" symbol is a stream extractor. These are the same symbols used for the shift left and shift right operations. In fact, they are nothing but *overloaded* operators. The process of overloading an operator gives it a special meaning when used with a particular object. In the next lesson, you will learn how to overload operators and write your own inserters and extractors.

When applied to the streams classes, inserters and extractors understand only the basic data types in C++. By default, they write the data as strings. For example, if you write the following statements in your code, the inserter will write "42" as a string to the stream rather than a binary 42:

```
int iVal = 42;
cout << iVal;
```

For the standard input and output streams, this is no problem. But for a structured file, writing a string where a binary value should appear can cause your program to write and read some invalid values. That is why the project in the previous section used the *read()* and *write()* member functions instead of using an inserter.

Inserters and extractors have a very low ranking on the operator precedence list. This prevents them from interfering with normal arithmetic operations yet still operate on streams. In addition, your program will evaluate inserters and extractors from left to right. It will evaluate the left-most operation before moving on to the next operation to the right.

What You Must Know

In this lesson, you learned how to declare and use objects using the Visual C++ *streams* classes. You learned how to open files and read information from the file and write information back to the file. By using a stream in a window, you were able to read a text file into an Edit Box control in the window and then edit the contents and write the new contents back to the file. You also learned how to use sequential and random input and output using streams. Finally, you learned that stream extractors and inserters are overloaded operators that read information from a stream or write information to a stream. In Lesson 35, "Overloading Functions and Operators," you will learn how to overload function names and operators and how to write your own inserters and extractors for streams classes. Before you continue with Lesson 35, however, make sure you understand the following key points:

◆ A *stream* is the flow of data from one place in your computer to another place. The ends of the streams may be files or devices such as the keyboard or display.

◆ Your program may open a stream to a device or file by naming the device or file and specifying whether it is an incoming stream *(ios::in)* or an outgoing stream *(ios::out)* or both *(ios::in | ios::out)*.

◆ When you open a stream in text mode, the stream will translate the end of line characters to the operating system default. When you open a stream in binary mode, the stream writes your data in the form you specify. When moving files from one operating system to another, such as from Windows to Linux, you should use binary mode.

◆ The *cin, cout,* and *cerr* standard I/O streams are stream *objects* that use the Visual C++ *stream* classes to read from the keyboard and write to the console screen.

Lesson 35

Overloading Functions and Operators

Most languages require that all of your functions, procedures, or subroutines have unique names, even though several functions may serve the same purpose but use different data types in their parameter list. Thus, you would need separate functions such as *IntOperation()* to perform an arithmetic operation of variables of type *int* and another, *DoubleOperation()*, to perform the same operations on variables of type *double*. Without a strict naming convention, this can make the names of the functions difficult to remember. In Visual C++, so long as the number or type of parameters, or both, are different, you may use the same name for similar functions. This is the process of *function overloading*. In addition to overloading functions, Visual C++ lets you redefine operators to perform special operations when used with an object. This is *operator overloading*. In this lesson, you will learn how to overload both functions and operators. By the time you finish this lesson, you will understand the following key concepts:

♦ The Visual C++ compiler identifies functions by their *signature,* which is a combination of a function's name and parameter list.

♦ If the signature of a function definition is unique, the Visual C++ compiler will permit the definition even if the function's name is the same as that of another function.

♦ Overloading a function is the process of declaring and defining more than one function with the same name but with different signatures.

♦ A function's return type is not a part of a function's signature because C++ lets you discard the return value.

♦ Operators as well as functions may be overloaded to provide special operations when used with C++ objects.

♦ The C++ *stream* inserters and extractors are examples of operator overloading. You may write your own inserters and extractors to use with your classes and structures.

Understanding Overloading

When you compile a program in Visual C++, the compiler keeps track of functions according to the *signature* of the functions. The signature is a combination of the name of a function and its parameter list. If the compiler encounters two or more functions with identical signatures, it cannot tell the difference between them, and it cannot tell which function your program intends to call. It then issues an error message, and the compilation of your program will fail.

If, however, the signatures of two functions are different even though the function names are the same, the Visual C++ compiler will allow you to declare and define both functions. This is because it can identify the functions as unique because of their signatures.

This process is *function overloading,* and it lets you define and use functions using the same name but different parameter lists. For two functions with the same name, the parameter list must differ in the number or data type of the parameters:

```
void Func (int x);
void Func (double x);
```

You should be aware that neither the return type nor the names of the parameters are part of a function's signature. The return type is not a part of the signature because Visual C++ lets you discard a return value by not assigning it to a variable, and thus the compiler cannot know which function you intend to call. The parameter names are not a part of the signature because Visual C++ lets you call functions with variables that have names different from the parameter names.

Normally, you would use overloaded functions to perform similar operations on different data types. Visual C++ does not require that you perform similar operations. Overloaded functions could perform very different operations, but that would only tend to make your programming confusing.

The following program, *Overload.cpp,* shows how you could use two functions, both named *Square( ),* to return the squares of an *int* data type and a *double* data type.

```
#include    <iostream.h>

int Square (int val);
double Square (double val);

void main (void)
{
    int iVal = Square (9);
```

```
    cout << "The square of 9 is " << iVal << endl;
    double fVal = Square (5.2);
    cout << "The square of 5.2 is " << fVal << endl;
}


int Square (int val)
{
    cout << "int Square(int val) called." << endl;
    return (val * val);
}


double Square (double val)
{
    cout << "double Square(double val) called." << endl;
    return (val * val);
}
```

When you compile and run this command-line program, you should see the following output:

```
int Square(int val) called.
The square of 9 is 81
double Square(double val) called.
The square of 5.2 is 27.04
```

Even though the functions you called have the same name, *Square,* the compiler was able to distinguish between them by the data types of the parameter lists.

You encountered a form of function overloading in Lesson 23, "Understanding Constructors and Destructors," when you declared multiple constructors for some of the classes in your *Shapes* project. Overloading constructor functions is a common use of function overloading. You cannot overload destructors, however, because Visual C++ does not allow you to pass arguments to destructor functions.

Overloading Functions

To overload a function, simply declare or define a function with the same name as another function, but with a different parameter list. The parameter list must have different data types or a different number of parameters.

You cannot count default values as part of the parameter count or types when overloading functions. The following function declarations, for example, would cause the compiler to generate and print error messages:

```
void Func (int x, double y = 24.8);
void Func (int x, char y = 'c');
void Func (int x, int y = 2);
```

By allowing default values, your program could call any of these functions with something like *Func(42)*. The compiler would not be able to distinguish between the three function declarations, and thus would generate an error:

```
stuff.cpp
stuff.cpp(12) : error C2668: 'Func' : ambiguous call to overloaded function
```

However, you could declare the functions so that only one of them has a default parameter:

```
void Func (int x, double y);
void Func (int x, char y);
void Func (int x, int y = 2);
```

The Visual C++ compiler will permit this declaration because it can distinguish between the function calls. When you call *Func(42)*, it can only mean the third function in the list.

Overloading Operators

You can overload functions even if the functions are not members of a class. For example, you can have global overloaded functions so long as the declarations and definitions of the functions meet the guidelines for function overloading.

Sometimes the C++ operators do not perform exactly as you would like when dealing with classes and other objects such as structures. In this case, you may redefine many of the operators to perform the tasks you need to do. This process is *operator overloading*.

For example, suppose you have a class that allocates memory for a string in the constructor, then deletes the memory allocation in the destructor:

```
class CEmployee
{
public:
```

```
    CEmployee ()
    {
        m_szName = NULL;
    }
    CEmployee (char *szName);
    ~CEmployee();
private:
    char *m_szName;
};
CEmployee::CEmployee (char *szName)
{
    m_szName = new char [strlen (szName) + 1];
    strcpy (m_szName, szName);
}
CEmployee::~CEmployee ()
{
    delete [] m_szName;
}
```

Then in your program code you call a function that assigns one class to another. This is a valid operation in C++:

```
void SomeFunction (CEmployee& Employee1)
{
    CEmployee Employee2 = Employee1;
    // some other code
}
```

The first line of the function assigns the contents of *Employee1* to a new variable, *Employee2*. However, the string variable is a pointer to heap memory allocated by the first variable. When *Employee2* goes out of scope, the destructor will delete the allocated memory, leaving the first variable, *Employee1*, with a pointer to unallocated memory. When your first class object tries to access the memory, it will get an invalid pointer error. Or when the second object goes out of scope, its destructor will attempt to release memory that has been freed already. Either way, your program is going to bomb.

You can overcome this problem by overloading the assignment operator, the equals sign, and make it allocate a new block of memory for the second variable:

```
const CEmployee& CEmployee::operator=(const CEmployee &Old)
{
    delete [] m_szName;
    m_szName = new char [strlen (Old.m_szName) + 1];
    strcpy (m_szName, Old.m_szName);
    return (*this);
}
```

In Lesson 24, "Understanding Class Scope and Access Control," you created a similar class that used an array of 20 characters for the employee's first and last names. This effectively limited the length of a name that you could enter to 19 characters plus one for the '\0' terminator. Now that you have learned how to allocate memory dynamically and how to overload an operator, you can redefine the class and create the following program, *Employee.cpp*:

```
/*
    Employee.cpp — Testing operator overloading.
 */
#include    <stdio.h>
#include    <iostream.h>
#include    <string.h>

class CEmployee
{
public:
    CEmployee (int ID, char *First, char *Last);
    CEmployee ()
    {
        m_EmployeeFirst = NULL;
        m_EmployeeLast = NULL;
    }
    ~CEmployee ();

    int GetID () {return (m_EmployeeID);}
    char *GetFirstName () {return (m_EmployeeFirst);}
```

```
    char *GetLastName () {return (m_EmployeeLast);}
    void PutNewData (int NewID = 0,
                     char *NewFirst = NULL,
                     char *NewLast = NULL);
    const CEmployee& operator= (const CEmployee &);
private:
    int      m_EmployeeID;
    char     *m_EmployeeFirst;
    char     *m_EmployeeLast;
};


int main ()
{
CEmployee emp[] =  {
                    CEmployee (1641, "Thomas", "Jefferson"),
                    CEmployee (1802, "George", "Washington"),
                    CEmployee (1732, "John", "Adams"),
                    CEmployee (1752, "Andrew", "Jackson"),
                    CEmployee (2401, "Elsie", "Smith")
                    };
//
// Thomas Jefferson got married and wants to change his
// last name to "Skelton." We need to save the old record,
// so create a new one
    CEmployee NewEmp;
// Copy the data in emp[0] to NewEmp
    NewEmp = emp[0];
    NewEmp.PutNewData(0, NULL, "Skelton");
// Print the results
    printf ("%s %s employee ID is %d (emp[0])\n",
            emp[0].GetFirstName(),
            emp[0].GetLastName(), emp[0].GetID());
    printf ("%s %s employee ID is %d (NewEmp)\n",
            NewEmp.GetFirstName(),
            NewEmp. GetLastName(), NewEmp.GetID());
    return (0);
```

```
}

CEmployee::CEmployee (int ID, char *First, char *Last)
{
    m_EmployeeID = ID;
    m_EmployeeFirst = new char [strlen (First) + 1];
    strcpy (m_EmployeeFirst, First);
    m_EmployeeLast = new char [strlen (Last) + 1];
    strcpy (m_EmployeeLast, Last);
}

CEmployee::~CEmployee ()
{
    delete [] m_EmployeeFirst;
    delete [] m_EmployeeLast;
}

void CEmployee::PutNewData (int NewID, char *NewFirst,
                           char *NewLast)
{
    if (NewID)
        m_EmployeeID = NewID;
//  If there already are names in the employee name
//  variables, delete them first, then reallocate memory
//  to hold the new names.
    if (NewFirst != NULL)
    {
        delete [] m_EmployeeFirst;
        m_EmployeeFirst = new char [strlen (NewFirst) + 1];
        strcpy (m_EmployeeFirst, NewFirst);
    }
    if (NewLast != NULL)
    {
        delete [] m_EmployeeLast;
        m_EmployeeLast = new char [strlen (NewLast) + 1];
        strcpy (m_EmployeeLast, NewLast);
```

```
        }
}


const CEmployee& CEmployee::operator=(const CEmployee &Old)
{
//   Make sure the employee name variables are empty. These
//   should have been set to NULL in the constructor, but you
//   may be reusing an existing class object.
     delete [] m_EmployeeFirst;
     delete [] m_EmployeeLast;
//   Reallocate memory for the names
     m_EmployeeFirst = new char
                          [strlen (Old.m_EmployeeFirst) + 1];
     m_EmployeeLast = new char
                          [strlen (Old.m_EmployeeLast) + 1];
     strcpy (m_EmployeeFirst, Old.m_EmployeeFirst);
     strcpy (m_EmployeeLast, Old.m_EmployeeLast);
     m_EmployeeID = Old.m_EmployeeID;
     return (*this);
}
```

To overload an operator, you declare a function as a member of the class but name the function using the *operator* keyword, followed immediately by the operator symbol that you want to overload, and then the parameter list. Then you must write the function that implements the operator.

You may overload most of the Visual C++ operators, but some of them may not be overloaded. The following lists those operators that may be overloaded:

```
+        -        *        /        %        &        |        ^        !        ~
<        >        <<       >>       =        +=       -=       *=       /=       %=
^=       &=       |=       <<=      >>=      ==       !=       <=       >=       &&
||       ++       -        ,        ->       ()       []       new      delete
* (indirection)
```

Writing Your Own Stream Extractors and Inserters

In previous lessons, you used inserters to place information into the output stream, which then wrote the information to the screen. You also used extractors to read information from the keyboard and to place that information into variables.

Inserters and extractors are examples of overloaded operators. To provide an extractor or inserter, you must write the code that you intend to execute when your program encounters the operator. The inserters and extractors provided with the streams class understand only the basic C++ data types. While you could use an inserter, for example, to write a string to a file, as in *cout << string,* you could not use the inserter with a class. Suppose you had a class named *CEmployee,* and you wanted to write it to the screen. The following code would not work because the streams classes have no knowledge of your class definitions:

```
CEmployee Emp;
cout << Emp;
```

To provide this capability, you would have to write inserters and extractors for your own class. In this section, you will modify the *Random* project to use a *CEmployee* class rather than an *EMPLOYEE* structure. Then you will add an inserter and an extractor to let you read and write the data file without using the streams *read( )* and *write( )* member functions.

Unlike other overloaded operators, inserters and extractors never are members of a class. They are global functions. Instead of declaring them as members of a class, your class definitions identifies them as *friend* functions so they may access *private* members. They take as parameters a reference to the stream on which they operate and a reference to the class with which you are using them. They return a reference to the stream.

Add the following class to the *Random* project. The new code is on the companion Web site *(http://www.prima-tech.com/books/book/5536/903).* The header and source files are shown here. The following listing is for the *Employee.h* file (be sure to add *fstream.h* to the include files in the header file):

```
#include    <fstream.h>


class CEmployee
{
public:
   CEmployee();
    virtual ~CEmployee();


    friend fstream& operator<<(fstream& o, CEmployee& emp);
```

```
    friend fstream& operator>>(fstream& o, CEmployee& emp);
    const CEmployee& operator=(const CEmployee &Old);

    int      m_iNumber;
    char     m_szFirstName[24];
    char     m_cMiddleInitial;
    char     m_szLastName[24];
    float    m_fSalary;
};
```

The following listing of the *Employee.cpp* file shows the code for the *CEmployee* class. Although the inserters and extractors are global functions, is is common practice to define them in the same file that implements the class code.

```
// Employee.cpp: implementation of the CEmployee class.
//
//////////////////////////////////////////////////////////

#include "stdafx.h"
#include "Random.h"
#include "Employee.h"

#ifdef _DEBUG
#undef THIS_FILE
static char THIS_FILE[]=__FILE__;
#define new DEBUG_NEW
#endif


//////////////////////////////////////////////////////////
// Construction/Destruction
//////////////////////////////////////////////////////////

CEmployee::CEmployee()
{
    memset (m_szFirstName, '\0', sizeof (m_szFirstName));
    memset (m_szLastName, '\0', sizeof (m_szLastName));
```

```
    m_iNumber = 0;
    m_cMiddleInitial = '\0';
    m_fSalary = 0.0;
}


CEmployee::~CEmployee()
{
}


const CEmployee& CEmployee::operator=(const CEmployee &Old)
{
    strcpy (m_szFirstName, Old.m_szFirstName);
    strcpy (m_szLastName,Old.m_szLastName);
    m_cMiddleInitial = Old.m_cMiddleInitial;
    m_iNumber = Old.m_iNumber;
    m_fSalary = Old.m_fSalary;
    return (*this);
}


fstream& operator<<(fstream& o, CEmployee& emp)
{
    if (!o.is_open ())
        return (o);
    o.write ((char *) &emp.m_iNumber, sizeof (int));
    o.write (emp.m_szFirstName, sizeof (emp.m_szFirstName));
    o.write (&emp.m_cMiddleInitial, sizeof (char));
    o.write (emp.m_szLastName, sizeof (emp.m_szLastName));
    o.write ((char *) &emp.m_fSalary, sizeof (float));
    return (o);
}


fstream& operator>>(fstream& o, CEmployee& emp)
{
    if (!o.is_open ())
        return (o);
    o.read ((char *) &emp.m_iNumber, sizeof (int));
```

```
    o.read (emp.m_szFirstName, sizeof (emp.m_szFirstName));
    o.read (&emp.m_cMiddleInitial, sizeof (char));
    o.read (emp.m_szLastName, sizeof (emp.m_szLastName));
    o.read ((char *) &emp.m_fSalary, sizeof (float));
    return (o);
}
```

By reading and writing the file this way, you will not be able to use the old data file that you used to read and write structures. When you use a structure, the Visual C++ compiler will adjust the member variables so they fall on convenient boundaries in memory. Thus, the size of a structure usually will be larger than the sum of the sizes of the member variables. In this code, you are reading and writing the class members individually, so your data file will be slightly more compact.

In the *CEmployeeDlg* class, remove the definition of the *EMPLOYEE* structure. Add *Employee.h* to the list of include files. Finally, change the *m_Employee* member function to be of type *CEmployee* rather than *EMPLOYEE*.

You will not need to change the *CEmployeeDlg* class, but you will have to make some changes to the *OnInitDialog(), OnNewrecord(), OnEditrecord(),* and *OnDeleterecord()* functions in the *CRandomDlg* class to take advantage of your overloaded operators. Rather than repeat the entire code, those four functions are shown here (to keep the listing short, many of the comment lines from Lesson 34 have been removed; the comments still apply, however):

```
BOOL CRandomDlg::OnInitDialog()
{
    CDialog::OnInitDialog();

    // Set the icon for this dialog.  The framework does
    // this automatically
    //  when the application's main window is not a dialog
    SetIcon(m_hIcon, TRUE);          // Set big icon
    SetIcon(m_hIcon, FALSE);         // Set small icon

    // TODO: Add extra initialization here
    fstream Stream ("Employee.dat", ios::in | ios::binary);
    if (!Stream.is_open ())
    {
        AfxMessageBox ("Open failed for Employee.dat");
```

```
            return (FALSE);
        }
    while (1)
    {
        CEmployee Employee;
        long pos = Stream.tellg ();
// Use the extractor to read the stream information into
// the CEmployee class variables.
        Stream >> Employee;
        if (Stream.eof())
            break;
        if (!Employee.m_iNumber)
            continue;
        CString strEmployee = _T(Employee.m_szFirstName);
        strEmployee += ' ';
        if (isalpha(Employee.m_cMiddleInitial))
        {
            strEmployee += Employee.m_cMiddleInitial;
            strEmployee += ". ";
        }
        strEmployee += Employee.m_szLastName;
        int iIndex = m_EmployeeList.AddString (strEmployee);
        m_EmployeeList.SetItemData (iIndex, (DWORD) pos);
    }
    Stream.close ();
    UpdateData (FALSE);

    return TRUE;
}


void CRandomDlg::OnNewrecord()
{
    CEmployee Employee;
    fstream Stream ("Employee.dat", ios::out | ios::in
                                  | ios::binary);
    if (!Stream.is_open ())
```

```
        return;
    DWORD pos;
    while (1)
    {
        pos = Stream.tellg();
//  Use the extractor to read the stream information into
//  the CEmployee class variables.
        Stream >> Employee;
        if (Stream.eof())
            break;
        if (!Employee.m_iNumber)
            break;
    }
    CEmployeeDlg ed;
    memset (&ed.m_Employee, '\0', sizeof (CEmployee));
    ed.m_strTitle = _T("New Record");
    if (ed.DoModal () == IDCANCEL)
        return;
    memcpy (&Employee, &ed.m_Employee, sizeof (CEmployee));
    Stream.clear ();
    Stream.seekg(pos, ios::beg);
    Stream << Employee;
    CString strEmployee = _T(Employee.m_szFirstName);
    strEmployee += ' ';
    if (isalpha(Employee.m_cMiddleInitial))
    {
        strEmployee += Employee.m_cMiddleInitial;
        strEmployee += ". ";
    }
    strEmployee += Employee.m_szLastName;
    int iIndex = m_EmployeeList.AddString (strEmployee);
    m_EmployeeList.SetItemData (iIndex, pos);
    Stream.close ();
}


void CRandomDlg::OnEditrecord()
```

```
{
    int iIndex = m_EmployeeList.GetCurSel ();
    if (iIndex < 0)
        return;
    fstream Stream;
    Stream.open ("Employee.dat", ios::out | ios::in
                                | ios::binary);
    if (!Stream.is_open ())
    {
        AfxMessageBox (_T("Could not open data file"));
        return;
    }
    CEmployee Employee;
    DWORD dwRecord = m_EmployeeList.GetItemData (iIndex);
    Stream.seekg (dwRecord, ios::beg);
    Stream >> Employee;
    CEmployeeDlg ed;
    ed.m_Employee = Employee;
    ed.m_strTitle = _T("Editing Record");
    if (ed.DoModal () == IDCANCEL)
        return;
    Stream.seekg (dwRecord, ios::beg);
    Employee = ed.m_Employee;
    Stream << Employee;
    Stream.close ();
    m_EmployeeList.DeleteString (iIndex);
    CString strEmployee = _T(Employee.m_szFirstName);
    strEmployee += ' ';
    if (isalpha (Employee.m_cMiddleInitial))
    {
        strEmployee += Employee.m_cMiddleInitial;
        strEmployee += ". ";
    }
    strEmployee += Employee.m_szLastName;
    iIndex = m_EmployeeList.AddString (strEmployee);
    m_EmployeeList.SetItemData (iIndex, dwRecord);
```

```
}

void CRandomDlg::OnDeleterecord()
{
    int iIndex = m_EmployeeList.GetCurSel();
    if (iIndex < 0)
        return;
    CString strName;
    m_EmployeeList.GetText (iIndex, strName);
    CString strText;
    strText.Format ("Are you sure you want to delete\n"
                    "employee %s", (LPCSTR) strName);
    if (AfxMessageBox (strText, MB_YESNO) == IDNO)
        return;
    DWORD dwRecord = m_EmployeeList.GetItemData (iIndex);
    if (dwRecord == LB_ERR)
        return;
    fstream Stream ("Employee.dat", ios::out | ios::in
                                    | ios::binary);
    CEmployee Employee;
    Stream.seekg (dwRecord, ios::beg);
//  Use the inserter to write the CEmployee class variables
//  into the stream
    Stream << Employee;
    Stream.close ();
    m_EmployeeList.DeleteString (iIndex);
}
```

This is really powerful magic. Your classes now have the ability to read and write themselves, and you need only code a single line to perform the operation. You will see these overloaded operators often when you read about "persistent" data. Inserters and extractors are not limited to streams. Because they are overloaded operators, you could write inserters and extractors, for example, to write or read from a database.

What You Must Know

You have learned how to write functions that have identical names but different parameter lists through *function overloading*. You learned about the *signature* of a function and how the Visual C++ compiler uses the signature to identify functions. Even though overloaded functions have the same function name, they must have different signatures to be unique to the Visual C++ compiler. In this lesson, you also learned how to overload operators such as the equality operator (=) to provide actions that are specific to your class. You also learned how to overload the shift operators (<< and >>) to provide stream extractors and inserters to read information from a file to your class variables and to write information from your class variables to a stream. In Lesson 36, "Handling Exceptions," you will learn how to handle critical errors in your program by catching and processing *exceptions*. Before you continue with Lesson 36, however, make sure you understand the following key points:

◆ The *signature* of a function is a combination of the name of the function and the function's parameter list.

◆ The Visual C++ considers a function declaration and definition to be valid if its signature is unique even if the function name is the same as that of another function.

◆ Function overloading involves writing functions using the same function name but with different parameter lists. Overloaded functions should provide similar operations on the parameters to avoid confusion.

◆ You may overload operators to provide special operations when you use the operators with C++ objects.

◆ The inserters and extractors used with Visual C++ streams are overloaded operators that let you specify how you will write information to a stream and how you will read information from a stream.

Lesson 36

Handling Exceptions

Errors happen. No matter how carefully you design and write your program, there always is the possibility that some unforeseen event will occur that will make it impossible for your program to continue. Often the causes of these errors may be beyond your control. The computer on which your program is running may not have enough memory. A device attached to the computer might return an unexpected error. Whatever the reason, these errors are caused by exceptional events that you could not have foreseen when you wrote your program, but the net result is that your program must recover from the error or exit gracefully. Visual C++ provides the mechanism for trapping and responding to unforeseen errors through *exceptions*. An exception is the interruption of a program caused by an unexpected or abnormal event. If your program does not respond to the condition, Windows will display an error message and your program will end abruptly. In this lesson, you will learn how to "catch" exceptions in your program and respond to the conditions that caused the error. By the time you finish this lesson, you will understand the following key concepts:

◆ When your program encounters certain problems, the Visual C++ run-time code will generate and return an error to your program.

◆ An *exception* is the result of an unforeseen or unexpected error that might prevent your program from continuing. When such an error occurs, some the Visual C++ library functions will "throw" an exception.

◆ When Visual C++ throws an exception, it gives your program a chance to "catch" the exception and handle the problem in your program code.

◆ If your program does not catch an exception, your program cannot continue running, and the Visual C++ run-time code will force the program to terminate.

◆ You handle exceptions in your program by using *try ... catch* blocks. If an exception occurs in a *try* block, the program control will transfer to a *catch* block.

◆ By using multiple *catch* blocks, your program can respond to more than one error possibility.

Understanding Exception Handling

Sometimes your program will encounter errors that you just did not expect. Your code may be correct, but some condition on the computer might cause some expected operation to fail. When this happens, some library functions often will generate—or "throw"—an *exception*.

An *exception* is an interruption of the normal program flow resulting from an unexpected or abnormal event. Exceptions are a part of the C++ language specification and give the programmer an opportunity to handle these conditions rather than simply halting the program because of the error condition. If the programmer doesn't handle the exception, generally the exception will cause the program to terminate.

An *exception handler* allows you to provide an alternate block of code to handle the condition and allow your program to recover from it gracefully.

Your program may generate an exception under three conditions:

♦ Your program may throw an exception as the result of a hardware problem, such as an attempt to divide by zero or to access an invalid memory address.

♦ The program may encounter a problem that keeps it from completing a task, such as a request to allocate an invalid block of memory or an attempt to access memory through an invalid handle or pointer.

♦ Finally, you may choose to throw an exception to signal an error condition as a means of aborting a block of code. For example, if a file that you need for a block of code does not exist, you may throw an exception that will execute a block of code to create the file first.

You don't *have* to handle an exception. If you don't, you'll usually get an error message from the run-time code, and your program will terminate. However, C++ provides a simple method for you to "catch" and adjust to these conditions.

Your program can catch an exception by executing a *guarded section* of code within a *try* block and then providing a *catch* block of code to handle the exception. As you will see, you can have multiple catch blocks to handle different types of exceptions that may be thrown.

Throwing an Exception

Several of the Visual C++ library routines may throw exceptions when error conditions arise. However, your program may throw an exception itself at any time by using the *throw* keyword. You may use this keyword to force your program to execute an alternate block of code when you detect an error.

For example, your program may need to retrieve some basic operating conditions from an initialization file that must be in a particular format. If this is the first time the program has been run, the file may not exist yet; or a user might have deleted it; or it may be corrupt, and the operating system cannot open the file.

The following program, *Except1.cpp*, attempts to open a file. If the file does not exist—which it probably does not—the program will throw an exception:

```
#include  <fstream.h>
//
//  except1.cpp. Test program for exception handling.
//  compile this program with the following command line
//
//          cl -GX except1.cpp user32.lib
//
//  The -GX enables exception handling. The user32.lib
//  provides the MessageBox function.
//
void main (void)
{
    fstream Stream;
    Stream.open ("xyzzy.dat", ios::in | ios::nocreate);
    if (!Stream.is_open())
        throw (-1);
    cout << "Program terminated normally" << endl;
}
```

Assuming the file *xyzzy.dat* does not exist, when you compile and run this program, it will end abruptly with the message "abnormal program termination." When you get this message, it usually is because a function, perhaps a library function, threw an exception that your program did not catch. In this program, the code never gets a chance to execute the statement that tells you the program terminated normally.

Now change the code to catch the exception as in the following *Except2.cpp* program. Be sure to include the *window.h* include file:

```
#include   <windows.h>
#include   <fstream.h>
//
//  except2.cpp. Test program for exception handling.
//  compile this program with the following command line
//
//            cl -GX except2.cpp user32.lib
//
//  The -GX enables exception handling. The user32.lib
//  provides the MessageBox function.
//
void main (void)
{
    fstream Stream;
    try
    {
        Stream.open ("xyzzy.dat", ios::in | ios::nocreate);
        if (!Stream.is_open())
            throw (-1);
    }
    catch (int x)
    {
        MessageBox (NULL, "XYZZY.DAT does not exist",
                    "File not open", MB_OK);
    }
    cout << "Program terminated normally" << endl;
}
```

Compile this program with the following command line. The "-GX" option enables exception handling in your program, and the *user32.lib* module causes the Visual C++ compiler to include the *MessageBox()* function in your code.

```
C:>cl -GX except2.cpp user32.lib
```

Now when you compile and run the program, instead of the rude "abnormal program termination" message, you will get a Windows message box telling you that "XYZZY.DAT does not exist." When you press the Enter key to dispatch the message box, the final line of the program will tell you that the "Program terminated normally."

You should notice that the *throw* statement in the program passed a parameter of −1, and the *catch* block declared an *int* parameter. This makes the exception an *integer exception*. As you will see later, you may have different *catch* blocks using different data types. To catch an exception, your *catch* block must declare a parameter of the same data type used by the *throw* statement.

What to Do When C++ Throws Exceptions

Many libraries written in C++ use exceptions to signal abnormal errors that might prevent a function from continuing. Exception handling is a clean and elegant method of handling potential problem spots in your program. Control passes quickly and automatically to a known block of code, which usually is designed specifically to handle potential problems.

Your first option, of course, is to ignore the exception. In this case, your program will shut down in an abrupt and not-so-elegant manner. Your second option is to catch the exception and process the problem in a *catch* block.

When you write the code in the *catch* block, you have three possibilities to consider:

◆ If the error is not serious, you can make adjustments for it and continue the program. If it is a simple matter of not being able to open a file, you can provide some means for the user to enter a different path or file name. A memory allocation error, on the other hand, might be more serious, and you might want to consider more drastic action.

◆ You can do some cleanup tasks, close open files, deallocate memory the program allocated, and exit the program if the error is so severe that the program cannot continue. After cleanup, you can terminate the program by calling the *exit()* function.

◆ Finally, you may decide to let another exception handler make the decision. You might have a handler in a function where the guarded section calls another function that contains an exception handler. That handler will get the first chance to handle the exception. If it cannot handle it adequately, you can execute the *throw* statement to rethrow the exception. The *catch* block will terminate and control will then pass to the next higher exception handler. If none is found, an abnormal program termination will result.

The following sample, *Except3.cpp,* shows how a *catch* block in a function can pass an exception back to the caller:

```
#include  <windows.h>
#include  <fstream.h>
//
//  except3.cpp. Test program for exception handling.
//  compile this program with the following command line
//
//           cl -GX except3.cpp user32.lib
//
//  The -GX enables exception handling. The user32.lib
//  provides the MessageBox function.
//
void ExceptTest ();

fstream Stream;

void main (void)
{
    try
    {
        ExceptTest();
    }
    catch (int x)
    {
        MessageBox (NULL, "XYZZY.DAT does not exist",
                    "Main", MB_OK);
    }
    cout << "Program terminated normally" << endl;
}

void ExceptTest ()
{
    try
    {
```

```
        Stream.open ("xyzzy.dat", ios::in | ios::nocreate);
        if (!Stream.is_open())
            throw (-1);
    }
    catch (int x)
    {
        cout << "This block will not handle the exception"
            << endl;
        throw;
        MessageBox (NULL, "XYZZY.DAT does not exist",
                "ExceptTest", MB_OK);
    }
}
```

Notice from the title bar that the message box displays is from the statement in *main()*. Also, notice that the *throw* statement in *ExceptTest()* does not include an argument. Executing the *throw* statement without an argument rethrows the exception in the current block. You should be aware that executing the *throw* statement without an argument outside an exception-handling block will throw an undefined exception that you may not be able to catch.

Using *try* and *catch* Blocks

Exceptions are an effective method of checking that the constructor function of a class object executes correctly. You will remember that constructor functions do not have return types, and Visual C++ will generate an error if you attempt to return a value from a constructor function.

By throwing an exception in a constructor when an object creation attempt fails, control returns to the function that created the object. You can take corrective measures at that point.

The Microsoft Foundation Class uses this technique in several places. The *CFile* class, for example, has an overloaded constructor that takes as arguments the name of a file and a set of open flags. On construction, it attempts to open the file. If it fails, it creates an *exception object,* an instance of the *CFileException* class, and throws an exception using a pointer to this object. Control then returns to your program code.

MFC provides a number of exception classes and some macros to help make the exception process even easier to use. Using the MFC exception macros is not much different from using the exception statements built into the C++ language. The MFC macros do have the advantage of automatically deleting the exception object when one of the MFC exception classes is used.

In the last section, you saw how to construct *try* and *catch* blocks using the standard C++ keywords. To use the MFC macros instead, use the following steps:

1. Start the *try* block with an uppercase *TRY.* Write the *TRY* block code as you normally would, but using calls to MFC objects. For example, to open a file, you would use the MFC *CFile* class rather than call a function that uses the C *fopen()* function or a C++ streams object.

2. For the *catch* block, use an uppercase *CATCH.* Two arguments are required, however. The first is the MFC exception class being used, and the second is a pointer to an exception class object. You can define your own exception classes, but if you are going to use them in a *CATCH* macro, they must be derived from the MFC *CException* class.

3. Finally, end the *CATCH* block using the *END_CATCH* macro. This will end the exception block and assure that the MFC code deletes the exception object automatically.

If you need to rethrow an exception within an MFC block, use the *THROW_LAST* macro rather than the *throw* statement.

Suppose you are using MFC and want to open a file using the *CFile* class. *CFile* throws a *CFileException* if it cannot open the file, so you want to declare the object at least in function scope and call the *Open* member function in a guarded section of code. Here is what it would look like:

```
CFile   file;

TRY
{
    file.Open ("XYZZY.dat", CFile::modeRead
                        | CFile::typeBinary);
}
CATCH (CFileException, e)
{
    // write code here to process a failed open
}
END_CATCH
```

Notice that in the *CATCH* parameters the *e* parameter does not have a data type. Typing the object is part of the MFC macro. In the next section, you will learn how to create your own exception object.

MFC contains several exception classes. To get a list of these classes and how to use them, select the Help menu in the Visual Studio, then select the Index item. When the MSDN Library window appears, type **MFC exceptions** in the Keyword field and press the Enter key.

Later in this lesson, you will learn how to create your own exception classes and use them in your program code.

Understanding Scope in Exception Blocks

When you use exception-handling blocks, you should be aware that both the *try* and *catch* keywords require compound statements. You *must* use the open and close braces even if your exception code contains only one statement. Any variables you declare within the compound statements follow the C++ rules that determine the scope of variables.

Any variables that you declare within a *try* or *catch* block will go out of scope when the block ends. If you create a variable within a *try* block and an exception occurs, the variable will go out of scope when your program transfers control to the *catch* block.

```
try
{
    int iVar = 0;   // declared in the try block
}
catch (int x)
{
    // The iVar variable in the try block is out of
    // scope and not available here.
}
```

If you need to use the same variable in both the *try* and *catch* blocks, you should declare the variable *before* entering the *try* block. You also may create objects on the heap in the *try* block and pass a pointer to the *catch* block, as you will do shortly when you create your own exception object. When you create objects on the heap, your program is responsible for releasing the memory, however.

You have used the *throw* and *catch* statement using an *int* as the argument, but C++ allows you to use any data type, even user data types such as a class, as the argument in a *throw* and *catch* sequence. This lets you provide exception objects that return more than just a simple error code. When you use an object this way, you should create the object on the heap so that it remains in memory when the *try* block ends. The following example, *Except4.cpp*, defines a class, *COpenException*, that stores an error code and presents the user with a chance to select another file:

```
#include     <windows.h>
#include     <stdio.h>
#include     <iostream.h>
//
//   except4.cpp. Test program for exception handling.
//   compile this program with the following command line
//
//              cl -GX except4.cpp user32.lib comdlg32.lib
//
//   The -GX enables exception handling. The user32.lib
//   provides the MessageBox function. comdlg32 is used
//   for the open/save file common dialog box.
//
FILE *TestFileFunc (char *szFile);
//
// Define the class to use as an exception object.
//
class COpenException
{
    public:
        COpenException();
        ~COpenException();

        OPENFILENAME m_ofn;

        int m_errno;
        int GetFileName (char *szName, int nSize);
};

main ()
{
    char fn[_MAX_PATH] = {"DooWop.Diddly"};
    FILE *fp;
    while (1)
//
//   Try to open the file in a guarded block
```

```
//
    {
        try
        {
            fp = TestFileFunc (fn);
            break;
        }
//
//  The program enters the catch block when TextFileFunc()
//  throws an exception.
        catch (COpenException *of)
        {
            int nResult = of->GetFileName (fn, _MAX_PATH);
//
//  TestFileFunc() created the "of" object on the head,
//  so you must delete it in the catch block.
            delete of;
//  If the user pressed the cancel key on the file dialog
//  box, exit the program by returning an error code.
            if (nResult == IDCANCEL)
                return (-1);
        }
    }
//
//  Close the file. we're not really going to do anything
//  with it in this program.
    fclose (fp);
    cout << "Open file " << fn << endl;
//
//  Return with a success code.
    return (0);
}

FILE *TestFileFunc(char *szFile)
{
    FILE *fp = fopen (szFile, "rb");
```

```
    if (fp == NULL)
    {
        int err = errno;
//
//  Create an exception object and set the error value
        COpenException *of = new COpenException;
        of->m_errno = err;
//
//  Throw an exception using the object.
        throw (of);
    }
    return (fp);
}


COpenException::COpenException()
{
    memset (&m_ofn, '\0', sizeof (OPENFILENAME));
    m_ofn.lStructSize = sizeof (OPENFILENAME);
}


COpenException::~COpenException()
{

}


int COpenException::GetFileName (char *szName, int nSize)
{
    m_ofn.lpstrFile = szName;
    m_ofn.nMaxFile = nSize;
    m_ofn.lpstrTitle = "Open a File";
    m_ofn.lpstrFilter = "All files (*.*)\0*.*\0";
    BOOL bResult = GetOpenFileName (&m_ofn);
    return (bResult ? IDOK : IDCANCEL);
}
```

In this program, the code attempts to open a file in a *try* block by calling the *TestFileFunc()*. If the file does not exist, *TestFileFunc()* creates a *COpenException* object on the heap, sets an error code in the object, and then throws an exception using a pointer to the object. In *main()*, the *catch* block catches exceptions that have a *COpenException* object. The *catch* block calls the object's *GetFileName()* member function, which displays a dialog box to let the user enter another file name.

The *try* and *catch* blocks are enclosed in a "forever" loop. The only two ways out of the loop are to enter a valid file name, in which case the program continues normally, or to press the Cancel button on the file dialog, in which case the program exits.

Notice that the *catch* block is responsible for deleting the exception object when that object no longer is needed.

Catching an Exception

When you write the *catch* block of an exception handler, you must include a parameter of the same data type as the type of value passed by the *throw* statement. If the data types are not the same, your *catch* block will not trap and process the exception:

```
try
{
    throw ((long) -1);
}
catch (int x)
{
    // This catch block declares an int parameter so it
    // will not catch the above exception, which passes
    // a long value.
}
```

There are times when you may find yourself having to catch exceptions, but you may not know the data type at the time you write your code. A special case of the *catch* statement allows you to catch every exception regardless of the data type. You write this form using the ellipsis as the argument to the *catch* statement:

```
try
{
    //  code for the guarded block.
}
catch (...)
```

```
{
    // This catch block will process exceptions thrown
    // using any data type.
}
```

As you will see later in this lesson, this form of the *catch* statement is useful as the last block in a series of *catch* statements.

Terminating a Program in an Exception Block

If a part of your program throws an exception and your code does not handle it in *try* and *catch* blocks, your program is going to terminate, and rather rudely from the user's standpoint. Any information in your program's memory will be lost, including perhaps some important information the user might have entered.

If the problem that caused the exception is so severe that your program cannot continue, you can use the *catch* block to terminate your program gracefully, saving any information or text the user might have entered.

This does not mean that every statement in your program should be protected by a *try* block. A statement such as x = y / 2 is not going to throw an exception. However, key operations that your program needs in order to function—such as accessing a hardware port or opening a file—should be guarded in a *try* block.

If your program cannot continue because of the exception, you can terminate your program at any point by calling the *exit()* function. In your code so far, the functions you have written all returned to the *main()* function before terminating the program. The *exit()* function lets you terminate your program at any point:

```
void Func()
{
    try
    {
        throw (-1);
    }
    catch
    {
        //  Clean up code here
        exit (-1);
    }
}
```

This will cause your program to terminate normally. Your function does not have to return to the *main()* function. In this example, the return code for your program will be *-1*, the argument you passed to the *exit()* function.

You also may specify a function that you want your program to call before it exits. To do this, you set the function name by calling the *atexit()* function, passing the name of the function as an argument. The function must not have a parameter list:

```
#include   <iostream.h>

void CleanUp(void);

void main (void)
{
    atexit (CleanUp);
}

void CleanUp ()
{
    cout << "Cleaning up" << endl;
}
```

After executing the *atexit()* function, this program will call the *CleanUp()* function before it exits. You should understand that *CleanUp()* will execute only if your program calls the *exit()* function or it terminates normally. If the program terminates abruptly because of an unhandled exception, *CleanUp()* will not execute. In the next section you will look at other methods to terminate your program.

Understanding the *unexpected()* and *terminate()* Functions

When your program ends prematurely because of an unhandled exception, the run-time code calls a function named *terminate()*. It is the *terminate()* function that actually prints the "abnormal program termination" message on your screen.

Visual C++ provides another function that you may call to end your program. This is the *unexpected()* function. The *unexpected()* function will call the *terminate()* function, so even by using *unexpected()*, you will get the abnormal terminate messages.

However, you may specify one function that *terminate()* will call before ending the program. In addition, you may specify another function that *unexpected()* will call before it calls the *terminate()* function.

If this sounds confusing, it is easer to visualize in program code:

```
#include  <iostream.h>
#include  <eh.h>
//
//  except5.cpp. Test program for exception handling.
//  compile this program with the following command line
//
//           cl -GX except4.cpp
//
//  The -GX enables exception handling.
//
// Declare a function that will execute when the program
// calls terminate()
void TerminateCleanUp(void);

// Declare a function that will execute when the program
// calls unexpected()
void UnexpectedCleanUp(void);

void main (void)
{
// Set the program to execute when terminate() and
// unexpected() are called.
    set_terminate (TerminateCleanUp);
    set_unexpected (UnexpectedCleanUp);

// call unexpected(). This will call terminate()
// automatically.
    unexpected();
    cout << "Program has ended" << endl;
}
```

```
void TerminateCleanUp ()
{
    cout << "Cleaning up as a result of a "
        << "call to terminate()" << endl;
}

void UnexpectedCleanUp ()
{
    cout << "Cleaning up as a result of a "
        << "call to unexpected()" << endl;
}
```

Notice the addition of *eh.h* to the include files at the top of the source code file. When you compile and run this program, you will see the following output:

```
Cleaning up as a result of a call to unexpected()
Cleaning up as a result of a call to terminate()

abnormal program termination
```

You still get the abnormal termination message, but at least your program can call two functions to provide cleanup code before it terminates.

Using Multiple *catch* Blocks

You will remember from Lesson 11, "Making Decisions within a Visual C++ Program," that your program can respond to multiple *if* conditions by chaining together a sequence of *else if* statements. When the program found a condition that was *true,* it would execute the statements for that condition and ignore all other conditions.

The *catch* block works similarly to the *else if* structure. You may chain together several *catch* statements. Your program will test each statement to see if it matches the type of exception that was thrown, and execute only one block of code when it finds a match.

The following program chains multiple *catch* blocks to handle various exceptions. Notice that the program forces a divide-by-zero error, which is caught by the general purpose exception handler. This is because divide-by-zero is a hardware error generated by the processor chip rather than by your source code.

```
#include  <windows.h>
#include  <iostream.h>
//
//  except6.cpp. Test program for exception handling.
//  compile this program with the following command line
//
//            cl -GX except4.cpp user32.lib
//
//  The -GX enables exception handling. user32.lib provides
//  the MessageBox function.
//

void main (void)
{
    try
    {
// Force a divide by zero exception.
        int x = 0;
        int y = 24 / x;
    }
    catch (int x)
    {
        MessageBox (NULL, "Integer exception caught",
                    "Integer", MB_OK);
    }
    catch (float x)
    {
        MessageBox (NULL, "Floating point exception caught",
                    "Float", MB_OK);
    }
    catch (long x)
    {
        MessageBox (NULL, "Long exception caught",
                    "Long", MB_OK);
    }
    catch (char *szString)
```

```
{
    MessageBox (NULL, "String exception caught",
                "String", MB_OK);
}
catch (double x)
{
    MessageBox (NULL, "Double exception caught",
                "Double", MB_OK);
}
catch (...)
{
    MessageBox (NULL, "General exception caught",
                "Catch All", MB_OK);
}
}
```

You should realize that the general purpose *catch(...)* statement must be at the end of your chain of *catch* statements if you use it. If any other *catch* blocks follow, the compiler will generate errors, and your compilation will fail.

Try changing the code in the *try* block to throw different types of exceptions, such as *throw(1)*, *throw((long) 1)*, or *throw(1.0)* to see which of the *catch* blocks executes.

What You Must Know

C++ exception handling gives your program the ability to handle unexpected problems gracefully when those problems might otherwise end your program abruptly. In this lesson, you learned how to use exceptions by providing guarded code in a *try* block and catching exceptions in a *catch* block. You learned the basics of the Microsoft Foundation Class library's exception-handling macros and classes. You also learned how to provide alternate functions to allow your program to provide some cleanup code when it encounters an unhandled exception. In Lesson 37, "Writing Functions with a Variable Argument List," you will learn how to declare and call functions that have an undetermined number of arguments. Before you continue with Lesson 37, however, make sure you understand the following key points:

◆ An exception is an unexpected error that might prevent your program from continuing.

◆ You may generate your own exceptions by using the *throw* statement.

◆ A *catch* block will execute only if the parameter type is the same as the argument passed in the *throw* statement.

◆ You may chain multiple *catch* blocks together to catch various types of exceptions.

◆ The "catch all" block—*catch(...)*—statement may be used to catch exceptions of any type. If this block is part of a chain of *catch* statements, it must be the last in the chain.

◆ An unhandled exception calls the *terminate()* function. You may specify a function to execute before *terminate()* forces your program to end.

Lesson 37

Writing Functions with a Variable Argument List

In previous lessons, you have learned how to declare and use functions in your programs and how to pass a fixed set of arguments to the functions. You learned how to overload functions to provide similar functions for different data types and how to provide default parameters for functions. In each of these cases, however, the parameter list was fixed. You had to call the functions with certain data types in a certain order. There are times when you will not know in advance the exact type and number of arguments your function will need. In such situations, you may declare a variable argument list. In this lesson, you will learn how to use variable arguments in your program. By the time you finish this lesson, you will understand the following key concepts:

◆ Visual C++ gives you the ability to declare and define functions with a variable argument list.

◆ To use variable arguments in a function, you must include the *varargs.h* or *stdarg.h* header file in your program.

◆ The C function *printf()* is an example of a function that uses variable arguments.

◆ Before you can access the arguments in a variable argument list, you must establish a *list marker*.

Including the *varargs.h* and *stdarg.h* Header Files

Sometimes you just cannot know in advance the data types and the order in which you will pass arguments to a function. This is especially true when you are writing information to a file or to the screen. At one point, a function may have to write an integer value, and at another point in your program, that same function may have to write a string.

The Visual C++ environment provides the means to declare and use functions with an unknown—or variable—argument list. Early in your C++ lessons, you met the *printf()* function. Although you used it only to write a string ("Hello, World!") to your screen, *printf()* actually accepts a variable argument list:

```
int x = 12;
double y = 3.2;
printf ("The result of %d times %f is %f\n", x, y, x * y);
```

The first parameter is a *format* string that includes formatting characters that let the variable argument functions determine the number and type of arguments that follow. The "%d" indicates an integer value, and the "%f" indicates a float value. You will learn about other formatting characters later in this lesson.

To declare a function with a variable argument list in your program, you must include the *varargs.h* or *stdarg.h* header file in your program. The *stdarg.h* is the preferred file because it is compatible with older C code.

```
#include     <stdio.h>
#include     <iostream.h>
#include     <stdarg.h>


void LogMessage (char *fmt, ...);


void main (void)
{
    LogMessage ("%s %c %d %ld %2.2f",
                "Test", 'c', 42, 24L, 36.3);
}


void LogMessage (char *fmt, ...)
{
 va_list ap;
```

```
    va_start (ap, fmt);
    vprintf (fmt, ap);
    va_end (ap);
}
```

In this program, the *LogMessage()* function has a variable argument list. When you compile and run the program, you should see the following output:

```
Test c 42 24 36.30
```

The *LogMessage()* function used the *fmt* parameter to print the variable argument list to you screen using the formatting information contained in the string.

Declaring a Function with Variable Arguments

You must prototype a function with a variable argument list the same way as you would prototype any ordinary function. To declare the variable arguments, you use an ellipsis in the parameter list:

```
void LogMessage (char *fmt, ...);
```

Your declaration must include one fixed parameter in addition to the ellipsis, and the ellipsis must be the last parameter in the list. The first parameter normally is a character string that contains formatting information for the variable argument functions. You may include more than one fixed argument, but the ellipsis that represents the variable arguments must be the last parameter:

```
void AnotherLog (fstream& Stream, char *fmt, ...);
```

If you try to include any parameters after the ellipsis, the compiler will generate and print an error because it expects the variable parameters to be the last in the list.

Using Variable Arguments in a Function

To use variable arguments in a function, you first must establish a *list marker* by using the *va_start()* function. You then retrieve the arguments one by one using the *va_arg()* function. When you are finished using the variable arguments, you release the list marker by calling the *va_end()* function.

The following program, *Varg1.cpp,* calls a function using variable arguments. The first argument is a string that identifies each variable type. It then prints a message to your screen depending upon the variable type:

```
/*
 * varg1.cpp. Demonstrates the use of a format string with
 * variable arguments.
 */
#include   <iostream.h>
#include   <stdarg.h>

void Show (char *fmt, ...);

void main (void)
{
    char *fmt = "icsdl";
    Show (fmt, 42, 'X', "Test", 25.84, 96L);
}

void Show (char *fmt, ...)
{
    va_list ap;
    va_start (ap, fmt);
    char *s = fmt;
    while (*s)
    {
        cout << "The argument is ";
        switch (*s)
        {
            case 'i':
            {
                int i = va_arg(ap, int);
                cout << "an integer: "  << i << endl;
                break;
            }
            case 'c':
            {
                char c = va_arg(ap, char);
                cout << "a char: "  << c << endl;
                break;
```

```
        }
        case 's':
        {
            char *str = va_arg(ap, char *);
            cout << "a string: "  << str << endl;
            break;
        }
        case 'd':
        {
            double d = va_arg(ap, double);
            cout << "a double: "  << d << endl;
            break;
        }
        case 'l':
        {
            long l = va_arg(ap, long);
            cout << "a long: "  << l << endl;
            break;
        }
    }
    ++s;
    }
    va_end (ap);
}
```

When you compile and run *varg1.cpp*, the program will produce the following output on your screen:

```
The argument is an integer: 42
The argument is a char: X
The argument is a string: Test
The argument is a double: 25.84
The argument is a long: 96
```

Visual C++ contains a number of built-in functions that will format a string using variable arguments. For example, *vprintf()*, which you saw earlier in this lesson, will format a string and write it to the console device. Other functions include *vfprintf()* to write to a file and *vsprintf()* to write the result to a string.

You must pass these built-in functions a format string. The string must identify argument types by preceding a character with a percent sign (%). The combination of a percent sign and a character is an *escape sequence*. This is the same scheme used by the standard library functions *printf()* and *scanf()*. For example, use "%d" or "%i" to signify a decimal value, "%o" an octal value, and "%x" or "%X" a hexadecimal number. The characters you may use with the percent sign are summarized in Table 37.1.

Table 37.1. Formatted Text Escape Sequences

Character	Argument Type	Conversion
d,i	*int*	Signed decimal.
o	*int*	Unsigned octal. Used without a leading 0.
x,X	*int*	Unsigned hexadecimal. Used with a leading 0X. Uppercase X is used to output hex characters in uppercase.
u	*int*	Unsigned decimal.
c	*int*	Single character (after conversion to unsigned *char*).
s	*char pointer*	The characters in the location identified by the pointer are printed until a terminating '\0' is encountered or the precision limit is reached.
f	*double*	Decimal floating point.
e,E	*double*	Decimal exponential. The precision determines the number of decimal places printed.
g,G	*double*	Decimal floating point or decimal exponential. If the exponent is less than -4 or greater than or equal to the precision, %e or %E is used. Otherwise %f is used.
p	*void pointer*	Prints the value of the pointer. Not available with all compilers.
n	*int*	*printf* maintains a count of the number of characters output during the current call. The %n sequence causes *printf* to write the value at the point specified into a variable. The parameter is a pointer to a type *int* variable.
%	none	None. %% causes a single % to be printed.

You may precede the *d, i, o, u,* and *x* letters by an *h* to indicate a short *int* value or by the letter *l* to indicate a long *int* value:

```
LogMessage ("%s %c %d %ld %f",
          "Test", 'c', 42, 24L, 36.3);
```

You should notice that there is no type *float* in the table. When you pass a type *float*, the variable argument functions automatically promote *float* types to *double*, which also is a floating-point data type.

You also may set the *precision* of the conversion by passing flags to the formatting functions. The following list summarizes the sequence and meaning of the various components of a format. Afterward, some examples will show you how to use the formatting and precision characters together.

The percent character symbolizes a formatting sequence to follow. If it is followed by another percent character, no formatting is performed, and a single percent character is output.

One or more of the following flags, in any order:

A minus sign (–) to specify the argument is to be placed in the left of the field.

A plus sign (+) to indicate a number is to be printed with a sign, even if positive.

A space. If the first character is not a sign (+ or –), a space is output to preserve column alignment.

The digit 0 to pad the spaces in a number field with leading zeroes (0).

The poundal (#) to specify alternate output for octal, hexadecimal, and exponential output. For an octal argument, a leading 0 will be output. For hexadecimal, a *0x* or *0X* will be output if the argument is non-zero. For exponential and floating-point numbers, the output will always have a decimal point. For the double g or G, trailing 0s will not be stripped.

Any number specifying a minimum field width. If the space required to print the number is less than this value, a wider field will be used.

A period if precision value is specified.

An optional precision value. For a string, this number specifies the maximum number of characters to print. For an integer, this number specifies the maximum number of characters to print, including leading zeroes (0). For floating-point or exponential numbers, it specifies the maximum digits to print after the decimal point. For the g or G conversion, it specifies the number of significant digits to print.

◆ A length modifier. A lowercase *h* indicates the argument is to be printed as a short or unsigned short. A lowercase *l* indicates a long or unsigned long, and an uppercase *L* indicates a long double.

◆ The conversion character itself, from Table 37.1.

Obviously the number of formatting possibilities is very large and very flexible. The following command-line program, *Vargs2.cpp*, uses the *printf()* function to show some of the possible combinations:

```
/*
 * vargs2.cpp. Demonstrates the use of precision formatting
 * for functions that use variable arguments.
 */
#include  <stdio.h>

void main (void)
{
    printf ("To print a percent sign: %%\n");
    printf ("To print the first 10 characters of a string:"
            "(%.10s)\n", "This is a string");
    printf ("To print a string to the right of a field: "
            "(% 25s)\n\n", "This is a string");
    printf ("To print a string to the left of a field: "
            "(%-25s)\n", "This is a string");
    printf ("To pad an integer with leading zeros: "
            "(%05d)\n", 42);
    printf ("To pad an integer with leading spaces: "
            "(% 5d)\n\n", 42);
    printf ("To print a double with two digits after the "
            "decimal: %.2f\n\n", 3.2);
    printf ("To pad a double with leading zeros: "
            "(%08.2f)\n", 3.2);
    printf ("To pad a double with leading spaces: "
            "(%8.2f)\n", 3.2);
    printf ("To print a double to the left of a field: "
            "(%-8.2f)\n", 3.2);
}
```

When you compile and run this program, you should see the following output on your screen. As an experiement, try modifying the program to use other formatting with different width and precision modifiers.

```
To print a percent sign: %
To print the first 10 characters of a string: (This is a )
```

```
To print a string to the right of a field: (        This is a string)

To print a string to the left of a field: (This is a string        )
To pad an integer with leading zeros: (00042)
To pad an integer with leading spaces: (   42)

To print a double with two digits after the decimal: 3.20

To pad a double with leading zeros: (00003.20)
To pad a double with leading spaces: (   3.20)
To print a double to the left of a field: (3.20    )
```

When your program uses the Microsoft Foundation Class library, you may use the *CString* class to format your string using the same precision statements. The *CString* class includes a member function, *FormatV()*, for variable arguments. *FormatV()* uses the same escape sequences as the *printf()* and other variable argument functions.

What You Must Know

In this lesson you learned how to declare functions that use a variable argument list. This is handy when you do not know ahead of time what type or how many arguments you will need to pass to a function. You learned how to use *escape* sequences to format the output for variable argument functions that write to your screen or to a file. You also learned how to set the *precision* for the output to control the appearance of the output from the *printf()* family of functions. This is the last lesson in this book. Programming in Visual C++ is a broad topic, and no single book could ever hope to cover all aspects of the C++ language. Hopefully, what you have learned in this book will start you on the programming road, and give you some tricks and functions that you may use in later programs. From the topics in this lesson, you should understand the following key points:

◆ Variable argument lists let you declare and define a function even if you do not know the data type and number of parameters the function will need.

◆ The *stdarg.h* and *varargs.h* header files contain the declarations you need to use variable arguments.

◆ You may use escape sequences beginning with a percent sign to format arguments using the variable argument functions.

◆ The escape sequences let you set the precision of the output from a variable argument.

Index